The Traveler's Companions
ARGENTINA • AUSTRALIA • BALI • CALIFORNIA • CANADA • CHINA • COSTA RICA •
CUBA • EASTERN CANADA • ECUADOR • FLORIDA • HAWAII • HONG KONG • INDIA •
INDONESIA • JAPAN • KENYA • MALAYSIA & SINGAPORE • MEDITERRANEAN FRANCE •
MEXICO • NEPAL • NEW ENGLAND • NEW ZEALAND • PERU • PHILIPPINES • PORTUGAL •
RUSSIA • SOUTH AFRICA • SOUTHERN ENGLAND • SPAIN • THAILAND • TURKEY •
VENEZUELA • VIETNAM, LAOS AND CAMBODIA • WESTERN CANADA

Traveler's Eastern Canada Companion

First Published 1998
Second Edition 2003
The Globe Pequot Press
246 Goose Lane, PO Box 480
Guilford, CT 06437 USA
www.globe-pequot.com

© 2003 by The Globe Pequot Press, Guilford CT, USA

ISBN: 0-7627-2332-7

Created, edited and produced by
Allan Amsel Publishing, 53, rue Beaudouin
27700 Les Andelys, France.
E-mail: AAmsel@aol.com

Editor in Chief: Allan Amsel
Editor: Anne Trager
Picture editor and book designer: Roberto Rossi

This edition updated and revised by Melissa Shales

Authors' Acknowledgments
A multitude of individuals and organizations contributed to this book with their generosity,
hospitality and expert advice. This list is far too long to include here, but the authors remember
and thank each one of them. Special thanks goes to Carol Sykes for all her hard work and dogged
determination to hunt down obscure facts, and to the national, provincial and local Canadian
tourist-information providers.

Printed by Samhwa Printing Co. Ltd., Seoul, South Korea

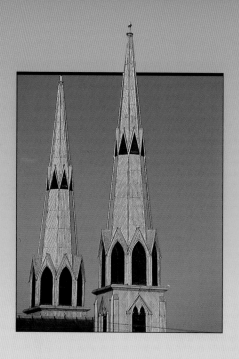

TRAVELER'S
EASTERN
CANADA
COMPANION

by Laura Purdom and Donald Carroll

Photographed by

Robert Holmes and Nik Wheeler

The
Globe
Pequot
Press

GUILFORD
CONNECTICUT

Contents

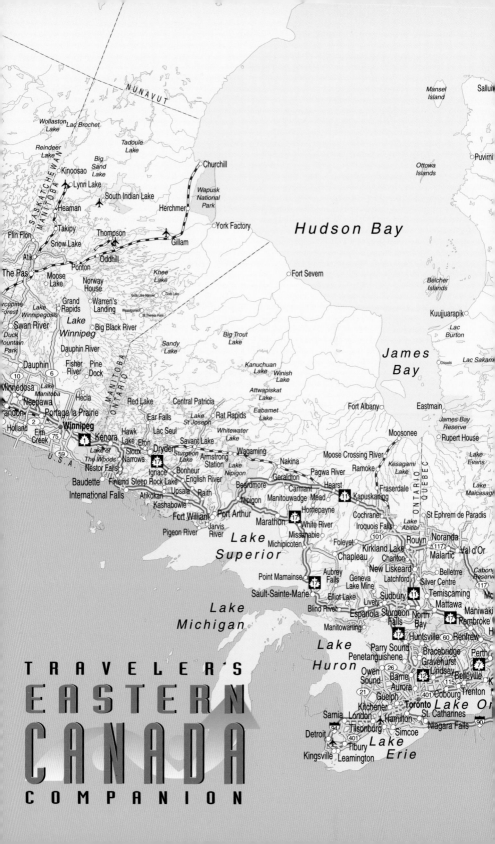

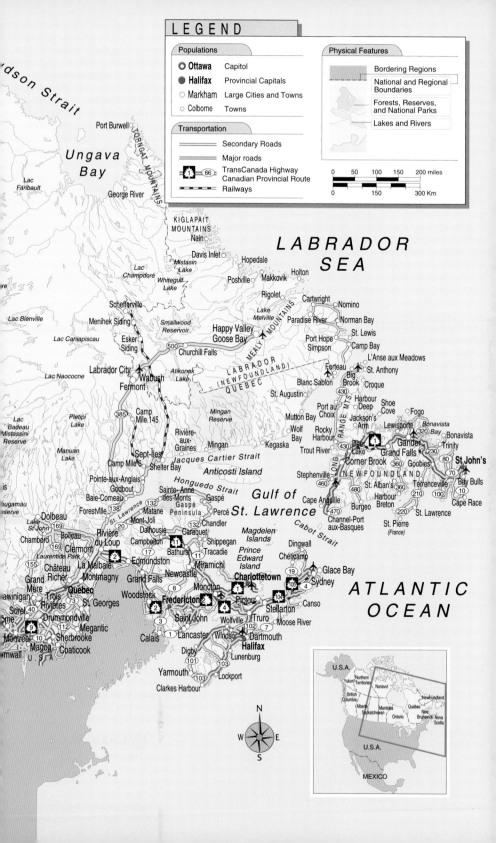

TOP SPOTS

Into the Mist

"Ladies and gentlemen… this is Niagara Falls!" announces the captain as the *Maid of the Mist* chugs toward the roaring heart of one of the world's natural wonders. Clad in blue ponchos, we cling to the sides of the little boat and watch the spectacle in silent amazement. Niagara from this vantage point is like some terrible archangel: terrifying in its power, yet clothed in an ethereal robe of white vapor. The voyage is a total sensory experience — we not only see the falls and hear their roar, but we feel them, smell them, even taste them as the mist washes over us.

Formed as the waters of Lake Erie race downhill to join Lake Ontario, Niagara Falls plunges over limestone cliffs at the rate of one trillion liters (almost three billion gallons) a minute. Sightseers, like pilgrims to a shrine, have been flocking to this thundering cataract since the infancy of North American tourism. And since 1846, *Maid of the Mist* boats have been carrying them to the base of the falls and back — very awed and slightly damp.

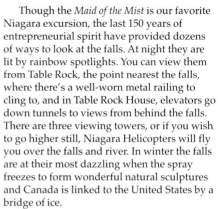

Though the *Maid of the Mist* is our favorite Niagara excursion, the last 150 years of entrepreneurial spirit have provided dozens of ways to look at the falls. At night they are lit by rainbow spotlights. You can view them from Table Rock, the point nearest the falls, where there's a well-worn metal railing to cling to, and in Table Rock House, elevators go down tunnels to views from behind the falls. There are three viewing towers, or if you wish to go higher still, Niagara Helicopters will fly you over the falls and river. In winter the falls are at their most dazzling when the spray freezes to form wonderful natural sculptures and Canada is linked to the United States by a bridge of ice.

Niagara, Ontario, is a stone's throw from Niagara, New York, which has still more viewing angles. After you've wandered along the promenade on the Canadian side, with its spectacular panorama of both the American and Horseshoe Falls, cross the Rainbow Bridge by car or on foot and, for a quarter, you can go through a door labeled: "Exit to the USA." On the American side the falls are surrounded by gentle green parkland — the first state park to be created in the United States (1885: the same year Banff was founded in Alberta). There is an interpretive center, and it's possible to get close to the breaking edge of the falls. Those who can't get enough of meeting the falls head on can cross over to Goat Island from the American side, where you can make the hike (after donning a yellow slicker and nor'easter) down to the base of the falls along a wooden stairway … into the mist once more.

The *Maid of the Mist* ℂ (905) 358-5781 WEB SITE www.maidofthemist.com operates daily from April to October, with departures every 15 minutes.

Niagara Falls — spectacular, no matter how you look at them. OPPOSITE: The American Falls gush over limestone cliffs. ABOVE: The *Maid of the Mist* chugs headlong into the thundering cataract.

Explore Historic Québec

Every English schoolchild learns how a certain dashing General Wolfe and his men scaled a cliff and defeated the French on the Plains of Abraham, after blockading the town for months. From the top, the 110-m-high (350-ft) cliff doesn't seem quite that tall. In fact, the battle only lasted 20 minutes, during which time both generals lost their lives.

Nevertheless, that British victory at Québec City was to alter the entire course of Canadian history. Today the Plains of Abraham lie under the watchful eyes of silent cannons. In winter, ski trails crisscross the snow not far from towering palaces and intricate sculptures of snow and ice. On Terrasse Dufferin, beneath the baronial towers of Château Frontenac, skaters drift across an outdoor rink and children whoop it up on a cliff-top toboggan run. People dressed in bright jackets and wearing heavy boots wait for the bus out to the ski slopes. Old women in sensible shoes and fur coats pick their way cautiously across the icy cobbles. Young backpackers puff steam and wrap frosted fingers around cups of soup and hot chocolate as they gaze over the balcony to the St. Lawrence Seaway, where huge ships carve jade-green clear water channels through the sludgy ice.

Québec City is not only one of the most beautiful cities in North America, and the only walled city on the continent north of Mexico,

but the first city in North America to have been designated a World Heritage Site by UNESCO. As Charles Dickens wrote, "It is a place not to be forgotten, or mixed up in the mind with other places." How could one forget a walled, cliff-top city with cobbled streets, many seventeenth- and eighteenth-century stone buildings, stunning views, lively bistros and outdoor cafés, magnificent churches — a city redolent of history, a city that not only speaks but breathes in French — and all in North America?

At the foot of the cliff, Basse-Ville, the harborfront site of the original settlement, offers action to the street-scene aficionado. Basse-Ville's picturesque Place Royale is at the heart of the city's street life, with performers in summer and ice sculptures in winter. When the chill gets to you, cozy cafés abound along Boulevard Champlain and Rue St-Paul.

In summer, the streets of this enchanting city heave with tourists visiting the sites or just wandering, shopping and eating — its French heritage has assured Québec a

Québec City, old and new — ABOVE LEFT: The Basilique Notre-Dame was rebuilt in 1922, in strict accordance with the original 1647 plans. RIGHT: Winding narrow streets seem made for wandering. OPPOSITE TOP: The Musée du Québec's modern façade. BOTTOM: Rue du Trésor, once the site of Québec's royal treasury, has now become a treasure trove of souvenirs.

gastronomic legacy. But the city really comes to life each year in February, when the Québecois transform the legendary pre-Lenten Carnaval d'Hiver (Winter Carnival) ((418) 621-5555 TOLL-FREE (866) 422-7628 WEB SITE www.carnaval.qc.ca into the world's largest winter festival, a 17-day extravaganza of epic proportions led by a mascot snowman, Bonhomme Carnaval. Nearly a million visitors flock into the city for a riotous collection of parades, fancy-dress balls, canoe and dogsled races, an international ice sculpture competition and a host of wintery entertainments, games and sports.

And if that is not enough, you can head out of town to the Ice Hotel ((418) 875-4522 TOLL-FREE (877) 505-0423 WEB SITE www.ice-hotel-canada.com, where everything from the beds to the glasses and chandeliers are made of ice, and activities range from snow shoeing and skiing to dog sledding.

Jet the Lachine Rapids

"It's like a submarine ride in a convertible!" bellows Jack Kowalski at a crowd of men, women and children gathered at Montréal's waterfront to shoot the Lachine Rapids with Saute Moutons (Wave Jumpers) — a fleet of hydro-powered jet-boats. (In French *mouton* refers to "sheep" as well as to the foamy whitewater that typifies rapids.) "Two things are certain," continues Kowalski to the adventurers who've lined up to take the plunge, "you *will* get wet, and you *will* have the time of your life."

Though the St. Lawrence River is "like bathwater" in summer, thrillseekers must nevertheless don woolen army sweaters. Then on top of a lifejacket goes a yellow hooded rain slicker. The flat-bottomed aluminum boats are specially made for the ride. Their shallow draft allows them to take on the roughest parts of the water, but even with their 1,100-horse-power engines, the boats are at times suspended, running against the awesome currents of the Lachine.

These currents were enough to stop explorer Jacques Cartier when he arrived at the native encampment of Hochelaga in 1535, not far from the present-day Montréal, on his quest for a route to the Orient. He named them, wistfully, *Lachine* (*la Chine* is French for China). Later *voyageurs* (fur traders) portaged the rapids before paddling their way across the Great Lakes on their way to trading posts in the interior. It wasn't until the Victorian era that steamboats regularly traversed the rapids, shepherded by daredevil native pilots with

names like Big John Canadian and Baptist Taiaiake. Eventually, the Lachine Canal bypassed the rapids, providing safety for shipping, and creating Montréal's most thrilling adventure playground.

Half historic sightseeing excursion and half thrill ride, Saute Moutons leap headlong through this untamed section of the mighty St. Lawrence River — right into the heart of cosmopolitan Montréal. Founded in the early 1980s, Jack Kowalski's jet-boat ride is one of Montreal's most popular attractions.

Jet-boats depart from the Montréal's Quai de l'Horloge (Clock Tower Pier) in the Vieux Port every two hours for the hour-and-a-half trip to the rapids and back. Trips run several times daily from May to October, between 10 AM and 6 PM. For information and to make reservations, contact Saute Moutons–Lachine Rapids Tours ((514) 284 9607 FAX (514) 287-9401 WEB SITE www.jetboatingmontreal.com, 47 rue de la Commune ouest. The same company also offers rafting trips (minimum age 14) through the Lachine Rapids, as well as rides on a high-speed chase boat, the *Jet St. Laurent*, along the St. Lawrence River, and a similar jet-boat ride, the *Whirlpool Jet*, at Niagara-on-the-Lake ((905) 468-4800 FAX (905) 468-7004, George III, 61 Melville Street, Niagara-on-the-Lake, Ontario.

OPPOSITE: A Québec City *calèche*.
ABOVE: Jet-boaters ride the last untamed section of the St. Lawrence River in Montréal.

See the Wonders of Witless Bay

Just south of Newfoundland's capital city of St. John's, along the lyrically named Irish Loop, lies the hamlet of Bay Bulls, the jumping off point for boat tours to the Witless Bay Ecological Reserve, where a trio of attractions bring visitors in droves each spring.

The islands of Witless Bay are off-limits to humans, set aside since the 1920s for the sea birds of this island province. Over two million birds arrive here in early May, including 500,000 Atlantic puffins, one of the largest puffin colonies on earth. They come to nest and to feed on capelin — the sardine-sized fish that cruise the bay in sparkling schools. The capelin also attract a somewhat larger predator — humpback whales. But Newfoundlanders know that spring has truly arrived when icebergs sail like ghost yachts into the bays.

Tour boats ply the waters of Witless Bay and approach the islands, giving passengers a close-up view of the busy puffins, along with other bird populations including murres, kittiwakes and a variety of gulls. Throughout the two-and-a-half-hour tour the sky is alive with beating wings, and from time to time the sea — of an almost surreal blue — seethes with the bobbing heads of puffins as they surface from their marathon dives into the icy water.

When icebergs are in the water, the boat gets close enough to feel the chill, and passengers can break off pieces and taste the pure, blue-hued ice. The 'bergs are "calves," sundered from their mothers in the Arctic ice fields. They make their way along the northern Canadian coast and out into the Gulf Stream, where they melt in the warm water. On their long journey to the open sea, the 'bergs take on fantastic forms; resembling anything from shark fins to gothic cathedrals.

The puffins arrive in early May and the icebergs are not far behind. A couple of weeks later, Newfoundland welcomes the whales. Humpbacks pass within meters of the tour boats, giving passengers up-close views of giant corrugated flippers and massive flukes (tails). Occasionally the leviathans lunge out of the water, launching their 36 tons into the air. Tour boats keep a respectful distance, but at times the animals move close enough that passengers can smell the whale's salty breath as the spray from a blow passes over the boat.

Contact Witless Bay Ecological Reserve at ((709) 729 2424 WEB SITE www.gov.nf.ca/parks &reserves. Gatherall's Puffin & Whale Watch ((709) 334-2887 TOLL-FREE (800) 419-4253 WEB SITE www.newfoundland-whales.com operates six tours daily from May to October, departing from Gatherall's wharf in Bay Bulls (30 minutes south of St. John's on Route 10). Reservations are requested, but walk-aboard passengers can usually be accommodated (see page 206 under THE AVALON PENINSULA).

Tower over Toronto

"How'd they build it? Well, basically, they just poured concrete nonstop for 40 months," explains our youthful guide. We're looking up — way up — at the world's tallest freestanding structure: Toronto's CN Tower ((416) 868-6937 WEB SITE www.cntower.ca, 301 Front Street West.

Before we know it we're preparing to be whisked up the tower's ultramodern elevator, which will take a mere 58 seconds to deliver us to the Space Deck, a 360-degree panorama viewing platform two-thirds of the way up the 553.33-m-tall (1,815-ft) tower — a privilege for which we've paid $16 (plus tax). The budget option, says our statistic-spouting guide, is to climb the 1,796 steps to the top. No thanks.

The CN Tower is a "tourist attraction" *par excellence*, but there is no denying that the view is superb, showing us the north shore of Lake Ontario, commuter planes landing and taking off on the Toronto Islands, and the great sprawl of the city fanning north, west and east. There is Horizons, "the only café in Toronto that is 1,136 ft high." Upstairs is the award-winning, revolving 360 Restaurant ((416) 362-5411, where diners pay a bit more to munch on blue-crab cakes and watch the world pass by. Stop by the PhotoFX booth and you can get an instant photo of your party looking wide-eyed at a digital representation of — you guessed it — the CN Tower.

We head downstairs to the Glass Floor and outdoor observatory, a magnet for daredevils of various stripes. Some people stand on the

glass — on thin air it seems — looking down a dizzying 340 m (1,115 ft) and waving for the camera; some walk along the girders that crisscross the glass, holding hands, laughing nervously; the rest of us cling to the opposite wall and turn green — despite the fact that our guide has assured us that the glass used in this floor is three times stronger than concrete (and strong enough to support the weight of 14 large hippos).

It takes another elevator (and fee) to get up a further 33 stories to the seemingly flimsy Sky Pod, at 447 m (1,465 ft) the highest point accessible to the public. The view on a good day stretches as far as Niagara.

At the base of the tower are plenty of activities to distract visitors from the disturbingly breathtaking views, including a visitor center, two simulation theaters, a games arcade, a cinema, a food court and a vast souvenir shop. All in all, there is plenty at Toronto's CN Tower to keep visitors of many tastes entertained for an hour or so. Even if you don't care for interactive video games, digital souvenirs and glass floors — go for the view.

The tower opens daily 8 AM to 11 PM, although most attractions close at 9 PM. A complicated system of admission tickets allows you to choose which, if any, of the extra attractions to add to the basic viewing platform.

OPPOSITE: Gulls roost in cliffside niches at Witless Bay Ecological Reserve, Newfoundland. ABOVE: Toronto's CN Tower, Ontario.

YOUR CHOICE

The Great Outdoors

Extending from the densely populated 49th parallel into the empty reaches of the north, Canada — the world's second-largest country — encompasses not only a stunning breadth of wilderness, but also a mind-boggling variety of terrains. Eastern Canada in particular spans from treeless far northern tundra to sea-battered fjords, from boundless prairie wheat fields to lake-dotted interiors, picket fences and potato patches, and great deciduous forests.

Canada has a total of 39 national parks and many provincial parks. While these parks serve to protect the natural habitat, most are accessible to travelers, and most offer an array of facilities and activities. Boating, biking, skiing, dog sledding … take your pick. But a stout pair of hiking boots is all that is really required to experience many of Canada's wide-open spaces.

THE NATIONAL PARKS
Undoubtedly top of the list are the Rocky Mountain parks that straddle the western provinces of Alberta and British Columbia. However there are also many fine parks in eastern Canada.

Rich and varied in its landscape, Québec is Canada's largest province, with no fewer than 25 national parks of varying sizes. On the Gaspé Peninsula, **Parc de la Gaspésie** is laced with trails leading into mountainous territory where Arctic flora grows. Further east, on the tip of the peninsula, **Parc National Forillon** has a craggy coastline from which walkers can spot whales in spring and fall.

Fundy National Park encompasses some of New Brunswick's loveliest shoreline, where the country's most extreme tides rise and fall. With forested hills and gorges as well, the park is crossed by 128 km (78 miles) of hiking trails, most of which are short, easy walks of no more than three hours. Long-distance backpackers link these to walk the 50-km (30-mile) Fundy Circuit.

Some of eastern Canada's most dramatic scenery is found in Newfoundland's fjord-creased **Gros Morne National Park** where splendid hiking abounds, particularly at Rocky Harbour and Bonne Bay. **Terra Nova National Park** on Bonavista Bay is popular for its rugged treks such as the Outport Trail, an 18-km (11-mile) walk along the south shore of the fjord.

Eastern Canada has its long-distance trails, too. In Ontario, the **Rideau Trail** follows paths and side roads for 386 km (232 miles) between Ottawa and Kingston, and the **Bruce Trail** runs

OPPOSITE: Autumn colors frame a backcountry waterfall in New Brunswick. ABOVE: Canoeing pristine waters at Old Fort William on Thunder Bay, Ontario.

690 km (414 miles) from Queenston on the Niagara River to Tobermory on the Bruce Peninsula, while the **Voyageur Trail** runs along the north shores of lakes Superior and Huron.

One of the jewels of central Canada, **Riding Mountain National Park** has 40 hiking and cycling trails traversing Manitoba's highlands — where bison, moose, elk and white-tailed deer roam, along with dozens of less easily spotted species from enormous black bears to tiny frogs.

Bisected by the Arctic Circle, on Baffin Island in Nunavut, **Auyuittuq National Park Reserve** is an international draw for climbers and hikers, who follow traditional Inuit routes marked by *inukshuks*, rock cairns resembling human figures.

In addition to local tourist information centers, park centers are often equipped with adequate trail maps. If you are venturing into the backcountry, you'll need a topographical map. The **Canada Map Office** produces an excellent series, available from all good map retailers.

WILDLIFE

Canada's tundra, mountains, forests and prairies support a profusion of wildlife. Point Pelee National Park, in southern Ontario, dips into Lake Erie at Canada's southernmost reach. This peninsula attracts some **350 species of birds** each spring and fall, and thousands of **monarch butterflies** gather here before their annual migration to Mexico each September.

North of Québec City, Tadoussac is an excellent place to spot beluga, humpback, minke and finback **whales** in summer months, and **snow geese** flock to Cap-Tourmente, north of Québec City, each autumn.

One of North America's highest concentrations of **bald eagles** is found on Cape Breton Island, Nova Scotia. July and August are the best time to see them. Nearby Bird Island is the place to see seabirds, including the **Atlantic puffin** and the endangered **piping plover**.

Newfoundland and New Brunswick are **whale** territory, with yearly migrations of humpback, right, finback and minke whales. Newfoundland is also well known for its seabirds: **Atlantic puffins**, **murres** and **black kittiwakes** can be observed from boats at the Witless Bay Ecological Reserve (see THE WONDERS OF WITLESS BAY, page 16 in TOP SPOTS, for more on this area). Cape St. Mary's on Newfoundland's southern Avalon Peninsula is a major nesting site for **gannets**, and Baccalieu Island has the world's largest colony of **Leach's stormy petrels** (three million pairs).

Newfoundland also has around 150,000 **moose** and the country's most southerly herd

of **caribou**. Meanwhile Churchill, Manitoba, is the **polar bear** capital of the world, and polar bears are abundant along Nunavut's Arctic coast.

It isn't wildlife, but it is one of the world's most spectacular natural phenomena — the **Northern Lights** (Aurora Borealis) play across the skies in most of northern Canada, but if you want to be sure of seeing them, head for Labrador, where there is a show on for a stunning 240 nights a year.

Sporting Spree

Whatever your sporting passion, be it curling or croquet, watching a beer-soaked hockey match or skiing solo down a pristine mountainside, Canada is likely to offer a time and a place for it.

CANOEING, KAYAKING AND RAFTING

Canada is the world's most watery land, with lakes and rivers that contain half of the world's supply of fresh water, and with more than 240,000 km (151,000 miles) of coastline. With so much H_2O, it's no surprise that Canada's shores and inland waterways are an irresistible draw for paddlers from all over the world.

Along the Québec and Ontario border, the **Jacques Cartier River** and **Rivière Rouge** in Les Laurentides offer first-class rafting, as does the **Ottawa River** in Ontario. There's even a whitewater trip in the downtown heart of Montréal where Saute Moutons–Lachine

Northern Ontario — OPPOSITE: A sled team takes a break TOP. The stark beauty of day's end at Algonquin National Park BOTTOM. ABOVE: A colony of gannets nesting on the Gaspé Peninsula in Québec.

Rapids Tours runs jet boats through **Lachine Rapids** (see JET THE LACHINE RAPIDS, page 15 in TOP SPOTS).

Moving east, New Brunswick's **Fundy National Park** has facilities for river, lake and ocean canoeing and kayaking, and there are jet boats through the Reversing Falls in **Saint John**. **Kejimkujik National Park** in Nova Scotia is a splendid place to paddle through the islets in Kejimkujik Lake or up the River Mersey beneath a canopy of red maples.

SKIING

In this land of legendary winters, where snow covers hill and vale for five months (or more!) of the year, skiing is a good way to stay warm. Good skiing can be had in just about every province and territory, but it is in British Columbia and the Rockies that you find ski slopes of a variety and grandeur unsurpassed anywhere in the world. In eastern Canada, head to Québec.

Québec's **Laurentides** (Laurentians) have been attracting thousands of visitors each year ever since the early days of skiing in North America. There are some 20 downhill ski stations within a 50-km (32-mile) region, all within a two-hour drive from Montréal. Cross-country skiers are very well served here too, with 1,200 km (755 miles) of groomed trails. The heart of the action is at **Mont Tremblant**, a teeming town of shops, après-ski spots and slope-side hotels. It's the largest station in Les Laurentides, with 77 ski runs, and the steepest,

with vertical drops of 650 m (2,132 ft). There are dozens of other ski resorts, including **Mont Ste-Anne**, only 40 km (24 miles) east of Québec City, with its 56 runs and vertical drops of 625 m (2,050 ft), and a Montréaler favorite, **Le Chantecler** (see FAMILY FUN, page 26) on Lac Ste-Adèle, with 22 ski runs, half of which are lighted so skiers can remain on the slopes until 10 PM.

Perhaps the best part of the Canada ski report is that skiing doesn't have to be an expensive undertaking. Many resorts, hotels and bed-and-breakfast inns offer affordable packages. Some hostels even offer ski packages. Contact Hostelling International ((613) 237-7884 FAX (613) 237-7868 E-MAIL info@hostellingintl.ca WEB SITE www.hostellingintl.ca, 400-205 Catherine Street, Ottawa, Ontario K2P 1C3 for details.

The Open Road

Al Capone once said, "I don't even know what street Canada is on." Everyone laughed, but old Scarface had put his chubby finger on one of Canada's most pressing needs: transportation. Nor could he have known that after his death Canada would come to live on one principal street, the **TransCanada Highway (TCH)**.

Completed in 1962, the TCH is only two lanes for much of its 6,978-km (4,361-mile) length from St. John's, Newfoundland, to Victoria, British Columbia. With more than

90 percent of all Canadians living within 80 km (50 miles) of this road, it truly is the country's main street. What's more, most of the major tourist attractions are within easy reach of the TransCanada Highway.

Adventurous vacationers and those with more time to spend will want to get off this well-beaten track to experience the country's more remote regions, including its incomparably beautiful national parks in the central and northern regions of the provinces.

If you're not bent on making one of Canada's many epic-length road trips, plenty of scenic loops and Sunday drives remain to be enjoyed. You will find many of them described in the regional chapters.

Backpacking

Perhaps it is the length and harshness of northern winters, but when summer rolls around, Canadians just can't stay indoors. **Québec** and **Montréal**, in particular, are perfect for visitors on shoestring budgets — who can savor the city's vibrant street-life and many summer outdoor festivals without spending a *sou*. Elsewhere too, penny-pinching travelers find much to like in Canada.

ACCOMMODATION
Canada's **hostels** are usually the least expensive places to lay your head down — especially for solo travelers — costing from $13 to $25 per night, per person. They also provide good company, a refreshing change from the isolation of hotels. Many of them have cooking facilities for self-catering, offering additional savings on food cost.

Those who plan to do a fair amount of hostelling will benefit by becoming members of **Hostelling International** WEB SITE www.hi hostels.ca. There are 12 regional offices across Canada, as well as branches in many other countries around the world. Membership of your home association offers full benefits in Canada, including reducing nightly fees at hostels and discounts at many local businesses. Ask when joining for a copy of the *Official Guide to Hostels in Canada and the United States of America*.

YMCA and **YWCA** residences can be found in many Canadian cities. They are often quite comfortable, with extras such as inexpensive cafeterias, fitness facilities and swimming pools. Though some residences offer dormitory accommodation for as little as $20, others can cost as much as a budget hotel. **YMCA Canada** ((416) 967-9622 FAX (416) 967-9618 WEB SITE www.ymca.ca, 42 Charles Street East, Sixth

Floor, Toronto, Ontario M4Y 1T4, will send you the *YMCA-YWCA Residence Directory*, a complete list of all YMCA-YWCA residences in the country.

Some **university campuses** open their dormitories to travelers from May to August. Anyone can use the facilities, though preference is often given to students. Rates for single and double rooms start at $35 to $40. Most universities have an office that handles reservations, and it's a good idea to book well in advance. You'll find university accommodation contact numbers listed under WHERE TO STAY in the regional chapters.

GETTING AROUND
Canada is big, and the largest part of your traveling budget will undoubtedly be transportation. Distances are vast; gasoline is expensive in comparison to United States prices, although much cheaper than in Europe; and trains can be outrageously expensive, although there are some excellent value passes available. Internal airfares are generally fairly high. **Greyhound Canada** TOLL-FREE (800) 661-8747 WEB SITE www.greyhound.ca and the other bus lines ply just about every route in the country and are almost always cheaper than rail, air or driving, unless you are traveling in a group of three or more. Greyhound offers

OPPOSITE: Ice climbers scale Montmorency Falls near Québec City. ABOVE: Hanging out in sight of Old City Hall, Toronto.

a wide range of discounts and passes, so don't buy a ticket until you've explored the possibilities thoroughly.

In Québec, Allo-Stop arranges **ride-sharing** (in Québécois, "*covoiturage*"): putting drivers who want company together with riders who need a lift. You can, for example, get a one-way ride between Montréal and Québec for an initial one-year membership fee of $6 and $15 for the ride. Visit their WEB SITE www.allostop .com or one of the following local offices: Québec City ℂ (418) 522-0056, 665 rue St-Jean, or Montréal ℂ (514) 985-3044, 4317 rue St-Denis. Phone for a list of contacts in smaller places.

Living It Up

While some vacationers come to Canada to test themselves against the great outdoors, others come to soak up the scenery at the country's luxury hotels and resorts. And, short of palm-shaded tropical beaches, Canada has just about everything the sybaritic swinger could want.

EXCEPTIONAL HOTELS

There is a common theme running through the best hotels in Canada. Many, although by no means all, are the historic railway hotels now run by Fairmont WEB SITE www.fairmont.com. Their prices are not cheap, but there is a level of elegance and service matched by few other large hotels.

Our pick of Toronto's many luxury hotels is the **Fairmont Royal York**, mainly because of its terrific location in the vibrant core of the city's shopping district. Competition comes from the gorgeously ornate **King Edward Hotel Meridian** and its turn-of-the-century splendor, with columns, marble, polished wood and beautiful ceilings. It has some of the finest dining in the city and a lounge serving high tea. The **Windsor Arms** is a tiny gem of understated elegance, with all the amenities of a much larger hotel.

In Ottawa, the **Fairmont Château Laurier** is the city's most luxurious and memorable hotel, the old Canadian Pacific building's fairytale roofline mirroring the Parliament Buildings right next door. At the opposite end of the scale, **Arc – the Hotel** is a trendy minimalist boutique hotel.

Niagara Falls draws thousands of tourists each year, but overnight visitors often prefer the tranquil charms of nearby Niagara-on-the-Lake, where the **Prince of Wales** hotel offers guests excellent cuisine, an idyllic setting and exceptional comfort.

Ask a Montréaler for a recommendation and you are likely to hear about one of Vieux Montréal's small inns, where Old World charm and excellent food are found at prices well below the large luxury hotels. The enchantingly French **Auberge du Vieux-Port** has 27 rooms on five floors of a renovated nineteenth-century warehouse. Rooms have stone or brick walls and brass beds, exposed wooden beams, tall windows and views of the Vieux Port. Downstairs is the highly regarded French restaurant, Les Remparts. Another charmer, the nine-room **Les Passants du Sans Soucy**, is a former furrier's warehouse. Its foundations date to 1684, making it the oldest hotel in the city. The **Fairmont Queen Elizabeth** is inevitably at the head of the list of larger hotels, a more modern building than many of its counterparts, but with the same superb levels of comfort and service and a convenient downtown location.

With its distinctive copper roofs towering over Québec's romantic walled quarter, Québec City's **Fairmont Château Frontenac** has been setting standards of excellence since 1893. The **Hotel Dominion 1912** in the old port at the foot of the cliff couldn't be more different, a sleek, modern boutique hotel oozing stylish sophistication.

EXCEPTIONAL RESTAURANTS
Toronto, with its rich cultural diversity, offers a profusion of excellent dining choices. **North 44** serves exceptional international cuisine, including such dishes as fried oysters with jalapeño cream and roasted rack of lamb. From its fifty-fourth-floor perch, the **Canoe Restaurant Bar & Grill** serves modern and traditional Canadian cuisine and luscious desserts along with impressive views of the city lights. **Oro** is one of the city's newer restaurants — sleek and sophisticated with contemporary Italian food made with fresh Canadian ingredients.

In Ottawa, the presence of so many politicians and diplomats ensures a high level of fine dining and a wide choice of restaurants. Among the finest, **Le Jardin** is an award-winning haute cuisine French restaurant, with one of Canada's best wine lists. **Signature** is the public restaurant of the local cookery school. In exchange for letting the students practice on you, you can expect a fabulous meal at a remarkably affordable price.

Montréal is lucky enough to have two of North America's finest restaurants. The first, the **Beaver Club** (in the Fairmont Queen Elizabeth) serves superb continental and Québec regional cuisine in a nineteenth-century style wood-paneled dining room. The second, **Nuances** (Casino de Montréal), also has wood paneling, along with a fine view, exquisite presentation, excellent service and fine food. Montréalers love it and claim that the desserts here are "built, not made." For those who prefer a more contemporary feel, **Toqué** means "loony" in French, and you would be crazy to pass up a chance to dine there; it is one of Montréal's most fashionable

restaurants, where the contemporary Québec-Montréal cuisine is as good as it gets. **Area** is one of the city's newer restaurants, with a pleasing ambiance, mouth-watering fusion cuisine (French, Italian and Asian) and an impressive wine list. Down in the old town, **Chez L'Epicier** is a mind-blowing combination of specialty delicatessen and an ultra-modern chic restaurant serving contemporary Québecois cuisine.

Québec City also has so many excellent restaurants that it is difficult to know where to eat. Although a different chef is now in charge of the kitchen, **À la Table de Serge Bruyère** remains one of the city's finest restaurants, with several options on the premises: from the informal elegance of the Café European to the hushed white-linen ambiance of La Grande Table, or the cozy second-floor bistro, Chez Livernois. At the Chateau Frontenac, chef Jean Soulard has raised the already fine restaurant, **Le Champlain**, to new heights of excellence, using herbs grown in his own gardens on the hotel roof. Giving him a run for his money, **St Amour** is discreetly tucked away in an old period home with a bright and airy winter garden. It serves wonderful local produce with imagination and flair — the dessert menu is positively poetic.

OPPOSITE AND ABOVE: Be it silver service scones, and *petits fours*, or country-style French courtyard dining, travelers find small luxuries throughout eastern Canada.

Family Fun

The bad news is: there is no Disneyland Canada. Or is this the good news? Whatever your opinion, this fact points to an essential, if subtle, difference between Canada and the United States when it comes to family vacations. The United States may have bigger thrill rides, glitzier cartoon characters, better-known superstars, but Canada has a small-town warmth and friendliness that we believe makes it just right for kids. It's safer, too. Canada, claims one of our American friends, reminds him of the United States of the 1950s. So, put Beaver and Wally in the car …

As long as there is snow on the ground, children seem to be impervious to the cold. So, why not take a winter vacation in Canada? If school schedules allow, visit Québec City during the first two weeks of February for the wonderful **Carnaval d'Hiver**, when a potbellied snowman named Bonhomme Carnaval reigns as ambassador. Though Québec's is the most famous, many cities across Canada have terrific winter carnivals (see FESTIVE FLINGS, below).

Skiing, as you might expect, is very big in Canada. In eastern Canada, Chantecler TOLL-FREE (800) 363-2450 in Ste-Adèle, Québec, about an hour from Montréal, is a laid-back resort perfect for families. Active teenagers will appreciate this resort's new snowboarding facilities. If your tastes run to adventure, your Canadian winter break might include **dog sledding, snowmobiling, backcountry skiing** or **winter camping** in one of the country's national parks.

When the snow melts, Canada's vacation offerings multiply. Teenagers are thrilled by **rafting** trips in Québec's Laurentides and along the Ottawa River. Whether you join a tour or go it on your own, possibilities for **hiking** and **backpacking** are virtually endless and can be easily combined with **off-road biking** and **paddling** in Canada's lakes, rivers and along its seashores. **Ranch vacations** and **farm stays** in Quinte's Isle (Ontario) give everyone in the family a chance to share in the day-to-day operations of working ranches and farms: guests help with chores, ride horses and round up cattle, and can participate a variety of leisure activities (see SPECIAL INTERESTS, below).

Children (and adults) are always delighted with **animal encounters**. Each of Canada's provinces and territories has its characteristic populations (see THE GREAT OUTDOORS, page 21), and an entire family vacation can easily be planned around wildlife watching.

And if the weather turns nasty, there are plenty of indoor attractions from children's **museums** at Toronto's Royal Ontario Museum and Ottawa's Museum of Civilization to a large collection of excellent hands-on science centers.

Cultural Kicks

Canada is a mosaic of cultures, an assembly of immigrant groups and native peoples, many of whom have maintained their uniqueness rather than merging into a national Canadian identity. This makes Canada in many ways a more exciting cultural destination than its southern neighbor, where ethnic origins have been obscured by the "melting pot."

You can take a trip around the world in Toronto with its patchwork of lively ethnic neighborhoods — from Italian to Chinese,

Portuguese, German, Jewish, Hungarian, Greek, Indian, West Indian, Vietnamese, Thai and French Canadian. Québec City needs no introduction, and Montréal is not only very French, but also very cosmopolitan, with a broad mix of ethnic communities. You'll note a strong Scottish influence in the Maritime Provinces (Nova Scotia translates as "New Scotland" in Latin) — evident from the brogue you'll hear in the more remote of parts the islands, and in the Highland games staged in various communities (see FESTIVE FLINGS, below).

Canada's **First Nations peoples** are as culturally varied as the country's immigrant groups. In this spectrum of native bands, it is the Inuit and the Pacific Northwest Coast natives whose art first garnered international attention. The **Inuit** are known for their carvings on soapstone, ivory, antler and whalebone, as well as for their printmaking.

With the rising popularity of Inuit art, there are frequent temporary shows in galleries and museums throughout Canada. Less known, outside the pages of fiction, are the cultures of the Plains Indians including the Blackfoot, the Algonquin groups of tribes such as the Cree and Mi'kmaq and the Iroquois (Huron and Mohawks), who inhabit the eastern provinces. A huge number of often small-scale community-based developments are now being created alongside set showpieces such as the excellent First Nations galleries in many major museums. Tourism Québec now produce a brochure specifically about First Nations cultural tourist projects, from canoe trips to museums or traditional camping.

Montréal's splendid Basilique Notre-Dame. The stained-glass windows tell of the city's religious history.

First Nations individuals and groups are also active in the performing arts. One of the best ways to see and learn about native art and artists is to go to the **Great Northern Arts Festival** that takes place in Inuvik, Northwest Territories, each July, or to attend the **Canadian Aboriginal Festival** (November) in Toronto (see FESTIVE FLINGS, below).

European-Canadian painters began to distinguish their art from its continental influences at the beginning of the twentieth century, when the Group of Seven emerged as an artistic force, creating a uniquely Canadian school of landscape painting. Today, painters and sculptors are exhibiting

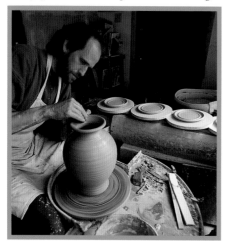

their work in galleries and museums throughout Canada and the world. Eastern Canada's outstanding museums include Toronto's **Art Gallery of Ontario** and the **Royal Ontario Museum**; the **McMichael Canadian Art Collection** in Kleinburg, Ontario; the **National Gallery of Canada** and the **Museum of Civilization** in Ottawa; Montréal's **Musée des Beaux Arts** and the **Musée de la Civilisation** in Québec City.

All three of Canada's international **ballet** companies are in the east: the Royal Winnipeg Ballet, Manitoba, the Grands Ballets Canadiens of Montréal, and the National Ballet of Canada, based in Toronto. Widely acclaimed **modern dance** troupes include the innovative La La La Human Steps and O Vertigo. Most other major cities have professional dance companies, along with **opera** companies (the Canadian Opera Company in Toronto is one of the best), symphony orchestras and smaller ensembles, and theaters with resident and touring **theater** companies. Toronto, Montréal, Ottawa and Winnipeg have **symphony orchestras** of international status. The Shaw and Stratford **theater festivals** are well known abroad, and avant-garde theater companies such as Carbone 14 and UBU tour the world and receive critical acclaim wherever they go. Montréal's **Festival International de Jazz** is a must on the itinerary of all jazz fans, while the **Cirque du Soleil** (also Montréal) is credited with revolutionizing the circus. Under its yellow and blue big top the troupe presents a

show that is known as much for its drama, cutting edge music and fabulous costumes as for its acrobatics.

Shop till You Drop

The rule to remember is: look for local specialties. This means that in the **Maritime Provinces** check out the hand-knit sweaters, hunting jackets and fishermen's gear such as oilskins. **Québec** is a good place to shop for Canadian crafts, and you will be amazed to learn how many things can be made from maple syrup. Another of the specialties of the region is salmon, which you can buy smoked and gift-packed.

In Québec *aubaine* means "a good bargain" and Montréalers are passionate about shopping for them. There are overwhelming numbers of boutiques, shopping malls and department stores catering to every need or whim. In **Ontario** look for native basketwork and, in the Kitchener area, Mennonite quilts. In the **Prairie Provinces**, such as Manitoba, you will find every sort of cowboy attire you could possibly want.

Nova Scotia has a keen craft tradition, producing excellent knitting, pottery, quilts and wooden carvings. In the **Northwest Territories** and **Nunavut**, in addition to wonderful Inuit carvings, seek out Dene specialties: snowshoes, baskets and drums, as well as traditional clothing such as parkas,

mitts and moccasins. Also in the north, Fort Liard is noted for its birch-bark baskets, and Fort Simpson for the now-rare art of moose-hair tufting.

There are two caveats to bear in mind when shopping for native Canadian arts and crafts. Although these items, when genuine, are among the loveliest things to buy in Canada, they are often swamped by cheap imitations. Be suspicious of any handcrafted article that strikes you as a bargain. To be certain that you are getting the real thing, buy from the artist or from a crafts guild or cooperative, or from a museum shop.

Short Breaks

Few visitors attempt to take Canada in as a whole. Nor is there a single entry-point at which all international flights arrive. In the east, Montréal and Toronto serve as the main **transportation hubs**. Both of these cities have their own unique attractions, and both have the distinct advantage of being within easy striking distance of the great outdoors, making them excellent choices for short vacations. Both

OPPOSITE: A souvenir shop in the Quartier Petit-Champlain, Basse-Ville, Québec City. BOTTOM: Tim Alexander forms a vase in Rossport, Ontario. ABOVE LEFT: Montréal's Botanical Gardens. RIGHT: In Québec City, choices abound for a taste of France

as L'Estrie) is a rural area bordering Vermont, New Hampshire and Maine. Skiing here is less crowded and less commercialized than it is in Les Laurentides. In both of these regions in early spring the sugar shacks are busy with maple syrup. In summer boating, swimming, sailing, golf, in-line skating, hiking and bicycling take over. Every fall the inns are booked solid with leaf peepers eager to take in the brilliant foliage.

Festive Flings

No matter what the season, Canadians love a party. Every province has an extraordinarily full calendar of festivals and events, covering almost every day of the year. There are over 400 in Newfoundland and Labrador alone. We have pulled out a few of the highlights.

WINTER
In **Québec**, Québec City goes wild with Carnaval d'Hiver (February) ((418) 621-5555 TOLL-FREE (866) 422-7628 WEB SITE www.carnaval .qc.ca, a riotous two-week festival of winter sports, ice-sculpting, cross-country skiing, barrel-jumping, dog sledding and ice canoe races, while La Fête des Neiges (January/ February) ((514) 872-4537 WEB SITE www.parc jeandrapeau is Montréal's salute to winter. This is followed swiftly by Montréal High Lights (February) ((514) 288-9955 TOLL-FREE (888) 477-9955 WEB SITE www.montrealhigh lights.com, a celebration of the finer things in life, with art, music, dance, haute cuisine and spectacular street lights.

Ontario has the Niagara Falls Winter Festival of Lights (November to January) ((905) 356-6061 TOLL-FREE (800) 563-2557 WEB SITE www.niagarafallstourism.com with fireworks, caroling and light shows featuring the falls. Ice boating, ice sculpting and snowshoe races are part of the fun during Ottawa's **Winterlude** (February) ((613) 239-5000 TOLL-FREE (800) 465-1867 WEB SITE www.capcan.ca and the Toronto Winterfest (February) ((416) 395-0490 WEB SITE www.city.toronto.on.ca/winterfest.

Manitoba celebrates the region's early French fur-trading history in Winnipeg during the Festival du Voyageur (February) ((204) 237-7692 WEB SITE www.festivalvoyageur.mb.ca, staged in Fort Gibraltar. Although it's not compulsory, many participants dress the part and it's all great fun, with such events creating gigantic snow sculptures and racing motorcycles on the iced-over river.

Newfoundland celebrates winter with the 10-day Corner Brook Winter Carnival (February) ((709) 632-5343 E-MAIL cbwc@nf.aibn.com.

cities are also within an hour's drive of the United States border — over which vast numbers of Americans flock to Canada each year.

Many visitors combine a trip to **Toronto** with an excursion to nearby **Niagara Falls**. This is can be accomplished as a daytrip, or you can take a more leisurely approach and include a tour of Niagara's wine country. You should plan to stay overnight in **Niagara-on-the-Lake** at one of the quaint bed-and-breakfast inns; take in a play at the **Shaw Festival** if your schedule allows. **Ottawa** is less commonly on people's list, but this is a capital city with style — and a great many excellent museums and galleries.

A less-obvious, but no less enjoyable, Toronto-based vacation would be to divide a week between Toronto's urban pleasures and the outdoor delights of the **Bruce Peninsula**, where two of Ontario's most impressive parks are found: Bruce Peninsula National Park and Fathom Five National Marine Park.

With **Montréal** as your entry point into Canada, if you've never been there, you must see **Québec City**. From Montréal, a four-hour train ride whisks you into its Old World atmosphere. Take a late afternoon train, splurge on first-class tickets, and enjoy dinner on the way.

One of the world's oldest mountain ranges, **Les Laurentides** is a rippling landscape of undulating hills and valleys. Just 56 km (35 miles) from Montréal, they are home to some of North America's best-known ski resorts. **Les Cantons de l'Est** (formerly known

SPRING

All over the region, there are maple syrup festivals, of which the biggest and best known is in **Ontario** at Elmira (April) ((519) 669-2605 WEB SITE www.ontariotravel.net. The renowned Shaw Festival (April-November) ((905) 468-2172 TOLL-FREE (800) 511-7429 WEB SITE www.shawfest .sympatico.ca, 10 Queen's Parade, Niagara-on-the-Lake, opens its season with plays by George Bernard Shaw and his contemporaries. Three million blossoms herald spring at the Canadian Tulip Festival (May) ((613) 567-5757 WEB SITE www.tulipfestival.ca in Ottawa, and the Stratford Shakespeare Festival (May-November) ((519) 273-1600 TOLL-FREE (800) 567 1600 WEB SITE www.stratfordfestival.ca opens its much-anticipated season.

SUMMER

The summer season starts in St. Catharine's, **Ontario**, with the 16-day Niagara Folk Arts Festival (May–June) ((905) 685-6589 TOLL-FREE (866) 801-1102 WEB SITE www.famc-stcath.org, Canada's oldest heritage festival. Ottawa turns musical in July with Bluesfest ((613) 233-8798 WEB SITE www.ottawa-bluesfest.ca closely followed by the Ottawa International Jazz Festival ((613) 241-2633 WEB SITE www .ottawajazzfestival.com and the Ottawa Chamber Music Festival ((613) 234-8008 WEB SITE www.chamberfest.com. The Changing of the Guard ((613) 239-5000 TOLL-FREE (800) 465-1867 WEB SITE www.capcan.ca begins in mid-June at Ottawa's Parliament Buildings

and continues through August. The Toronto Downtown Jazz Festival (June) ((416) 928-2033 WEB SITE www.torontojazz.com regularly includes over 1,600 performers in some 60 venues. The Toronto International Carnival (August) ((416) 285-1609 TOLL-FREE (888) 210-8789 WEB SITE www.torontointernationalcarnival .info, formerly Caribana, celebrates Toronto's vibrant West Indian community with North America's largest Caribbean carnival.

In **Québec**, Montréal's Festival International de Jazz (June and July) ((514) 871-1881 TOLL-FREE (888) 515-0515 WEB SITE www.montrealjazz fest.com is one of Canada's best parties, attracting both internationally known and local players, while Just for Laughs (also July and also in Montréal) ((514) 790-4242 (information) or (514) 845-2322 (box office) TOLL-FREE (888) 244 3155 WEB SITE www.hahaha .com has become one of the world's largest and most prestigious celebrations of comedy. In late July / early August, Divers Cité Montréal ((514) 285-4011 WEB SITE www.diverscite.org is one of North America's largest gay pride festivals.

Québec City's two-week Festival d'Eté International (International Summer Festival) (July) ((418) 529-5200 TOLL-FREE (888) 992-5200 WEB SITE www.infofestival.com steps up the fun in the city's lovely parks.

Montréal — OPPOSITE: A girl wears the fleur-de-lys at the Festival of St. Baptiste. ABOVE: Revellers color Boulevard Réné-Levesque.

In **Manitoba**, the Winnipeg Folk Festival (July) ℂ (204) 231-0096 WEB SITE www.Winnipeg folkfestival.ca, held in Birds Hill Provincial Park, features over 80 concerts, with all forms of popular music. Eclectic crafts, many weird, are also on show and there are some 30 or 40 restaurants serving good quality food from around the world. The National Ukrainian Festival (August) ℂ (204) 622-4600, in Dauphin, presents costumed interpreters, fiddling contests, dancing and workshops. Winnipeg celebrates its rich ethnic heritage with the colorful two-week-long Folklorama (August) ℂ (204) 982-6210 WEB SITE www.folklorama.ca, the largest multi-cultural festival in the world. Very authentic.

In **New Brunswick**, the Shediac Lobster Festival (July) ℂ (506) 532-1122 WEB SITE www .lobsterfestival.nb.ca takes place in "the Lobster Capital of the World." The province also hosts ethnic festivals galore, including the Miramichi Irish Festival (July) ℂ (506) 887-8810 WEB SITE www.canadasirishfest.com, Fredericton's New Brunswick Highland Games and Scottish Festival (July) ℂ (506) 452-9244 TOLL-FREE (888) 368-4444 WEB SITE www.nbhighlandgames.com, Foire Brayonne (July to August) ℂ (506) 739-6608 WEB SITE www.foire-brayonne.nb.ca in Edmundston, and the Acadian Festival (August) ℂ (506) 727-2787 in Caraquet, the heart of French-speaking New Brunswick.

In **Newfoundland and Labrador**, the village of Twillingate throws the Fish, Fun and Folk Festival (July) ℂ (709) 884-2678 WEB SITE www.fishfunfolkfestival.com, and the Festival of Flight (July to August) ℂ (709) 651-5927 WEB SITE www.gandercanada.com takes place each year in Gander, when hot-air balloons and traditional music float on the breeze. Summer in the Bight (June to October) ℂ (709) 464-3847 TOLL-FREE (888) 464-3377 WEB SITE www.risingtide theatre.com is a summer-long theater festival in Trinity Bight. The Royal St. John's Regatta (August) ℂ (709) 576-8921 WEB SITE www.infonet .st-johns.nf.ca is North America's oldest sporting event (it began in 1826). St. John's, known for its year-round folk music scene, is also the venue for the Newfoundland and

Labrador Folk Festival (August) ((709) 576-8508 WEB SITE www.sjfac.nf.net, when musicians and dancers converge for a lively weekend. The Labrador Straits Bakeapple Folk Festival (August) ((709) 931-2545 in southern Labrador pays homage to this delicious fruit.

In **Nova Scotia**, the Halifax Nova Scotia International Tattoo (July) ((902) 451-1221 TOLL-FREE (800) 563-1114 WEB SITE www.nstattoo .ca is North America's largest indoor show, with over 2,000 performers offering pageantry, pipes and family entertainment. Also in July, Halifax holds the Atlantic Jazz Festival TOLL-FREE (800) 567-5277 WEB SITE www.jazzeast.com, while in August, the Halifax International Busker Festival brings in street performers from across the world. Elsewhere on the island, the Festival Acadien de Clare (July) is Canada's largest celebration of Acadian culture, with different events in a string of east coast villages. In Lunenburg, there is the Folk Harbour Festival (August) ((902) 634-3180 WEB SITE www .folkharbour.com, with island folk music and traditional foods. Chester Race Week (August) ((902) 275-3876 is the largest sailing regatta in the Maritime Provinces.

On **Prince Edward Island**, the Charlottetown Festival (June to mid-October) ((902) 566-1267 TOLL-FREE (800) 565-0278 WEB SITE www.confeder ationcentre.com opens with its annual production of the musical version of *Anne of Green Gables*. The Summerside Highland Gathering (June) ((902) 436-5377 TOLL-FREE (877) 22467473 WEB SITE www.collegeofpiping.com is a weekend of nonstop Celtic events. Street performers and fireworks top the festivities at Charlottetown's Festival of Lights (Canada Day weekend — July 1) ((902) 629-1864 TOLL-FREE (800) 955-1864 WEB SITE www.visitcharlottetown .com. The Indian River Festival (August) ((902) 836-4933 TOLL-FREE (800) 565-3688 WEB SITE www .indianriverfestival.com is a wonderful four-day series of chamber music, choral music and jazz, attracting international artists.

Throughout the country, **Canada Day** (July 1) is celebrated by fetes, processions, parties and picnics.

FALL

In late August, Montréal, **Québec**, again takes center stage for the Montréal World Film Festival ((514) 848-3883 WEB SITE www.ffm-montreal.org.

Ontario makes merry throughout the fall with the Canadian National Exhibition (August) ((416) 263-3800 WEB SITE www.TheEx.com, in Toronto, which incorporates everything from a horse show to an air show, with music and heritage festivals; the Toronto International Film Festival (September) ((416) 967-7371

WEB SITE www.bell.ca/filmfest; the Niagara Grape and Wine Festival (September) ((905) 688-0212 WEB SITE www.grapeandwine.com, in St. Catharines; the world's second-largest Oktoberfest (October) ((519) 570-4267WEB SITE www.oktoberfest.ca in Kitchener; and the Royal Agricultural Winter Fair (November) ((416) 263-3400 WEB SITE www.royalfair.org in Toronto. The Canadian Aboriginal Festival (November) ((519) 751-0040 WEB SITE www .canab.com, held each year at the Toronto SkyDome, is a celebration of First Nations' heritage, culture, fashions, food, theater, films, literature and arts.

Fredericton, **New Brunswick**, is the venue for the Harvest Jazz and Blues Festival ((506) 454-2583 WEB SITE www.harvestjazzblues.nb.ca (September).

On Cape Breton Island, **Nova Scotia**'s Celtic Colors Festival (October) ((902) 562-6700 WEB SITE www.celtic-colours.com is still a relative newcomer, but has stormed through to become one of the premier festivals of Celtic culture in the world, attracting international performers and huge audiences.

Galloping Gourmet

It must be said that Mobil-star-spangled restaurants are few and far between in Canada. But that is not to say that you can't eat wonderfully well in every part of the country. In all the major cities, up-market restaurants are following the global culinary trends, but the real key to good eating is to concentrate on regional specialties.

You will want to sample some of the many seafood dishes, and seal flipper pie and cod tongues, which Newfoundland has made famous. In Nova Scotia, you must try the clam chowder, Digby scallops, Lunenberg sausage and "Solomon Gundy," a pickled-herring-and-chopped-meat concoction that is much better than it sounds. In Prince Edward Island, the Malpeque oysters and the local cheeses are the star attractions. In New Brunswick, go for the broiled Atlantic salmon and the steamed fiddleheads, which are the new shoots of an edible fern unique to the region. In all of the Maritimes you should treat yourself to the glorious desserts made with any of the local berries. And, in all of these eastern provinces you will find some of the finest (and most affordable) lobster in the world. In Nova

Specialty of the house — fiddlehead ferns in a New Brunswick market. Take them home and sauté in butter.

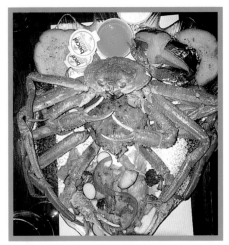

Scotia, they are so plentiful that even McDonalds weighs in with the McLobster!

Québec, once the heart of New France, would be called New Normandy if it were named after its stomach, for its cuisine remains based on the French peasant cooking of its early Norman (and, to a lesser extent, Breton) settlers. Not that you can't find classic or nouvelle French cuisine in Québec — you can, famously, in both Montréal and Québec City. But you can find that in New York, Los Angeles or Mexico City, or in dozens of other cities around the world. What makes Québec special is the way provincial French recipes have been adapted to Canadian foodstuffs. A few examples: *soupe aux pois*, a thick pea soup; *tourtières*, delicious minced meat pies (the meat is usually pork, but can be hare or even venison); *cretons*, pork pâté that is usually served with rye bread; *cipaille*, a pastry-layered game-and-potato pie; and *trempette*, fresh baked bread saturated with maple syrup and covered in whipped cream. Maple syrup, in fact, is a theme running through (or over) almost all of Québécois cooking — in sauces, desserts and cured ham — which is hardly surprising, given that the province oozes with maple syrup.

What is perhaps surprising is that Montréal rivals New York as a Mecca for worshippers of the great deli sandwich and the humble bagel, while other snack options include *poutines* (chips doused in gravy and cheese) and *beavers' tails* (sugary pastries eaten with a wide range of toppings from lemon or cinnamon to berries and cream).

ABOVE: King crab in St. John's, Newfoundland. OPPOSITE: At Old Fort William, Ontario, you can see natives and traders going about their daily business.

Happily, the French influence — and the maple syrup — doesn't stop when you get to Ontario, although here the culinary emphasis shifts to the province's game birds — you must try the Haliburton pheasant — and its dazzling variety of freshwater fish from Ontario's countless lakes and rivers. There is also, in Toronto and Montréal, a wide array of first-rate ethnic restaurants: Greek, Italian, Chinese, Indian, Polish, Hungarian, Japanese and so forth.

Tuck into the red meat when you get to Manitoba. Across all the Prairie Provinces the beef is exceptional — as is the freshwater fish from the thousands of lakes and rivers carved into the prairies. In Manitoba, you should try bison: lean and flavorful, preferably accompanied by the local wild rice, which is grown by First Nations peoples. Watch out, too, for the Saskatoon berry, unique to Western Canada, which resembles a small blueberry — it's full of flavor and generally used for desserts rather than being eaten as fruit. In these provinces, too, you will come across a sort of Borscht Belt, where the large Ukrainian population has left its mark on the menus in the form of spicy sausages, dumplings and a variety of cabbage dishes.

On the other hand, if you are just looking for a pit stop where you can refuel quickly, you will find coffee shops, diners and fast-food places just about everywhere you go.

As in the United States, Canadian restaurants tend to be informal and welcoming. They also tend to serve meals at earlier hours than Europeans are used to, so if you are counting on having a late dinner you would be wise to check on kitchen closing times first.

DRINKING

The first time I visited Canada I asked a shopkeeper where I might find a bottle of liquor. This simple question caused utter consternation, followed by endless consultations, followed by — blank. The reason was, it turned out, that spirits may only be purchased from specially licensed liquor stores. To buy liquor by the bottle in many parts of the country, except in parts of Québec, you have to go to one of these official stores. This interferes with one's budgeting more than with one's drinking, because even the happiest of Happy Hours is not as economical as a couple of self-catered cocktails, and a Rémy in your room is better value than any postprandial drink in a restaurant. Fortunately most hotels and restaurants are licensed.

Even the most convivial imbibing is complicated by local laws, which come in various shades of blue. In some places the

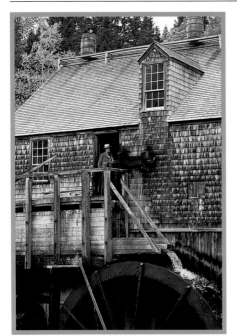

bars close at midnight, in other places they stay open as late as 4 AM. In most places, on Sundays you can only order a drink at a restaurant or a hotel dining room, and then only if you order a meal. In a few places you can't buy a drink — period — whatever day it is. The drinking age in Quebec, Alberta and Manitoba is 18; in all other provinces it is 19. Minors are not admitted into licensed nightclubs.

Canadians are not great whisky drinkers, even though they make some excellent whiskies — Nova Scotia has the continent's only single malt distillery. But they are great beer drinkers, and good local brews are available from Toronto to Whitehorse.

Canadian wines don't have an international reputation, there are many which are up to world standard. The great wine-producing areas are British Columbia, with wineries such as Quails' Gate, Cedar Creek and Mission Hill, and the St. Catharine's–Niagara area of southern Ontario. Among the many small boutique wineries to look out for here are Colio, Southbrook, Château des Charmes, Strewn and Stoney Ridge. Nova Scotia also has a few small vineyards. A true Canadian specialty is the very sweet "ice wine" is

enjoyed as a dessert wine or liqueur, which is made from grapes that are left on the vine until frozen.

Special Interests

LEARNING VACATIONS
From absorbing French language and culture in a Québec café to practicing your "Eskimo roll" in a Yukon kayaking class, Canada is a veritable universe of learning opportunities.

French Canadians recommend Québec City for **language learning**. It offers more of an "immersion" experience — as opposed to cosmopolitan Montréal where 80 percent of the downtown population is fully bilingual. Berlitz ((609) 514-3136 TOLL-FREE (800) 457-7958 WEB SITE www.berlitz.com, 94 Cumberland Street, Toronto, Ontario, tempts Francophiles with its "Learn French in Romantic Places" program. Two weeks of private or group instruction in Québec or Montréal might not have you conjugating like a native, but it will be fun, and you'll make progress.

Outward Bound Canada Western School ((604) 737-3093 TOLL-FREE (888) 688-9273 FAX (604) 737-3109 WEB SITE www.outwardbound .ca offers challenging **mountaineering** courses. Ice, snow and rock climbing, off-trail hiking, backcountry navigation, first aid and minimum-impact camping are all part of the curriculum.

With Voyageur Outward Bound School ((612) 338-0565 TOLL-FREE (800) 328-2943 E-MAIL vobs@vobs.com, canoers and kayakers can perfect their Eskimo roll on Madawaska Kanu Centre's ((613) 594-KANU weekend and five-day whitewater **paddling** courses in the warm waters of the Madawaska River in southern Ontario.

Ecological study tours are the specialty of Earthwatch ((617) 926-8200 TOLL-FREE (800) 776-0188 E-MAIL info@earthwatch.org, whose volunteers get a chance to contribute to ongoing studies by assisting researchers in the field. In Newfoundland it's possible to study minke, humpback and other species of **whales** for a week with Wildland Tours ((709) 722-3123 FAX (709) 722-3335 E-MAIL wildtour@nfld.com WEB SITE www.wildlands.com, 124 Water Street, St. John's, Newfoundland. Participants also have the opportunity to see puffins and gannet colonies, caribou and seals.

Elderhostel ((613) 530-2222 TOLL-FREE (877) 426-8056 offers learning vacations for the 55-and-older set. Their "Take a Closer Look at Canada" series encompasses a variety of weeklong tours that explore the **culture and history** of the country from Saskatchewan's Mounties to

ABOVE: The old sawmill at King's Mill Landing Historical Settlement, New Brunswick. OPPOSITE: Trinity, Newfoundland — St. Paul's Anglican Church TOP; a historic cedar-shingle residence BOTTOM.

Nova Scotia's maritime communities. Also offered are tours to the Arctic where you can learn about Inuktitut history and modern Arctic life. Elders of these First Nations communities often take part in providing the experience. Costs are very reasonable.

Anishinabe Village ((204) 925-2026 FAX (204) 925-2027 E-MAIL avi@mts.net WEB SITE www.wredco.com, 36 Roslyn Road, Winnipeg, operates Shawenequanape Kipichewin Camp, (/ FAX (204) 848-2815 from mid-May through mid-September, offering visitors the opportunity to learn, first-hand, the **culture and crafts of the Ojibway aboriginals,** by living as they did (but with a few extra amenities). Three days is enough to learn the how (and why) of erecting a tipi, preparing hides, making weapons and cooking traditional dishes. If you can extend your stay, optional excursions to First Nation villages add to the overall experience.

FARM AND RANCH VACATIONS
Canada's guest farms and ranches range from working cattle ranches, where guests can try their hand at cattle drives or branding, to remote lodges in pristine backcountry, and to luxury resorts complete with room service.

In Ontario, **Travelinx** TOLL-FREE (800) 668-2746 WEB SITE www.canadatravel.ca lists farm vacation operations in many provinces. You can also contact the **Bruce County Office of Tourism and Agriculture** ((519) 534-5344 FAX (519) 534-2442 TOLL-FREE (800) 268-3838 WEB SITE www.naturalretreat.com, 578 Brown Street, PO Box 129, Wiarton, Ontario N0H 2T0, for a list of independent operators, or the **Ontario Farm and Country Accommodations** (no phone number available) WEB SITE www.countryhosts.com, c/o Samme Putzel, Rural Route 2, Vankleek Hill, Ontario K0B 1R0. Note that these associations are not booking agents, but merely provide information; reservation booking is done directly with farms and ranches.

Manitoba vacation farms can be found through the **Manitoba Country Vacations Association (MCVA)** (/ FAX (204) 776-2176 E-MAIL ffamfarm@escape.ca WEB SITE www.countryvacations.mb.ca.

WINE TASTING AND TOURS
The East's wine country is the Niagara Peninsula. Contact the **Wine Council of Ontario** ((905) 684-8070 WEB SITE www.wineroute.com, 110 Hanover Drive, Suite B205, St. Catharines, Ontario L2W 1A4, which has maps of the wine region, including locations of individual wineries and information on summer happenings in wine country. Several wineries offer wine tasting and tours; call for details at the following well-known Ontario

wineries: **Château des Charmes Wines Ltd.** ((905) 262-4219 WEB SITE www.chateaudescharmes.com, 1025 York Street, Niagara-on-the-Lake; **Hillebrand Estates Winery** ((905) 468-7123 TOLL-FREE (800) 582-8412 WEB SITE www.hillebrand.com, 1249 Niagara Stone Road, Niagara-on-the-Lake; **Iniskillin Wines** ((905) 468-3554 WEB SITE www.inniskillin.com, Line 3 at the Niagara Parkway, Niagara-on-the-Lake; **Konzelman Winery** ((905) 935-2866 WEB SITE www.konzelmannwines.com, 1096 Lakeshore Street, Niagara-on-the-Lake; and **Reif Winery** ((905) 468-7738 WEB SITE www.reifwinery.com, 15608 Niagara Parkway, Niagara-on-the-Lake.

Taking a Tour

Ready for adventure? Whether your idea of a thrill is dog mushing through the Arctic or riding a luxury bus through wine country, Canada has a tour for you.

ADVENTURE
Butterfield & Robinson's ((416) 864-1354 TOLL-FREE (800) 678-1147 FAX (416) 864-0541, 70 Bond Street, Suite 300, Toronto, Ontario, offers leisurely paced strolls through Nova Scotia's valleys and villages with stops along the way for meals of fresh lobster, mussels and scallops. Other tours include biking and walking trips.

Backroads ((510) 527-1555 TOLL-FREE (800) 462-2848 FAX (510) 527-1444, 801 Cedar Street, Berkeley, California, specializes in active adventures in an irresistible framework of luxury lodging and gourmet dining. Trips include bicycling Nova Scotia's Evangeline Trail and hiking New Brunswick's Fundy Coast.

In summer (June to August) **G.A.P Adventures** ((416) 260-0999 TOLL-FREE (800) 465-5600 FAX (416) 260-1888 E-MAIL adventure @gap.ca WEB SITE www.gapadventures.com offers a selection of cycling in Nova Scotia and on Prince Edward and Cape Breton Islands, hiking and kayaking in Newfoundland, and multi-activity trips in the Canadian Rockies and Newfoundland.

Each February and March hundreds of thousands of harp seals enter the Gulf of St. Lawrence to bear their young on the vast floating ice fields west of the Magdalen Islands. **Natural Habitat Adventures** ((303) 449-3711 TOLL-FREE (800) 543-8917 FAX (303) 449-3712 WEB SITE www.nathab.com, 2945 Center Green Court, Suite H, Boulder, Colorado 80301, takes participants by helicopter to the ice floes to walk among the mother seals and white coated pups. The tour

is part of a project to protect these endangered animals. The same company takes amateur naturalists out to track gray wolves in Québec's Jacques Cartier Park. Eight-day trips take place in February and March.

From May to mid-October **Equitour/FITS** ((307) 455-3363 TOLL-FREE (800) 545-0019 FAX (307) 455-2354 E-MAIL equitour@wyoming.com WEB SITE www.ridingtours.com, 10 Stalnaker Street, Dubois, Wyoming 82513, has two-day horseback riding trips along the upper St. Lawrence, with stops for swimming and trout fishing along the way. In August and September riders can explore the wild country of the Canadian Appalachians on old woodcutters' trails.

You can follow the trail of the old fur traders on a six-day kayaking trip on Georgian Bay with **Black Feather Wilderness Adventures** ((705) 746-1372 TOLL-FREE (800) 574-8375, Rural Route 3, Parry Sound, Ontario. Black Feather also offers canoeing on the Nahanni River in the Northwest Territories combined with a four- to five-day alpine hike in the Cirque of the Unclimbables, as well as rugged 16-day kayaking and hiking trips on Ellesmere Island — the top of the world.

There are a number of excellent First Nations-owned and run tour companies. One of the longer-established of them is the **Arctic Tour Company** ((867) 977-2230 FAX (867) 977-2276 E-MAIL atc@auroranet.nt.ca, Tuktoyaktuk, Northwest Territories, which offers various winter and summer tours, including dog-team and snowmobile excursions, wildlife viewing and bird watching, Northern Lights viewing, camping, hiking and community tours, along with native cultural and traditional tours.

GUIDED BUS AND CRUISE TOURS

Globus Tours ((303) 797-2800 TOLL-FREE (800) 851-0728 EXTENSION 7518 WEB SITE www.globus journeys.com, is a Swiss-owned company offering deluxe bus tours. Their sister company, **Cosmos** (contact Globus) WEB SITE www.cosmos vacations.com offers bargain-priced bus tours with accommodation in modest hotels. **Maupintour** ((913) 843-1211 TOLL-FREE (800) 255-4266 FAX (913) 843-8351 WEB SITE www .maupintour.com and **Tauck Tours** ((203) 226-6911 TOLL-FREE (800) 468-2825 FAX (203) 221-6828 WEB SITE www.taucktour.com are two more well-established luxury bus-tour operators with many Canadian destinations.

The city-sized ships of **Holland America** WEB SITE www.hollandamerica.com ply the North Atlantic and North Pacific coastlines. Otherwise there is an abundance of cruises that chug along the gorgeous glacier-bound west coast of British Columbia, typically making their way to Alaska. The cruise season is generally late May through early September.

Life in the tidal pool at Montréal's Biodôme, located in the Olympic Park.

Welcome to Eastern Canada

If you like the idea of a gigantic country that can be enjoyed without a gigantic wallet, a New World nation that has taken care not to squander its Old World inheritance, a place where the dazzle of the landscape is matched by the kaleidoscopic mix of peoples who inhabit it, then you will like Canada — a lot.

And there is a lot of it to like. Covering almost 10 million sq km (3.9 million sq miles), it is the second largest country in the world (after Russia). Unlike Russia, however, or its next-door neighbor to the south, Canada has only 30.3 million inhabitants — slightly more than California. While the land extends northward well into the Arctic Circle, the vast majority of the population is concentrated in a narrow band along the long border with the United States.

From a strictly demographic point of view, the two most striking things about this population are that it is overwhelmingly urban — over 75 percent of Canadians live in cities or towns — and surprisingly heterogeneous. Unlike their American counterparts who have been historically quick to jettison their cultural baggage in the rush to become assimilated, immigrants to Canada have tended to cherish and safeguard their distinctive traditions, preserving the old in order to civilize the new. Thus it is not uncommon to see signs in Finnish by Lake Superior or to hear Ukrainian spoken on the Manitoban prairies. Likewise, members of various other nationalities and ethnic groups in Canada have created cheery enclaves without the dreary ghettos.

It's a pity that United States president John F. Kennedy appropriated the phrase "a nation of immigrants" to describe the United States, because it applies more accurately to Canada. Whereas the United States may have been founded by immigrants, and substantially populated by them for a century or more, Canada is still being shaped by immigration. At the beginning of the nineteenth century the country had a population of barely five million; since then two tidal waves of immigrants — the first before World War I and the second following World War II — have washed up on Canada's shores, helping to boost the population to its present level and helping to determine what kind of nation has entered the twenty-first century. Even today, people continue to pour in, including recently many Hong Kong Chinese. Canada, with land to spare and a great heart, is not only a generous contributor of aid to the developing world, but one of few countries genuinely welcoming to refugees.

There are, of course, problems. Many First Nations peoples are still fighting through the courts and parliament for the return of their traditional lands — or suitable compensation. The creation of the territory of Nunavut ("Our Land" in Inuit) in 1999 was one triumph. Meanwhile,

friction still exists between the two predominant cultures, the British and the French, although calls for Québec to tear itself away from the Confederation seem to have died back to a murmur, for the moment. And, inevitably, the arrival of new, often poor and ill-educated people from the developing countries has put a drain on social resources and blue-collar jobs in some cities. However, what is remarkable is that with most other Western countries foaming at the mouth about economic migrants, in Canada, there really are relatively few serious racial tensions.

Perhaps the achievement the Canadians themselves rate most highly has been their ability to share a continent with the United States without

becoming totally Americanized, something that is not always easy, particularly given the imbalance in population numbers and the sheer volume of American media that floods across the longest unguarded national boundary in the world. Canadians seem to be forever worrying about their national identity being obliterated by the long shadows cast by the colossus to the south. As former Prime Minister Pierre Trudeau, in a celebrated quip, told Americans on a visit to Washington in 1969, "Living next to you is in some ways like sleeping with an elephant. No matter how friendly and even-tempered the beast, one is affected by every twitch and grunt."

OPPOSITE: The Montréal antiques district TOP and a Toronto Greek neighborhood BOTTOM. ABOVE: In the town of Niagara Falls, motels and restaurants shout their welcome.

Most Canadians live within reach of American radio and television stations, a major concern of Canadian intellectuals for the better part of the twentieth century. The worry first surfaced in the 1920s, when Canada was absorbed into the American radio system at a time when the United States was beginning to flex its imperial muscles. Then, after the end of World War II, when America was at the zenith of its power and influence, there came the new threat of cultural annexation by television.

So seriously was this threat viewed that no fewer than three royal commissions were set up between 1949 and 1961 to address "the problem of American culture in Canada," and specifically to seek ways of organizing "resistance to the absorption of Canada into the general cultural pattern of the United States." There was little the commissioners could do, however, apart from encouraging the Canadian Broadcasting Corporation (CBC) to feature homegrown material. Even this rearguard action, faithfully pursued by the CBC since its creation in 1936, has never received wholehearted government support. Recent surveys show that 80 percent of total television viewing in the big metropolitan areas near the border is of American programs; even in Edmonton, which receives only Canadian stations, the figure reached 66 percent.

Nor is the cross-border invasion limited to the airwaves. American films occupy most of the cinema screens, American magazines dominate the newsagents and American clothes line the shelves of the stores. Even Canadian sports have not escaped American colonization. All of the top ice hockey teams — the one sport Canadians are passionate about — play in America's National Hockey League, and Canada's major baseball teams compete in the American major leagues. Perhaps the only sport that Canadians have managed to remain somewhat aloof about is American football, but that's only because they enthusiastically embraced the game, made a few minor adjustments, and renamed it Canadian football.

Sporting rivalry is just one way Canadians find of coping with being considered by the world as nicer, quieter versions of the Americans, their accent rarely differentiated when overseas, and their dollar treated as a slightly discounted version of the real thing. There was countrywide ecstasy when the United States and Canada met head-to-head in the Olympic ice hockey finals in 2002 — and Canada took the gold!

When I told a prominent Canadian businessman over lunch (truthfully) that I had never met a Canadian I didn't like, he reacted with exasperation bordering on disgust. "That's precisely our problem," he said. "Nobody dislikes us, because nobody knows us."

It is true that most Canadians are incredibly friendly, welcoming and hospitable people, and many Canadians have chosen to reach back, sometimes way back, into their colonial past for a suitable identity. There are parts of the country where stylized versions of the British and French ways of life have been lovingly, not to say fanatically, preserved.

Canada's multi-ethnic population, British monarch, ongoing ties to Europe and active role in the Commonwealth all play a decisive role in shaping the national psyche, making them more outward looking and worldly wise than many Americans. Canada has a strong European-style social security and health system, which it guards jealously against the American capitalist model. The homegrown media is markedly different from the United States version. Not only is there a strong French-language broadcast culture, but much of the news and discussion on CBC TV and radio is

set up on decidedly British lines, coverage of international events is broader and more objective, humor is gently sophisticated and ironic.

In the end, for all the agonizing over their soft-focus national profile, the great majority of Canadians sensibly realize that they quite probably live in the best of all possible worlds. After all, their country has only one neighbor — and that one is so friendly that neither of them has ever bothered to put up a fence. They have the luxury of living in cities that are not only handsome and comfortable but come equipped with the world's largest backyard, in the form of wilderness areas of awe-inspiring beauty. Their society has the civilizing patina of history while enjoying all the benefits of modern technology.

In this book we explore eastern Canada, from Newfoundland's Cape Spear — the easternmost point in the nation — west to Winnipeg, the cultural capital in the heart of the prairie. To cover every town and every place of interest in a country as rich as this would be impossible without writing a 24-volume encyclopedia, but we attempt to bring you the best of what is on offer. The great preponderance of major tourist attractions in eastern Canada are within easy reach of the Trans-Canada Highway. As we journey along the nation's "Main Street," we pause en route to explore the byways that lead to towns and cities of unusual charm and scenic areas of exceptional loveliness, both rugged and gentle. We also head briefly up to the far northern regions of Churchill, Manitoba, Nunavut and the Northwest Territories.

Canadians have managed to establish cheery enclaves without creating dreary ghettos.

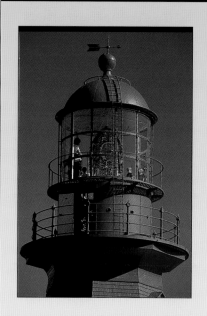

The
Country
and Its
People

HISTORICAL BACKGROUND

Just when people first came to Canada is a matter of considerable debate — some experts say it could have been up to 40,000 years ago, while others insist that it was no more than 11,000 years ago — but there is no argument over who they were or where they came from. They were nomadic tribes from Asia, principally Siberia and Mongolia, who came into North America during successive ice ages across a land bridge over the Bering Strait. This migration, often imagined as a mass exodus like Moses crossing the Red Sea, in fact happened gradually as bands of hunters traveled east in

tablished a settlement at the site of present-day L'Anse aux Meadows. Unfortunately, the archeological remains don't tell us how long the settlement survived or what finished it off, but it is generally assumed that a combination of the harsh winters and clashes with the region's indigenous populations drove the settlers away before they had a chance to establish a viable colony.

Thing then went quiet for nearly five centuries. In the fourteenth century, Portuguese, Basque and Breton fishermen discovered the Grand Banks fishing grounds off the coast of Newfoundland to be among the richest in the world. Then, in 1497, the Venetian John Cabot (*né* Giovanni Caboto) arrived in Newfoundland, and then Nova Scotia,

search of game. And the land bridge from Asia, now referred to as Beringia, was actually hundreds of miles wide, more like a small continent.

Over thousands of years, these bands and their descendants fanned out across North America, establishing different Amerindian societies and civilizations, which in some cases became highly developed as early as the eighth millennium BC.

THE FIRST EUROPEANS

There is evidence, although inconclusive, that the first European to set foot in North America was a sixth-century Irish monk who, according to legend, landed briefly on the coast of Newfoundland. Vikings sailing from Greenland around AD 1000 made the earliest verified landing. Arriving at the northwestern tip of Newfoundland, which they named Vinland ("land of grapevines"), they es-

to claim these new-found lands for England and Henry VII. The next claimant to what was already shaping up as another stage for the longstanding Anglo-French rivalry was the Breton Jacques Cartier, who in 1534 sailed into the Gulf of St. Lawrence, landing at Prince Edward Island (which he named Île St-Jean) and the Gaspé Peninsula before sailing down the St. Lawrence as far as a native village in the shadow of an impressive hill, which he named *Mont Réal* (royal mountain). He claimed the entire area for France, referring to it by the Algonquin word for "settlement": Kannata.

NEW FRANCE

Since Cartier didn't return to France laden with the hoped-for gold and gems, French interest in Canada quickly waned, only to be revived at the start of the seventeenth century by, of all things, the demands of haute couture. In a word, furs.

In 1605 French explorer Samuel de Champlain established the first permanent European settlement in Canada at Port Royal, Nova Scotia, on the Bay of Fundy, in hopes of trading with the natives for beaver pelts. Three years later Champlain founded another settlement on a plateau overlooking the St. Lawrence River at the bend where the river suddenly narrows. He named the village Québec, and as the center of the fur trade, it rapidly grew into the most important city in New France.

Following in the footsteps of the explorers and the fur traders, the Jesuits swiftly began the

because it may have held the long-sought Northwest Passage to the Orient. Gradually, however, it began to dawn on them that Canada, or New France, possessed its own treasure trove of riches — and Britain had the key to the back door.

In 1610 the English navigator Henry Hudson sailed into the giant bay that now bears his name. Sixty years later Hudson Bay in turn gave its name to a commercial enterprise, the Hudson's Bay Company, which was to leave an indelible mark on the history of Canada. Formed by British fur merchants to provide an alternative to Québec as an outlet for the fur trade, it was granted by Charles II right to all the lands drained by rivers flowing into Hudson Bay. Thus backed by a

spiritual and intellectual colonization of the region. Their more contemplative lay counterparts, the Société de Notre-Dame, moved in on Cartier's "royal mountain" and founded the settlement of Montréal in 1642. Before long it had supplanted Québec as the center of the fur trade in New France.

The two decades spanning the middle of the seventeenth century were difficult ones for the French settlers, as they became inexorably drawn into the bitter tribal conflicts between the Hurons, their principal trading partners, and the warlike Iroquois. But the real threat to their colonial supremacy came, as always, from the British. The British had watched uneasily as New France expanded, but their primary concerns remained settling and securing their American colonies and exploiting the fertile fishing grounds off the Canadian coast. Canada itself was of interest only

solicitous sovereign and a powerful navy, it was to become the largest fur trading company in North America, and today is still a force to be reckoned with in Canadian retailing.

Although British military activity in Canada was minimal during the War of the Spanish Succession (1701–13), under the Treaty of Utrecht France was forced to relinquish all claims to Hudson Bay and Newfoundland, and to give up Acadia, which the British promptly renamed Nova Scotia ("New Scotland"). The Catholic French farmers, who refused to swear an oath of loyalty to the British crown, were evicted. Some later returned, but many made their way south to Louisiana, where they became known as Cajuns.

OPPOSITE: A bridal party of Kwakiutl Indians, photographed by Edward Curtis in 1914, arrives at the groom's village. ABOVE: Yukon native women and their children.

There was a period of relative peace and tranquility for the next 40 years, broken only in 1744 by the British seizure of the French fortress of Louisbourg on Cape Breton Island. It was handed back four years later under the Peace of Aix-la-Chapelle.

The Seven Years' War, known in America as the French and Indian War, was to be the decisive turning point in Canadian history. The war began well for the French and their native allies, as in battle after battle the British forces showed themselves to be tactically unprepared for what amounted to quasi-guerrilla warfare. But the tide began to turn in 1758 with the arrival of British land and naval reinforcements. A successful siege

had fallen. Both Wolfe and Montcalm were killed. The battle had lasted 20 minutes.

Although it was one of the shortest battles on record, its consequences ultimately reverberated around the world. The fall of Québec effectively marked the fall of New France, and when the French handed over all of Canada under the terms of the Treaty of Paris in 1763, the British were left as undisputed masters of the entire North American continent. Some historians argue, however, that it was a Pyrrhic victory in that the British were also left overconfident and overstretched, not to mention out-of-pocket, while the many American colonists who fought on the British side, including one George Washington, had gained

of the fortress at Louisbourg led to its recapture, giving the British control of the entrance to the Gulf of St. Lawrence, while at the Lake Ontario end of the St. Lawrence River the British took the vital Fort Frontenac. Then, in the summer of 1759, an assault force under the command of 32-year-old General James Wolfe, the youngest general in the British army, sailed from the Atlantic down the St. Lawrence to Québec. All summer long Wolfe's artillery pounded the city, reducing it to rubble, but without budging the French forces under the Marquis de Montcalm in their citadel atop the steep cliffs above the town. Then, on the night of September 12, Wolfe tried a daring maneuver. He led a force of 5,000 infantrymen in boats to a point behind the city, where they silently scaled the cliffs and assembled on the Plains of Abraham. The next morning, the startled French forces, flushed out of their fortified redoubt, were slaughtered. Québec

wartime experience as well as insights into British military strategy that would prove invaluable a few years later when the Americans launched their War of Independence.

BRITISH CANADA

The conquest of Canada brought another problem for Britain: what to do about the predominantly French population in the new territory over which they now ruled. In the end, they did the decent thing — and paid dearly for it. By passing the Québec Act of 1774, the British gave the French Canadians the right to continue using their own language, the secure ownership of their property, the primacy of French civil law, as well as the freedom to practice the Roman Catholic religion (including the Church's right to collect tithes). This did not go down at all well with the overwhelmingly Protestant population in the 13 American colonies, who were already incensed over what they considered unjust taxes imposed by Britain to help pay for the war against France. When the boundaries of the province of Québec were extended to protect the French Canadian fur traders operating in the Ohio and Mississippi River valleys, the American colonists decided that they had had enough.

The colonial rebellion became the American Revolution late in 1775 with attacks on Montréal and Québec City which, had they been successful, would almost certainly have heralded a fairly swift victory for the Americans. In fact, the attack on Montréal was successful, but so brutish was the behavior of the "liberators" that most French Canadians decided they would prefer not to be thus liberated and went on to fight fiercely alongside the British, thus denying the Americans an early knockout.

By the time the war ended in 1783, Canadians had a new neighbor, the United States of America, and also a lot of new Canadians, for about 50,000 Americans who remained loyal to the British Crown had fled northwards. Most of them settled in Nova Scotia and what is now New Brunswick, although about 7,000 made their way to present-day Ontario. More still arrived at the end of the war claiming to be Loyalists, but their devotion to George III might possibly have been influenced by the offer of free land to Loyalist immigrants. In any case, as a result of the American Revolution, Canada received a large transfusion of English-speaking immigrants, many of whom were well-educated and had occupied positions of responsibility and influence under the old colonial regime. The balance of power shifted abruptly away from the French to the Anglo Canadians.

In the years following the war Canada was transformed both politically and territorially. In 1791 the province of Québec was divided into Upper Canada (mainly English-speaking: now Ontario) and Lower Canada (mainly French-speaking: now Québec), each with its own Lieutenant Governor and parliament. Meanwhile, the vast and hitherto neglected lands to the west were gradually being opened up in the wake of the pioneering explorations of Alexander Mackenzie, who in 1793 became the first white man to cross Canada all the way to the Pacific coast, and Simon Fraser and David Thompson, who were the first to map the great mountains and rivers from the Rockies to the Pacific.

The War of 1812 was the last neighborhood brawl before the United States and Canada settled down to live together more or less happily ever after. The war had a number of causes: border disputes, British interference with American shipping, fierce rivalry in the lucrative fur trade,

American claims that the British were behind native raids on American border settlements, British claims that Americans were trying to export republicanism to Canada, and so forth. Whatever the justice of any of these claims, they added up to war. Although both sides suffered some telling blows — the Americans captured Toronto (or York, as it was then called) and burned it to the ground, whereupon the British retaliated by capturing Washington and burning the White House — neither side really seemed to have much appetite for the fight. The Americans wanted to get on with nation-building and the British wanted to get on with countering the Napoleonic threat at home, while the Canadians wanted to be left in peace. In 1814 they got together and declared the war over.

Not surprisingly, considering the enormous size of the two countries, the border issue was not resolved immediately. The first major step was taken in 1818 when they agreed on the 49th parallel as their mutual border from the Great Lakes to the Rockies, but it was not until 1842, after much haggling and a little skirmishing, that the Canadian border with the New England states was established. The last link, the border with the Oregon Territory west of the Rockies, was established along the 49th parallel in 1846.

As increased immigration swelled the population, French Canadians became convinced that the British were deliberately trying to dilute their power by swamping them with English-speaking newcomers. As a result, in 1837 French Canadians under the leadership of Louis-Joseph Papineau demanded autonomy for Lower Canada (Québec) so that they could establish an independent republic. When the British refused, a violent rebellion broke out which was not finally defeated until 1838. It was the first time that the call for an independent Québec had been heard. It would not be the last.

Nor were the French Canadians the only ones growing impatient with British rule around this time. In Upper Canada (Ontario) a rough and ready coalition of economic have-nots led by newspaper editor William Lyon Mackenzie rose up against the oligarchic Tory establishment and demanded that the government be remodeled along American lines. When these demands, predictably, were not met, Mackenzie too resorted to armed rebellion, with even less success than Papineau whom he soon joined in exile in the United States.

Although both insurrections had been easily put down, they succeeded in lighting an anticolonialist fuse that would prove unquenchable.

Nevertheless, Canada at mid-century was a picture of expansion and growth. New waves of immigrants boosted the population of the Mari-

Expo '86 in Vancouver.

time Provinces, which were beginning to prosper as a result of their flourishing lumber, fishing and shipbuilding industries. The population explosion also led to the creation of settlements further westward, in addition to providing the labor needed to build the canals, roads and railways that made the westward expansion possible. In less than 20 years, over 3,000 km or 2,000 miles of railroad tracks were laid. All that was needed for Canada to become a truly coast-to-coast country was for some sort of tug to be exerted from the other side of the Rockies. That tug, when it came, turned out to be a powerful yank: in 1858 gold was discovered in the Fraser River valley.

The gold rush that followed was so frenetic, and so dominated by Americans rushing northwards to stake their claims, that Britain quickly proclaimed a new Crown colony, British Columbia, to control the stampede into the territory.

British colonies now straddled the continent from the Atlantic to the Pacific.

THE DOMINION OF CANADA

With the old Anglo-French tensions still causing problems, and the turmoil to the south caused by the American Civil War, not to mention the ordinary growing pains brought on by rapid population growth and territorial expansion, it was widely felt that the colonies should come together and forge a stronger union among themselves. So in 1864, delegates from the various colonies convened in Charlottetown, Prince Edward Island, to begin laying the groundwork for a new confederation. Three years later, the British North America Act of 1867 created the Dominion of Canada, in which the colonies of Nova Scotia, New Brunswick, and Québec became provinces in a confederated union with self-rule under a parliamentary system of government. Manitoba joined the Confederation in 1870, British Columbia in 1871 and Prince Edward Island in 1873. The Yukon, formerly a district of the Northwest Territories, was made a separate territory in 1898 at the height of the Klondike gold rush. Alberta and Saskatchewan, also carved out of the old Northwest Territories, joined in 1905; Newfoundland, typically, held out until 1949, when it finally became Canada's tenth province.

As important as this political union was to Canada's development, it was more symbolic than real so long as there was no corresponding physical link between the provinces. In fact, three of the provinces — Nova Scotia, Prince Edward Island British Columbia — only agreed to join the Confederation on condition that a transcontinental railway was built to tie the new nation together. Work on this mammoth project began in 1881 and, incredibly, was completed in only four years. In 1885, at Rogers Pass in the Selkirk Mountains,

the last spike was driven: the Canadian Pacific Railway was in business.

As was to be expected, however, this mighty triumph of engineering was not achieved without casualties. The coming of the Iron Horse meant the virtual disappearance of the buffalo, the driving of natives from their ancestral homelands, and the deaths of hundreds of (mostly Chinese) laborers on the railroad itself. It also precipitated a bloody uprising in 1885 on the part of the Métis, who were the descendants of French trappers and Cree women, aided and abetted by several tribes of Plains natives, all of whom felt threatened by the armies of new settlers swarming over their land.

Already driven out of Manitoba as far west as the southern banks of the Saskatchewan River, the Métis and their native allies, under the leadership of Louis Riel, overwhelmed the Mounted Police post at Duck Lake, attacked the town of Battleford, and captured and burned Fort Pitt. But

their successes were short-lived. Before long they were subdued by the superior firepower of the Canadian forces, and Riel was hanged. His execution became another source of resentment both among First Nations people and French Canadians, who felt that he would not have been treated so harshly had he not been a Roman Catholic of French ancestry.

With the country now linked literally and politically from sea to sea, the final years of the nineteenth century saw Canada blossom dramatically as a nation. As thousands upon thousands of new immigrants arrived, new lands were settled and cultivated, hydroelectric projects were initiated, new manufacturing industries were started up alongside the already-thriving industries of lumbering, fishing, mining, pulp and paper. Above all, agriculture boomed as the Prairie Provinces became one of the great grain-producing areas of the world. And, for icing on the national cake, in

1896 gold was discovered in the Klondike, setting off one of the biggest gold rushes in history as 100,000 (mainly American) fortune-seekers poured into the Yukon. These were heady times.

THE TWENTIETH CENTURY

Thus Canada entered the twentieth century in a buoyant mood. It was also blessed from 1896 to 1911 with one of its greatest prime ministers, Sir Wilfrid Laurier, a French Canadian and Roman Catholic who set himself the Herculean task of ending the antagonism and suspicion between Canada's English and French communities. But World War I came along and deepened the rift: French Canadians violently objected to military conscription, which was introduced in 1917 after the Canadian volunteer forces fighting along-

The entrance to Ottawa's Confederation Building.

side the British in the trenches had suffered such appalling losses that there were no volunteers left to fight. The French Canadian point of view — that the war had nothing to do with them, and therefore they shouldn't be drafted to fight in it — left much residual bitterness on both sides after the war was over.

A happier legacy of the war was an economy enriched by a vastly increased manufacturing capacity, streamlined industrial development, expanded mining activity and burgeoning exports of wheat. Along with Canada's postwar prosperity came growing independence from Britain, acknowledged by the British at the Imperial Conference of 1926 when Canada was granted the right

to conduct its own international affairs without reference to London, and sealed by the Statute of Westminster in 1931, which made Canada an independent nation.

Then came the Depression, which was even worse in Canada than in the United States. Suddenly the Promised Land was a ravaged land, as drought erased the wheat fields and unemployment stalked the cities. The misery of the "Dirty Thirties," as the Canadians called the decade, lasted until September 1939, when Hitler marched into Poland. Canada, following Britain's lead, immediately declared war on Germany, whereupon the economy coughed, spluttered, then roared back to life.

Also revived, sadly, was the bitter Anglo-French debate over military conscription, which once again split the country, even though one of the aims of the war was to liberate occupied France. Again, Canada suffered battlefield losses out of all proportion to its population. On the other side of the ledger, the Canadian economy prospered out of all proportion to its prewar capacity, as almost 10 percent of the population were engaged in war-related industries. Thanks to the war, Canada became one of the world's major industrial nations as well as an important military power, a cofounder of the United Nations, and a member of NATO.

Peace was as good to Canada as the war had been. A huge oil field was discovered near Edmonton, Alberta, in 1947. Giant uranium deposits were discovered in Ontario and Saskatchewan, and its extraordinary mineral riches made Canada the world's leading producer of nickel, zinc, lead, copper, gold and silver. Its inexhaustible water resources made countless hydroelectric projects possible, its forests made it the world's foremost exporter of newsprint, and its oceans made it the world's foremost exporter of fish. As if that weren't enough, Canada was fortunate in having the world's best customer for raw materials right on its doorstep.

Another milestone in Canada's rise among the world's top industrial nations was the opening in 1959 of the St. Lawrence Seaway, a joint United States–Canadian project that made possible shipping from the Great Lakes to the Atlantic. Three years later the TransCanada Highway was completed, a concrete link spanning all 10 provinces.

In 1967 Canada celebrated its hundredth birthday by throwing itself a big party in the form of a World's Fair — Expo '67 — in Montréal. Canadians had much to celebrate: a vigorous and rapidly expanding economy, one of the highest standards of living in the world, advanced social welfare programs providing health care and other benefits for all citizens, virtually unlimited natural resources, and a history of international conduct such that Canada had managed to join the front rank of the world's nations without making any enemies. What better reasons to have a party?

QUÉBEC AND THE CANADIAN FEDERATION

Alas, there was a ghost at the birthday party. The old specter of separatism, which had haunted the federation during the entire century of its existence, was suddenly summoned up in a speech by visiting French President de Gaulle. Speaking to a large throng outside the Montréal City Hall, he declared, "*Vive le Québec libre!*" Considering that he was present in Canada as a guest of a nation celebrating its "unity through diversity," this was mischief-making on an epic scale.

With their clamoring having thus been endorsed by the President of France, Québec's separatists found new heart for the struggle to wrench the province away from the rest of the nation. With the ultimate goal of full independence, the Parti Québécois (PQ) was formed under the leadership of René Lévesque. The PQ won 23 percent of the vote in the 1970 provincial elections. That same year the separatist movement turned nasty around its fringes, as the *Front de Liberation du Québec* (FLQ) kidnapped and murdered the province's Minister of Labor, Pierre Laporte. Prime Minister Pierre Trudeau responded by invoking the War Measures Act and sending 10,000 troops into the province, an unpopular action that ultimately benefited the PQ, who came to power in 1976. They set about developing the province's economy, instituting educational reforms, and making Québec monolingual, all the while pressing for a referendum and secession from the Canadian federation. But, in 1980, when the referendum came, 60 percent of the province voted "*non*" to secession.

At the next election Lévesque's separatists were voted out of office. In 1987 the Conservative government of Brian Mulroney made a significant gesture towards the Québécois when the prime minister signed a document recognizing them as a "distinct society." The following year, in what seemed like a reciprocal gesture of appreciation, Québec gave Mulroney's Conservatives a large part of their majority in the national elections. It seemed, at last, that the flames of separatism had finally been extinguished.

Not so. As before, the desire for separation among the Québécois smoldered unnoticed, waiting to be re-ignited into the burning issue it had so often been in the past. Sure enough, it blazed back into prominence at the start of the 1990s. This time, however, nobody was able to say precisely what set it alight. The best explanation we heard came from Don Johnson, a columnist for the Toronto *Globe and Mail*. "We are merely advised that Québeckers feel humiliated, the status quo is unacceptable and unhappiness prevails," he said with a helpless shrug. He then went on to compare it to the breakdown of a marriage — "where neither party can point to a specific cause, but there is a general feeling that a divorce would be preferable."

In 1992 and again in 1995, referenda for sovereignty were held in Québec. In both cases, the electorate rejected the idea. But the 1995 vote was nearly a dead heat with 51 percent against. It is almost certain that at some point in the future, another "neverendum" — as Canadians have named them — will be called. For the moment, the stuffing has been knocked out of the cause and most Québécois seem happier with the status quo. Independence is on the backburner, and the small Maritime Provinces, desperately worried that an independent Québec would cut them off physically from the rest of Canada, too small and poor to survive alone, can rest that bit more easily.

CANADA TODAY

While the future of the federation is one of Canada's prime political issues, economics are seen as a more burning issue. In 1989, the free trade agreement with the United States (NAFTA) was pushed through parliament by Prime Minister Brian Mulroney, causing the loss of thousands of jobs and exposing the country's industries to American competition. The collapse of the North Atlantic cod fishing industry brought hard times

to Newfoundland and Nova Scotia, where unemployment now runs very high. In 2002, a series of political scandals rocked the administration, leaving an increasingly cynical population struggling to believe in any of their politicians.

One thing, however, is clear: after centuries of exploitation and marginalization, Canada's native peoples are beginning a new and happier era. Having gained political strength throughout the late 1960s and early 1970s, the First Nations of the north launched a series of land claims against the Canadian government in the late 1970s, demanding financial compensation, funding for social programs, hunting rights and a greater role in wildlife management and environmental protection.

The success of these land claims has led to a native cultural revival and, finally, to redrawing the very map of Canada. On April 1, 1999, Canada — formerly comprised of 10 provinces and two territories — gained a new territory, when the Northwest Territories was divided in two. The eastern half is now known as Nunavut, "Our Land" in the Inuit language. The western lands are still called the Northwest Territories.

Both in the north and throughout the rest of the country, native Canadians (excluding the Inuit) number around 282,000 and are members of 574 separate communities, called "bands." Ethnically, many of Canada's native peoples have the same heritage as certain United States tribes: Cree, Sioux and Blackfoot, for example, are found in both countries. In Canada, native people belong to 10 linguistic groups, each of which has many local dialects.

Since 1973, when the Canadian government accepted a proposal by the National Indian Brotherhood, increasing numbers of bands manage their own schools. These schools have introduced new curricula, which often include the history of native Canadians and native-language courses.

The maple leaf or the fleur-de-lys? Will it be the national or the provincial flag that flies over Québec in future?

GEOGRAPHY AND CLIMATE

William Lyon Mackenzie King, Canada's longest-serving prime minister (1921–30, 1935–48), observed in 1936: "If some countries have too much history, we have too much geography."

It's hard to argue with that. Spread over almost 10 million sq km (3.6 million sq miles), Canada stretches more than 5,500 km (3,400 miles) from Cape Spear, Newfoundland, in the east, to the Alaskan border in the west, and 4,600 km (2,900 miles) from Lake Erie's Pelee Island in the south to Cape Columbia on Ellesmere Island in the north (just 800 km or 500 miles from the North Pole).

Within this vastness one finds stunning topographical extremes. Almost half the country, for example, is forested — one single forest zone of conifers extends for 6,000 km (3,730 miles) in a wide sweep from Newfoundland to the far north — while similarly enormous tracts of land are empty, treeless prairies. There are millions of acres of flood plains and marshy lowlands, and there are the majestic Rocky Mountains, though Canada's highest peak, Mount Logan (6,050 m / 19,844 ft), is not in the Rockies but in the St. Elias Mountains of southwestern Yukon.

And then there is the water. Canada is awash in lakes and rivers; they account for over seven percent of the country's total area. There are 400,000 of them in Ontario alone. Three of the 20 longest rivers in the world are to be found in Canada. In all, the country has a staggering 25 percent of the world's fresh-water resources.

Geologically, Canada can be divided into five distinct regions, not counting the archipelago of islands inside the Arctic Circle. The Appalachian region is that hilly, wooded part of the country bounded on the west by the St. Lawrence River and on the east by the Atlantic. It includes the Maritime Provinces, Newfoundland, and the Gaspé Peninsula, and belongs to an ancient mountain system, now eroded to modest elevations, that reaches as far south as Alabama.

The St. Lawrence Lowlands comprise the swath of land from the mouth of the St. Lawrence River to the Great Lakes. This fertile floodplain is home to most of Canada's people, industry and commerce.

The prairies spread across the provinces of Manitoba, Saskatchewan and Alberta, and on up into the Northwest Territories. The rich soil in the southern reaches, where the prairies join the Great Plains of the United States, yields great golden seas of wheat, which gradually dry up in Alberta, giving way to huge cattle ranches.

The Western Cordillera is bounded on the east by the Rocky Mountains and on the west by the Coast Mountains. In between is the spectacular diversity of British Columbia, a province of soaring mountain peaks, alpine lakes and meadows, large boreal forests, intricate networks of rivers, deep blue lakes, hot springs and long green valleys.

The fifth region, the Canadian Shield, encompasses everything else: the immense, horseshoe-shaped land mass that surrounds Hudson Bay, and stretches from the coast of Labrador down to the St. Lawrence Lowlands, over to the prairies, and up to the Arctic. Covering some 4.7 million sq km (1.8 million sq miles), about half the entire area of Canada, this rough-hewn, rock-strewn, lake-pitted wilderness is one of the oldest sections of the earth's crust.

The flora and fauna vary from region to region, however some animals can be found just about everywhere: squirrels and chipmunks, rabbits and hares, porcupines and skunks. Equally widespread throughout the country's forests and woodlands are deer, moose, black bears, beavers, wild geese and ducks. The richest fishing grounds in Canada — possibly in the world — are to be found in the Gulf of St. Lawrence and the waters of the continental shelf off Newfoundland: though cod stocks have been wiped out by over-fishing, the area still teems with herring, mackerel, tuna, oysters, clams, lobsters and scallops, along with some 800 other species of edible marine life.

In the St. Lawrence Lowlands, the coniferous forests of spruce, firs, and pines that sweep from Labrador to the Rockies begin to be infiltrated by aspen, birch, oak, elm, beech, hemlock and ash. In southern Québec the sugar maples appear, and in southwestern Ontario the walnut and tulip trees, the hickories and dogwoods. As for animal life, the region is better known for bipeds than quadrupeds.

In the prairies, one animal is conspicuous by its absence: the plains buffalo (bison). The few that have survived are in national parks or specialist ranches, while great herds of cattle have taken their place. Denizens of the semiarid southern prairie grasslands include kangaroo rats, hares, pronghorn antelopes and the ranchers' nemesis, coyotes.

In the mountain ranges of the Western Cordillera one can find, if one tries hard enough, brown bears, elk, mountain goats, bighorn sheep and the bosses of the upper slopes, grizzly bears. In the lakes and rivers there is some of the best trout and salmon fishing to be found anywhere in the world.

The great expanse of forests across northern Canada shelter large concentrations of fur-bearing

that guarantees Vancouver milder winters than, say, Dallas. True, the eastern coast takes a beating from the Atlantic, but parts of it are also caressed by the Gulf Stream, creating swimming beaches equal to any in the Mediterranean.

Having said that, one has to admit that for much of the year Canada is a theme park called Winter. Harold Town, one of Canada's leading artists, once said: "We are a nation of thermometers monitoring cold fronts. We jig to the crunch of snow." Indeed, over a third of the annual precipitation in Canada falls as snow, compared to a worldwide average of five percent. The only national capital city colder than Ottawa is Ulan Bator, in Mongolia; Winnipeg is the coldest city

animals: mink, ermine, marten, muskrat, beaver, river otter, lynx, bobcat, wolves and wolverines. In the northern tundra are arctic foxes, lemmings, musk oxen and caribou, snow geese and trumpeter swans. Still further north the frigid waters are full of whales, seals, and walrus, and the mighty polar bear patrols the ice packs of the Arctic.

Because words like "frigid," "polar," "ice" and "Arctic" — and even the subtly prejudicial "north" — are all words that we readily associate with Canada, most foreigners think that Canada's climate can probably be summed up in one word: cold. This is a mistake. True, Canada occupies the northern — and therefore colder — part of the continent, but this ignores the fact that Pelee Island, Ontario, is on the same latitude as Rome. True, the dominant images of western Canada are the snow-capped peaks of the Rockies, but this obscures the fact that those same Rockies form a protective wall

in the world with a population of more than half a million; and residents of Montréal shovel more snow every year than residents of any other city.

But there is a bright side. It's just that: brightness. Canada may be refrigerated half the time, but it is sunlit most of the time. Which means that it is beautiful all the time, brilliantly white in winter, infinitely and variously green the rest of year — except for the fall in the southeast and maritime provinces, which are cloaked in a gaudy display of reds and golds to rival the best in New England. What's more, its meteorological diversity mirrors its geographical diversity, so that the visitor has the luxury of choosing not only the scenery and activities that most appeal, but also the precise climate in which to enjoy both. In Canada there is truly a time and place for everything.

OPPOSITE: Canada — a land called Winter.
ABOVE: The Canadian prairies in bloom.

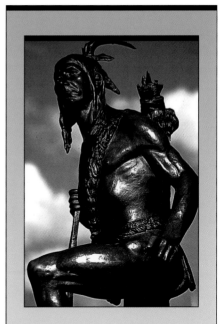

Ontario

Ontario is by far the richest, most populous and most visited province in Canada. It is home to a third of all Canadians. It has more mineral resources than any other province, some of the most fertile farmland in the country, and the longest frost-free season in which to cultivate it. As the country's industrial heartland, it produces half of Canada's manufactured goods. It is also home to the country's capital, Ottawa, and its largest city, Toronto. And it has approximately 400,000 freshwater lakes, covering some 200,000 sq km (77,000 sq miles). In a word, it has everything.

Originally part of New France, then of the British colony of Canada, it became a separate province in 1791 when the Constitutional Act

divided the colony into the predominantly French-settled Lower Canada (Québec) and the Loyalist-dominated Upper Canada (Ontario). Its first capital was Niagara-on-the-Lake, but in 1793 Toronto became the capital and was promptly renamed York. In 1813, invading Americans burned the town to the ground. (A year later the British retaliated by burning, or at least blackening, the White House.) When York was rebuilt it expanded rapidly, helped by a tide of immigration from Britain and Europe, and in 1834 was incorporated as a city, reverting to its original native name of Toronto.

When the British North America Act of 1867 created the Dominion of Canada, Upper Canada joined the Confederation as the new province of Ontario, a name derived from an Iroquois word variously translated as "shining waters" and "high rocks standing near the waters" and thought

to refer to Niagara Falls. Ottawa became the capital of the newly confederated Canada, with Toronto remaining the provincial capital. Since then Ontario has gone from strength to strength, becoming the economic center of the nation.

Although Ontario is Canada's second largest province, after Québec, with 1,068,587 sq km (413,000 sq miles), its industrial and commercial preeminence is due almost entirely to that chipped-arrowhead-shaped peninsula that begins at Toronto and extends southwest to the point where it pokes into Detroit. This is Canada's machine room. But that is not all. Low-lying and lapped by three of the Great Lakes (Ontario, Erie and Huron), it has extremely rich soil, making it an agricultural center as well. Add to all this Toronto's dominance as a commercial and banking center, and you can see why the province prospers.

OTTAWA

In almost every sense, Ottawa is the ideal capital city. It is imposing: its neo-Gothic government buildings are set high on a bluff overlooking the Ottawa River. It is beautiful: its many official buildings and handsome residential neighborhoods share the city with numerous parks, lakes and open spaces, all surrounded by a four-kilometer-wide (two-and-a-half-mile) greenbelt and overhung by clear, unpolluted air. It is cultured: its six national museums and stunning National Arts Centre are only the "official" end of a cultural spectrum that is varied and impressive. It is cosmopolitan: it is the most completely bilingual city in Canada, and it boasts some of the best hotels and restaurants. And it is fun: the original reason for Ottawa's existence, the Rideau Canal that sweeps through the heart of the city, is a summer-long haven for boating and canoeing enthusiasts, while in winter it becomes the world's longest skating rink.

Yet only 150 years ago this was a rough-and-ready, brawling backwoods village of French lumberjacks and Irish construction workers. In those days it was known as Bytown, after the man who built the canal. In 1855 it changed its name to Ottawa when Queen Victoria chose it to be the capital of the short-lived United Province of Canada, before it became the national capital when the Confederation came into being 10 years later. This was a widely unpopular choice, and a long time passed before Canadians stopped referring scornfully to "Westminster-in-the-Wilderness." Nevertheless, the people of Ottawa immediately began erecting buildings worthy of a national capital and — perhaps equally important — set about changing their image. If they were tolerably successful in

Ottawa in bloom — OPPOSITE TOP: Spring arrives in Rockcliffe Village neighborhood. ABOVE: The Parliament building presides over the Tulip Festival BOTTOM.

the former pursuit, they were too successful in the latter. For almost a century Ottawa was noted for its sobriety, propriety, dignity and decorum — in other words, for being numbingly boring. Then in the 1960s the city suddenly seemed to get its second wind. New buildings went up, the city's cultural life was reinvigorated, the entertainment scene expanded, recreational facilities proliferated — it was as if the city had decided, all of a sudden, to start enjoying itself.

BACKGROUND

When Philemon Wright arrived from New England in 1800, the region was inhabited by a band

of Outaouaic natives, after whom the place was named. Wright established a small settlement at the confluence of the Ottawa, Rideau and Gatineau Rivers, which he rightly considered an ideal spot from which to ship timber to Québec. In 1826 the settlers were joined by Colonel John By and a group of Royal Engineers, accompanied by a small army of mostly Irish laborers, who had been sent by the Duke of Wellington to build a canal. After the War of 1812, concerned that a long stretch of the St. Lawrence was within easy reach of American guns, Wellington decided to construct an alternative waterway from the Ottawa River to Lake Ontario. The project, which was completed in 1832, resulted in a 200-km (125-mile) system of canals, rivers, locks, dams and lakes stretching from Bytown, as the village had come to be known, to Kingston, Ontario. It was called the Rideau Canal.

By the mid-1830s, Bytown had a thriving industry producing and shipping squared timber. But something else led to its becoming the capital of Canada. Distressed by the bitter rivalry between the larger cities of Upper and Lower Canada over which should be the capital of the new United Province of Canada, in 1855 Queen Victoria selected Bytown because it was situated on the border between the two provinces. Having been thus honored, the people of Bytown changed its name to Ottawa and began preparing this one-industry (timber) town to handle a second industry: government.

Today, the fourth-largest metropolitan area in Canada is actually made up of Ottawa and ten outlying municipalities, along with Gatineau and surrounding towns across the river in Québec. In spite of the urban sprawl, the people here still gloat over living in the seat of political power, yet within a short drive of genuine, beautiful wilderness. It has proven a happy combination.

GENERAL INFORMATION

The **Capital Infocentre** ((613) 239-5000 TOLL-FREE (800) 465-1867 WEB SITE www.canadascapital .gc.ca, 90 Wellington Street, provides information on Ottawa and Gatineau-Hull.

The best way of sightseeing in Ottawa is on foot, as the major attractions are all within easy walking distance of one another. However, sightseeing trolleys and double-decker buses leave from Confederation Square; contact **Grayline** ((613) 725-1441 TOLL-FREE (800) 297-6422 WEB SITE www.grayline.ca or **Capital Trolley Tours** ((613) 749-3666 TOLL-FREE (800) 823-6147 WEB SITE www .ottawatours.com. **Canada Ducks** ((613) 792-3825 WEB SITE www.canadaducks.ca operates amphibious city tours from the corner of Sparks and Metcalfe (May to October). **Blue Umbrella Tours** ((613) 232-0344 WEB SITE www.blueumbrellatours .com runs a wide variety of walking tours, from crime and scandal trails to pub crawls (May to October). Other tours include the **Haunted Walk of Ottawa** ((613) 232-0344 WEB SITE www.haunted walk.com and **Ottawa Walks** ((613) 744-4307. The **Ottawa Riverboat Company** ((613) 562-4888 WEB SITE www.ottawariverboat.ca and **Paul's Boat Lines** ((613) 225-6781 run boat cruises along the Ottawa River and Rideau Canal in summer.

WHAT TO SEE AND DO

Undoubtedly, Ottawa's main sight is **Parliament Hill** WEB SITE www.parl.gc.ca, the very heart of Ottawa. Here, high above the Ottawa River, stand some splendid sandstone structures capped with green copper roofs: a neo-Gothic extravagance of towers and pinnacles. A huge fire in 1916 destroyed most of the original buildings, and they were rebuilt a few years later with the addition of the soaring 92-m-high (302-ft) **Peace Tower** at the center, a monument to Canadians who died in World War I. Take a trip up the tower (there is an elevator) for some excellent views over Ottawa. The **Parliament Buildings** (or "Centre Block") house the Senate and the House of Commons. When Parliament is in session you can sit in the public galleries to watch. The offices of the **East and West Blocks** are closed to the public. The **Parliamentary Library**, the one place that escaped the 1916 fire, is a polygonal domed building with an impressive, paneled interior. From late June to late August, the **Changing of the Guard** WEB SITE www.capcan.ca takes place daily at 10 AM on the

FREE (800) 465-1867 WEB SITE www.capcan.ca. Also between Parliament Hill and the Château Laurier, the **Canadian Museum of Contemporary Photography** ((613) 990-8527 WEB SITE www.cmcp .gallery.ca, 1 Rideau Canal, showcases a magnificent collection of over 160,000 photographs in a series of constantly changing exhibits.

Across the canal between George and York Streets, **Byward Market** was once a down-to-earth farmers' market that had been here since 1840. Joined by local artists and artisans, food stores and restaurants, this has become one of the trendiest areas in the city and a thriving nightlife center.

Looking east from the Parliament Buildings you'll see the steel and glass **National Gallery of**

lawns in front of the Parliament Buildings, with military music, colorful uniforms and a magnificent backdrop. From July to September, a half-hour sound-and-light show highlights Canada's history for half an hour every evening. There are also free concerts of the Peace Tower's 53-bell carillon daily in July and August at 2 PM, and September to June weekdays at noon.

To the east lies the **Rideau Canal**, which stretches 200 km (125 miles) between Ottawa and Kingston and is now used purely for recreational purposes. Lined by gardens and trees, in summer it's a lovely place for walks and boating, while in winter skaters glide along it. There is a flight of nineteenth-century locks with an interpretive center between the Château Laurier and Parliament Hill. Over the first three weekends in February, the canal is the center of Ottawa's huge winter festival, **Winterlude** ((613) 239-5000 TOLL-

Canada ((613) 990-1985 TOLL-FREE (800) 319-2787 WEB SITE www.national.gallery.ca, 380 Sussex Drive, home to the finest and most complete collection of Canadian art in the world. Nearby, the moving **Canadian War Museum** ((819) 776-8600 TOLL-FREE (800) 555-5621 depicts Canada's role in modern conflicts across the globe. This museum is due to move; phone first to check location.

The **Aboriginal Experiences First Nations' Village** ((613) 564-9494 TOLL-FREE (877) 811-3233 WEB SITE www.aboriginalexperiences.com, stands on Victoria Island in the Ottawa River near Parliament Hill (open mid-May to mid-October). Although touristy, it offers an entertaining look

OPPOSITE: The "world's longest skating rink" — the Rideau Canal in winter. ABOVE and OVERLEAF: Ottawa's Parliament Buildings — "a neo-Gothic extravagance of towers and pinnacles" — have weathered many years and many seasons.

at First Nations' lifestyle, arts and crafts, with storytelling, song and dance on the program.

Across Alexandra Bridge from the National Gallery is the **Canadian Museum of Civilization** ((819) 776-7000 TOLL-FREE (800) 555-5621 WEB SITE www.civilisation.ca, 100 Laurier Street, Gatineau. This enormous building contains such exhibits as a Pacific Northwest Coast native village with totem poles, six life-size longhouses and life-size reconstructions of an archaeological dig. The First People's Hall offers an excellent explanation of native culture alongside galleries about the incoming settlers, while hands-on participation, an excellent Children's Museum and an Imax cinema make it a good place to take the whole family.

art and an extensive collection of 120 aircraft that traces the history of aviation from the early 1900s to the present day.

Gatineau Park, 318 Meech Lake Road, is only a few kilometers (a couple of miles) northwest of the city center. With woodlands, lakes and hills, it is an ideal place for fishing, boating, swimming, camping and hiking in summer, and cross-country skiing in winter.

SPORTS AND OUTDOOR ACTIVITIES

Several companies running one- or two-day of **whitewater rafting** trips, such as Owl Rafting ((613) 238-7238, 39 First Street. There are several

The **Canadian Museum of Nature** ((613) 566-4700 TOLL-FREE (800) 263-4433 WEB SITE www.nature .ca, Macleod and Metcalfe Streets, is housed in a Victorian building. As its name suggests, it is concerned with the formation of the earth and its life forms. There's a dinosaur section that rarely fails to delight children.

Popular with children and adults, the **Canada Science and Technology Museum** ((613) 991-3044 WEB SITE www.nmstc.ca, 1867 Boulevard St-Laurent, has hands-on displays from magnificent old steam engines, vintage cars and machinery to samples of all kinds of technology, including the Apollo 7 space capsule.

Moving northwards a little, the **Canada Aviation Museum** ((613) 993-2010 TOLL-FREE (800) 463-2038 WEB SITE www.aviation.nmstc.ca, at Rockcliffe and Aviation parkways, features a Harrier jump jet, the Virtual Glider, an exhibit of aviation

places where you can rent **boats**, **canoes** and **paddleboats** along the Rideau Canal, such as Dow's Lake Pavilion ((613) 232-1001, 1001 Queen Elizabeth Drive.

In winter there's **skiing** at Mont Cascades ((819) 827-0301, 30 minutes north of Ottawa on Highway 307. The longest run is 670 m (2,067 ft). During the summer you can cool off at the water park with its six slides. Also in winter, the Rideau Canal becomes the world's longest **skating** run, stretching from The National Arts Centre ((613) 996-5051 to Dows Lake. You can rent skates and towing sleds from Silver Skates ((613) 825-4145 WEB SITE www.silver-skates.com, across from the Arts Centre.

The **Capital Pathway** is a network of 65 km (40 miles) of parkways, walking and jogging trails, and cycle paths closed to motorized traffic every Sunday morning in summer.

Ottawa's NHL-affiliated **hockey** team, the Senators ((613) 599-0250 TOLL-FREE (800) 444-7367 WEB SITE www.ottawasenators.com, play at Corel Centre ((613) 599-0100 WEB SITE www.corelcentre.com, while Jetform Park is home to the Ottawa Lynx AAA **baseball** team ((613) 747-5969 TOLL-FREE (800) 663-0985 WEB SITE www.ottawalynx.com.

NIGHTLIFE AND THE ARTS

The city after dark has changed for the better in recent years. The free monthly magazine *Where* has good general listings of what's on. Also look for local free weeklies, such as the *Ottawa Xpress*.

The **National Arts Centre** ((613) 947-7000 WEB SITE www.nac-can.ca, 53 Elgin Street, has a 2,300-seat opera auditorium, a 950-seat theater, the smaller Studio for experimental works, the Atelier (which seats only 150) and the Fourth Stage, used by local community groups. The Centre has its own National Arts Centre Orchestra and bilingual theatrical company.

You can listen to rock at **Barrymore's** ((613) 996-5051, 323 Bank Street, Irish folk music at **Molly McGuire's** ((613) 241-1972, 130 George Street, or blues upstairs at the **Rainbow Bistro** ((613) 541-5123, 76 Murray Street, which puts on free matinees between 3 PM and 7 PM, Thursday, Friday and Saturday. **Patty's Place** ((613) 730-2434, at 1070 Bank Street, is an Irish pub that serves fish-and-chips and Irish stew. The **Collection & Bar** ((613) 562-1120 has live DJs, an eclectic restaurant serving excellent food, and a bar serving impressive martinis.

The **Casino de Lac-Leamy** ((819) 772-2100 TOLL-FREE (800) 665-2274 WEB SITE www.casinos-quebec.com, across the river in Gatineau, is usually still known to locals as the Casino de Hull. Under either name, it has become one of the city's top attractions, with performances, gaming and excellent dining.

WHERE TO STAY

Expensive

The renowned **Fairmont Château Laurier** ((613) 241-1414 TOLL-FREE (800) 441-1414 FAX (613) 562-7031 WEB SITE www.fairmont.com, 1 Rideau Street, is a beautiful castle-like building which opened in 1912. Guests have included the rich, the famous and the royal. Situated at the bottom of Parliament Hill on Confederation Square, many of its 429 rooms and suites offer beautiful views. Among its facilities are an indoor swimming pool, one of the city's finest restaurants, Epic, and the elegant Zoe's lounge.

Built in the 1960s, the **Sheraton Ottawa Hotel** ((613) 238-1500 TOLL-FREE (800) 489-8333 FAX (613) 235-2723 WEB SITE www.sheraton.com, 150 Albert Street, offers 236 attractive rooms, an indoor pool

and fitness center, a wine bar and a restaurant, and every modern convenience and comfort.

Connected to the Rideau Centre, the 24-story **Westin Ottawa** ((613) 560-7000 TOLL-FREE (800) 937-8461 FAX (613) 234-5396 WEB SITE www.westin.com, 11 Colonel By Drive, overlooks the Rideau Canal. It has 487 tastefully decorated rooms, squash courts, a gym, an indoor pool and restaurants.

The **Ottawa Marriott** ((613) 238-1122 TOLL-FREE (800) 853-8463 FAX (613) 783-4229 WEB SITE www.marriott.com, 100 Kent Street, is another modern high-rise hotel with 480 large and well-equipped rooms, an indoor swimming pool, a piano bar, a café and a revolving restaurant with great views. The **Minto Place Suite Hotel** ((613) 782 2350 TOLL-FREE (800) 267-3377 WEB SITE www.mintohotel.com, 433 Laurier Avenue West, has 418 suites of varying sizes, with all conveniences, very well-equipped kitchens and comfortable living rooms. With its special weekend rates, children under 18 stay free of charge, and there is a kids' club for the younger ones.

Arc — The Hotel ((613) 238-2888 TOLL-FREE (800) 699-2516 FAX (613) 235-8421 WEB SITE www.arcthehotel.com, 140 Slater Street, is an ultra-chic boutique hotel, with 110 rooms and a fitness center. Evening canapés and a continental breakfast are included in the rate. The **Carmichael Inn and Spa** ((613) 236-4667 FAX (613) 563-7529 WEB SITE www.carmichaelinn.com is a restored heritage property with only 10 antique-furnished rooms and a wraparound porch. It also has a full service spa.

Mid-range

The **Lord Elgin** ((613) 235-3333 TOLL-FREE (800) 267-4298 FAX (613) 235-3223 WEB SITE www.lordelginhotel.ca, 100 Elgin Street, offers very good value. Built in 1940, this stately stone building near Parliament Hill has 315 rooms. The **Capital Hill Hotel & Suites** ((613) 235-1413 TOLL-FREE (800) 463-7705 FAX (613) 235-6047 WEB SITE www.capitalhill.com, 88 Albert Street, is a popular choice close to Parliament Hill, with 150 rooms, a restaurant, a coffee shop and a fitness center. Nearby the **Crowne Plaza** ((613) 237-3600 FAX (613) 237-2351 WEB SITE www.crowneplazaottawa.com, 101 Lyon Street, which has undergone extensive renovation, offers 411 rooms with good facilities, including an indoor pool, a fitness center and two popular restaurants.

The **Howard Johnson** ((613) 237-9300 FAX (613) 237-2163 WEB SITE www.hojo.com, 123 Metcalfe Street, is a fine, centrally located nineteenth-century hotel (formerly the Roxborough), with 132 rooms, a cozy bar and a restaurant. Alternatively the **Bostonian** ((613) 594-5757 FAX (613) 594-3221 WEB SITE www.thebostonian.ca, 341 Maclaren Street, is one of the new breed of boutique hotels, with 117 elegant executive suites designed for business travelers, with in-room Internet connections, work stations and kitchenettes, in addition to the usual facilities.

The **Cartier Place Suite Hotel** ((613) 236-5000 TOLL-FREE (800) 236-8399 FAX (613) 236-3842 WEB SITE www.suitedreams.com, 180 Cooper Street, has 253 comfortable and well-equipped apartments of differing sizes with maid service and dry cleaning included in the cost. Facilities include an indoor pool, a fitness center and a restaurant. Under-14s stay free of charge in their parents' room.

Lower down the financial scale, the **Days Inn Downtown Ottawa** ((613) 789-5555 TOLL-FREE (800) 789-6196 FAX (613) 789-6196 WEB SITE www.daysinn.com, 319 Rideau Street, offers clean and comfortable, if bland, accommodation in a central location.

Inexpensive

Downtown the Swiss-style **Gasthaus Switzerland** ((613) 237-0335 TOLL-FREE (888) 663-0000 FAX (613) 594-3327 WEB SITE www.gasthausswitzerland.com, 89 Daly Avenue, has 22 rooms, some with private bath. At the high end of inexpensive range, the **Travelodge Hotel Ottawa West** ((613) 722-7600 TOLL-FREE (800) 267-4166 FAX (613) 722 2542 WEB SITE www.thetravelodge.com, 1376 Carling Avenue, is 10 minutes west of the town center. It offers attractive rooms with balconies and use of an outdoor swimming pool.

Even more affordable, the **Econolodge Ottawa Downtown** ((613) 789-3781 TOLL-FREE (800) 553-2666 FAX (613) 789-0207 WEB SITE www.econolodge.com, 475 Rideau Street, is central, clean and comfortable if somewhat Spartan. Continental breakfast, local phone calls and parking are included in the rate.

The **Ottawa International Hostel** ((613) 235-2595 TOLL-FREE (800) 663-5777 FAX (613) 235-9202 WEB SITE www.hostellingintl.on.ca, 75 Nicholas Street, is housed in an eighteenth-century jail. It's within walking distance of the major sites and is open year-round. In addition to the dormitory, private rooms are available. For budget accommodation from May to August, try **Carleton University Residence** ((613) 788-5609, 223 Commons Building, 1233 Colonel By; by **Algonquin College Residence** ((613) 727-7698 TOLL-FREE (877) 225-8664 FAX (613) 727-7647, 1385 Woodroffe Avenue, Nepean; and the **University of Ottawa** ((613) 564-5400 FAX (613) 562 5157 E-MAIL clc@uottawa.ca, 90 University Street.

There are also many excellent bed and breakfasts in the city. For listings, contact **Ottawa Area Bed & Breakfast** ((613) 563-0161 TOLL-FREE (800) 461-7889 WEB SITE www.bbcanada.com or www.bedandbreakfasts.ca, 488 Cooper Street, or the **Ottawa Tourism and Convention Authority** ((613) 237-5130 WEB SITE www.tourottawa.org or www.ottawagetaways.com, 130 Albert Street.

WHERE TO EAT

Expensive

The small **Opus Bistro** ((613) 722-9549, 1331 Wellington Street, Westboro, is elegant in its simplicity. The menu features the best of contemporary cuisine (open Tuesday to Saturday for dinner only). **Le Jardin** ((613) 241-1424, 127 York Street, is in a nineteenth-century house with a particularly beautiful upstairs dining room and is known for reliable quality (open daily for dinner only).

Signatures ((613) 236-2499 TOLL-FREE (800) 457-2433, 453 Laurier Avenue, is the extremely fine French restaurant of the Cordon Bleu Culinary Arts Institute. The students cook up a storm, and if you wish, there are plenty of short courses on offer as well.

In Gatineau, **Le Baccara** ((819) 772-6210, Casino de Lac Leamy, is the city's only five-diamond restaurant, where superb food is served in serene surroundings. The **Café Henri Burger** ((819) 777-5646, 69 Laurier, which first opened in the 1920s, continues to enjoy a well-deserved reputation for high quality cuisine in pleasant surroundings. There's French cuisine in a relaxed, intimate atmosphere at **La Tartuffe** ((819) 771-1689, 133 rue Notre-Dame, and it's worth the short drive into the Gatineau Hills to enjoy the beautiful setting and the superb French food at **L'Orée du Bois** ((819) 827-0332, Kingsmere Road, Old Chelsea.

Moderate

There's a distinctly English feel about **Friday's Roast Beef House** ((613) 237-5353, 150 Elgin Street, where steaks and ribs again predominate in a very Victorian setting. **Le Café** ((613) 594-5127, in the National Arts Centre on Rideau Canal serves Canadian food and Canadian wines. It's a pleasant spot for any meal of the day and stays open quite late Monday to Saturday. For Indian food try the smart and popular **Haveli** ((613) 241-1700, 87 George Street, Market Mall. **Kinki** ((613) 789-9559, 41 York Street, is an excellent Asian-fusion sushi and tempura restaurant in Byward Market.

Those who really want a view should try **Le Merlot** ((613) 238-1122, 100 Kent Street, the revolving restaurant at the top of the Marriott Hotel. **Bravo Bravo** ((613) 233-7525, 292 Elgin Street, is a good Italian restaurant with Tuscan decor, an attractive outdoor terrace and a fine line in weekend brunches, including a Sunday gospel brunch.

Inexpensive

The **Elephant & Castle** ((613) 234-5544, 50 Rideau Street, is a popular and central meeting place

TOP: Byward Market. BOTTOM: The start of the bed race during the Winterlude Festival.

where pub-style food is served, and it's open all day every day. One of the best-value Chinese restaurants in town is **Shanghai** ((613) 233-4001, 651 Somerset Street West, near Bronson. For Italian, there's **The Ritz 3 Uptown** ((613) 789-9797, 89 Clarence Street, with other locations scattered around Ottawa.

There are several good eateries in the Byward Market area. **Memories** ((613) 232-1882, 7 Clarence Street, is an attractive bistro–café serving light lunches and sandwiches as well as weekend brunch. You can go back in time to the 1950s at **Zak's Diner** ((613) 241-2401, 16 Byward Market, where there's lots of vinyl, chrome, and 1950s music on the jukebox.

If all you need is munchies, join the line at **Market Beavertails** ((613) 230-1230, 69 St. George Street, for a taste of Ottawa's signature pastries, or stop in at **Cows** ((613) 244 4224, 43 Clarence Street, for around 50 flavors of ice cream. Both are in Byward Market.

How to Get There

Ottawa's **Macdonald-Cartier International Airport** ((613) 248-2125 is conveniently located 15 km (eight miles) south of the city, about 25 minutes from downtown. Buses, taxis and **shuttle services** ((613) 736-9993 run to downtown.

VIA Rail ((613) 244-8289 WEB SITE www.viarail .ca has several trains daily to and from Toronto and Montréal. The station is near Riverside Drive, off Highway 417, just east of downtown.

Buses all run from the **Ottawa Bus Central Station** ((613) 238-6668, 265 Catherine Street, near the Kent Street exit from Highway 417, on the edge of downtown. **Voyageur Colonial** ((613) 238-5900 operates a bus service that links Ottawa with other Canadian cities.

The TransCanada Highway (Route 417) is the principal east–west highway into and out of Ottawa. Approaching from the south you will want to take Route 16, which crosses the border at Ogdensburg, New York, and also connects with Route 401, the main Toronto–Montréal highway.

SOUTHWEST OF OTTAWA

Stretching from the dazzling, sophisticated city of Ottawa to the sprawling, wealthy metropolis of Toronto, the people of this part of Ontario, especially in Kingston and Quinte's Isle, have managed to preserve the character and quiet dignity of an earlier age.

KINGSTON

Strategically sited where Lake Ontario meets the St. Lawrence River, Kingston was an important native trading center long before the French fur

traders arrived in the early seventeenth century. Although the French immediately coveted the spot, constant fighting between the Iroquois and the Hurons prevented them from establishing a trading post until 1673, when a lull in the hostilities allowed Louis de Buade, Comte de Frontenac, to establish a fortified settlement here. Fort Frontenac, as it was known, survived for almost a century before falling to a force of British-American troops in advance of the Treaty of Paris, which in 1763 ceded control of all of Canada to Britain.

Resettled in the 1780s by self-exiled Loyalists, who gave it the name Kingston, the town rapidly became a key British naval base and home to a large shipyard. Kingston survived the War of 1812 unscathed, and went on to enjoy two significant boosts to its economy: in 1832, when it became the southern terminus of the newly completed Rideau Canal, and again in 1841, when it became, briefly, the capital of both Upper and Lower Canada.

Already a prospering military center, Kingston soon became an important academic center with the founding of Queen's University.

Since then, Kingston has remained remarkably unchanged in several respects, although it's now a thriving city of around 143,000 people. Even today there are few buildings more than two or three stories tall, while eighteenth-century Brock Street remains an important commercial thoroughfare and still has some of the same stores it had two centuries ago. Kingston has also retained its strong military connections: the Royal Military College, the National Defence College and the Canadian Army Staff College are all located here. But most noticeably, it has preserved — and in many instances restored — not only its graceful gray limestone public buildings, but also its many fine Victorian private residences.

Finally, Kingston has also retained its strategic importance: it lies, conveniently, almost exactly halfway between Montréal and Toronto. Equally conveniently, it is ideally placed for boat excursions on Lake Ontario and sightseeing trips to the Thousand Islands region.

The **Kingston Tourist Information Office** ((613) 548-4415 WEB SITE www.kingston-ontario .com is at 209 Ontario Street. A **Visitor's Day Pass** ($5) entitles you to entry to many of the city's sights and bus transportation, or you could take the **Confederation Trolley Tour** ((613) 548-4453, 29 Ontario Street (mid-May to September).

What to See and Do

Stout and forbidding **Fort Henry** ((613) 542-7388 WEB SITE www.forthenry.com, just east of the city off Route 2, glowers over Kingston from a high hilltop (open mid-May to early October). This massive fortification was completed in 1836 to

Kingston: an oasis of Victorian serenity.

defend the naval dockyard at Point Frederick. A regiment of costumed interpreters and a busy program of special events and demonstrations show what life was like for the nineteenth-century guardsmen. In July and August there are weekly evening Sunset Ceremonies (call for schedule).

Across Navy Bay on Point Frederick stands the **Royal Military College**, with **Fort Frederick Museum (** (613) 541-6000 (late-June to September). Displays cover the history of the college and, somewhat bewilderingly, the small arms collection of General Porfirio Diaz, who was the President of Mexico from 1886 to 1912. **Murney Tower Museum (** (613) 544-9925, King West at Barrie Streets, is a splendid martello tower built in 1846 (open mid-May to August).

City Hall ((613) 533-2190, 216 Ontario Street, was built in 1843, when Kingston was capital of the United Province of Canada, and this grand domed building is one of the country's finest examples of classical architecture. In front of City Hall, **Confederation Park** stretches down to the water's edge and is the site of concerts and other open-air events in the summer. Eastward along the waterfront, the **Marine Museum of the Great Lakes (** (613) 542-2261 WEB SITE www.marmus.ca, 55 Ontario Street, is devoted to the history of shipping on the lakes from the seventeenth century to the present day, including the history of shipbuilding in the area. Among the exhibits is a 3,000-ton icebreaker.

One of the town's odder museums is the **Correctional Service of Canada Museum (** (613) 530-3122, 555 King Street West, an exhibition about the country's prison service, in an 1873 mansion, built as the prison governor's residence (April to August).

The **Kingston Archeological Centre (** (613) 542-3483 WEB SITE www.carf.info, 370 King Street West, is primarily a research center, coordinating archeological studies on the local Cataraqui people, but also has a small exhibition on the history of the local area, from its very earliest days. A lovely nineteenth-century house is the setting for the recently renovated **Agnes Etherington Art Centre (** (613) 533-2190 WEB SITE www.queensu .ca/ageth, University Avenue at Queen's Crescent. The wide-ranging collection includes Canadian, African and European art and antiques.

Bellevue House ((613) 545-8666 WEB SITE www .parkscanada.gc.ca, 35 Centre Street, is an extravagant green-and-white Tuscan-style villa set in attractive grounds (open April to October). Built in 1840 by a wealthy merchant, its elaborate appearance quickly earned it the nicknames "Pekoe Pagoda" and "Tea Caddy Castle." In 1848 and 1849 it was home to Canada's first prime minister, John A. Macdonald, and the interior has been restored and furnished to that period.

East of Kingston in the St. Lawrence River lie the **Thousand Islands**, which in fact number more than 1,000, ranging in size from quite large to a mere few meters. **Wolfe Island** is the largest. Some are forested and verdant, and the houses on them range from humble to palatial. This beautiful 80-km (50-mile) stretch of the St. Lawrence has long been a popular vacation spot, and there are quite a number of cruises and tours of the islands in operation (**Kingston Island Cruises (** (613) 549-5544 offers a range of cruises). **St. Lawrence Islands National Park (** (613) 923-5261, 2 Country Road 5, Mallorytown, encompasses 17 of the islands and part of the mainland at Mallorytown Landing, where the park has its visitor centre (mid-May to mid-October). While you're here, take a look at the wreck of the **HMS *Radcliffe***, a gunboat that saw action in the 1812 war and is kept in a shelter close to the Interpretive Centre.

For some more of the outdoor life, **Frontenac Provincial Park (** (613) 376-3489 TOLL-FREE (888) 668-7275, 1090 Salmon Lake Road, Sydenham, offers untouched wilderness in Canadian Shield country where you can bird-watch, hike, canoe or, when the weather's right, cross-country ski. **Frontenac Outfitters (** (613) 376-6220, in Sydenham, rent out camping gear, canoes and kayaks.

Where to Stay and Eat

Rosemount Bed & Breakfast Inn ((613) 531-8844 TOLL-FREE (888) 871-8844 FAX (613) 544-4895 WEB SITE www.rosemountinn.com, 46 Sydenham Street South, is an expensive Tuscan-style villa built in 1850 and beautifully restored and furnished with antiques. Luxuries include a mini-spa and wonderful food.

Hochelaga Inn (/FAX (613) 549-5534 TOLL-FREE (877) 933 9433 WEB SITE www.someplaces different.com, 24 Sydenham Street South, is another attractive Victorian-era house with 23 well-equipped rooms, handsomely decorated with period pieces (mid-range). Off-shore, on Wolfe Island, **General Wolfe Hotel and Restaurant (** (613) 385-2611 TOLL-FREE (800) 353-1098 FAX (613) 385-1048 WEB SITE www.generalwolfehotel.com is basically all about wonderful food, with three dining rooms producing everything from salads to flambées via classic nouvelle cuisine, in a property built in 1860 in a glorious island setting (moderate to expensive). There are only nine rooms, so book ahead.

Particularly good for families, **Seven Oaks Motor Inn (** (613) 546-3655, 2331 Princess Street, has 40 accommodations set in acres of land with a large swimming pool. Near Fort Henry, the **Highland Motel Five (** (613) 546-3121, 725 Highway 15, offers 45 rooms and facilities that include tennis courts and an outdoor pool.

Louise House Summer Hostel ((613) 531 8237 WEB SITE www.hostellingintl.ca, 329 Johnson Street, has good facilities. Alternatively, check the listings at **Kingston Area Bed and Breakfast** ((613) 542-0214 WEB SITE www.bbcanada.com.

Kingston is surprisingly lacking in fine dining opportunities, with the notable exception of the General Wolfe. For good (expensive) Italian food go to **Gencarelli** ((613) 542-7976, 629 Princess Street, where in warm weather you can eat on the pleasant rooftop terrace. **Shoeless Joe's** ((613) 547-1555, 371 Princess Street, is part of an international chain providing excellent steak, burgers and other all-American staples (moderate). The inexpensive **Kingston Brewing Company** ((613) 542-4978, 34 Clarence Street, serves basic bar food amid the tanks in which their own very commendable beer and lager are brewed.

QUINTE'S ISLE

Surrounded by the waters of Lake Ontario, Quinte's Isle is a pastoral idyll floating offshore. It, too, was settled by Loyalists, who took advantage of the island's position and rich soil to make it a quiet farming paradise. Today it produces more vegetables and fruit than almost any other area of comparable size in Ontario — much of which is grown by descendants of the original settlers. The island is dotted with roadside stands selling fresh produce.

It is also increasingly dotted with art galleries and craft shops, as many artists and artisans have come here to get away from the rigors and distractions of life on the other shore. The great Canadian artist D.R. Dawson, for example, settled in the town of Picton, having lived for years on a Greek island. Inevitably, too, the island has be-

gun to undergo the experience of being "discovered," and consequently now has facilities and developments geared to the tourist trade. But it remains largely unspoiled — and thoroughly pleasant.

For visitor information concerning Quinte's Isle, contact the **Prince Edward County Chamber of Tourism and Commerce** ((613) 476-2421 TOLL-FREE (800) 640-4717 WEB SITE www.pec.on.ca, 116 Main Street, Picton.

What to See and Do

Quinte's Isle is a restful place with quiet roads and old settlements. It is also a recreational area where the flatness of the land makes for good bicycling, while the waters offer sailing and fishing opportunities.

The small town of **Picton** is the largest in the area and the hub of the island. It's an attractive, quiet town with some interesting old buildings and a deep-water harbor. You can pick up maps and guides in the local tourist office and take a look at some of the many crafts that are produced here. Each summer it becomes the center of a music festival called **Quinte Summer Music**, in which top Canadian performers participate. Nearby **Bloomfield**, first founded in the early nineteenth century, is a good place for crafts, pottery and antiques. **Consecon** is a small and picturesque village with a millpond and some delightful views over the water.

East of Picton, Route 33 brings you to the **Lake on the Mountain**, a small lake 60 m (197 ft) above Lake Ontario. Its origins are unknown, but legend has it that the lake is fed from Niagara Falls. This spot is well worth a stop for the spectacular views over Lake Ontario.

West of Picton you'll find **Sandbanks** and **North Beach Provincial Parks**, ideal for picnicking, sailing and swimming. Sandbanks is a huge sandbar that extends across a bay and has dunes that reach up to 24 m (80 ft) in height. North Beach is good for swimming, windsurfing and sailing; there's also a place that rents out equipment and gives lessons. For information on the parks call Sandbanks Provincial Park headquarters ((613) 393-3319.

Bloomfield Bicycle Co. ((613) 393-1060, 225 Main Street, Bloomfield, rents bicycles and offers guided cycle tours of the area. **Bernie Gray Kayaking** ((613) 961-1552, Still Water Basin Marina, 383 Dundas Street West, Belleville, organizes kayaking trips at all levels. The **Diamond J Ranch** ((613) 476-4595, Salmon Point Road near Cherry Valley, offers beach and bush horseback riding. **Prince Edward Sailing Charters** ((613) 476-4595 offer a day's sailing on a tall ship.

Bellevue House in Kingston remains rooted in the mid-nineteenth century.

Where to Stay and Eat
Isaiah Tubbs Resort ((613) 393-2090 TOLL-FREE (800) 724-2393 WEB SITE www.someplacesdifferent .com, Rural Route 1, West Lake Road, Picton, offers rooms and suites in the restored 1820s inn, as well as lodges and seasonal cabins, all with excellent facilities (mid-range to expensive).

There's an old-fashioned coziness about **Waring House Restaurant and B&B** ((613) 476-7492 TOLL-FREE (800) 621-4956 FAX (613) 476-6648 WEB SITE www.waringhouse.com, Loyalist Parkway, just west of Picton on Rural Route 1. This is in an 1835 stone house with delightful antique-furnished guest rooms. It specializes in European cuisine, with home-baked breads and pastries. The dining

packages. It also has a good casual restaurant and fine rose gardens. **Merrill Inn** ((613) 476-7451 WEB SITE www.merrillinn.com, 343 Main Street East, Picton, is a charming hotel dating from the 1870s. Each of the 15 rooms is individually decorated with antiques and is also furnished with modern conveniences (mid-range).

Tara Hall Bed & Breakfast ((613) 399-2801 TOLL-FREE (877) 233-4612 WEB SITE www.magma .ca / tarahall, 146 Main Street, Wellington, is a lovely landmark house with decorative detail throughout and three guestrooms (inexpensive). In Bloomfield, **Mallory House** ((613) 393-3458, Rural Route 1, offers some of the most charming accommodation on the island (inexpensive). This

room, with its open fireplace and polished wooden floor, quite literally exudes warmth (rooms moderate; meals expensive). The owners also run a year-round cooking school.

Bloomfield Inn ((613) 393-3301 TOLL-FREE (877) 391-3301 WEB SITE www.angelines-inn.com, 29 Stanley Street West, Bloomfield, has nine rooms, one of the best restaurants in the area, **Angéline's**, and a lovely café (rooms moderate, meals expensive). It's an attractive old house with a warm and welcoming interior. The chef's specialties include freshwater fish and pheasant, and his Austrian origins are in evidence when his wonderful pastries are served for afternoon tea.

The mid-range **Tip of the Bay Motor Hotel** ((613) 476-2156 TOLL-FREE (888) 955-5030 E-MAIL tip@reach.net, 35 Bridge Street, Picton, which overlooks Picton Bay, has its own dock and offers fishing

early nineteenth-century farmhouse set in attractive grounds has three guestrooms.

HOW TO GET THERE

Most people arrive in Kingston by car. Situated on Route 401 midway between Montréal and Toronto, it is an easy morning's (or afternoon's) drive from either city — and even quicker to reach from Ottawa or Syracuse, New York. To reach Quinte's Isle from Kingston, take Highway 49 south off Route 401.

Kingston is also well served by **Voyageur Colonial** ((613) 547-4916 buses from Montréal, Ottawa and Toronto. **VIA Rail** ((613) 544-5600 operates a daily service through Kingston from Montréal and Toronto.

Muster ceremony at Kingston's Fort Henry.

ONTARIO

MANITOBA

Lake Winnipeg

nnipeg

Lake of The Woods
Island

Deer Lake
Oldshoe Lake
Stout Lake

Big Trout Lake

JAMES BAY

44

1

Keewatin
Minaki
Reddit
Kenora
Clay Lake
Goldpines

McKenzie Island
Red Lake
Red Lake
Trout Lake
Birch Lake
Casummit Lake

Wapikopa Lake
Kanuchuan Lake

Akimiski Island

Vermillion Bay

Lac Seul

Dryden
Hudson
Sioux Lookout

Lake St Joseph

Pickle Crow
Rat Rapids

Mameigwess Lake
Winisk Lake

Fort Albany
Normansland Point

Baudette

17

Minnitaki
Raleigh
Ignace

Savant Lake
Savant Lake

Shabuskwia Lake

Attawapiskat Lake

Atikokan

English River

Armstrong Station

Makokibatan Lake

Missisa Lake

Ekwan River

Rainy Lake
Manitou Lakes
International Falls

Quetico Park
Upsala

Wagaming Lake

Kagianagami Lake

Eabamet Lake

Whitewater Lake

Attawapiskat River

Kashabowie
Mabella
Raith

Nipigon

Wabimeig Lake

James Bay

Otter Lake
Sturgeon Lake

Whitefish
Kakabeka Falls
Pine Portage

Beardmore

Nakina

Albany River

Jaab Lake

Fort Albany

Port Arthur
Nipigon
Thunder Bay
Fort William
Jarvis River

Bankfield
Rossport
Longlac
Carmant
Schreiber
Middleton

Pagwa River

Charlton Island

Lake Superior

Marathon
Hemlo
White River

Manitouwadge
Hornepayne
Hearst

Lac Sainte Therese

Moosonee

Moose Crossing River

Mead

11

Opasatika
Lepage

Ramoke

Michipicoten
Michipicoten Bay
Wawa

Missanabie
Dalton

Moonbeam
Fauquier

Fraserdale

Kesagami Lake

QUEBEC

Lake Michigan

Agawa Bay
Point Mamainse
Gros Cap
Sault-Sainte-Marie
Echo Bay

Goulais River
Devon

Chapleau
Foleyet

101

Smooth Rock Falls

Cochrane
Brower

Hunta

Devonshire

U.S.A.

Schumacher
South Porcupine
Gogama
Rann Mine

Monteith

Lake Abitibi

Bruce Mines
Thessalon
Blind River
Meldrum Bay
Evansville

Iron Bridge
Spagge

Aubrey Falls

Westree

Elk Lake

Kirkland Lake

Charlton

Englehart

17

Espanola

Cartier
Milnet

Latchford

New Liskeard
Ville Marie

Providence Bay

Sudbury
Burwash

Markstay

117

Lake Huron

Killarney

Espanola

11

Sturgeon Falls

Temiscaming

Tobermory
Lion's Head
Oliphant

French River

Lake Nipissing
Nipissing

North Bay

Mattawa
Deux Rivières

17

Parry Sound

11

Burks Falls

Algonquin Park

17

Deep River

Kincardine
Kinloss

21

Owen Sound
Penetanguishene

Huntsville

Pembroke

Bayfield
Mildmay
Milverton

26

Midland

11

Gravenhurst

Eagle Lake

60

Renfrew

6

10

Shelburne

Barrie

35

Bancroft

62

60

Arnprior

Sarnia
Exeter
Watford

Waterloo
Guelph

400

Newmarket

Lake Simcoe

Lindsay

Peterborough

Almonte

OTTAWA

Detroit
Dresden
Windsor
Tilbury
Kingsville
Leamington
Blenheim

402
401

Stratford
Kitchener

Aurora

Perth
Smith Falls

17

403

London
Brantford

401

Brampton

Cobourg

7

94

3

Eagle

Simcoe
Hamilton

Toronto

Port Hope

Belleville

9

Niagara

St. Catherines

Picton

Kingston

Brockville

401

Montreal

Fort Erie

Niagara Falls

Trenton

81

Lake Erie

Lake Ontario

U.S.A.

0   50   100 miles
0   50   100   150 Km

TORONTO

However hard one struggles to be open-minded, one cannot help but arrive in a new place with certain preconceived ideas. We arrived in Toronto thinking of Peter Ustinov's description of it as "New York run by the Swiss." But what we hadn't counted on was its amazing accuracy. Toronto's buildings are not just tall, they do indeed scrape the sky; its crime rate is not just low, it's the lowest of any major city in North America; its streets are not just clean, we actually saw two city workers outside our hotel scrubbing a municipal litter bin with soap and water — in the rain!

With a metropolitan population of around 4.2 million and an urban area of some 630 sq km (230 sq miles), Toronto stands (and sprawls) as a gleaming, humming rebuttal to those who argue that big cities must inevitably become breeding grounds of corruption, poverty and violence. Toronto does have a lot of concrete, but it also has over 200 verdant parks. It does have a lot of shiny new skyscrapers, but it also has many lovingly preserved old buildings. It is certainly growing rapidly, but its growth is carefully controlled so that adequate provision is made for housing in any development involving new office space. It is large, but it has excellent public transportation, including a sparkling, efficient subway system. Its schools are good, its cultural amenities are first-rate, its services are efficient, its streets are not only clean but safe, and its citizens are orderly and polite. No wonder people flock to live here.

While the spirit of the city is symbolized by the soaring CN Tower, its enterprising character is represented by a vast subterranean city — the PATH — with over 10 km (six miles) of underground shops, restaurants, cinemas and cafés. Once best known for its suffocating sense of propriety — for many years it had "blue laws" restricting drinking — Toronto is now a lively recreational, cultural and entertainment center with more theaters than any other city in North America except New York and a thriving film industry. But perhaps the best measure of the extent to which Toronto has managed to achieve just the right balance between the old and the new, between dynamism and tradition, is the fact that it strikes American visitors as a British city while to Europeans it seems very American. As for the locals, they pride themselves on having over 100 different ethnic communities. Which probably makes it the most *Canadian* city in Canada.

Today, the city is not only the largest in Canada, but has two superlatives: the CN Tower, which is the world's tallest building, and Yonge Street, the city's main strip, which actually runs from the lake at Queen's Quay for a staggering 1,900 km (1,190 miles) up to Rainy River into northern Ontario, making it the world's longest street.

BACKGROUND

Toronto got off to a slow start. The Huron, who named the site (it means "meeting place"), saw the spot merely as the first (or last) link in a land chain connecting Lake Huron with Lake Ontario, as did the early French fur traders. In the first half of the eighteenth century the French decided that it might be worth building a fort to protect their traders, but it was destroyed during the Seven Years' War. After the war, the victorious British showed no interest in developing the site until 1793, when the Lieutenant Governor, John Graves Simcoe, decided to establish a town there. Soon thereafter it became the capital of Upper Canada in place of Niagara-on-the-Lake, which was thought to be too dangerously close to the American border. It was renamed York after George II's son, the Duke of York.

York's early days as a capital were inauspicious. Its few dirt streets resembled bogs while one of its earliest industries — livestock slaughtering — led to the sobriquet "Hogtown." Then, in 1813, an American force attacked the town and burned down every building of any size. York's next 20 years were marked by such economic and popu-

OPPOSITE: Glass and concrete office buildings can't hide the world's tallest free-standing structure, Toronto's CN Tower, seen here from Front Street. ABOVE: The entrance to the Canadian National Exhibition Center.

lation growth that in 1834 it was incorporated as a city and given back its original name, Toronto.

For better or worse, economic and political power in Toronto — indeed in the province as a whole — was held almost exclusively by an elite group of wealthy businessmen, known as the Family Compact. This small "club" exercised such power that its influence extended far beyond the boundaries of government and commerce to have a determining impact on every aspect of life in the city. Because these men were Anglophilic as well as Anglophone, Toronto became English in character as well as in language. And because they were puritanical and philistine, it became "Toronto the Good," most righteous of cities — and most boring. While its population expanded rapidly throughout the remainder of the nineteenth century — thanks largely to the arrival of Scots fleeing the Highland clearances and Irish fleeing the potato famine — its horizons didn't

expand much until after World War II, when a tidal wave of immigrants from all over the world enlarged and enlivened the city, transforming it from a dull gray zone of strictly enforced virtue into the ethnically diverse, vibrant, cosmopolitan city it is today.

GENERAL INFORMATION

For province-wide information, visit the drop-in **Information Centre** at Toronto Eaton Centre, Level 1, 220 Yonge Street. For information on Toronto contact **Tourism Toronto** ((416) 203-2500 TOLL-FREE (800) 363-1990 FAX (416) 203-6753 WEB SITE www.torontotourism.com, 207 Queen's Quay West, Suite 590. There is also an **Info T.O. Booth** at the Metro Toronto Convention Centre (near the CN Tower), 255 Front Street West.

 Green Tourism Association ((416) 392-1288 FAX (416) 392-0071 WEB SITE www.greentourism.ca,

To rent a bicycle, a conveniently located place is **Wheel Excitement** ((416) 260-9000, 5 Rees Street, behind the Skydome.

Sightseeing Tours

Narrated sightseeing tours of Toronto, with entertaining and informative guides, are offered by **Gray Line Sightseeing Tours** ((416) 594-0343, WEB SITE www.grayline.ca. You can spend the day hopping on and off the bus at various stops for the single adult fare of $29. To see the city from the air, to make a longer trip over the Niagara Falls, or to go heliskiing, contact the **Helicopter Company** ((416) 203-3280 TOLL-FREE (888) 445-8542 WEB SITE www.helitours.ca or **National Helicopters Inc.** TOLL-FREE (866) 361-1100 WEB SITE www.nationalhelicopters.com. For a wide variety of walking and cycle tours in the neighborhoods, contact **A Taste of the World** ((416) 923-6813 WEB SITE www.torontowalksbikes.com.

There are regular one-hour Toronto Harbour cruises with **Mariposa Cruise Line** ((416) 203-0178 WEB SITE www.mariposacruises.com, which also runs longer lunch and brunch cruises. **Canada Ducks** ((416) 487-8687 WEB SITE www.canadaducks.ca, 47 Delhi Avenue, and **Toronto Hippo Tours** ((416) 703-4476 TOLL-FREE (877) 635-5510 WEB SITE www.torontohippotours.com, 31a Parliament Street, both run entertaining amphibious tours of the city.

Seaflight 2000 ((416) 504-8825 TOLL-FREE (877) 504-8825 WEB SITE www.seaflight2000.com, at 249 Queen's Quay West, Suite 109, operates hydrofoil tours of the harbor and a high-speed ferry service across Lake Ontario to Niagara-on-the-Lake and Niagara Falls that departs from 339 Queen's Quay West, beside Fire Station No. 9.

590 Jarvis Street, Fourth Floor, provides information about the city's 8,100 hectares (20,000 acres) of green space and all associated events, as well as a variety of eco-friendly tourist projects in and around the city.

Getting Around

The Toronto Transit Commission (TTC) ((416) 393-4636 operates streetcars, buses and subways. Day passes and single-ride tickets are sold at subway stations and some convenience stores. A family day pass for unlimited travel is $7.50; adult fare is $2.25. There are three subway lines, and the system is relatively easy to use.

The Toronto Islands are reached by **ferry** ((416) 392-8193 from the docks at the foot of Bay Street. Below the downtown financial district is a 10-km-long (six- mile) network of underground walkways known as **PATH**. Color-coded signs show the way.

WHAT TO SEE AND DO

The Waterfront Area

The most conspicuous feature of the Toronto skyline is **CN Tower** ((416) 868-6937 WEB SITE www.cntower.ca, 301 Front Street West. A tall, slim concrete structure that resembles a giant needle, the tower, built as a transmitter mast, stands 553.33 m (1,815.39 ft) high, making it the world's tallest freestanding structure. Glass elevators shoot you skywards to the revolving restaurant, and observation platforms lay the most spectacular and giddy view of the city literally at your feet. In the basement are various other attractions, from simulators to movies and shopping (see TOWER OVER TORONTO, page 17 in TOP SPOTS).

Close by on Front Street is the remarkable **SkyDome** ((416) 341-2770 WEB SITE www.skydome.com, 1 Blue Jays Way, a domed sports stadium with

The Skydome, home of the Blue Jays, Toronto's National League baseball team.

an ingeniously designed 86-m-tall (282-ft) retractable roof. It is home to the Canadian football team the Argonauts, and the baseball team Blue Jays. It seats up to 50,000 spectators and has the world's largest scoreboard. There's a restaurant with a huge seating capacity and a 364-room hotel with 70 rooms overlooking the playing field.

From the CN Tower it's a pleasant stroll through parkland to the old streetcar roundhouse that is now home to a microbrewery called **Steam Whistle Brewing** (416) 362-2337 WEB SITE www.steam whistle.ca, 255 Bremner Boulevard. It's just steps from the brewery to the **Harbourfront Centre** ((416) 973-4100 WEB SITE www.harbourfront.on.ca, 235 Queen's Quay West, an urban park providing shopping, recreation and cultural events — many of them free. To get there, walk down York Street and pass through the Teamway, a well-lit, soundproofed tunnel under the railway tracks that separate downtown from the harbor.

Queen's Quay Terminal ((416) 203-0510 WEB SITE www.queens-quay-terminal.com, 207 Queen's Quay West, has galleries and shops, with a books court and stores featuring Canadian products, crafts and souvenirs. At the **York Quay Centre** there's an art gallery and theater, and nearby **Pier 4** has sailing schools and equipment stores. A few blocks further west is the **Harbourfront Antique Market** ((416) 260-2626 TOLL-FREE (888) 263-6533 WEB SITE www.hfam.com, Canada's largest antiques market, with over 100 dealers.

You can find out about some of Toronto's most dramatic history at **Fort York** ((416) 392-6907, 100 Garrison Road (take the streetcar from Bathurst or Union subway stations). Built in 1793 to defend the town, in 1813 the Americans captured the city and the retreating British blew up fort's magazine, killing 300 Americans and 150 British. It was rebuilt in 1816 and restored in the early 1900s. It offers the visitor a good picture of the life of the British soldier in the early nineteenth century, with its furnished officers' and soldiers' quarters, and military drills performed by authentically uniformed men during the summer months.

Continuing west along the waterfront, the **Marine Museum of Upper Canada** ((416) 392-1765, Exhibition Place, traces the history of shipping and trade in the area. During the summer the *Ned Hanlan*, a restored 1932 tugboat, is open to the public.

Built on three artificial islands on the lake, **Ontario Place** ((416) 314-9900 TOLL-FREE (866) 663-4386 WEB SITE www.ontarioplace.com, 955 Lake Shore Boulevard West, is an indoor-outdoor entertainment complex (open mid-May to September). Futuristic pod-like structures on tall steel legs house theaters where shows and films on Ontario can be seen. In addition to the Molson Amphitheater, there is also an Imax cinema, as well as over 30 rides. The Children's Village is a well-designed, supervised play area. All age groups enjoy a visit to the HMS *Haida*, a Canadian destroyer used in World War II and the Korean War.

You can take a boat trip out to the **Toronto Islands** from the dock at the foot of Bay Street near the Westin Harbour Castle Hotel. These small islands off the downtown waterfront offer recreational possibilities such as swimming, fishing, boating and cycling, and are a popular retreat from the summer heat for Torontonians and visitors alike. **Hanlan's Point** has tennis courts and a pleasant clothing-optional beach. **Ward's Island** is good for swimming. But the most popular is **Centreville** ((416) 203-0405 WEB SITE www.centreville.ca, on Centre Island, a theme park designed to look like an Ontario village of 100 years ago.

Downtown
Toronto's King and Bay Street area is its financial center. **Stock Market Place** at the Toronto Stock Exchange ((416) 947-4676 WEB SITE www.tse.com/ visitor, Exchange Tower, 130 King Street West, is a fun, interactive gaming center where the excitement of the Stock Market comes alive. Of the bank towers, the most striking are the two triangular towers of gold reflecting glass at **Royal Bank Plaza**, Front and Bay Streets. A true cathedral of commerce, it contains an international art collection that includes a vast sculpture by Jesùs Soto composed of 8,600 aluminum tubes.

Heading north on Bay Street from the Royal Bank Plaza is the **Toronto-Dominion Centre** ((416) 982-8473, 55 King Street West. Mies van der Rohe designed this austere complex of five buildings, and inside is the **Gallery of Inuit Art** and the impressive Toronto-Dominion Bank's art collection, which focuses on Canada's northern frontier.

The city's most famous shopping arcade — and top tourist attraction — is the vast **Eaton Centre** ((416) 598-8560 WEB SITE www.torontoeatoncentre.com, Yonge and Dundas Streets, a shoppers' paradise with several floors of famous names interspersed with smaller up-market boutiques.

BCE Place, 10 Front Street West, is an arcade whose interior resembles the ribs of a capsized ship. It incorporates the façade of the Canadian Chamber of Commerce Building (1845), which was disassembled, moved and reconstructed on its present site. Within the arcade are the Heritage Square Shops, a Mövenpick theme restaurant and the **Hockey Hall of Fame** ((416) 360-7735 WEB SITE www.hhof.com, 30 Yonge Street.

Heading east along Front Street, colorful **St. Lawrence Market**, between Church and Jarvis Streets, is a farmers' market housed in Toronto's first city hall building (1899). **Kensington Market**, between Spadina Avenue and Bathurst Street, is also fascinating. It's especially lively in the early mornings when merchants, their wares, and livestock create quite a scene.

In the heart of downtown, **New City Hall** ((416) 392-9111, 100 Queen Street West, with its two curved towers, is a highly acclaimed piece of modern architecture. So futuristic is its design that it even made an appearance on *Star Trek*. In front of the building stands a Henry Moore sculpture, known locally as The Archer. Nearby on Albert and Bay Streets stands **Old City Hall**, designed by E.J. Lennox (who also designed Casa Loma; see below). Because of years of delays and a $2.5 million budget overrun, Lennox was refused payment by the city. He promptly sued and won. In retaliation, the city forbade Lennox to take credit for the building, but Lennox got the last laugh by finishing the façade with gargoyles

sculpted to resemble the leading city politicians of the day. He also carved his initials in the building; the letters are visible along the Bay Street side. The Old City Hall now functions as a courthouse.

A couple of blocks east of the city halls, Victorian **Mackenzie House** ((416) 392-6915, 82 Bond Street (subway: Dundas), was the home of William Lyon Mackenzie, Toronto's first mayor and leader of the 1837 rebellion. Following the rebellion he lived in exile in the United States — when he was able to return to the city his friends gave him this house. Now restored and furnished in mid-nineteenth-century style, the house has displays telling the story of his life. Various other historic homes around the city are open to the public; ask the tourist office for the brochure *Discover the Toronto Story* for full details.

To the west of New City Hall, the **Art Gallery of Ontario** (AGO) ((416) 979-6648 WEB SITE www .ago.net, 317 Dundas Street West, houses one of the country's most important art collections. The Henry Moore Sculpture Centre, with over 300 exhibits, has the largest public collection of Moore's works in the world. The European Collection covers movements in art from the seventeenth century through to the early twentieth century, while three galleries are devoted to the comprehensive Canadian Collection. Adjoining the Art

Gallery building is a beautiful Georgian brick house known as **The Grange** ((416) 979-6648. Toronto's oldest brick residence, The Grange was once the home of the prominent Boulton family, and later became the first home of the Art Gallery; it has now been restored to the elegance of an 1830s residence (subway: St. Patrick or Dundas).

Queen's Park Area

Around Queen's Park, the **Royal Ontario Museum (ROM)** ((416) 586-8000 WEB SITE www.rom .on.ca, 100 Queen's Park, is Canada's largest public museum and one of its most wide ranging, covering art, archeology and the natural sciences. Among its most famous features are its Chinese art treasures, its Ming Tomb, the Dinosaur Gallery, a huge replica of a bat cave complete with special effects, and the popular hands-on Discovery Gallery. The **Sigmund Samuel Building** ((416) 586-5549, 14 Queen's Park Crescent West, houses a large collection of Canadiana, including room settings and folk-art. The **George R. Gardiner Museum of Ceramic Art** ((416) 586-8080 WEB SITE www.gardinermuseum.on.ca, 111 Queen's Park, includes extensive collections of Pre-Columbian pottery, Italian majolica, English Delftware and eighteenth-century European porcelain.

West of the ROM, the **Bata Shoe Museum** ((416) 979-7799 WEB SITE www.batashoemuseum .com, 327 Bloor Street West, takes a street-level look at art with its exposition of footwear dating back to 4,500 years. It's a social history of shoes, from fashion statement to religious symbol. Also on display are celebrity shoes that have touched the toes of the likes of Madonna, Elvis, Elton John and John Lennon.

Moving south of the ROM to Queen's Park, you will find the late-nineteenth-century **Ontario Provincial Parliament Building** ((416) 325-7500, a Romanesque pink sandstone building. You can attend parliamentary sittings when the house is in session.

Neighborhoods

Toronto's immigrant communities have been encouraged to maintain their cultural individuality, and the result is a rich and colorful ethnic patchwork. Around Dundas Street East is one of several **Chinese** communities; another is along Dundas Street West; a third hugs University Avenue. There's a large **Italian** community at St. Clair Avenue West and Dufferin Street — an area rumored to have more Italians than Florence — and along Gerrard Street East you'll find **Little India**. Between Pape and Woodbine Streets, bouzouki music can be heard in the **Greek** district known as "the Danforth," while between Bathurst and Spadina Streets, south of College Street, is the lively open-air Kensington Market, with its distinctly **Portuguese** accent.

Some of Toronto's other neighborhoods are characterized by lifestyle or income rather than by nationality, such as the genteel **Forest Hill** area or the wealthy **Rosedale** area. The **Beaches** area, situated along Queen Street East at Woodbine, has a touch of California about it. It's largely a professional neighborhood with a beach and lakeside parkland, a boardwalk and a core of cafés, shops and restaurants. The area bordered by Parliament Street, the Don River, Danforth Avenue and Gerrard Street is known as **Cabbagetown**. Originally built to provide housing for factory workers, it was a rundown slum area by the 1960s but then underwent extensive renovation to become a very pleasant residential and commercial district.

On and around Bloor Street, Yorkville Avenue, Hazelton Avenue and Cumberland Street, are Canada's most exclusive shops. Here you'll find such famous names as Chanel, Cartier, Hermès and Louis Vuitton. There are shopping malls including the **Holt Renfrew Centre (** (416) 922-2333, 50 Bloor Street West, and **Hazelton Lanes (** (416) 968-8600, 55 Avenue Road, and attractive old houses that now contain small art galleries, boutiques and cafés.

Avenue Road is well known for its **flower markets**, especially along the block between Davenport Road and Bernard Avenue. You will find more flowers west of Avenue Road in the Annex, a pretty, residential area.

Queen Street West is Toronto's equivalent of New York's Bleaker Street, with its trendy clubs, boutiques, galleries, bistros, restaurants and bars concentrated on the section of Queen Street West lying between University Avenue and Bathurst Street. Close to the College of Art, the street has developed a certain bohemian air and it's great fun to wander around. The City Officials touted Queen Street west of Bathurst as the **Gallery District**. This strip of the street contains nearly 20 art galleries, interior design shops, Canadian Fashion shops and many antique dealers.

Moving from the hip to the seriously chic, **Bloor-Yorkville** is the smartest part of town. The area — bounded by Charles Street, Davenport Road, Yonge Street and Avenue Road — was once a downbeat, dilapidated hippie hangout, but after renovation it is now filled with art galleries, cafés, restaurants and upscale shops.

South of Bloor Street on Markham Street there's an altogether different kind of atmosphere at **Mirvish Village**, where entrepreneur Ed Mirvish has his flagship store, the brash and breezy **Honest Ed's (** (416) 537-1574, 581 Bloor Street West. Walking around this huge bargain store with its lights and signs can be overwhelming, but there are some good buys to be found. Ed has become a well-known patron of the arts, and was responsible for the rejuvenation of this block of pleasant Victorian buildings containing restaurants, bars and shops selling antiques, books and art.

Outside Downtown

The eccentrically splendid **Casa Loma (** (416) 923-1171 WEB SITE www.casaloma.org, 1 Austin

OPPOSITE: 360 Restaurant at the top of Toronto's CN Tower is the perfect place to watch the world go by. ABOVE: Another bird's eye-view of the skyline.

Terrace, Davenport and Spadina Roads (subway: Dupont), sits atop a hill with commanding views over the city. This 98-room, baronial-style mansion was the folly of Sir Henry Pellatt, a financier, who built it between 1905 and 1911 for $3.5 million, and with its cellars, towers, secret passageways and stables, it's rather like a set for an old Hollywood movie. Its wood paneling, massive ballroom and marble-floored conservatory with stained-glass dome are examples of the unfettered extravagance which eventually reduced Sir Henry to surrender his glorious dream palace to the city in payment of back taxes. Be sure to climb up to the turrets for a view over the city.

herons, swans and ducks, and the fox and rabbit populations are increasing. It is open to the public only on weekends and is situated south of the junction of Leslie Street and Queen Street East.

About 11 km (seven miles) north of downtown in the Don River Ravine stands the splendid **Ontario Science Centre** ((416) 696-3127 WEB SITE www.osc.on.ca, 770 Don Mills Road. Another of architect Raymond Moriyama's triumphs, the museum integrates beautifully with its environment and its series of buildings are linked by enclosed escalators and ramps that allow the visitor to enjoy stunning views. Moriyama's respect for the natural beauty of the site is rumored to have extended to penalty clauses in building con-

At **High Park**, Bloor Street West you can play a game of tennis, enjoy the gardens and picnic grounds, go fishing or boating, take the children to the zoo, and on a summer's day watch Shakespeare in the open air. It is the city's largest park and at its center is **Colborne Lodge** ((416) 392-6916 (subway: High Park), a lovely Regency villa bequeathed to the city by its architect/owner John George Howard. This elegant home contains some watercolors of Toronto painted by Howard himself. He was also an engineer and his house boasts what was the first indoor flush toilet in Ontario.

For wildlife watchers and those who just enjoy a peaceful retreat, **Tommy Thompson Park** (also known as Leslie Street Spit) might be the place to go. Landfill from building sites created the spit that extends out into the lake and, unexpectedly, the wildlife literally flocked to it. It is now a sanctuary for birds such as gulls, geese,

tracts for each tree destroyed. This hugely popular museum presents science and technology in a way that demonstrates its everyday relevance and encourages viewer participation, with over 800 interactive exhibits and an Omnimax cinema. Allow plenty of time to look around, and remember that it gets very busy on weekends.

Excursions from Toronto

To see what life was like in rural Ontario during the nineteenth century, take a trip to the **Black Creek Pioneer Village** ((416) 736-1733 WEB SITE www.trca.on.ca, 1000 Murray Ross Parkway, 29 km (18 miles) northwest of downtown (May to December). This recreated village includes a blacksmith's shop, a mill and a general store, all run by costumed villagers.

Paramount Canada's Wonderland ((905) 832-8131 WEB SITE www.canadaswonderland.com, Highway 400, exit at Rutherford Road, 40 minutes from downtown, is a massive theme park, covering over 148 hectares (370 acres) (June to September).

North of Highway 401, in the Rouge Valley, 35 km (22 miles) northeast of downtown, is the **Toronto Zoo (** (416) 392-5929 WEB SITE www.toronto zoo.com, 361a Old Finch Avenue. Natural habitats have been recreated to allow the animals greater freedom. Around the zoo, an area of untouched land provides the setting for North American wildlife and can only be visited by monorail. In the winter you can follow a cross-country skiing trail to visit the zoo.

The superb **McMichael Canadian Art Collection (** (905) 893-1121 TOLL-FREE (888) 213-1121

As everywhere in Canada, the city is ringed by **golf** courses.

Bicyclists will find plenty of trails around the parks, and there's no shortage of places renting out cycles. **Fishing** enthusiasts should bear in mind that pollution in Lake Ontario means they have to be very careful about eating anything caught there, but each year the Great Salmon Hunt attracts anglers to try their luck at landing the biggest salmon.

Toronto has over 100 natural and manmade **skating rinks**, both indoor and outdoor, so you're never far from one. For information on any city rink call **(** (413) 392-1111. **Cross-country skiing** is a favorite Torontonian pastime, and there are trails

WEB SITE www.mcmichael.com, 10365 Islington Avenue, Kleinburg, about 40 km (25 miles) north of the city, houses the most important collection of works by the Canadian painters known as the Group of Seven. These artists were a revolutionary force in Canadian art, the first to produce uniquely Canadian painting inspired by the unspoiled beauty of the northern Ontario landscape. Also represented here are wonderful collections of Inuit and other native art.

SPORTS AND OUTDOOR ACTIVITIES

Toronto offers great opportunities for all kinds of outdoor activities. The **Ministry of Tourism and Recreation (** (416) 314-0944, Queen's Park, can supply details, and **Metro Region Conservation (** (416) 661-6600 has tips on swimming areas, sledding, cross-country skiing, fishing and boating.

throughout the city, some of which go out onto the lake.

For **spectator sports**, the Air Canada Centre **(** (416) 815-5500 WEB SITE www.theaircanada centre.com, 40 Bay Street, behind Union Station, is used by the Toronto Maple Leafs NHL hockey team **(** (416) 815-5700 WEB SITE www.mapleleafs .com, and the Toronto Raptors Basketball Club **(** (416) 815-5600 TICKETS (416) 872 5000 WEB SITE www.raptors.com. The Skydome **(** (416) 341-3000 WEB SITE www.skydome.com, 1 Blue Jays Way, is home to the Toronto Bluejays Baseball Club **(** (416) 341-1000 TICKETS (416) 341 1234 TOLL-FREE (888) 654-6529 WEB SITE www.bluejays.com, and the Toronto Argonauts (Canadian Football League).

OPPOSITE: The Hockey Hall of Fame catalogs the feats of the men of ice. ABOVE: The Blue Jays take to the field at Toronto's Skydome.

NIGHTLIFE AND THE ARTS

Toronto is a lively place after dark and offers a wide choice of entertainment. For details of what's on, check listings in the *Toronto Star* on Thursday, the *Globe and Mail* on Saturday, the monthly *Toronto Life* magazine, and the free weeklies *Now* and *eye* or call the **Toronto Theatre Alliance** hotline ((416) 536-6468 extension 40 WEB SITE www.theatreintoronto. Tickets for a range of plays, shows and concerts can be bought through **Ticketmaster** ((416) 872-2222, and many half-price tickets are available on the day of the show, for cash, from the **T.O. Tix booth**, inside Eaton Centre Level 2 Dundas Mall Corridor.

Toronto has a large, lively and varied **theater scene**, with over 100 theaters and 200 professional theater and dance companies, while the annual Fringe Festival in July showcases cutting-edge theater from across the world. The **Royal Alexandra**,

260 King Street West, stages Broadway, London and Canadian productions, and has been beautifully restored to its Victorian-era splendor. Another magnificently restored theater in Toronto is the **Canon Theatre**, 244 Victoria Street, which was home to *Phantom of the Opera* for over 10 years. The **Princess of Wales Theater** ((416) 872-1212, 300 King Street West, features Broadway Blockbusters. All three can be booked through ((416) 872-1212 TOLL-FREE (800) 461 3333 WEB SITE www.mirvish.com.

The **Elgin & Winter Garden Theatres** ((416) 314-2871 (tours) or (416) 872-5555 (tickets), 189 Yonge Street, present musicals and theater pieces. They also offer guided tours on Thursday at 5 PM and Saturday at 11 AM. The larger Elgin theater has been restored to the gilt and grandeur of the Edwardian era, while the upstairs Winter Garden is a smaller theater, whimsically decorated to look like an English garden. At the **St. Lawrence Centre for the Arts** ((416) 366-7723, Front and

Scott Streets, classics and Canadian plays are among the works performed by Toronto repertory companies. For innovative theater there's the **Théâtre Passe Muraille** ((416) 504-7529, 16 Ryerson Avenue. At the **Tarragon Theatre** ((416) 531-1827, 30 Bridgman Avenue, excellent Canadian works are performed. You mustn't miss seeing Toronto's legendary **Second City** ((416) 343-0011 WEB SITE www.secondcity.com, 56 Blue Jays Way. This sketch comedy troupe has an illustrious list of alumni, many of whom went on to star in *Saturday Night Live* and *SCTV*. The troupe's impressive home in the heart of the entertainment district has, in addition to the main stage, a smaller cabaret stage where other excellent comedy acts perform.

Those who like dinner theater have several options available. The most lavish is, without doubt, the extraordinary **Medieval Times** ((416) 260-1170 TOLL-FREE (888) 935-6878 WEB SITE www.medievaltimes.com, where an "authentic" dinner comes complete with a spectacular tournament and jousting.

The **Canadian Opera Company** ((413) 363-6671 WEB SITE www.coc.ca is based at the 3,200-seat **Hummingbird Centre for the Performing Arts** ((416) 872-2262 WEB SITE www.hummingbirdcentre.com, 1 Front Street East. The company also presents a series of free outdoor performances during the summer at Harbourfront. The Hummingbird Centre is also home to the highly acclaimed **National Ballet of Canada** ((416) 345-9686, with performances in November, December, February and May. The innovative **Toronto Dance Theatre** ((416) 973-4000 is the city's leading contemporary dance company.

The **Toronto Symphony** ((416) 593-7769 WEB SITE www.tso.on.ca has its home at **Roy Thomson Hall** ((416) 593-4828 (tickets) or (416) 593-4822 (tours) WEB SITE www.roythomson.com, 60 Simcoe Street, and plays here from September to May when not touring. The 2,850-seat Roy Thomson Hall is also home to the **Toronto Mendelssohn Choir** ((416) 598-0422, and it attracts top names in music of all kinds. There's also a broad range of music from rock to classical on offer at **Massey Hall** ((416) 593-4828 WEB SITE www.masseyhall.com, 178 Victoria Street, and chamber music and recitals at the St. Lawrence Centre for the Arts (see above). Concerts, from gospel to opera, take place at the **Toronto Centre for the Performing Arts** ((416) 872-2222, 5040 Yonge Street.

Looking for Jazz? Toronto is home to two international festivals in July, and the **Top O' the Senator** ((416) 364-7517, 253 Victoria Street, is one of its foremost jazz venues, with a reputation for presenting exciting new talent. You can also hear jazz at the Roy Thomson Hall and the Massey Hall (see above). The **Air Canada Centre** and **Skydome** (see above) are both used as venues for major events including pop concerts.

Many top bands have played over the years at the major rock venue, **El Mocambo** ((416) 968-3566, 464 Spadina Avenue, or at the blues and rock venue, the **Horseshoe Tavern** ((416) 598-4753, 370 Queen Street West. For 1960s R&B and blues, try the **Orbit Room** ((416) 535-0613, 580a College Street. There's World music at **Bamboo** ((416) 593-5771, 312 Queen Street West.

Clubs here, as everywhere else, change with frequency, and you need to check the listings for details. Among those that currently attract the crowds are **Tonic** ((416) 204-9200, 117 Peter Street, with a multimedia light show and 72 televisions hanging over the central dance floor/performance space; the **Court House Chamber Lounge** ((416) 214-9379, 10 Court Street, a historic building with retro fittings including vintage mirrors, and a

Morning breaks at Union Station on Toronto's Front Street.

favorite haunt of 30- to 40-somethings, with music to match; the **Eleventh Hour** ((416) 599-4687, 184 Pearl Street, where basic black, Martinis and professional chic are the order of the day, and the music ranges from house to R&B; **Easy and the Fifth** ((416) 979-3000, 225 Richmond Street, where local business-types unwind to Top 40, reggae and blues; and the spectacular **Atlantic Pavilion** ((416) 260-8000, Ontario Place West Entrance, 955 Lakeshore Boulevard West, with a club, bar and restaurant, live theater and rooftop patio. There are also several good DJ lounges including the **Fluid Lounge** ((416) 593-6116, 217 Richmond Street West, and the **Gypsy Co-op** ((416) 703-5069, 817 Queen Street West.

Of the gay clubs, the most entertaining is probably **El Convento Rico** ((416) 588-7800, 750 College Street, which features Latin drag on Friday and Saturday nights.

WHERE TO STAY

Accommodation in Toronto can become quite scarce at the peak of the summer season, so reservations are recommended. **Tourism Toronto/ Accommodations Toronto** ((416) 203-2500 TOLL-FREE (800) 363-1990 FAX (416) 203-6753 WEB SITE www.torontotourism.com, Queen's Quay Terminal, 207 Queen Street West, can help you find the right accommodation and provides a free booking service; most rates offered here are better than hotel rack rates. Discounts are usually offered over weekends and for senior citizens.

Expensive

As befits one of Canadian-Pacific's gloriously extravagant hotels, the **Fairmont Royal York** ((416) 368-2511 TOLL-FREE (800) 441-1414 FAX (416) 368-2884 WEB SITE www.fairmont.com, 100 Front Street West, stands opposite Union Station. One of Toronto's best-known — and best — hotels, it was the tallest structure in the British Empire when built in 1929. It has magnificent public areas, 1,356 rooms (which tend to be on the small side) and excellent facilities including a pool, a fitness center, a spa, a business center, shops and several places to eat — among them the superb *Epic* restaurant and the *Library Bar*, whose martinis regularly win awards. There is a rooftop herb and vegetable garden.

For modern luxury in the heart of the city, **Toronto Marriott Eaton Centre** ((416) 597-9200 TOLL-FREE (800) 905-0667 FAX (416) 597-9211 WEB SITE www.marriotteatoncentre.com, 525 Bay Street, can't be beat. Rooms and suites have views over the busy commercial and cultural area of Eaton Centre and are very comfortable. The suites have larger bedrooms than most other Toronto hotels. The indoor rooftop swimming pool offers a fabulous view of the city.

Close to the downtown theater district, **Le Royal Meridien King Edward** ((416) 863-3131 TOLL-FREE (800) 543-4300 FAX (416) 367-5515 WEB SITE www.lemeriden-kingedward.com, 37 King Street East, is a truly grand hotel. The rooms are beautiful, spacious and well equipped.

Dominating the Harbourfront skyline are two more top-of-the-line hotels: **Radisson Plaza Admiral Harbourfront** ((416) 203-3333 FAX (416) 203-3100 WEB SITE www.radisson.com, 249 Queen's Quay West, is conveniently located close to Harbourfront entertainment and cultural activities. The 157 rooms have harbor views, and there's also a lounge with lovely views over the marina. The **Westin Harbour Castle** ((416) 872-1212 TOLL-FREE (800) 461-3333 FAX (416) 361-7448 WEB SITE www.westin.com, 1 Harbour Square, has 980 comfortable and well-equipped rooms with views of either the lake or the skyline. It has some good restaurants including the Lighthouse, one of Toronto's two revolving restaurants, and a free shuttle service will take you downtown.

Next to the CN Tower, the **Crown Plaza Toronto Centre** ((416) 597-1400 TOLL-FREE (800) 422-7969 FAX (416) 597-8128 WEB SITE www.crowneplaza toronto.com, 225 Front Street West, is ideally suited for business people. All 587 rooms and suites are spacious and have computer ports and work desks.

Moving midtown near Queen's Park, **Sutton Place Hotel** ((416) 924-9221 TOLL-FREE (800) 268-3790 FAX (416) 924-1778 WEB SITE www.suttonplace .com, 955 Bay Street, maintains extremely high standards. Its rooms are furnished in elegant French style and have the usual array of facilities. The nineteenth to thirty-second floors are given over to the luxuriously appointed apartments of **La Grande Résidence** ((416) 324-6432 TOLL-FREE (800) 268-3790.

In Yorkville, the **Four Seasons Hotel Toronto** ((416) 964-0411 TOLL-FREE (800) 819-5053 FAX (416) 964-2301 WEB SITE www.fourseasons.com, 21 Avenue Road, manages to surpass the expected high standards of this superb chain. The hotel has 210 attractive and very comfortable rooms, many of which offer excellent views of the city, and there is a swimming pool and restaurants.

The **Old Mill Inn** ((416) 236-2641 TOLL-FREE (866) 653-6455 FAX (416) 236-2749 WEB SITE www .oldmilltoronto.com, 21 Old Mill Road, only 15 minutes from Toronto Airport, bills itself as a country hideaway. It is hardly that, but this small neo-Tudor hotel, set in delightful gardens, has 60 elegant rooms and suites, a full spa, and even such treats as a full Victorian afternoon tea and a lavish Sunday brunch, all served with fine views along the Humber Valley.

Only five minutes from the airport, the **Courtyard by Marriott Toronto Airport** ((416) 675-0411 TOLL-FREE (800) 321-2211 FAX (416) 675-0433 WEB SITE www.courtyard.com, 231 Carlingview Drive, is designed mainly for business travelers, with 168 comfortable and well-appointed rooms, all with large work stations, that include a modem connection with hotel fax, and printing services.

Mid-range

Conveniently located in downtown, **Delta Chelsea Inn** ((416) 595-1975 TOLL-FREE (800) 268-9070 FAX (416) 585-4375 WEB SITE www.deltachelsea .com, 33 Gerrard Street West, is a very busy hotel with 1,600 modern rooms, some with kitchen facilities. It has three restaurants, three lounges, an adults-only health club, a supervised children's program, and a family pool area.

Fitness and sports fanatics will love the **Inn on the Park** ((416) 444-2561 TOLL-FREE (877) 644-4687 FAX (416) 446-3308 WEB SITE www.innonthepark toronto.com, 1100 Eglinton Avenue East, northeast of downtown near the Ontario Science Centre. It is beautifully positioned above a ravine and is set in 200 hectares (500 acres) of land. The rooms are not terribly special, but it has swimming pools, tennis courts, squash and racquetball courts, aerobics classes and horseback riding. There are supervised activities for children throughout the day.

About 16 km (10 miles) outside the city, the **Guild Inn** ((416) 261-3331 FAX (416) 261-5675, 201 Guildwood Parkway, Scarborough, offers a beautiful and unusual setting. In 1932 this manorial building

If you're planning a cultural binge, **Hotel Victoria Downtown** ((416) 363-1666 TOLL-FREE (800) 363-8228 FAX (416) 363-7327 WEB SITE www .toronto.com/hotelvictoria, 56 Yonge Street, might be of particular interest as it's very close to both the O'Keefe and St. Lawrence Centres. There are 48 small, modern rooms, a dining room, a bar and an elegant reception area.

The **Strathcona Hotel** ((416) 363-3321 TOLL-FREE (800) 268-8304 FAX (416) 363-4679 WEB SITE www.thestrathconahotel.com, 60 York Street, is an older hotel, opposite the Royal York and offering excellent value. There are 200 rooms with private bath and television, a bar and a café. The central, recently renovated **Comfort Hotel Downtown** ((416) 924-1222 TOLL-FREE (800) 221-2222 FAX (416) 927-1369 WEB SITE www.nhgi.com/comfort, 15 Charles Street East, is a delightful place with friendly service and 108 spacious rooms.

housed the art-and-craft workshops of the Guild of All Arts; its popularity brought about the need for guestrooms and attracted many famous visitors. Spread over the 37-hectare (95-acre) grounds are important architectural fragments salvaged from old Toronto buildings that were pulled down to make way for new developments. The hotel has a good dining room, a verandah where you can take cocktails, an outdoor swimming pool and a tennis court.

Inexpensive

Bond Place ((416) 362-6061 TOLL-FREE (800) 268-9390 FAX (416) 360-6406 E-MAIL bondplaceresvn @on.aibn.com, 65 Dundas Street East, is convenient

Vestige of another era: When it was built in 1929, the Royal York Hotel was the tallest structure in the British Empire.

to the Eaton Centre and has a restaurant/café, bar and lounge and 285 smallish but well-appointed rooms with air conditioning and television.

Hostelling International–Toronto ((416) 971-4440 TOLL-FREE (800) 668-4487 FAX (416) 971-4088, 76 Church Street, is centrally located and open year-round. There are 88 beds, a kitchen, laundry facilities and family rooms, and city tours are offered.

Several local universities offer cheap downtown accommodation from mid-May to August, including **Neill-Wycik College Hotel (** (416) 977-2320 TOLL-FREE (800) 268-4358 FAX (416) 977-2809 E-MAIL hotel@neill-wycik.com, 96 Gerrard Street East; **Ryerson University (** (416) 979-5296 FAX (416) 979-5212 WEB SITE www.ryerson.ca/conference; and **Victoria University (** (416) 585-4524 FAX (416) 585-4530 E-MAIL accom.victoria@utoronto.ca, 140 Charles Street West.

For lists of bed-and-breakfast accommodation contact **Bed and Breakfast Homes of Toronto (** (416) 363-6362 WEB SITE www.bbcanada.com, College Park, 777 Bay Street; the **Bed and Breakfast Association of Downtown Toronto (** (416) 410-3938 FAX (416) 368-1653 WEB SITE www.bnb info.com; or **Across Toronto Bed and Breakfast (** (705) 738-9449 TOLL-FREE (877) 922-6522 FAX (705) 738 0155 WEB SITE www.torontobandb.com. You can also write the **Federation of Ontario Bed and Breakfast Accommodation** (FOBBA) WEB SITE www.fobba.com, PO Box 437, 253 College Street, Toronto M5T 1R5, for a copy of its booklet *Ontario Bed and Breakfast*, or pick one up at any provincial travel information center.

WHERE TO EAT

Dining in Toronto is a delightful experience, not only because it has over 6,000 restaurants, but because of the many ethnic groups that make up the population. In the various ethnic neighborhoods you'll invariably find good, moderately priced restaurants. King, Bloor and Queen Streets are particularly good hunting grounds; Kensington Market is great for Chinese food; the area around Church Street and Wellesley Avenue has some excellent eateries.

Expensive

Topping the list are a triumvirate of grand hotel restaurants — **Truffles** at the Four Seasons Hotel, **Epic** at the Fairmont Royal York, and **Commodore's** at the Radisson Plaza Admiral Harbourfront (see WHERE TO STAY, above).

Then there are several restaurants with superb city views, starting with **360 Restaurant (** (416) 601-4729, on the observation platform of the CN Tower, 301 Front Street West, which offers mouthwatering regional cuisine and an award-winning wine list. The **Canoe Restaurant Bar & Grill (** (416) 364-0054, 66 Wellington Street West, has

a Canadian-themed menu along with top-notch desserts and a top-floor view of the city. Continental food is served in candlelit elegance at **Scaramouche (** (416) 961-8011, 1 Benvenuto Place. The food is of the highest quality both in the main restaurant and the less formal Pasta Bar.

At the award-winning **Auberge du Pommier (** (416) 222-2220, 4150 Yonge Street, classic French-Mediterranean cuisine is simply and beautifully presented in a romantic 1860s mill workers' cottage, with a garden terrace in summer. The smooth service and simple elegance of **Avalon (** (416) 979-9918, 270 Adelaide Street West, make it a Toronto favorite. Try the wood-grilled sardines, *foie gras* with caramelized quince and brioche, or the grilled yellowfin with potato gnocchi and roasted-tomato sauce.

Eclectic North American cooking is to be had at **North 44 (** (416) 487-4897, 2537 Yonge Street, in attractive surroundings of burnished metal, etched glass and mosaic tiling. An exceptional wine list rounds out the inventive menu. The chic **Centro Grill and Wine Bar (** (416) 483-2211, 2472 Yonge Street, offers fine Italian dining with a Californian flare in light and airy surroundings, bright with mirrors and strong colors. Open for dinner Monday to Saturday

At **Susur Restaurant (** (416) 603-2205, 601 King Street West, you need to concentrate on the wonderful seven-course set meal of classic European and Asian cuisine. Sleek and sophisticated **Oro (** (416) 597-0155, 45 Elm Street, is one of the city's newer restaurants, with superb contemporary Mediterranean-fusion food made with the freshest Canadian ingredients avaialable.

Moderate

Bistro 990 ((416) 921-9990, 990 Bay Street, is the place to go star-spotting. The food is good, uncomplicated bistro style and comes with a fine selection of wines. The place has the look of a grand wine cellar with arches and unusual pictures lining the walls. Leave room for the delicious desserts.

Joe Badali's ((416) 977-3064, 156 Front Street West, is a large, warm and cheerfully noisy Italian restaurant with an excellent array of soups, salads and wraps along with more substantial meals. Also handily placed for theaters and shops, the award-winning **Zoom Caffe and Bar (** (416) 861-9872, 18 King Street East, features a regional American menu of architecturally designed food with bold flavors (reservations recommended).

Mistura Restaurant ((416) 515-0009, 265 Davenport Road, manages to combine an elegant candlelit atmosphere, contemporary Italian cuisine and an attentive, knowledgeable staff. **Sotto Sotto Trattoria (** (416) 962-0011, 116 Avenue Road, Lower Level, serves Italian regional cuisine and an excellent international selection of wines.

Rain ((416) 599-7246, 19 Mercer Street, is a restaurant/lounge that goes out of its way to help you make friends, with a large communal table. The food is Asian. **Amber** ((416) 926-9037, 119 Yorkville, is in a windowless basement, but with a calm Japanese ambiance and muted colors along with a menu that combines Japanese and eastern Mediterranean cuisines.

Arlequin ((416) 928-9521, 134 Avenue Road, serves French bistro food from *croques monsieurs* (like a grilled cheese sandwich) to *steak-frites* (steak and french fries) as well as North African dishes such as chicken *tagine*.

For Asian food, the **Bangkok Garden** ((416) 977-6748, 18 Elm Street, is a very good and popular Thai restaurant, where the waiters are extremely helpful and the setting is somewhat exotic. **Katsura** (Westin Prince Hotel) ((416) 444-2511, 900 York Mills Road, is an excellent Japanese restaurant that serves traditional Japanese food, teppanyaki and sushi, while **Edo** ((416) 322-7679, 484 Eglinton Avenue West, serves both sushi and other traditional Japanese fare such as tempura and teriyaki. There's a wide variety of northern Indian dishes at **Cuisine of India** ((416) 229-0377, 5222 Yonge Street, including tandooris and excellent homemade breads.

The **Fish House** ((416) 595-5051, on 144 Front Street West, with its seafaring decor, has excellent specials created from the daily catch, as well as an oyster bar.

Inexpensive
Patriot Restaurant (416) 922-0025, 131 Bloor Street West, Second Floor, is a popular Canadian bistro; the trendier **Jump Cafe & Bar** ((416) 363-3400, Commerce Court, is a lively North American café that comes up with some innovative dishes and stylish presentation.

Tiger Lily's ((416) 977-5499, 257 Queen Street West, is a noodle shop with dim sum-fusion brunch on Saturday and Sunday. This tiny and unpretentious storefront café is on the edge of the theater district.

For traditional deli fare try "Canada's Cornbeef King," **Shopsy's** ((416) 365-5333, 33 Yonge Street. Opened by the Shopsowitz family in 1922 as an ice cream shop, this Toronto institution has a voluminous menu including all the classics, plus sandwiches such as the Royal Canadian Mounted Beef: with sautéed peppers, Bermuda onions, and mushrooms with melted mozzarella and cheddar cheese. Breakfast is served all day.

Sai Woo ((416) 977-4988, 130 Dundas Street West, is one of the city's oldest and best-known Chinese restaurants, serving good Cantonese food in busy, basic surroundings. Dim sum is served at lunchtime on weekdays, and twice a year they hold banquets where as many as 15 courses may be served.

The handsome **Indian Rice Factory** ((416) 961-3472, 414 Dupont Street, offers a small but excellent menu which includes a selection of vegetarian dishes. There's Moroccan cuisine served in exotic surroundings at the **Sultan's Tent** ((416) 961-0601, 1280 Bay Street, Yorkville, with live music and belly dancing.

HOW TO GET THERE

Toronto's **Lester B. Pearson International Airport** WEB SITE www.gtaa.com, 27 km (17 miles) from downtown, handles both foreign and domestic flights. The drive takes about 20 to 45 minutes (longer in rush hour); taxis cost around $40. The **Airport Express** ((905) 564-6333 TOLL-FREE (800) 387-6787 WEB SITE www.torontoairportexpress .com operates buses to three subway stops each hour from 8 AM to 11:30 PM. The service to and from selected downtown hotels operates every 20 minutes.

VIA Rail ((416) 366-8411 TOLL-FREE (888) 842-7245 WEB SITE www.viarail.ca operates inter-city trains from Toronto Union Station (which is also the hub of the GO Train network). VIA Rail and **Amtrak** TOLL-FREE (800) 872-7245 WEB SITE www .amtrak.com jointly operate trains from Union Station to New York and Chicago.

The **Greyhound** terminal ((416) 367-8747 TOLL-FREE (800) 667-0882 WEB SITE www.greyhound .ca is at 610 Bay Street, north of Dundas Street, near Eaton Centre. Several other companies offer a variety of bus routes, arriving and departing from the Bay Street terminal.

If you are driving from Detroit/Windsor in the west or Montréal in the east you will want Route 401. From Niagara Falls, take Queen Elizabeth Way, which turns into the Gardiner Expressway as it enters Toronto.

THE GOLDEN HORSESHOE

"The Golden Horseshoe," the sliver of land that arcs around from Oshawa, east of Toronto, to Niagara Falls, is so called because, in addition to being horseshoe-shaped, it is one of the wealthiest regions in the country. A large proportion of Canada's manufacturing industry is concentrated here, especially in and around the steel-making city of Hamilton.

If Hamilton is Canada's Pittsburgh, the Niagara peninsula is its Napa Valley: nearly 80 percent of Canada's wine grapes are grown here. There is also history among the vines, for it was here that Laura Secord snuck away from the American-held village of Queenston and set out on her 30-km (19-mile) hike through the bush to warn the British of American plans for a surprise attack. Her home still stands in Queenston, as does a monument to General Isaac Brock, who died leading the first counterattack against the Americans in the War of 1812.

But however much blood and wine may have flowed here, it's still the water that brings the tourists: Niagara Falls and Niagara-on-the-Lake, two of the most beautiful spots on earth.

HAMILTON

Hamilton, population 650,000, sits at the western corner of Lake Ontario, on a landlocked harbor spanned at the lakeside by a sandbar, cut through to allow ships into the port. Across this sandbar sweeps Burlington Skyway, a section of the Queen Elizabeth Way that links Toronto with Niagara Falls.

Hamilton is Canada's steel-producing capital and its heavy industry has brought more than its fair share of pollution. It's not all a landscape of satanic mills, however, and the Hamilton Place Arts Center and a number of small museums have helped put Hamilton on the cultural map. For information, contact **Hamilton Tourism** ((905) 546-4222 TOLL-FREE (800) 263-8590 FAX (905) 546-4107 WEB SITE www.city.hamilton.on.ca, 1 James Street, Eighth Floor.

Like Toronto's Yorkville, **Hess Village** at Hess and George Streets is a very pleasant area of renovated clapboard buildings that now house shops, restaurants and cafés. Nearby, local produce is displayed in the huge, bustling indoor **Farmer's Market** ((905) 546-2096, 55 York Boulevard. A striking modern building houses the **Art Gallery of Hamilton** ((905) 527-6610 WEB SITE www.art galleryofhamilton.on.ca, 123 King Street West, which has an important and impressive collection of historic and contemporary Canadian and American art. The university art collection, at the **McMaster Museum of Art** ((905) 525-9140, at 1280 Main Street West, is also worth a visit, with some 6,000 works including European Old Masters, Canadian works and a collection of Inuit art. Hamilton is also home to the **Canadian Football Hall of Fame and Museum** ((905) 528-7566 WEB SITE www.footballhof.com, 58 Jackson Street West, which documents the history of the game back to 1860, with the aid of some 30,000 artifacts and old film footage.

Outside of town, **Dundurn Castle** ((905) 546-2872, York Boulevard, Dundurn Park, stands on a hill overlooking the bay. It is an impressive 35-room white stone mansion with a dignified columned portico, built in the 1830s by Sir Allan Napier MacNab, Prime Minister of the United Provinces of Canada from 1854 to 1856. It has been furnished in the style of the 1850s and restored to its former splendor. In the grounds is the **Hamilton Military Museum** ((905) 546-2872, dedicated to Canada's role in wars from 1812 to World War II.

The **Canadian Warplane Heritage Museum** ((905) 679-4183 TOLL-FREE (877) 347-3359 WEB SITE www.warplane.com, Hamilton International Airport, 9280 Airport Road, Mount Hope, is not the largest collection, but is certainly one of the most spectacular, with over 25 beautifully restored planes. You can clamber into the cockpits, use simulators, watch the planes fly and even take a ride in a bi-plane.

The **Royal Botanical Gardens** ((905) 527-1158 WEB SITE www.rbg.ca, at 680 Plains Road West, between Routes 2 and 6, cover 1,100 hectares (2,718 acres) of land along the lakeside. The greater part of this area is given over to natural parkland threaded with 32 km (20 miles) of trails, but among the most stunning sights are the Rock Garden, the Rose Garden and the gorgeous Lilac Garden in the Arboretum.

Stoney Creek has a number of fine historic houses, of which two are open to the public: the late-eighteenth-century **Battlefield House** ((905) 662-8458, 77 King Street West, in the grounds of Battlefield Park, site of the battle against the Americans in 1813; and the Victorian **Erland Lee House** ((905) 662-2691, 252 Ridge Road, home of Erland and Janet Lee, founders of the Women's Institute.

About 32 km (20 miles) northwest of Hamilton off Highway 8 is the **African Lion Safari** ((519) 623-2620 TOLL-FREE (800) 461-9453 WEB SITE www .lionsafari.com. You can take a safari tram through the various reserves where the animals roam free. Alternatively, you can drive your own car through the park. Convertibles are not allowed, for obvious reasons.

North of Hamilton, the **Great Canadian Balloon Adventure** ((905) 689-5764 offers hot-air-balloon flights over Flamorough and the Dundas Valley. **Wild Waterworks** ((905) 561-2292 TOLL-FREE (800) 555-8775 WEB SITE www.hamrca.on.ca, 585 Van Wagners Beach Road, Hamilton, is an excellent water park, with a range of rides and Canada's largest wave pool.

Where to Stay and Eat

The **Sheraton Hamilton** ((905) 529-5515 FAX (905) 529-2609 WEB SITE www.sheraton.com, centrally located downtown at 116 King Street West, has 300 modern rooms, nicely furnished and well-equipped (mid-range), an indoor pool with an attractive poolside area, a fitness center and two restaurants. There's a sense of grandeur about the **Royal Connaught Howard Johnson Plaza Hotel** ((905) 546-8121 TOLL-FREE (800) 446-4656 FAX (905) 546-8118 WEB SITE www.hojo.com, 112 King Street East, which first opened its doors in 1904 (mid-range). The entrance hall is lavishly decorated with chandeliers and columns, and the rooms all have luxuriously large bathrooms. There are two restaurants and an indoor swimming pool.

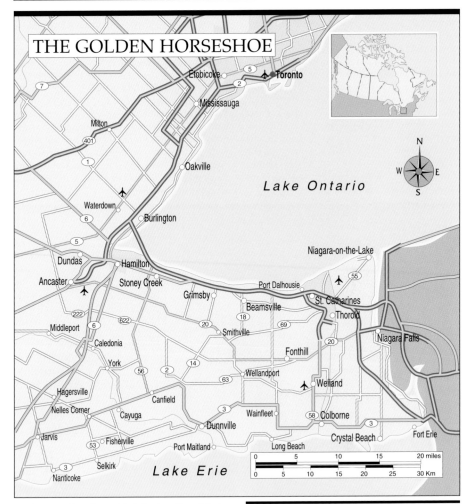

A comprehensive guide to bed and breakfasts, including those in Hamilton, is published by the **Federation of Ontario Bed and Breakfast Accommodation** ((416) 964-2566 WEB SITE www.fobba.com, PO Box 437, 253 College Street, Toronto M5T 1R5.

The **Sirloin Cellar** ((905) 525-8620, 14 1/2 James Street North, has been serving excellent steak and seafood since 1969, also offers pastas and Asian cuisine. **Wild Orchid** ((905) 528-7171, 286 James Street North, is a light, attractive Portuguese restaurant, with live jazz on Monday nights.

How to Get There

John C. Munro Hamilton International Airport ((905) 679-8359 WEB SITE www.yhm.com, Mount Hope, has services from various Canadian cities with Westjet, and from Pittsburgh, Pennsylvania with US Air. The **GO Centre** TOLL-FREE (888) 438-6646 WEB SITE www.gotransit.com, 36 Hunter Street East, Hamilton has VIA Rail and bus connections to Toronto, Niagara and other local destinations.

ST. CATHARINES

Founded in the late eighteenth century by Loyalists escaping the American War of Independence, in the 1820s St. Catharine's became an important stop on the Underground Railroad for escaping slaves. Ask for the booklet on *Niagara's Freedom Trail* to follow the route from the border at Fort Erie to the British Methodist Episcopal Church and Salem Chapel that were key staging posts. **Visitor Information** is available from City Hall ((905) 688-5601 WEB SITE www.st.catharines .com, 50 Church Street.

A decade later, the town's fortunes were transformed by the 42-km (26-mile) **Welland Canal**, completed in 1833, which connects Lake Ontario to the much higher Lake Erie through a series of eight locks. From nearby Port Weller it cuts through to Port Colborne on Lake Erie, allowing oceangoing ships to navigate the Great Lakes. The original canal was built in St. Catharines and at

Port Dalhousie you can see sections of the first three canals built in 1829, 1845 and 1887, where some of the locks, warehouses and other nineteenth-century structures still stand. At the **St. Catharine's Museum** ((905) 984-8880 TOLL-FREE (800) 305-5134, Lock 3, 1932 Government Road, you can watch the oceangoing giants pass through the locks and learn about the Underground Railway — and visit the Ontario Lacross Hall of Fame. Today, the town is in the heart of Ontario's fruit-growing region, and nowhere is this more evident than in the bustling outdoor **Farmer's Market** ((905) 688-5601, King and James Streets, near City Hall, where you see the abundance of the local produce.

FREE (877) 688-2324 FAX (905) 684-6432 WEB SITE www.ramadastcath.com, 327 Ontario Street. Conveniently situated in downtown, it has 125 comfortable rooms and an indoor pool, a video lounge and a bowling alley. Prices are within the mid-range category. The **Holiday Inn** ((905) 934-8000 TOLL-FREE (877) 688-2324 FAX (905) 934-9117 WEB SITE www.holidayinnstcath.com, 2 North Service Road, has 140 rooms with television and private bath, and indoor and outdoor swimming pools. Both hotels are mid-range. Lists of bed and breakfasts are available through **Bed and Breakfast Accommodations — St. Catharines and Niagara Region** ((905) 935-8248 or (905) 348-4063 E-MAIL efegan@miagara.com.

Take time to walk around the downtown area ((905) 685-8424 WEB SITE www.stcathdowntown.com, around St. Paul Street, which has many charming historic buildings, green spaces and boutiques. Self-guided walking tour brochures are available. Stop off en route for a taste and tour at the **Tate & Bate Brewery** ((905) 682-0268, 75 St. Paul Street, which was founded in 1834. Also worth visiting nearby are the historic towns of **Jordan** and **Port Dalhousie**.

This is a popular resting place for visitors to the area's many festivals and as a base from which to explore the vineyards of the Niagara Peninsula. The local tourist offices provide a detailed booklet of the local wineries that offer tastings and tours.

Where to Stay and Eat
St. Catharine's has several chain hotels including the **Ramada Parkway Inn** ((905) 688-2324 TOLL-

There are plenty of options for eating, with some 65 restaurants of varying sorts in the downtown area. **Freighters** ((905) 704-1705, Wellands Canal Centre, Lock 3, Government Road, offers a casual menu of steak, fish, chicken and salad, with a superb view of the traffic on the canal. More grown-up is the **Double Olive Martini Bar and Restaurant** ((905) 704-4549, 81 James Street at Market Square, which has live entertainment four nights a week, a patio, wine-tasting and good food.

NIAGARA-ON-THE-LAKE

At the meeting point of the Niagara River and Lake Ontario, delightful Niagara-on-the-Lake is one of North America's best-preserved nineteenth-century towns. Settled by Loyalists in the late eighteenth century, Niagara-on-the-Lake, then known as Newark, became the first capital of

Upper Canada in 1792. In 1813 it was completely destroyed by the Americans, but it was quickly rebuilt and seems to have changed very little since. Its attractive situation and pretty tree-shaded streets lined with clapboard and brick houses make it a delightful stopping point during a trip to Niagara Falls.

For information contact the **Niagara-on-the-Lake Chamber of Commerce** ((905) 468-1950 FAX (905) 468 4930 WEB SITE www.niagaraonthe lake.com, 26 Queen Street, PO Box 1043, Niagara-on-the-Lake L0S 1J0.

What to See and Do

Queen Street is the town's focal point, and the only part of it that gets busy. Its lovely old buildings house bakeries, teashops, restaurants and shops selling all manner of goods such as crafts, jams and confectionery. The splendid old **Niagara Apothecary Museum** ((416) 962-8641 dates from 1866 and maintains its original walnut counters, beautifully labeled drawers and old jars. It no longer dispenses medications, and looking at such remedies as "Dragon's Blood" or "Pink Pills for Pale People," you can't help but feel that it's probably just as well.

The town's main attraction is the annual **Shaw Festival** ((905) 468-2172 TOLL-FREE (800) 511-7429 FAX (905) 468-3804 WEB SITE www.shawfest.sympatico .ca, which draws theater-goers April to November, presenting top-name actors in a season of plays by George Bernard Shaw and his contemporaries. There are three theaters in the town, the main one being the **Festival Theatre**, a modern brick and glass structure with an attractive interior, at Queen's Parade and Wellington Street.

South of Niagara Parkway on River Road is **Fort George Historic Site** ((905) 468-4257 WEB SITE www.parkscanada.gc.ca (April to November). Built between 1797 and 1799, the fort was a major British post in the War of 1812. It was destroyed by the Americans in 1813, rebuilt in 1815 and later abandoned. It was restored in the 1930s. You can visit the officers' quarters, the soldiers' barracks, the forge and the powder magazine, and watch a display by the Fort George Fife and Drum Corps. The **Niagara Historical Society Museum** ((905) 468-3912, 43 Castlereagh Street, Davy, is one of the oldest and largest museums of its kind in Canada, presenting the social and military history of the region.

Near Niagara-on-the-Lake are several wineries that offer tasting tours, among them some of Canada's best-known labels such as **Peller Estates Winery** ((905) 468-4678 WEB SITE www.peller .com, 290 John Street; **Château des Charmes** ((905) 262-4219 WEB SITE www.chateaudescharmes .com, 1025 York Road; **Inniskillin Winery** ((905) 468-3554 WEB SITE www.inniskillin.com, Niagara Parkway and Line 3; and **Hillebrand Estates**

Winery ((905) 468-7123 WEB SITE www.hillebrand .com, 1249 Niagara Stone Road, an attractive vineyard that would not look out of place in the French countryside. The tourist office can provide a self-drive tour brochure; **Niagara Winery Tours** ((905) 374-8111 WEB SITE www.niagaraair bus.com offers vineyard tours — if you don't have to drive you are free to taste.

Steven Bauer Bike Tours ((905) 262-9898 WEB SITE www.stevebauer.com offers bike rental and guided bicycle tours of the Niagara Peninsula. The **Niagara Steamship Company** ((905) 468-8343 TOLL-FREE (888) 250-4572 WEB SITE www .niagarasteamship.com operates cruises on the Niagara River on the SS Pumper, a steamboat built

in 1903 (mid-May to mid-October). It departs from the Navy Hall Dock, just behind Old Fort George. **Whirlpool Jetboat Tours** ((905) 468-4800 TOLL-FREE (888) 433 4444 FAX (905) 468-7004 WEB SITE www.whirlpooljet.com, George III, 61 Melville Street, runs wild, high-speed whitewater rapid tours either in enclosed "jetdomes" or open boats.

Where to Stay

Niagara-on-the-Lake is a small town and most of its hotels are small and fill up in the summer, so try to book well in advance.

In the mid-range to expensive category, the **Prince of Wales** ((905) 468-3246 TOLL-FREE (888) 669 5566 FAX (905) 468-5521 WEB SITE www.vintage inns.com, 6 Picton Street, is a beautiful old inn with 108 rooms — including a royal suite which was once actually graced by royalty — all decorated with antique furniture and with large bathrooms. It combines Old World charm with a full range of facilities. The award-winning **Pillar & Post Inn** ((905) 468-2123 TOLL-FREE (888) 669-5566 FAX (905) 468-3551 WEB SITE www.vintageinns .com, 48 John Street, is another lovely hotel, with 123 spacious rooms furnished in early colonial

Niagara-on-the-Lake — OPPOSITE: A sailboat plies Lake Ontario. ABOVE: The Inniskillen Winery.

style, combining old-fashioned elegance with modern amenities. Another of the town's best hotels, belonging to the same group, the **Oban Inn** ((905) 468-2165 TOLL-FREE (888) 669-5566 FAX (905) 468-4165 WEB SITE www.vintageinns.com, 160 Front Street, is a delightful early eighteenth-century-style building overlooking the lake. It has beautiful gardens, 26 comfortable rooms with antique furniture, a piano bar, a good restaurant, and its very own ghost — so they say. In contrast, the **Gate House Hotel** ((905) 468-3263 FAX (905) 468-7400, 142 Queen Street, has 10 rooms decorated in chic, modern Milanese style. The **White Oaks Conference Resort and Spa** ((905) 688-2550 TOLL-FREE (800) 263-5766 FAX (905) 688-2220 WEB SITE www.whiteoaksresort.com, just outside the town at 253 Taylor Road, Rural Route 4, is a long way from all the "olde worlde" charm, but is equally beautiful, in a sophisticated, modern minimalist style. The real attraction lies in amenities such as its tennis courts (four outdoor and eight indoor), squash and racquetball courts, child-care facilities, a café and a restaurant.

The town also has many excellent bed and breakfasts, many in historic houses. The Chamber of Commerce (see above) operates an accommodation booking service. Alternatively, contact the **Niagara-on-the-Lake Bed and Breakfast Association** ((905) 468-0123 WEB SITE www.canvisit.com, PO Box 1228, Niagara-on-the-Lake L0S 1J0, or the **Federation of Ontario Bed and Breakfast Accommodation** ((416) 964-2566 WEB SITE www.fobba.com, PO Box 437, 253 College Street, Toronto M5T 1R5.

Where to Eat

There are quite a few good restaurants in the town, which is generally a much better place for dining than Niagara Falls. The **Oban Inn** ((905) 468-2165, 160 Front Street, has a reputation for moderately priced fine dining in tasteful surroundings. Traditional English dishes feature on the menu, and lunch and dinner are served in the cozy pub or the formal dining room. There's fine European cuisine in an elegant setting at the **Prince of Wales Hotel** ((905) 468-3246, 6 Picton Street. Escabèche, the elegant main dining room, is open daily for lunch and dinner (expensive). The Drawing Room is a wonderful setting for a full afternoon tea.

For a more raucous dining experience, **The Buttery** ((905) 468-2564, 19 Queen Street, offers casual dining through the week, but holds weekend Henry VIII banquets: costumed wenches serve old English food and minstrels supply entertainment (moderate).

The Olde Angel Inn ((905) 468-3411, 224 Regent Street, The Old Market Square, serves English pub food and 26 varieties of beer. The dining room serves continental food (inexpensive to moderate). Classic Italian food is served in chic, modern surroundings at **Restaurant Giardino**

((905) 468-3263, the Gate House Hotel, 142 Queen Street (inexpensive to moderate). If all you want is a light snack, try the **Country Cravings Deli** ((905) 262-1515, corner of York and Creek Roads, St. David's (inexpensive).

NIAGARA FALLS

Midway between Lake Erie and Lake Ontario, the Niagara River hurtles over a 57-m (188-ft) cliff at a rate of 130 million liters or 34 million gallons each minute, thus creating one of the greatest wonders of the world. Divided by a small island, the Canadian Horseshoe Falls are 670 m (2,200 ft) wide and the American Falls much less wide at 260 m (850 ft). The American Falls are also shorter, at 21 to 34 m (70 to 110 ft) high. At times over 75 percent of the rushing water is diverted by canals to power stations on both the American and Canadian sides, resulting in a variation of the water volume depending on time of day and year. It is said that the erosion caused by the plunging water will eventually flatten the falls, but it is estimated that this will take about 25,000 years to happen.

Since the seventeenth century, people have traveled huge distances to see the falls, and today an average of 15 million people on the Canadian side and a further five million on the American side come every year to wonder at the spectacle. No one quite knows why it has become a tradition for honeymooning couples to come here, but one legend has it that the idea caught on after Napoleon's brother brought his new bride here in 1804, riding all the way from New Orleans in a coach. Anyway, the falls themselves are everything they are cracked up to be — and more. One can only echo Rupert Brooke's feelings on seeing the falls: "I was so impressed by Niagara. I had hoped not to be, but I horribly was." So is everyone, it seems.

General Information

For information on the falls and the surrounding region, contact **Niagara Falls Tourism** ((905) 356-6061 WEB SITE www.discoverniagara.com, 5515 Stanley Avenue, or the **Niagara Parks Commission** ((905) 371 0254 TOLL-FREE (877) 642-7275 WEB SITE www.niagaraparks.com, 7400 Porage Road South, who offer a $13 Passport to all park properties. There are drop-in information centers in summer at Table Rock, Maid of the Mist Plaza, and the Rapids View Parking Lot.

Take to the skies with **Niagara Helicopters** ((905) 357-5672 TOLL-FREE (800) 281-8034 WEB SITE www.niagarahelicopters.com or **Skyway Helicopters** ((905) 641-2222 TOLL-FREE (800) 491-3117 WEB SITE www.skywayhelicopters.com. **Niagara Air Tours** ((905) 688-9000 operates 25-minute fixed-wing flights over the falls and area.

What to See and Do

There are dozens of ways to enjoy the falls, but however you look at them, they are hopelessly spectacular, even when surrounded by high-rise, down-market urban sprawl. Start at the top, along the rim of the Horseshoe Falls. Next head for the **Journey behind the Falls** ((905) 371-0254 TOLL-FREE (877) 642-7275, Queen Victoria Park, also next to the Horseshoe Falls, where elevators take you down to viewing points actually beneath the thunderous curtain of water. Expect long delays in high season.

Now you are ready for a boat trip on the *Maid of the Mist* ((905) 358-5781 WEB SITE www.maid ofthemist.com, which affords a tremendously exciting, if damp, experience. Kitted out in blue hooded raincoats, you are taken to the base of the American Falls, as close as you can get to its deafening might. The *Maid of the Mist*, operates daily from April to October, with departures every 15 minutes from 10 am, from the Maid of the Mist elevator at the foot of Clifton Hill. See INTO THE MIST, page 11 in TOP SPOTS.

For an aerial view of the falls, there are three towers, the best being the **Skylon Tower** ((905) 356-2651 TOLL-FREE (800) 717-4397 WEB SITE www .skylon.com, 5200 Robinson Street. Exterior elevators carry you to the top, where there's a Revolving Dining Room, the Summit Buffet and an indoor and outdoor viewing deck. In the basement you'll find a large souvenir shopping mall and an indoor amusement park, **Skyquest**. Several of the local hotels, including the Sheraton Fallsview and the Hilton, are a blot on the skyline from the outside, but offer superb views across the falls from their upper stories. Finally, go back at night to see the falls under a rainbow array of floodlights.

A funicular railway leads up the cliff from the falls to the downtown area of **Clifton Hill**, called "the street of fun at the falls," this is where visitors escape the stress of dealing with too much Nature. The town is, in many ways, a victim of its own success, and you may be dismayed at the heaving crowds and the tackiness of the neon-clad attractions such as The House of Frankenstein, The Haunted House and Ripley's Believe It Or Not, strung out along the strip between the souvenir shops, bars, fast-food joints and themed restaurants such as the Rainforest Café. Or you may really enjoy the buzz.

Sparkling **Casino Niagara** TOLL-FREE (888) 266-7258 WEB SITE www.casinoniagara.com, 5705 Falls Avenue, has an 8,900-sq-m (96,000-sq-ft) gaming area bursting with 2,700 slot machines and 135 gaming tables. Several restaurants and seven bars are found on the premises, so you won't have to go far to drown your sorrows.

A short way from the town center, **Canada One Factory Outlets** TOLL-FREE (866) 284 5781 WEB SITE www.canadaoneoutlets.com, 7500 Lundy's Lake,

off the Queen Elizabeth Way, is a factory outlet mall whose attractive prices, good range of designer labels and proximity to the United States border have helped turn it into one of the town's prime tourist attractions.

Marineland ((905) 356-9565 WEB SITE www .marinelandcanada.com, 7657 Portage Road, is an exciting theme park whose rides include the world's largest steel-framed roller-coaster; the aquarium complex houses sharks, a coral reef, dolphins and beluga and killer whales.

The **North Niagara Parkway** stretches between the falls to Niagara-on-the-Lake, a distance of 26 km (16 miles) following the river on its way to Lake Ontario. With its parks, gardens and historic buildings and sites, it makes a delightful drive or walk. The **Great Gorge Adventure** ((905) 354-5711 TOLL-FREE (877) 642-7275 is an elevator down to the bottom of the gorge for a close view of the rapids in violent action. At the bottom is a boardwalk along the river, with information points to show the various geological forms in the rock face.

A little further along, **Niagara Spanish Aero Car** ((905) 371-0254 TOLL-FREE (877) 642-7275 offers cable trips over the Whirlpool Rapids for some dramatic views of the swirling water below. At **Niagara Glen**, trails lead to the river's edge and the forest offers a lovely and peaceful retreat for the weary traveler. Nearby the **Niagara Parks Botanical Garden** ((905) 371-0254 TOLL-FREE (877) 642-7275 has beautiful gardens filled with shrubs and flowers maintained by students of the local Horticultural School. Within the grounds the spectacular **Butterfly Conservatory** is a huge greenhouse that is home to around 2,000 live tropical butterflies. Along the road nearby, look out for the **Floral Clock**, made up of some 1,900 plants.

A little further north is **Queenston Heights** ((905) 371-0254 TOLL-FREE (877) 642-7275, the place where in 1812 the British finally defeated the American attempt to take Queenston. It's now a peaceful park and a good spot for a picnic.

Where to Stay

The falls can easily be seen as part of a daytrip from Toronto. If you do plan to spend the night, you should consider staying at nearby Niagara-on-the-Lake (see NIAGARA-ON-THE-LAKE, page 94). There are, however, accommodation signs screaming at you everywhere around Niagara Falls. It's quite difficult to categorize accommodation in terms of price, as there's such a great fluctuation according to the time of year, added to which, prices seem to change according to daily demand. It really is worth bargaining. Niagara Falls Tourism can help in finding accommodation (see GENERAL INFORMATION, above).

For information on bed and breakfasts, contact the **Federation of Ontario Bed and Break-**

fast **Accommodation** ((416) 964-2566 WEB SITE
www.fobba.com, PO Box 437, 253 College Street,
Toronto M5T 1R5, or the tourist office.

MID-RANGE TO EXPENSIVE

The award-winning **Sheraton Fallsview** ((905)
374-1077 TOLL-FREE (800) 618-9269 FAX (905) 374-
6224 WEB SITE www.fallsview.com, 6755 Fallsview
Boulevard, is a 32-story hotel with 402 comfortable and well-appointed, if bland, rooms and
suites, an indoor pool, a fitness room, a restaurant and, above all, spectacular views. Almost next
door, the **Marriott Fallsview** ((905) 357-7300 TOLL-
FREE (888) 501-8916 WEB SITE www.niagarafalls
marriott.com, 6740 Fallsview Boulevard, is an
upmarket 23-story property whose 430 rooms all
have views of the falls. The **Hilton Niagara Falls**
((905) 354-7887 FAX (905) 374-6707 WEB SITE www
.hiltonniagarafalls.com, 6361 Fallsview Boulevard, has 516 rooms, a rooftop restaurant and
lounge, and a huge indoor pool complete with
spiral waterslide, whirlpools and a waterfall.

The **Sheraton on the Falls** ((905) 374-4444
TOLL-FREE (800) 263-7135 FAX (905) 371-0157 WEB
SITE www.niagarafallshotels.com, 5875 Falls Avenue, has 395 well-equipped rooms, some with
balconies and views of the falls. The **Old Stone
Inn** ((905) 357-1234 TOLL-FREE (800) 263-6208
FAX (905) 357-9299 WEB SITE www.oldstoneinn
.on.ca, 5425 Robinson Street, has 114 spacious,
modern rooms, although the building itself looks
like an old-fashioned inn, reflecting its age — it
first opened for business in 1904. The emphasis
is on couples at the **Travelodge Clifton Hill** ((905)
357-4330 TOLL-FREE (800) 668-8840 FAX (905) 357-
0423 WEB SITE www.travelodge.com, 4943 Clifton
Hill, where there are 80 units, some of which are
honeymoon suites.

Next door to the Sheraton, the **Brock Plaza
Hotel** ((905) 374-4444 TOLL-FREE (800) 263-7135
FAX (905) 357-4804 WEB SITE www.fallsavenue.com,
5685 Falls Avenue, is a less expensive alternative.
It has been in business since 1929 and there's some
elegance about it. About three-quarters of the
233 rooms look towards the falls, and there's a
restaurant with great views on the tenth floor. Less
expensive rooms come with an unfortunate view
of the parking lot.

INEXPENSIVE

The **Best Western Fallsview** ((905) 356-0551 TOLL-
FREE (800) 263-2580, 5551 Murray Street, is quite
centrally located with 233 modern rooms, some
of which are suites catering to the honeymoon
market; with round beds and large baths. North
of downtown, the **Ameri-Cana** ((905) 356-8444
TOLL-FREE (800) 263-3508 FAX (905) 356-8576 WEB
SITE www.americananiagara.com, 8444 Lundy's
Lane, offers motel accommodation set in large
grounds with tennis courts and indoor and out-

door swimming pools, a spa, coffee shop and restaurant (inexpensive). With self-catering facilities,
it's an appealing option for families. Another reasonable option in the same strip is the **Carriage
House Motor Lodge** ((905) 356-7799 TOLL-FREE
(800) 267-9887 WEB SITE www.falls.net/motel/
carriage, 8004 Lundy's Lane, with 120 rooms, a
coffee shop and pool.

Where to Eat

The town is awash with fast food, pizzerias and
steak houses. If you are looking for fine dining,
the place to start is probably at one of the hotels
(see above) or the casino. The moderately priced
Skylon Tower ((905) 356-2651 TOLL-FREE (800) 927-
2251, 5200 Robinson Street, has both an à la carte
dining room and the Summit Buffet. There's a
happy country atmosphere and international
cuisine at the **Old Stone Inn** ((416) 357-1234, 5425
Robinson Street.

The Niagara Parkway Commission owns **Table Rock** ((905) 354-3631, on the brink of the falls, where you can dine inexpensively inside or on an outdoor terrace. The Parkway Commission also runs the more formal, moderately priced **Queenston Heights** ((905) 262-4274, on Niagara Parkway North, which similarly offers a choice of indoor or outdoor dining, beautifully located with some great river views. **Betty's Restaurant** ((905) 295-4436, 8921 Sodom Road, is a mid-range eatery with generously portioned scallops, chicken and burgers.

Oh Canada Eh! Dinner Show ((905) 374-1995 TOLL-FREE (800) 467-2071, 8585 Lundy's Lane, has been a hit for years, a rousing dinner theater that tells the history of Canada with song, dance and a buffet meal.

As with hotels, many of the better, more charming restaurants are up the road in Niagara-on-the-Lake.

How to Get There

The nearest airport is Buffalo International, but Toronto is also within easy reach. **Niagara Airbus** ((905) 677-8083 FAX (800) 206-7222 WEB SITE www.niagaraairbus.com operates regular shuttle services to Niagara Falls from Toronto, Hamilton and Buffalo airports.

VIA Rail ((905) 685-9772 TOLL-FREE (888) 842-7245 WEB SITE www.viarail.com has several trains a day from Toronto to St. Catharine's and Niagara Falls, while **Amtrak** TOLL-FREE (800) 872-7245 FAX (215) 856-7954 WEB SITE www.amtrak.com, has frequent service from various American cities.

The major road linking all the towns and cities of the Golden Horseshoe, from Toronto to Niagara Falls, is Queen Elizabeth Way. Interstate 90 is the principal American highway lead-

Visitors enjoy the walkway above the American Falls in Niagara Falls, USA.

ing to the vicinity of the falls, from both the south-west and the southeast. Allow plenty of time at weekends, when the line to cross the border can cause serious delays. There is an hourly bus service between Toronto and Niagara Falls, and a bus twice daily between the falls and the Prince of Wales Hotel in Niagara-on-the-Lake. The station, however, is quite a hike from the tourist area.

SOUTHERN ONTARIO

Southern Ontario, the "land between the lakes," consists of miles and miles of gently rolling farmland laced with rivers and streams and sprinkled with charming towns and villages. Thanks to its rich alluvial soil and temperate climate, the area produces an abundance of fruit and vegetables. This means that the larger towns are genuine market towns, where you can find a fine selection of local produce. Almost anywhere you go you can find a welcoming array of inns and taverns, on the English model.

The region is a cultural as well as an agricultural seedbed, where the English way of life that was first supplanted here in the eighteenth century has blossomed in the form of communities called London, Windsor, Cambridge, Essex, Waterloo, Woodstock, Blenheim and Stratford — where the summer-long Shakespeare Festival provides a unique celebration of the Bard's work.

BACKGROUND

The Hurons were the first to appreciate the agricultural potential of this fertile region, but their efforts at farming were constantly interrupted by the belligerent, rampaging Iroquois. It wasn't until after the Anglo-French treaty in 1763 that settlers moved into the area, and not until after the American Revolution, when the Loyalists began arriving, that it acquired its distinctly British character. The first farming-based settlement was at Windsor; others followed at London and Stratford. At about the same time Germans settled in the area, as did many Mennonites from Pennsylvania, whose resolute pacifism during the American Revolution had made them unpopular with their American neighbors.

Today the German and Mennonite presence is still very marked, particularly in the Kitchener–Waterloo–St. Jacobs area. The Mennonite Story ((519)664-3518 WEB SITE www.stjacobs.com, 1406 King Street North, St. Jacobs, explains the history and lifestyle of the Mennonite people.

The peninsula as a whole remains what it was two centuries ago: still very pretty to look at, still very Olde English in outlook. For information about southern Ontario communities, contact the **Southern Ontario Tourism Organization** ((519) 756 3230 TOLL-FREE (800) 267-3399 FAX (519) 756-

3231 WEB SITE www.soto.on.ca, 180 Greenwich Street, Brantford ON N3S 2X6.

STRATFORD

Set in farmlands, this attractive town with a population of 26,000 has many far-from-accidental things in common with the famous English town of the same name. Back in 1830, proprietor William Sargint called his inn the Shakespeare Inn, which prompted the community to change its name to Stratford and the river's name to Avon. The most important link, however, was forged in 1953, with the inauguration of the world-famous Shakespeare Festival that is held here each summer and attracts a large international audience.

The **Shakespeare Festival** ((519) 271 4040 TOLL-FREE (800) 567-1600 FAX (519) 273-6173 WEB SITE www .stratfordfestival.ca, held early May to mid-November, was the dream of local journalist Tom Patterson, realized with the help of Sir Tyrone Guthrie in 1953, when the first festival productions were staged inside a tent. The idea took off, an award-winning theater was built, and the festival has grown in size, popularity and reputation. It now attracts an audience of around 500,000. While the plays performed are predominantly Shakespearean, other classic and contemporary works also feature. International stars appear in the highly rated productions.

There are three theaters in the town — the **Avon Theatre**, 99 Downie Street, the **Tom Patterson Theatre**, Lakeside Drive, and the **Festival Theatre**, 55 Queen Street, which was built in 1953, designed along the lines of the Elizabethan stage. A recent renovation to celebrate the festival's fiftieth anniversary added a more intimate **Studio Theatre** to the complex. The nearby **Queen's Park** provides a beautiful setting, with lawns stretching down to the riverside. Around here the river is dammed to form Victoria Lake, with swans and ducks to further the resemblance to England's Stratford. There are many pleasant walks and spots for picnicking. Footpaths lead beyond the dam through an old-fashioned gate into the delightful **Shakespeare Garden**, next to Huron Street Bridge, an English-style garden complete with a bust of the bard.

In an old building near Confederation Park, **Gallery Stratford** ((519) 271-5271 WEB SITE www .gallerystratford.on.ca, 54 Romeo Street North, often has temporary exhibitions of international modern painting and sculpture, plus lectures and films. There are three galleries, so there's always a choice of exhibitions.

The Shakespeare Garden in Queen's Park, Stratford, features a bust of the Bard RIGHT, as well as green lawns and swan ponds OVERLEAF.

Guided **walking tours** ((519) 271-5140 TOLL-FREE (800) 561-7926 leave from the Visitor Information Centre, York Street at Lakeside Drive (May to October). **Avon Boat Rentals** ((519) 271-8681 rent out pedal boats, canoes, kayaks and a tour boat (May to September). Or hop on a double-decker bus for a city tour with **Festival Tours** ((519) 273-1652 WEB SITE www.festivaltours.on.ca (tickets and departures from York Lane).

For visitor information, contact **Tourism Stratford** ((519) 271-5140 TOLL-FREE (800) 561-7926 FAX (519) 273-1818 WEB SITE www.city.stratford .on.ca, 47 Downie Street.

Where to Stay and Eat

One of the oldest hotels in Stratford, the mid-range **Queen's Inn at Stratford** ((519) 271-1400 TOLL-FREE (800) 461-6450 FAX (519) 271-7373, 161 Ontario Street, is conveniently central. It has 32 attractive, air-conditioned rooms and two restaurants. The similarly priced **Albert Place Hotel** ((519) 273-5800 FAX (519) 273-5008 E-MAIL albert@strat.net, 23 Albert Street, has 34 spacious, modern rooms with television and airconditioning, and some mini-suites are available. A sprawling low-rise complex set in gardens, the **Festival Inn** ((519) 273-1150 TOLL-FREE (800) 463-3581 FAX (519) 273-2111 WEB SITE www.festivalinnstratford.com, 1140 Ontario Street, has 182 moderate-to-expensive rooms and its own organic herb and vegetable garden.

For bed-and-breakfast accommodations, contact the **Stratford and Area Bed & Breakfast Association** WEB SITE www.bbcanada.com/associations/ stratford, or the **Federation of Ontario Bed and Breakfast Accommodation** ((416) 964-2566 WEB SITE www.fobba.com, PO Box 437, 253 College Street, Toronto M5T 1R5.

Serving fine French food in a converted nineteenth-century church, which retains its altar, stained glass and original woodwork, **Church Restaurant and Belfry** ((519) 273-3424, Brunswick and Waterloo Streets, is the best dining option, but reservations during the festival period, really do need to be made at the same time you book your theater tickets: up to six months in advance. The Belfry grillroom and bar upstairs offers a less expensive menu and snacks and drinks.

Rundles ((519) 271-6442, 9 Coburg Street, is another excellent restaurant, beautifully located by Victoria Lake (moderate to expensive). Its modern interior is adorned with contemporary paintings and sculptures, and the food is mouth-watering and imaginative: the three-course *table d'hôte* is recommended. They also prepare delicious packed lunches for festival-goers.

Local produce features largely on the menu at **The Old Prune** ((519) 271-5052, 151 Albert Street. The food is light, fresh and delicious, the building old; for dinner the menu is *prix-fixe*, but there is quite a wide choice (expensive).

LONDON

Situated at the fork of the River Thames (pronounced as it is spelled), London is the area's industrial center, and the province's fourth largest metropolitan area. However, this is not immediately obvious thanks to the town's attractive old houses, tree-lined streets and squares, and exceptional amount of greenery — a result of an extensive tree-planting scheme that started a hundred years ago and is still in progress.

Information and maps are available through **Tourism London** TOLL-FREE (800) 265-2602 WEB SITE www.londontourism.ca, 300 Dufferin Avenue, Suite 1110.

What to See and Do

Overlooking the river, **London Regional Art and Historical Museum** ((519) 672-4580 WEB SITE www.londonmuseum.on.ca, 421 Ridout Street North, is a striking modern building designed by Raymond Moriyama. This unusual structure is a series of interlocking barrel vaults that form large and airy galleries with domed skylights providing natural lighting. The gallery holds changing exhibitions of national and international work, and has its own large collection of Canadian art.

Children have a wonderful time at **London Regional Children's Museum** ((519) 434-5726, 21 Wharncliffe Road South, where they are encouraged to explore, participate and play. In the gallery called "The Street Where You Live" they can dress in costume and "be" a firefighter, a doctor or a builder. They can see what life was like in the past, explore the Computer Hall, or look into outer space. Children should also visit the **Storybook Gardens** ((519) 661-5770, Springbank Park, with delightful gardens, many themed on fairy stories and popular children's books; there is also a petting zoo and a small fairground (May to October).

For a glimpse of what life was like before the settlers arrived in southwestern Ontario, visit the **London Museum of Archeology** ((519) 473-1360 WEB SITE www.uwo.ca/museum, 1600 Attawandaron Road, where there are displays on the area's prehistory and a reconstructed Attawandaron Village. About 32 km (20 miles) southwest of the city, **Ska-Nah-Doht Village** ((519) 264-2420, 8449 Irish Drive, Mount Brydges, in the Longwoods Road Conservation area off Route 2, is a recreation of a prehistoric Iroquois village with exhibits and audiovisual presentations that show all aspects of everyday life.

Life in a pioneer community is recreated at the **Fanshawe Pioneer Village in** ((519) 457-1296 WEB SITE www.pioneer.wwdc.com, Fanshawe Park, 14 km (9 miles) northeast of the city. This reconstructed village consists of 30 buildings, with wagon rides and demonstrations of pioneer crafts (May to mid-December). The park covers 600 hectares (1,500 acres) of land, with a large lake and a pool where you can swim, fish, canoe, windsurf and sail.

Where to Stay and Eat

The best accommodation is probably **Idlewyld Inn** ((519) 433-2891 TOLL-FREE (877) 435-3466 WEB SITE www.someplacesdifferent.com, 36 Grand Avenue, a splendid 1878 mansion with tall windows, ornate woodwork and a grand central staircase. It has 27 guestrooms, each uniquely decorated and with a happy combination of antique furnishings and modern facilities. **Delta**

London Armouries Hotel ((519) 679-6111 TOLL-FREE (800) 668-9999 FAX (519) 679-6397 WEB SITE WWW .deltahotels.com, 325 Dundas Street, provides extremely comfortable accommodation in a thickwalled and turreted armory, built in 1905, above which rises a glass tower. Rooms are attractively furnished, all have private bath and television, and there's an indoor swimming pool. Just on the edge of town, the moderately priced **Windermere Manor** ((519) 858-1391 TOLL-FREE (800) 997-4477 FAX (519) 858-5189 WEB SITE www.windermere manor.com, 200 Collip Circle, has 48 comfortable rooms and suites that come complete with microwaves and computer terminals as well as the usual facilities.

For lists of bed and breakfasts contact the **London and Area Bed & Breakfast Association** ((519) 673-6797 WEB SITE www.bbcanada.com, 2 Normandy Gardens.

Chancey Smiths ((519) 672-0384, 130 King Street, Covent Garden Market, is the best of the local steak-and-seafood restaurants (moderate to expensive). The **Green Tomato** ((519) 660-1170, 172 King Street is a laid-back California-style bistro, with a wide range of vegetarian and non-vegetarian dishes and great desserts (moderate to inexpensive). Similarly priced is **Miestro's** ((519) 439-8983, 352 Dundas Street, where the menu features dishes from all around the world.

HOW TO GET THERE

Route 401 between Toronto and Windsor is the concrete spine of the peninsula. Driving along it, Kitchener is about an hour from Toronto, London an hour and a half from Kitchener, and Windsor about two hours from London. To continue on to Stratford, follow Highway 8 west from Kitchener onto Highway 7/8 west. If you are coming from the United States, Detroit and Windsor are connected by both a bridge and a tunnel.

Amtrak TOLL-FREE (800) 872-7245 WEB SITE www.amtrak.com, and **VIA Rail** ((519) 256-5511 TOLL-FREE (888) 842-7245 WEB SITE www.viarail.ca operates several trains daily along the Toronto–Kitchener–Stratford–London–Chicago route. The **Robert Q. Airbus** ((519) 673-6804 runs airport shuttles from Toronto and Detroit airports.

NORTHERN ONTARIO

Northern Ontario is generally considered to be everything north and west of Lake Nipissing, which lies between the Québec border and the northern tip of Georgian Bay. In other words, it is almost all of Ontario in terms of size, but very little of it in terms of interest to visitors. Thickly forested and thinly populated, this vast wilderness has no towns of any size except near rich mineral deposits and along the shores of Lake Huron and Lake Superior.

On the other hand, its many lakes and rivers and its forests teeming with wildlife make it ideal for the sportsperson who really wants to get away from it all.

SUDBURY

The town of Sudbury sits in the vast Sudbury Basin, a mineral-rich geological formation 37 km (59 miles) long that is the world's largest source of nickel. The resulting pollution has contributed to the bleakness that afflicts parts of the landscape. However, this is compensated for by the surrounding Canadian Shield countryside, wild and wonderful with its forests, rocks and lakes, offering the outdoor enthusiast all kinds of possibilities.

A demonstration in the Fanshawe Pioneer Village, northeast of London.

Of Sudbury's population of around 165,000, about a quarter are Francophone. Laurentian University, which is situated on the shores of Lake Ramsey, is bilingual, and French culture thrives here. For visitor information, get in touch with the **Sudbury Welcome Centre** ((705) 673-7133 TOLL-FREE (877) 304-8222 WEB SITE www .sudburytourism.ca.

What to See and Do
The major attraction here is **Science North** ((705) 522-3701 TOLL-FREE (800) 461-4898 WEB SITE www .sciencenorth.on.ca, 100 Ramsey Lake Road, just south of the TransCanada Highway, an impressive science center at the edge of Lake Ramsey. This dramatic building was designed by architect Raymond Moriyama and consists of two snowflake-shaped buildings set over a cavern in the rock. The smaller hexagonal structure is the reception area, linked to the larger "snowflake," containing the exhibition halls, by a tunnel through the rock. Watch a 3-D film of the Northern Ontario landscape before ascending to exhibition areas where a hands-on experience of science awaits you. Hour-long **cruises** on Ramsey Lake leave from the wharf next to Science North.

To the west of the town stands Sudbury's famous landmark, the nine-meter-tall (30-ft) **Big Nickel**, which once stood above the Big Nickel Mine. **Dynamic Earth**, due to open in 2003 under the auspices of Science North (phone for details), will offer a dramatic multimedia tour of the region's geology.

The town also has a series of small museums, which together make up the **City of Greater Sudbury Heritage Museum** ((705) 692-4448. They include the Anderson Farm Museum, Main Street, on an old dairy farm; the Centre Franco-Ontarien de Folklore, 38 Xavier Street, celebrating the Ontario's French heritage; the Flour Mill Museum, 245 St. Charles Street, a 1903 clapboard house, once the home of the local logging mill foreman; the Copper Cliff Museum, Power Street, Copper Cliff, an early twentieth-century log cabin; the Rayside-Balfour Museum, 239 Montée Principal, Centre Trillium, Azilda, with displays about local agriculture; and the Northern Ontario Railroad Museum and Heritage Centre, 26 Bloor Street, Capreol.

Lovers of the great outdoors will enjoy an excursion to the **Killarney Provincial Park** ((705) 287-2900, about 80 km (50 miles) southwest of Sudbury. It covers 363 sq km (140 sq miles) of rugged Canadian Shield wilderness at its most beautiful, against a backdrop of the snow-capped La Cloche Mountains. Apart from some campgrounds, there are few facilities here, and you make your way on foot, by canoe, or on skis. For fishing and whitewater canoeing, the place to go is **French River**, south of Sudbury, which runs

between Lake Nipissing and Georgian Bay. However, the countryside all around Sudbury offers endless opportunities for outdoor recreation, and there are plenty of lodges, camps and organized trips to ease the way.

Where to Stay
Most guest accommodation in Sudbury is in chain hotels such as the reliable downtown **Ramada Inn Sudbury** ((705) 675-1123 TOLL-FREE (800) 436-4449 FAX (705) 675-7727 WEB SITE www.ramada.ca, 85 St. Ann Road, with 145 rooms and an indoor swimming pool, and the **Howard Johnson Plaza** ((705) 522-3000 TOLL-FREE (866) 768-4947 WEB SITE www.hojosudbury.com, 1696 Regent Street, at the south end of town. Both hotels are mid-range.

SAULT STE. MARIE

Known as "the Sault" (pronounced "the Soo"), Sault Ste. Marie is separated from its twin town in the United States by the rapids of St. Mary's River, which links Lake Superior and Lake Huron. Long before the explorers came, the rapids were a meeting place for natives, who came here to catch whitefish. Established by Jesuit missionaries in 1668, Sault Ste. Marie has grown into an industrial town with a population of over 80,000. It has a large steelworks, pulp and lumber mills, and is also a very important shipping center. A series of locks on the St. Mary's River enables huge ships to pass between Lakes Huron and Superior, bypassing the rapids and making the canal the busiest section of the St. Lawrence Seaway, with 90 million metric tons (100 million tons) of cargo passing through annually. The Soo is also linked to its Michigan twin by road and railway bridges, and it's therefore a popular stopping place for travelers.

For visitor information, contact **Tourism Sault Ste. Marie** ((705) 759-5462 TOLL-FREE (800) 461-6020 FAX (705) 759-2185 WEB SITE www.sault-canada.com, 99 Foster Drive.

At the bottom of Huron Street you can watch the continuous stream of ships passing through from a viewing platform by the **Soo Locks**, around which are pleasant walking trails. There are four American locks and one Canadian — which dates from 1895 and is the oldest of the system. This Canadian lock, now operated by Parks Canada, is used only by pleasure craft, and has some lovely spots for picnicking. **Boat trips** on the MV *Chief Shingwauk* ((705) 253-9850 TOLL-FREE (877) 226-3665 WEB SITE www.locktours.com, run mid-May to mid-October from Roberta Bondar Dock, next to the Holiday Inn. The trip passes through all five locks and lasts about two hours.

The **Sault Ste. Marie Museum** ((705) 759-7258, 690 Queen Street East, is housed in the town's imposing former Post Office (1906). It has five well-laid-out galleries, telling the story of the region from prehistory to the present with various reconstructions, such as a First Nations birchbark dwelling, a blacksmith's shop and Soo as it would have been in 1912.

The **Ermatinger-Clergue Heritage Site** ((705) 759-5443, 831 Queen Street East, is a lovely Georgian building dating from 1814: the oldest surviving dwelling in Northern Ontario (open April to November). Built by wealthy fur trader Charles Oakes Ermatinger for his wife — who was an Ojibway princess — it served as a way station for many explorers. One floor has been restored and furnished in the style of the early nineteenth century, and the other floor houses a museum. Also

((705) 946-7300 TOLL-FREE (800) 242-9287 WEB SITE www.agawacanyontourtrain.com. The nine-hour, 114 km (68 miles) journey into beautiful Agawa Canyon takes in some spectacular scenery, plunging deep into the unspoiled wilderness, through forests, over rivers and gorges, along trestle bridges, on mountain ledges and around lakes. The trip allows two hours for exploring, fishing, camera clicking and climbing the 300 stairs up to the observation platform. A full breakfast and lunch menu are available. In winter, the **Snow Train** makes the same journey, when a lovely white mantel covers the landscape. Finally there is the 480-km (300-mile) excursion to the French-Canadian town of **Hearst**. An overnight stay in

at the site, **Clergue Block House** is the former powder magazine for the North West Fur Company, its wooden upper floor was added in 1894.

The **Canadian Bushplane Heritage Centre** ((705) 945-6242 TOLL-FREE (877) 287-4752 WEB SITE www.bushplane.com, Bay Street, is a vast historic hangar where the concept of water-bombing bush fires was developed. Today it pays fascinating homage to a variety of pioneer flying machines, with plenty of interactive displays on Canadian heritage.

Casino Sault Ste. Marie TOLL-FREE (800) 826-8946, 30 Bay Street East, has 450 slot machines, 30 gaming tables and a restaurant. **Circle H Ranch** ((705) 253-7055, 534 Case Road, offers horseback riding.

To the north of the city lies the unspoiled and untamed **Algoma** wilderness. The main attraction in the area is the **Agawa Canyon Tour Train**

modern accommodation is included in the fare. Those who wish to pay a premium can travel in the luxurious dome car, where the scenery can be appreciated in all its glory. The train is popular at all times, but reservations are essential in the fall, when this is a perfect way to enjoy the spectacular colors of the leaves.

To appreciate more natural beauty, take the TransCanada Highway (Route 17) 230 km (143 miles) north to Wawa, along the **Lake Superior Drive**. The route takes you by **Batchawana Bay**, with miles of sandy beaches. You'll find plenty of accommodation of all kinds here. Beyond the lovely **Alona Bay**, the road passes through **Lake Superior Provincial Park**, a majestic wilderness of cliffs and forests. Here, rising from the lake, is **Agawa**

Sudbury's famous Big Nickel, which once stood above the entrance to the Big Nickel Mine.

Rock, on which a series of native pictographs tell stories that were the inspiration for Longfellow's epic poem, *Hiawatha*.

For a spectacular view of the lake and St. Mary's River, go 26 km (16 miles) west of the town along Route 550 to **Gros Cap** ridge, where there's a marked trail along the shore.

Sports and Outdoor Activities

Lake Superior Provincial Park is a beautiful setting for **boating** and **canoeing**, and also offers **fishing**. At Batchawana Bay, the rivers offer good fishing and there are more opportunities during the two-hour stop on the Agawa Canyon trip. For **swimming**, Batchawana Bay has some lovely beaches although the waters are cool, and in the Kinsmen-Crystal Creek Conservation Area, also known as Hiawatha Park, a short drive northwest of town, there's a swimming pond and waterfalls.

Within the city limits, **Hiawatha Highlands** has many kilometers of cross-country ski trails. Cross-country and downhill skiing are also popular at the **Searchmont Resort (** (705) 781-2340 TOLL-FREE (1-800) 663-2546, about 30-minutes from the city on Highway 556. There are hundreds of kilometers of groomed **snowmobile** trails in the region.

Where to Stay

Close to the Algoma Central train station, **Holiday Inn (** (705) 949-0611 TOLL-FREE (888) 713-8482 FAX (705) 945-6972 WEB SITE www.holiday-inn.com, 208 St. Mary's River Drive, has an indoor pool, a restaurant and 195 rooms (moderate). Nearby, **Travelodge (** (705) 759-1400 TOLL-FREE (866) 759-1400 WEB SITE www.soonet.ca/tlodge, 332 Bay Street, has 47 rooms with free continental breakfast and in-room fridge and microwave, and a sauna and fitness room (moderate).

The Hostelling International-affiliated **Algonquin Hotel (** (705) 253-2311 TOLL-FREE (888) 269-7728 FAX (705) 942-0269 WEB SITE www.hihostels .ca, 864 Queen Street East (inexpensive), is near the harborfront, and the museum and art gallery. There are private rooms, a restaurant, a bar and on-site parking.

THUNDER BAY

The port of Thunder Bay stands on the shores of Lake Superior at the western end of the St. Lawrence Seaway, virtually at the exact center of Canada. It is the terminus for freighters and a pivotal point in the transportation of grain, forest products and other materials. Fifteen huge grain elevators dominate the skyline, although reduced grain shipments in recent years have meant a reduction in traffic through the **Lakehead**. However, the city's economy remains typically Canadian, being largely dependent on grains, forest products and mineral resources.

Jobs in shipping attracted many immigrants to Thunder Bay, which today has a population of around 130,000. There is a rich ethnic mix — including a large Finnish community and some 10,000 First Nations people. With the forest and mountains to the north, the wilderness is never far away, and it's not uncommon to see moose and bear wandering about the town.

In the days before the St. Lawrence Seaway, Fort William, as it was then known, was an important fur-trading center. Natives and trappers brought their furs here to the mouth of the Kaministikwia for their meeting — known as the Great Rendezvous — with the buyers who brought their European goods up the St. Lawrence. In 1801 the British built Fort William, which served as the headquarters of the North West Trading Company. Each summer more than 2,000 voyageurs met here for the Great Rendezvous, six weeks of discussion and celebration — and no insignificant

amount of drinking. Fort William remained a fur trading post until the late nineteenth century. In 1970, it merged with the community of Port Arthur to form the city of Thunder Bay.

Visitor information can be obtained from **Tourism Thunder Bay** ((807) 625-2149 TOLL-FREE (800) 667-8386 WEB SITE www.gottagonorth.com, 500 East Donald Street.

What to See and Do
The best way to get an idea of the city's economic role and its geography is to take a **harbor cruise**.

The **Thunder Bay Art Gallery** ((807) 577-6427, Confederation Campus, Edward or Balmoral Streets, focuses particularly on contemporary First Nations art, including the work of Norval Morrisseau, a well-known native artist who was born in Thunder Bay. The **Thunder Bay Museum** ((807) 623-0801, 425 Donald Street East, also mixes permanent exhibits, covering the history

and prehistory of the region, with a regular program of changing displays.

The huge glass-and-steel **Centennial Conservatory** ((807) 622-7036, Dease Street, is a greenhouse garden with paths winding through lush tropical foliage, changing floral exhibits, and a cactus house with some 280 different species — all rather astonishing and especially welcome in winter.

At the eastern end of the city, wooded **Centennial Park**, near Boulevard Lake, off Arundel Street, covers a 57-hectare (140-acre) area and has a logging camp, a museum and nature trails.

Further out to the east of the city is scenic **Sleeping Giant Provincial Park**, with trails, cliffs, woods and shoreline. At one end you'll see the Sleeping Giant rock formation stretching out into the lake, attached to which is a legend involving a silver mine, a treacherous native and a Great Spirit.

Kadabeka Falls, a few miles west of Thunder Bay.

Old Fort William Historical Park ((807) 473-2344 WEB SITE www.oldfortwilliam.on.ca, 16 km (10 miles) along Broadway Avenue (or take a boat from Port Arthur Marina), has become one of Canada's more popular tourist sights (mid-May to early October). You can see trappers, voyageurs, natives and traders going about their business.

Amethyst Mine Panorama ((807) 622-6908, Route 11 / 17, 56 km (35 miles) east of Thunder Bay, is a giant open-cast amethyst mine where you can tour the workings and dig out your own amethyst, or choose them from displays (mid-May to October). This is the largest deposit in North America.

Thunder Bay Charity Casino ((807) 683-1935 TOLL-FREE (877) 656-4263, Cumberland Street

South, has 14 gaming tables and 450 slot machines, a restaurant, a bar and a gift shop.

Sports and Outdoor Activities

There's good canoeing territory between the Lakehead and Rainy River, and at Centennial Park you'll find canoes and boats for rent. Sleeping Giant Provincial Park is a good spot for swimming, and there are beaches at **Kakabeka Falls** ((807) 473-9231 WEB SITE www .ontarioparks.com, 25 km (16 miles) west of town.

Long winters and short summers have given rise to the local saying that here there's "six months of good **skiing**, six months of poor skiing." Certainly, there is plenty of it. In the immediate vicinity are three downhill areas with excellent facilities and snowmaking equipment. There are also five cross-country trails close by, with plenty of après-ski and package deals to be had. The **Big Thunder**

Ski Jump, southwest of the city, is the world's largest with 90-m (295-ft) and 70-m (230-ft) jumps. The national ski-jumping team trains here.

Where to Stay and Eat

The **Valhalla Inn** ((807) 577-1121 TOLL-FREE (800) 964-1121 FAX (807) 475-4723 WEB SITE www.valhalla inn.com, 1 Valhalla Inn Road, is the town's largest and most up-market hotel, with 267 rooms and suites, two restaurants, a pool and a recreation area. Near the airport, **Travelodge Hotel Airlane** ((807) 473-1600 TOLL-FREE (800) 578-7878 FAX (807) 475-4852 WEB SITE www.airlane.com, 698 West Arthur Street, is one of the best in the area. It has 155 rooms, good service and a host of amenities.

The town's best restaurant is **Bistro One** ((807) 344-4682, 276 North Cumberland Street. For a light lunch, or casual fine dining on Saturday and Sunday evenings, head for the **Good News Café** ((807) 623-5001, north of the Arthur and Syndicates Street intersection (moderate). It is a bit of a drive, but **Karen's Kountry Kitchen** ((807) 977-2882, Pass Lake, 42 km (25 miles) east of Thunder Bay, is worth it, with delicious light lunches, sinful desserts and a lakeshore setting.

HOW TO GET THERE

The **Algoma Central Railway** ((705) 946-7300 TOLL-FREE (800) 242-9287 WEB SITE www.agawacanyon tourtrain.com operates trains service four times a week between Sault Ste. Marie and Hearst, Ontario (mid-May to mid-October only). There is a daily **VIA Rail** TOLL-FREE (888) 842-7245 WEB SITE www.viarail.ca train eastbound from Winnipeg that stops at Thunder Bay and Sudbury on its way to Ottawa and Montréal, and one westbound daily along the same route. There is also daily train service between Sudbury and Toronto.

Greyhound TOLL-FREE (800) 667-0882 WEB SITE www.greyhound.ca has frequent buses from major Canadian cities to Sudbury, Sault Ste. Marie and Thunder Bay, as well as daily buses to Sault Ste. Marie from Detroit and Chicago.

The TransCanada Highway (Route 17) links Sudbury, Sault Ste. Marie and Thunder Bay with each other as well as with eastern and western Canada. Approaching from the south, Sudbury can be reached by Route 69 from Toronto; Sault Ste. Marie by Interstate 75 from Detroit; and Thunder Bay by Interstate 35 from Minneapolis / St. Paul and Duluth, which becomes Route 61 when it crosses the border.

ABOVE: The windmill at Thunder Bay's Friendship Gardens. OPPOSITE TOP: Once an important fur trading post, Old Fort William has been reconstructed along with 50 village buildings where you can see trappers, voyageurs, natives and traders going about their business. BOTTOM: Boat-builder John DeForge plies his trade on Manitoulin Island.

Québec

Québec, the largest of Canada's provinces, is very large indeed: it covers over one and a half million square kilometers (nearly 600,000 sq miles), or one-sixth of Canada. It is twice the size of Texas and three times the size of France. But it is as "La Belle Province," a bastion of French culture in an Anglo-dominated continent, that Québec is best known. And rightly so, because for almost four centuries the people of Québec have stubbornly resisted every effort by others to interfere with their way of life — first by the natives who wanted to drive them out, then by the British who wanted to stamp them out, and latterly by their fellow Canadians, who have tried to buy them out. All to no avail. The Québécois are determined not to

surrender any part of the heritage left them by their ancestors. This determination is succinctly captured in the province's defiant motto, which is displayed on all Québec license plates: *Je me souviens* ("I remember").

They have much to remember. Although Jacques Cartier landed at Gaspé in 1534 and claimed the region for France, the French-speaking history of the province did not begin in earnest until 1608, when Samuel de Champlain established a small fur-trading post at a place on the St. Lawrence River that the natives called *Kébec*. Three years later he established another trading post on the river at a spot near modern Montréal. Permanent settlements followed at Trois Rivières in 1634 and Ville-Marie (now Montréal) in 1642. Although constantly raided by the hostile Iroquois, the settlements grew steadily and more were founded along the shores of the St. Lawrence. By 1700 there were 25,000 French colonists living along the St. Lawrence, while the colony of New France stretched from Hudson Bay to the Gulf of Mexico, and from the St. Lawrence almost to the Rockies.

French dominion over Québec continued more or less undisturbed for the next half-century, but the outbreak of the Seven Years' War in 1756 changed all that. The 20-minute battle on the Plains of Abraham, during which the British forces

under General James Wolfe routed the French under the Marquis de Montcalm, broke forever France's political hold on Québec. Under the Treaty of Paris in 1763, France ceded all its Canadian possessions to England. In 1774, Parliament passed the Québec Act, recognizing the right of French Canadians to keep their language, religion, property and legal system. Incensed by these and other concessions, especially regarding special advantages in the fur trade, the American colonists sent an army under General Richard Montgomery to attack Montréal and Québec City. Montréal fell, but Québec City held out, and the following year the British recaptured Montréal.

In 1791, Parliament passed the Constitutional Act dividing Québec into mainly English-speaking Upper Canada (present-day Ontario) and mainly French-speaking Lower Canada (present-day Québec). The arrangement worked reasonably well for the next four decades, despite growing resentment among the people of Lower Canada at being swamped by English-speaking immigrants, and at being governed by a British lieutenant governor with his handpicked legislative council. This led to a violent but unsuccessful rebellion by French Canadians in 1837. While the insurrection itself may have been put down, the desire for greater control over their own affairs would linger on. And on.

In 1867 the newly created provinces of Québec and Ontario joined Nova Scotia and New Brunswick in the confederated Dominion of Canada. Québec City became the provincial capital. For the rest of the century, Québec's economy remained largely dependent on trade and agriculture. Québec City consolidated its position as the center of government as well as chief custodian of French Canadian heritage and culture, while Montréal emerged as a great port and the province's financial and industrial center. By 1911, Montréal's population had reached half a million — and it doubled in the next two decades.

Unfortunately, the suspicions and enmities that had long bedeviled Québec's relations with the other provinces surfaced again, with renewed virulence, in 1917, when Canada was forced to introduce conscription to replace the horrific numbers of servicemen lost in the fighting in Europe. To the French Canadians, conscription was a sinister ploy to use them as cannon fodder in Britain's war with Germany. To the rest of Canada, the revolt of the Québécois against conscription was little short of treasonable.

The old wounds, thus reopened, never really healed. And when the Union Nationale party of Maurice Duplessis took control of the provincial government in the 1930s the estrangement looked set to become permanent — all the more so when the fight over conscription flared up again during World War II. Indeed, by 1960, when the Union

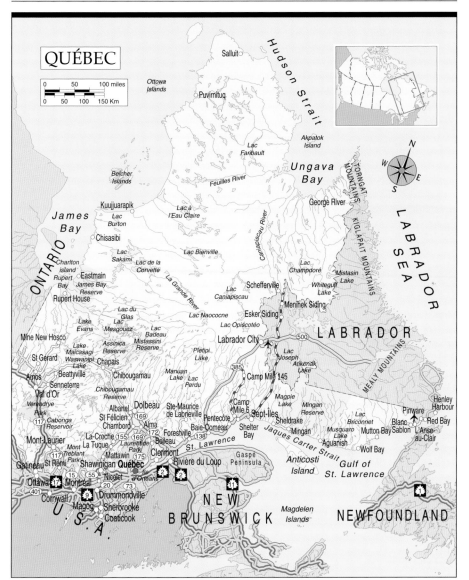

QUÉBEC

Salluit

Ottawa
Islands

Puvirnituq

Hudson Strait

Akpatok
Island

Lac
Faribault

Ungava
Bay

George River

TORNGAT MOUNTAINS

KIGLAPAIT MOUNTAINS

LABRADOR SEA

Belcher
Islands

Feuilles River

Kuujjuarapik

Lac à
l'Eau Claire

James
Bay

Lac
Burton

Chisasibi

Lac
Sakami   Lac de la
Corvette

Lac Bienville

Caniapiscau River

Lac
Champdoré

Mistasin
Lake

Charlton
island
Rupert Eastmain
Bay James Bay
Reserve
Rupert House

Lac du
Glas
Lac
Mesgouez

La Grande River

Lac
Caniapiscau

Schefferville

Whitegull
Lake

Menihek Siding

ONTARIO

Esker Siding

Lac Naococne
Lac Opiscotéo

LABRADOR

Mine New Hosco

Lake
Evans

Lac
Badeau
Mistassini
Reserve

Labrador City

500

MEALY MOUNTAINS

St Gérard

Lake
Malcasagi
Waswanipi
Lake

Assinica
Reserve

Chapais

Pletipi
Lake

385

Lac
Joseph

Atikonak
Lake

Amos
Beattyville

Senneterre

Chibougamau

Chibougamau
Reserve

Manuan
Lake Lac
Perdu

Camp Mile 145

Val d'Or

Vereodrye
Park
117 Cabonga
Reservoir

Albanel
St Félicien 169
Chambord

Dolbeau

Alma

Ste-Maurice
de Labrieville

Camp
Mile 6

Magpie
Lake

Mingan
Reserve

Lac
Briconnet

Pinware

Henley
Harbour

Blanc
Sablon

Red Bay

L'Anse-
au-Clair

Pentecôte

Sept-Îles

Sheldrake

172 Forestville

Mutton Bay

Mont-Laurier

La-Croche 155 169
Laurentide
Park

Baie-Comeau

Shelter
Bay

Mingan

Musquaro
Lake

Aguanish

Wolf Bay

Mont La Tuque
117 Treblant
Park

Boileau

138

Jaques Carter Strait

Gatineau St Rémi
Ottawa 17 Montréal
401
Cornwall

Shawinigan Québec
Mattawin 175
15 Clermont
55 Nicolet
20 73 Île
d'Orléans

Rivière du Loup

Gaspé
Peninsula

Anticosti
Island

Gulf of
St. Lawrence

St. Lawrence

Magog Sherbrooke
Drummondville
Coaticook

2

4

NEW
BRUNSWICK

11

Magdelen
Islands

1

NEWFOUNDLAND

U. S. A.

0 50 100 miles
0 50 100 150 Km

Nationale finally lost power to the Liberals, Québec was not only far apart from the rest of Canada, but far behind as well. Industrial expansion had been sacrificed in an attempt to preserve Québec's traditional agrarian economy; science and economics had been woefully neglected in the province's Church-run schools; and most progressive ideas for revitalizing the province had been successfully suppressed.

In 1960, however, the Liberals under Jean Lesage gained power and set in motion the "Quiet Revolution," an ambitious program of economic and social reform, which nudged Québec towards a modern society and a dynamic economy. At the same time it exposed the lack of French Canadi-

ans properly trained for managerial responsibilities, which meant that most of the bosses were Anglos — a situation guaranteed to sow further discord. And it did. In the late 1960s the separatist Parti Québécois rose to prominence under René Lévesque, taking 23 percent of the vote in the 1970 provincial elections and then, astonishingly, taking power in the 1976 elections. But Lévesque's radicalism, tinged with Anglophobia, frightened Anglo-run businesses out of the province, which in turn frightened the rest of the population. In a 1980 referendum the voters of Québec over-

A sylvan scene in the Laurentians, north of Québec City.

whelmingly rejected the idea of declaring independence, and in 1985 the Parti Québécois was turned out of office in favor of the Liberals.

In recent years, while the pendulum continues to swing gently, the threat of recession acted as a powerful wake-up call, and most Québécois seem to have lost interest in further autonomy or independent nationhood in favor of economic development. One thing is certain: Québec has the potential to be a formidable economic power. Its natural resources alone guarantee that. With 16 percent of the world's freshwater resources, it is able to generate (and sell) vast amounts of hydroelectric power. With its gigantic forests, it has a thriving lumber industry and is the top producer

of paper in North America. With more than its share of the ancient rocks of the Canadian Shield, it is rich in such minerals as iron, copper, gold, silver, lead, zinc and nickel; it is one of the world's foremost producers of aluminum. With the fertile flood plain of the St. Lawrence, its farmland supports a thriving agriculture industry. With all of these blessings, and with a population of only 7.4 million, it is no wonder that Québec is able to export 40 percent of its total production.

What to say of those seven million Québécois? To begin with, they are not as homogeneous as they may appear at first glance. At least 10 percent are of British ancestry, most of whom live in Montréal, and another 10 percent are immigrants from Europe, Asia, Latin America and the Caribbean. While French may be the official language of Québec, with English as the widely understood second language, over 35 other languages are

spoken in the province — such is the ethnic diversity of its immigrant population. Nor are the French-speakers the fanatical malcontents they are often portrayed to be. On the contrary, they are warm, garrulous, hospitable, informal and affectionate, with a *joie de vivre* that underlines their primarily Norman and Breton ancestry.

If it is their destiny to carry the torch of French civilization in the Americas, not only do they do it proudly, but with a big smile.

QUÉBEC CITY

The first European to visit the spot the natives called *Kébec* (meaning "the narrowing of the waters") was Jacques Cartier in 1535. Optimistically, he renamed the cliff Cap Diamants ("Diamond Cape") in honor of the great mineral wealth he hoped (and failed) to find there. When Samuel de Champlain arrived in 1608 he took a much more realistic view of the site's potential importance. Recognizing its strategic location, he established a trading post at the foot of the cliff, and then in 1620 built a fort at the summit. It was captured by the British under Admiral David Kirke in 1629, but was regained by the French three years later. For the next 130 years it found itself repeatedly under siege by either the British or the Iroquois, finally falling on the morning of September 13, 1759, when General Wolfe's troops surprised the French forces (under the Marquis de Montcalm) on the Plains of Abraham.

In 1763, with the signing of the Treaty of Paris, the city that had been the heart and soul of New France became the capital of a new British colony. After the American attack on the city in 1775 was repulsed, the British strengthened the fortifications and built the Citadel but, happily, they were never needed.

GENERAL INFORMATION

The **Maison du tourisme** ((418) 873-2015 TOLL-FREE (877) 266-5687 WEB SITE www.bonjourquebec.com, 12 rue Ste-Anne, at Place d'Armes across from the Château Frontenac, is the main drop-in information office for the city and province. For written or telephone information on the city, contact **Québec City and Area Tourist Information Centre** ((418) 649-2608 WEB SITE www.quebecregion.com, avenue Wilfred-Laurier, Haute-Ville.

Getting Around

Québec City has stairways and a funicular to bring you up (or down) the escarpment between Haute-Ville and Basse-Ville. With the attractive old stone buildings, narrow winding streets, pleasant squares and parks, there's a lot to see within a small area, which is comforting news for the visitor, as the narrow and sometimes pedestrian streets make walking by far the best means of getting about.

For a very relaxed (but expensive) sightseeing tour, take a ride in one of the **horse-drawn** *calèches* that you'll find waiting at Place d'Armes (see below) or on Rue d'Auteuil by the city walls, near the tourist information office. A 30-minute tour with an English-speaking driver costs around $50. They operate all year, rain, snow or shine.

For guided **walking or bus tours**, call Maple Leaf Guide Services ((418) 622-3677 TOLL-FREE (877) 622-3677 WEB SITE www.mapleleafservices .com. Les Tours du Vieux-Québec ((418) 664-0460 offer a variety of coach tours of the city and surrounding countryside, including whale-watching.

(Upper Town) includes the romantic and historic Vieille-Ville (Old City) with its walled fortifications, lovely residential areas and the Plains of Abraham, as well as some extramural concessions to the twentieth century, in the form of modern office buildings and shopping malls. Although the city has an official population of about 700,000, it never has that few people in it, as its attractions make it one of the most visited cities in the entire continent (see also EXPLORE HISTORIC QUÉBEC, page 12 in TOP SPOTS).

Basse-Ville

From Terrasse Dufferin, either the funicular or the Côte de la Montagne leading to the Escalier Casse-

One of the best and certainly the cheapest way to see the city from the water is to take the **ferry** that crosses every hour between Québec and Lévis ((418) 644-3704 or (418) 837-2408. Or you could try a longer, guided **river cruise** on the *Louis Jolliet* ((418) 692-1159 TOLL-FREE (800) 563-4643 WEB SITE www.croisieresaml.com (summer only). To rent a **bicycle** or **scooter**, call Vélo Passe-Sport Plein Air ((418) 692-3643.

WHAT TO SEE AND DO

When speaking of Québec City one should probably refer to it as Québec Cities. The city is clearly divided into two sections. At the foot of the cliff, the Basse-Ville (Lower Town) is the site of the original town and harbor, and extends into the valley of the Rivière St-Charles, where the industrial suburbs begin. Above it, the Haute-Ville

Cou (Breakneck Stairway) will bring you down to **Rue Petit-Champlain**, the oldest street in the city. It's a bustling, arty area with an abundance of craft shops and cafés.

The **Maison Chevalier** ((418) 646-3167 WEB SITE www.mcq.org, 50 rue du Marché-Champlain, is a former inn, built in 1752 for ship-owner Jean-Baptiste Chevalier. Handsomely restored, it now houses a museum with changing exhibits on Québec's history and culture. Texts are in French but English-language guidebooks are available.

North and slightly to the east is **Place Royale**, a small eighteenth-century square that was the hub of the city's thriving commerce until business moved away in the nineteenth century. Now the

Québec City — The airy spires of Haute-Ville OPPOSITE contrast with weighty Château Frontenac overlooking Basse-Ville and the St. Lawrence River ABOVE.

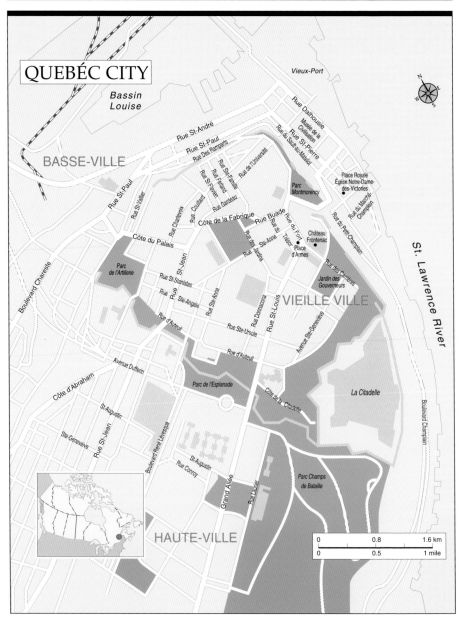

QUEBÉC CITY

Bassin
Louise

Vieux-Port

BASSE-VILLE

Rue St-André
Rue St-Paul
Rue Des Ramparts

Rue Dalhousie
Musée de la Civilisation
Rue St-Pierre
Rue du Sauw-au-Matelot

Rue St-Paul
Rue St-Vallier
Rue St-Flavien
Rue Ste-Famille
Rue de l'Université
Rue St-Paul
Rue Charlevoix
Rue Couillard
Rue Gardeau

Place Royale
Église Notre-Dame-
des-Victories

Rue du Petit-Champlain
Rue du Marché-
Champlain

Parc
Montmorency

Côte de la Fabrique
Rue Buade
Rue du Fort
Côte du Palais
Rue des Jacquis
Place
d'Armes
Château
Frontenac

Parc
de l'Artillerie
Rue St-Jean
Rue St-Stanislas
Rue Ste-Anne
Rue Ste-Angele
Rue Ste-Anne
Rue d'Auteuil
Rue Ste-Ursule
Rue St-Louis
Rue Donacona
Avenue Ste-Geneviève

Jardin des
Gouverneurs

VIEILLE VILLE

Rue des Carrières

St. Lawrence River

Rue d'Auteuil

Avenue Dufferin

Côte d'Abraham
St-Augustin
Ste-Geneveive
Rue St-Jean
Boulevard René Lévesque
Boulevard Charest
St-Augustin
Rue Conroy
Grand Allée

Parc de l'Esplanade

Côte de la Citadelle

La Citadelle

Boulevard Champlain

Parc Champs
de Bataille

HAUTE-VILLE

0		0.8		1.6 km
0		0.5		1 mile

whole area has been carefully restored, and in the square some of the beautiful steep-roofed buildings house museums, art galleries, restaurants and shops, making it once again the lively center of Basse-Ville.

On the south side of Place Royale stands **Église Notre-Dame-des-Victoires**. This little church was built in 1688 and extensively restored after the bombardment of 1759. It has some interesting features such as the fort-shaped altar and a wooden model of a boat hanging from the ceiling. These furnishings were brought here by the early settlers, as offerings to ensure safe voyages. Various activities are staged in the **Centre d'interprétation de Place-Royale** ((418) 646-3167 WEB SITE www.mcq.org, 27 place Royale.

Just north of Place Royale, in the Vieux-Port area, stands the excellent **Musée de la Civilisation** ((418) 643-2158 WEB SITE www.mcq.org, 85 rue Dalhousie, an interesting modern building designed to integrate with the surrounding architecture. It has some lively multimedia exhibitions, and a particularly good exhibition on Québec's history and society.

If you wander by the water's edge, you'll find **Le Vieux-Port**, a redevelopment of the old port area, with parks, restaurants and cafés — and in the summer months, boat tours, exhibitions and free open-air entertainment of all kinds and for all ages. The days when it functioned as one of the world's great ports are recalled in the **Centre d'interprétation du Vieux-Port (** (418) 648-3300 TOLL-FREE (800) 463-6769, 100 rue St-André (at Rioux), where Parks Canada offers a range of films, exhibits and demonstrations on shipbuilding and the lumber trade (May to November; by appointment the rest of the year). At the northwestern tip of the port is the **Marché du Vieux-Port**, where farmers sell their fresh produce daily year-round.

At the end of the Rue du Trésor, turn left onto Rue Buade, and at the corner of Côte de la Fabrique you'll find the **Basilique-Cathédrale Notre-Dame (** (418) 694-0665 WEB SITE www.patrimoine-religieux.com. This somber, gray stone cathedral has an ornate interior and some interesting paintings. The basilica was destroyed during the British invasion in 1759, subsequently rebuilt only to be destroyed by fire in 1922, following which it was rebuilt using the original 1647 plans. One of its unique features is the fabulous golden umbrella-like *baldaquin* (altar canopy). To the right of the nave is the tomb of François Xavier de Laval, Canada's first bishop. The map over Laval's sepulcher shows the outlines of the origi-

Further west is the **antique shop district** along Rue St-Paul: another reclaimed urban area whose cafés and galleries have made it one of the city's most fashionable spots.

Haute-Ville

Situated in the heart of Haute-Ville, the **Place d'Armes** is a good base for a walking tour. The square, and indeed the city, is dominated by the imposing Château Frontenac (see below).

On the far side of the square, look for the awning-covered **Rue du Trésor**, so named because the royal treasury once stood here. During the summer months the tiny alley is jammed with artists of varying talent displaying works and sketching visitors' portraits. Just off this little street is the entrance to Les Promenades de Vieux-Québec, an indoor retail area with shops and a 3D show entitled **"The Québec Experience" (** (418) 694-4000.

nal diocese of Québec, which stretched from Newfoundland to Louisiana. Most of the governors of New France are buried in the crypt: Samuel de Champlain may or may not be among them. A rather alarmingly colorful 30-minute sound-and-light show, **Feux Sacrés** (Heavenly Lights) (** (418) 694-4000 WEB SITE www.quebec experience.com, plays hourly May to October.

To the left of the basilica, the **Seminary**, 2 côte de la Fabrique, was founded in 1663 by Québec's first bishop, François Xavier de Laval, and developed into the Université Laval. It has a beautiful and tranquil inner courtyard and the main chapel is notable for its relics and the beautifully crafted tomb of Laval. Today it has become the home of the **Musée de l'Amerique Française (** (418) 692-

LEFT: Rue du Trésor, a miniature Montmartre.
RIGHT: Cobblestones and copper roofs —
a typical old Québec street scene.

2843 WEB SITE ww.mcq.org, with exhibits about the history and lifestyle of the French-speaking peoples of Canada.

Nearby the l'Hôtel-Dieu houses the **Musée des Augustines (** (418) 692-2492, 32 rue Charlevoix, dedicated to the Augustine nuns who founded it — the first hospital in North America — in 1639. It houses a collection of medical instruments, religious paintings and objets d'art. Just along the Rue des Jardins is the **Holy Trinity Anglican Cathedral (** (418) 692-2193, a fine building in the English baroque style. Built in 1804, it was the first Anglican cathedral built outside the United Kingdom, and contains many gifts presented by King George III (Mad King George).

Moving back south and still on a religious note, the **Couvent des Ursulines**, 12 rue Donnacona, was founded in 1693, and is the oldest girls' school in North America. The **Musée des Ursulines (** (418) 694-0694 WEB SITE www.museocapitale.qc.ca/014.htm lies within the convent walls. Displays show how the nuns lived under French rule. The **Chapelle des Ursulines** contains some interesting relics, and the Marquis de Montcalm is buried here — at least in part: his skull is in the museum.

Rue St-Louis is one of the city's main shopping streets, leading back up to Place d'Armes. The **Musée d'art Inuit Brousseau (** (418) 694-1828, at No. 39, is a wonderful private collection of over 450 Inuit sculptures, owned by the people who run the Inuit art shop next door. It's well worth looking, even if you can't afford to buy.

Back on the square, **Château Frontenac** (see WHERE TO STAY, page 125) is an enormous red-brick

structure with a profusion of towers, turrets and parapets that give it the air of a medieval castle. Built by Canadian Pacific as a railway hotel in the late nineteenth-century on the site of Château St-Louis, the residence of the governors of New France, it takes its name from a former governor, the Comte de Frontenac. Guided tours depart from the lobby.

Behind Château Frontenac you'll find the **Terrasse Dufferin**, a wide boardwalk stretching south, offering wonderful views of Basse-Ville, the St. Lawrence and the opposite shore. There are a couple of cafés, and in winter it has an open-air skating rink and toboggan run. At the far end is the **Jardin des Gouverneurs**, once the garden of the Château St-Louis. At the center of this little park stands a monument that pays tribute to both General Wolfe and the Marquis de Montcalm. In summer there's often some kind of entertainment to be found here. Beyond the garden, the **Promenade des Gouverneurs** is a stairway and boardwalk clinging to the edge of the cliff, leading you by La Citadelle and on to the Plains of Abraham. Running along the south side of the garden, the **Avenue Ste-Geneviève** is lined with European-style inns, behind which is hidden the lovely little **Parc du Cavalier du Moulin** with its vestiges of the seventeenth-century French fortifications.

The Fortifications

The Fortifications de Québec ((418) 648-7016 TOLL-FREE (800) 463-6769 WEB SITE www.parkscanada.risq.gc.ca/fortifications, 100 rue St-Louis, warrant a tour to themselves. Built mainly by the British to protect the city from American attack, the 4.6-km (2.9-mile) city wall encircles the old town and has four *portes*, or gates. Guided tours (90 minutes) leave from the Frontenac kiosk on Terrasse Dufferin.

Standing at the south end near Porte St-Louis is **La Citadelle (** (418) 694-2815, the large star-shaped fortress that looms high over the banks of the St. Lawrence. Based on designs by the great French military architect Vauban, it was constructed (1820–50) at great expense and is now occupied by the Royal 22nd Regiment, the only French-speaking regiment in the Canadian army, and its museum. You can watch the Changing of the Guard and Beating of the Retreat ceremonies during the summer. Near Porte St-Louis, the **Poudrière de l'Esplanade** (Powder Magazine), 100 rue St-Louis, now holds an interpretation center explaining the development of the fortifications.

Inside Porte St-Jean is the **Parc de l'Artillerie (** (418) 648-4205 TOLL-FREE (800) 463-6769, 2 rue d'Auteuil, a complex of buildings dating from the early eighteenth century, including the impressive Dauphine Redoubt, the Officers' Quarters, barracks and an old iron foundry. There's an interpretation center that offers guided tours with costumed interpreters. Throughout July and August there are daily musket demonstrations (phone for the schedule). Also in the grounds, **Les Dames de Soie Doll Museum** ((418) 692-1516 is one for the children — a charming doll workshop and museum.

Outside the Walls

West of the fortress is the 100-hectare (250-acre) **Parc des Champs-de-Bataille (National Battlefields Park)**, far better known as the Plains of Abraham. It was on this now pleasant green area, sprinkled with gardens and monuments and offering impressive views of the St. Lawrence, that the bloody battle of 1759 was fought. Two early

WEB SITE www.mdq.org occupies two buildings — a neoclassical structure and a former jailhouse — linked by a tall glass-roofed atrium. The museum houses North America's largest collection of Québécois art, in eight galleries containing works from the colonial era to the present. The jailhouse is a newish addition (one cellblock has been left intact as an exhibit). This building's four galleries host temporary shows, and the tower contains a David Moore sculpture called *Le Plongeur*.

From here, head back in the direction of the Old City towards the **Grande Allée**, the wide avenue that is alive with cafés, bars and restaurants, and at the north side near the corner of Avenue Dufferin you'll come to the **Hôtel du**

nineteenth-century Martello towers have displays on the battles waged here. The canons peering threateningly over the cliff have nothing to do with the battle or any previous city defenses, but were a private collection placed here because they looked good. Today the park is a popular destination for locals, with hiking trails and cross-country skiing in winter. The reception center, **Maison de la Decouverte** ((418) 648-4071 WEB SITE www.ccbn-nbc.gc.cq, 835 avenue Wilfred-Laurier, has a number of entertaining hi-tech presentations about the park and the history of French Canada, and offers guided walking and bus tours in summer; call for details. There are free summer concerts at the **Kiosque Edwin-Bélanger**, while the park is one of the main sites of the Winter Carnival (see CARNAVAL DE QUÉBEC, below).

At the south end of the park, the **Musée du Québec** ((418) 643-2150 TOLL-FREE (866) 220-2150

Parlement (National Assembly) ((418) 643-7239, a stately Renaissance-style building built between 1877 and 1886, and home of the provincial government. There are free guided tours of some of the most splendid rooms.

A couple of streets away, Rue St-Jean has become one of the trendiest in the city, with a delightful mix of restaurants, cafés and clubs that keep buzzing year-round. For sheer self-indulgence, stop off at the **Choco-Musée de la chocolaterie Erico** ((418) 524-2122, 634 rue St-Jean, where you can learn about the history of chocolate, watch it being made and, of course, enjoy the tasty results.

OPPOSITE: Why the sign? Imagine Québec under more than a meter of snow. Restaurants such asAux Anciens Canadiens ABOVE offer warm welcome and ancestral Québec cuisine.

Festive Québec

In early July, the town is busy with the annual **Festival d'Été de Québec** (Quebec Summer Festival) ((418) 529-5200 WEB SITE www.infofestival.com. It's a cultural celebration with concerts, theater, folk music, jazz and dancing. Book your accommodation in advance. In the last week of July and the first week of August, there are Wednesday and Saturday **firework displays** in Parc de la Chute-Montmorency TOLL-FREE (800) 923-3389 WEB SITE www.lesgransfeux.com. This is followed in August by the **Fêtes de la Nouvelle-France** ((418) 694-3311 WEB SITE www.nouvellefrance.qc.ca, a celebration of the French rule of Canada, and the **International Festival of Military**

gardens. The **Villa Bagatelle** ((418) 688-8074, 1563 chemin Saint-Louis, is a fine Victorian house that serves as a local art gallery and interpretation center for the local gardens (March to December). It also has its own particularly fine English gardens. **Parc Bois-de-Coulonge** ((418) 528-0773, 1215 chemin Saint-Louis, was a nineteenth-century botanical garden and became the residence of the governor-general for nearly a century, until the house burned down in 1966. The official residence of the Government of Québec, **Domaine Cataraqui** ((418) 681-3010, 2141, chemin Saint-Louis, was built in 1850 (March to mid-December). It has a garden museum, a series of exhibition halls incorporating

Bands ((418) 694-5757 WEB SITE www.fimmq.com/anglais/accueil/centre.html.

The **Carnaval de Québec** ((418) 626-3716 WEB SITE www.carnaval.qc.ca is an altogether more rambunctious affair. This 17-day celebration is held over three weekends in late January and early February, and it's when Québec really lets its hair down, the festivities overseen by a two-meter (seven-foot) snowman. Activities center around ice and snow sculptures. There are concerts, dances, parades, skiing, ice-skating and a plentiful supply of *caribou*, the local mixture of alcohol, wine and maple syrup that tastes something like a strong port. Book accommodation well in advance as this is a big event and the city is glazed with revelers.

Excursions from Québec City

In **Sillery**, 35 km (20 miles) from the city center, there are several wonderful old mansions and

a history of the property, and a variety of touring exhibitions, and there is a program of outdoor concerts through summer.

The last and possibly finest of the local gardens is in nearby Sainte-Foy. **Jardin Roger-Van Den Hende** ((418) 656-3410, Pavillon Envirotron, 2480 boulevard Hochelaga, displays more than 2,100 species (May to September).

A short distance east of Québec City lies **Île d'Orléans**, a rural oasis and a popular Québécois vacation spot. The island's winter population of approximately 6,000 doubles during summer, but it's still a tranquil escape from the city, with several charming small villages, one traffic light — at last count — and no movie theaters. The largest

OPPOSITE: Seen here from the Breakneck Stairway, Rue Petit-Champlain is the oldest street in the city. ABOVE: A footbridge crosses the falls at Parc de la Chute Montmorency, northeast of the city.

inn has 16 rooms and there are a couple of dozen bed and breakfasts.

Just beyond the bridge to Île d'Orléans is **Parc de la Chute-Montmorency** ((418) 663-3330 WEB SITE www.chutemontmorency.qc.ca, with its impressive 83-m (272-ft) falls — one and a half times the height of Niagara, although much narrower. A cable car will take you to the top, where you can cross over the falls on a suspension bridge. Pack a picnic or have a delightful gourmet lunch at **Manoir Montmorency** ((418) 663-3330. Québécois cuisine is featured and there are fine views of the St. Lawrence River, Île d'Orléans and the falls. The park is a 10-minute drive from downtown Québec.

North of Québec City is the Huron village of Wendake and **Jacques Cartier Park** ((418) 848-3169 WEB SITE www.sepaq.com, where activities include hiking, mountain biking, rock climbing and canoeing. **Réserve Faunique des Laurentides** ((418) 846-2112 WEB SITE www.sepaq.com is an 8,000-sq-km (3,088-sq-mile) wildlife reserve that has black bear and moose among its inhabitants.

SPORTS AND OUTDOOR ACTIVITIES

The Plains of Abraham ((418) 648-4071 is a good place for **jogging** and **bicycling**. There are 1.3 km (just under a mile) of **in-line skating** paths, with equipment rental available.

A little farther along lies the **Basilique Ste-Anne-de-Beaupré** ((418) 827-3781, 10018 avenue Royale, Sainte-Anne-de-Beaupré. This impressive medieval-style church was constructed in the 1920s and dedicated to Saint Anne as the patron saint of Québec. Pilgrim processions also take in Saint Anne's Museum and the huge panoramic painting, the Cyclorama de Jérusalem, and the Way of the Cross, lined with life-size bronze figures created in France between 1913 and 1946.

From here you can easily reach **Mont Ste-Anne**, renowned for its world-class skiing and year-round outdoor activities (see below), and the **Cap Tourmente National Wildlife Area** ((418) 827-4591, chemin du Cap-Tourmente, Saint-Jaochim a wonderful area for bird-watching, visited by hundreds of thousands of snow geese in migration season (late-September to mid-October). Guided tours are available.

The **ice-skating** season runs roughly from December until March. You can join the throngs in the Parc de l'Esplanade or Place de Ville. North of the city in St-Gabriel-de-Valcartier, at the **Village Vacances Valcartier** ((418) 844-2200 WEB SITE www.valcartier.com, 1860 boulevard Valcartier, there is a waterpark with rides, slides and a wave pool, horseback riding, and white-water rafting, while in winter you can skate through the woods or go **tobogganing**; there's also nighttime skating here. If you're a **skiing** enthusiast, the Plains of Abraham has cross-country skiing trails, as do many of the nearby parks. Call Regroupement des stations de ski de fond ((418) 653-5875 for further information. Visitors can enjoy **dog-sledding** in winter in the Parc de la Jacques-Cartier ((418) 848-3732 WEB SITE www.traineaux-chiens.qc.ca, 7600 Route 175 North, Stoneham, 20 minutes' drive north of the city.

Nearby, **Station Ecotouristique Duchesnay** ((418) 875-2122 TOLL-FREE (877) 511-5885 WEB SITE www.sepac.com, 143 route Duchesnay, Ste-Catherine-de-la-Jacques-Cartier, on Lake St-Joseph, offers a enormous array of winter and summer outdoor pursuits, including walking, fishing, canoeing, kayaking, cross-country skiing, dog-sledding and skating. It also has a lodge and in winter an ice hotel (see below). **Mont Ste-Anne** ((418) 827-4561 TOLL-FREE (418) 463 1568 WEB SITE www.mont-sainte-anne.com is northeast of Québec City along Route 360, with 56 downhill trails, 14 lifts and over 200 km (125 miles) of cross-country trails. Nearby Stoneham ((418) 848-2411 TOLL-FREE (800) 463-6888 WEB SITE www.ski-stoneham.com has 30 runs. Both are accessible by car or by the Winter Shuttle ((418) 525-4953 or (413) 525-5191, a taxi service that runs between major hotels in Vieux-Québec, the nearby suburb of Ste-Foy, and the ski stations. A little further away, **Le Massif** ((418) 632-5876 WEB SITE www.lemassif.com, Charlevoix, has 20 runs and the highest vertical drop east of the Rockies, at 770 m (2,526 ft).

If you want to go **fishing**, Québec authorities insist you have a permit. Most sports shops can provide one. Contact the Ministry of Wildlife and Environment ((418) 643-3127, 150 boulevard René-Lévesque est, for its pamphlet on fishing regulations, or pick one up at a tourist information office. Armed with the rules and your permit you can then go north to the lakes of the Réserve faunique des Laurentides ((418) 528 6868, about 50 km (30 miles) from the city via Route 73.

NIGHTLIFE AND THE ARTS

There's plenty to do in Québec City at night, mostly in or just outside the Old City. For events listings in English, check the *Québec Chronicle-Telegraph*, which comes out each Wednesday. The French-language daily *Le Soleil* lists events in their "Où Aller à Québec" section ("Where to Go in Québec"). *Voir* is a free, French-language weekly with arts events and reviews; it appears every Thursday. Finally, *Québec Scope* is a free, bilingual monthly listing events of all kinds.

You can purchase tickets for most shows at **Billetech**, Grand Théâtre de Québec ((418) 643-8131, 269 boulevard René-Lévesque est. Theater productions are all in French. At the **Grand Théâtre de Québec** ((418) 643-8131, 269 boulevard René-Lévesque est, classic and new plays are performed by the Théâtre du Trident. For cabaret and comedy in a casual café atmosphere go to **Maison de la Chanson** ((418) 692-2631, 78 rue Petit-Champlain. **L'Orchestre symphonique de Québec** ((418) 643-8131 plays at the Grand Théâtre de Québec.

Nightclubbing centers on the bars of Rue St-Jean. There are several good places for live rock music within the walls. **Restaurant Carthage** at No. 395 has belly dancing on Friday and Saturday nights, and good moderately priced Middle Eastern food.

The **Grande Allée** also has some lively bars and clubs that tend to attract a slightly younger crowd. Québec's jazz Mecca is the **Café Bar L'Emprise** ((418) 692-2480 in the Hôtel Clarendon, 57 rue Ste-Anne. The **Imax Cinema** ((418) 627-4629 (information) or (418) 627-4688 (tickets), at 5401 boulevard des Galeries, has the largest screen in Canada.

WHERE TO STAY

During Carnaval in February and in high summer hotels get booked up, so it's essential to book well in advance.

Expensive

Fairmont Le Château Frontenac ((418) 692-3861 TOLL-FREE (800) 441-1414 FAX (418) 692-1751 WEB SITE www.fairmont.com, 1 rue des Carrières, may no longer be the ultra-luxury hotel that it was in its heyday, but there's still an air of romance about staying in the most famous — and obvious — landmark in Québec City. Situated on Terrasse Dufferin, right by the Place d'Armes, its location could not be better. There's a huge ballroom, an indoor pool, a piano bar, a café, shops, a very good restaurant called Le Champlain, and an air of decaying splendor. The 618 units vary widely in size and location, but most have splendid views of the St. Lawrence and the Old City.

At Place d'Youville, just outside Porte St-Jean, **l'Hôtel du Capitole** ((418) 694-4040 TOLL-FREE (800) 363-4040 FAX (418) 694-1916 WEB SITE www.lecapitole.com, 972 rue St-Jean, is a dramatically postmodern 1992 renovation of the beautiful beaux arts-style theater building. The 40 rooms look out on the three-story atrium-lobby with its cascades of flowers and potted palms. Rooms and miniature suites are equipped with eiderdown quilts, whirlpools and compact disc players. The complex includes the gorgeously restored Théâtre Capitole and an Italian restaurant.

Outside the walls, the contemporary **Hôtel Radisson Québec** ((418) 647-1717 TOLL-FREE (888) 884-7777 FAX (418) 647-2146 WEB SITE www.radisson.com/quebeccityca, 690 boulevard René-Lévesque est, is a high-rise hotel which faces the Parliament buildings and has 377 rooms, an outdoor pool and a restaurant. The poured-concrete interior is less than inspirational, but the rooms are very spacious and the location is convenient. Nearby, at

Playbills announce the latest offerings at Palais Montcalm.

the **Hilton Québec** ((418) 647-2411 TOLL-FREE (800) 447-2411 FAX (418) 647-2986 WEB SITE www.hilton .com, 1100 boulevard René-Lévesque est, you'll find service that cannot be bettered. The rooms are spacious, the decor is modern, and the facilities are typically Hiltonesque. It has a bar and restaurant, and a heated outdoor pool in summer. For a superb view of the Old City, make sure you get a room on one of the upper floors.

Overlooking the Parc des Champs-de-Bataille, the **Hôtel Loews Le Concorde** ((418) 647-2222 TOLL-FREE (800) 463-5256 FAX (418) 647-4710 WEB SITE www.loewshotels.com/leconcor.html, 1225 Cours du Général-De Montcalm, is a pleasant walk from the heart of the city and ideally placed for the cafés and nightlife of Grande Allée. Among the luxury facilities there's an outdoor pool, VIP floors, a café terrace, a dance club and, perched on top of this soaring concrete tower, a revolving restaurant.

Hotel Dominion 12 ((418) 692-2224 FAX (418) 692-4403 WEB SITE www.hoteldominion.com, 126 rue St-Pierre, is totally different from everything else in town: a chic, ultra-modern boutique hotel in a renovated Basse-Ville office block, said to be the city's first tower block (nine stories high). There are 60 rooms that combine elegance, luxury and the necessities of modern business, along with fine views of the St. Lawrence Seaway.

For obvious reasons, the **Ice Hotel** ((418) 875-4522 TOLL-FREE (877) 505-0423 FAX (418) 875-2833 WEB SITE www.icehotel-canada.com, in the grounds of Station Ecotouristique Duchesnay, 143 route Duchesnay, Ste-Catherine-de-la-Jacques-Cartier, is only open a few months a year. Each year, it melts away and has to be rebuilt from scratch. This is an experience for the hardy, with literally everything from the beds to the bars, glasses and chandeliers carved from ice (there are furs on the beds to block the cold, at least partially). Those who want to have a look but still have their creature comforts can stay at the lodge of the Station Ecotouristique Duchesnay (see SPORTS AND OUTDOOR ACTIVITIES, above).

Mid-range

In the Upper Town, **Hôtel Clarendon** ((418) 692-2480 TOLL-FREE (888) 554-6001 FAX (418) 692-4652 WEB SITE www.familledefour.com, 57 rue Ste-Anne, is in itself a landmark. It's the city's oldest hotel, with a wonderful art deco interior and loads of character. It has 143 rooms, and boasts an excellent jazz bar, a cocktail lounge, and an atmospheric French restaurant. Further along the road, the **Hôtellerie Fleur de Lys** ((418) 694-0106 TOLL-FREE (800) 567-2106 FAX (418) 692-1959 WEB SITE www .hotelfleurlys.com, 115 rue Ste-Anne, is a bit of a surprise as it's a modern hotel in the heart of the Old City. Service is very good here, and there are 40 well-equipped and smartly decorated rooms, some with kitchenettes.

Hôtel Le Château de Pierre ((418) 694-0429 FAX (418) 694-0153, 17 avenue Ste-Geneviève, is a charming Victorian mansion, elegantly decorated throughout. Its 16 rooms have a genteel look but modern conveniences. The **Hôtel Manoir Ste-Geneviève** ((418) 694-1666 TOLL-FREE (877) 694-1666 FAX (418) 694-1666 WEB SITE www.quebecweb .com/msg, 13 avenue Ste-Geneviève, overlooks the Jardin des Gouverneurs. This early nineteenth-century building is filled with old English country furniture, creating a cozy and comfortable atmosphere. It offers nine accommodations, all air-conditioned and with television; some have kitchenettes.

Outside the city walls, **Hôtel Château Laurier** ((418) 522-8108 TOLL-FREE (800) 463-4453 FAX (418)

524-8768 WEB SITE www.vieux-quebec.com/laurier, 1220 place George V ouest, offers 154 well-equipped rooms, and the restaurants and nightlife of the Grande Allée are on the doorstep.

Inexpensive

Many small family-run hotels and guesthouses can be found on Rue St-Louis in the heart of the walled city, including the nineteenth-century **Auberge St-Louis** ((418) 692-2424 TOLL-FREE (888) 692-4105 FAX (418) 692-3797, at 48 rue St-Louis, which offers 27 very pleasant rooms and very good value; rates include breakfast. At the Victorian **Hôtel Le Clos St-Louis** ((418) 694-1311 TOLL-FREE (800) 461-1311 FAX (418) 694-9411 WEB SITE www.clossaintlouis.com, 69 rue St-Louis, rooms are clean and neat and the landlady is a real character. A good choice of similar accommodation can be found along peaceful rue Ste-Ursule: **Hôtel**

La Maison Demers ((418) 692-2487 TOLL-FREE (800) 692-2487 TOLL-FREE IN FRANCE (0800) 903187 FAX (418) 692-5009, 68 rue Ste-Ursule, offers eight cozy rooms; the **Hôtel Maison Ste-Ursule** ((418) 694-9794 FAX (418) 694-0875, 40 rue Ste-Ursule, has 15 rooms, most with private bathrooms.

Québec has plenty of options for backpacking travelers. The **Auberge de Jeunesse** (a member of Hostelling International) ((418) 694-0755 FAX (418) 694-2278 WEB SITE www.cisq.org, 19 rue Ste-Ursule, is housed in a former Ursuline girls' residence. The tidy dorm-style rooms sleep four to six and it has a billiards room and a picnic area. There is also the **Auberge de la Paix** ((418) 694-0735, 31 rue Couillard.

parts to this restaurant, of which the finest and most formal is **La Grande Table**. The last few years have brought on a clutch of other contenders for the city's best food, however, starting with **Le Champlain** ((418) 692-3861, at the Château Frontenac, where chef Jean Soulard creates culinary masterpieces from local ingredients including herbs grown on the château's roof. **Laurie Raphaël** ((418) 692-4555, 117 rue Dalhousie, is one of the hottest tickets in town, with a celebrated chef who serves contemporary Québécois food in a relaxed, friendly restaurant, with a patio for summer.

Situated in one of the city's seventeenth-century buildings, **Aux Anciens Canadiens** ((418) 692-1627, 34 rue St-Louis, serves a mix of ancestral Québec

The university offers **campus accommodation** from May 1 to August 22. For details contact Le Service des résidences de l'Université Laval ((418) 656-5632 FAX (418) 656-2335 WEB SITE www .ulaval.ca/sres, Pavillon Alphonse-Marie-Parent, bureau 1618, Cité Universitaire, Ste-Foy, Québec G1K 7P4.

Finally, there's also the **YWCA de Québec** ((418) 683-2155 FAX (418) 683-5526, 855 avenue Holland, which takes both sexes, with 15 rooms for single or double occupancy and an indoor pool.

WHERE TO EAT

Expensive

À la Table de Serge Bruyère ((418) 694-0618, 1200 rue St-Jean, is the city's most famous restaurant, serving French and Alsatian cuisine in an elegant nineteenth-century building. There are several

and nouvelle cuisine, from pea soup, *creton* and *tourtière* to sweet-and-sour duckling with maple syrup. The building is filled with period antiques, which gives it the look of an early settler's house.

French haute cuisine is at **Le St-Amour** ((418) 694-0667, 48 rue Ste-Ursule, an attractive restaurant with a warm and informal atmosphere and a retractable roof for summer evenings. Rabbit is always a good choice here, and the chocolate desserts are famous. **Au Parmesan** ((418) 692-0341, 38 rue St-Louis, offers fine Italian dining to the accompaniment, nightly, of an accordionist or singer. There's free parking with valet service here. **Louis Herbert** ((418) 525-6294, 668 Grande Allée, is a charming setting with a small cozy dining room

OPPOSITE: Chef Marie-Chantal Le Page presents excellent Québécois cuisine at Manoir Montmorency. ABOVE: Dining at the landmark Château Frontenac runs from casual to chic.

backed by a larger conservatory. It has become a popular lunch spot for locals, with friendly service and excellent international food.

Seafood Italian-style is the specialty at **Gambrinus (** (418) 692-5144, 15 rue du Fort (opposite the Château Frontenac). This cozy restaurant also serves meat dishes, but the pastas with seafood sauce are splendid. There is a singer-guitarist in the evenings. Probably the best seafood dishes are to be found at **Le Marie-Clarisse (** (418) 692-0857, situated in the Lower Town at 12 rue du Petit-Champlain (near the funicular). The fish is cooked to perfection and with great flair, but committed carnivores are also well catered to.

Moderate to Inexpensive

Serge Bruyère (see above) also houses the upper-floor **Chez Livernois**, a bistro with great views of the street and decor based on the lives of the photographer brothers who once worked here. The **Café du Monde (** (418) 692-4455, 57 rue Dalhousie, is a pleasantly relaxed bistro with good food, an excellent range of imported wines, hilarious waiters and piano music — ideal for a fun night out.

No prizes for guessing the cuisine at the **Café Suisse (** (418) 694-1320, 32 rue Ste-Anne. The extensive menu offers some particularly good fondues and raclettes, and with its sidewalk terrace and exceptionally late opening hours, it's become a favorite of the local arts crowd. **Le Parlementaire (** (418) 643 6640, in the Houses of Parliament, is sadly only open at lunchtime, as it is an excellent and relatively inexpensive restaurant, serving different Québécois regional cuisine amid a glorious beaux-arts decor. With its consignment shops, used-book stores, coffee shops and galleries, the St-Jean-Baptiste neighborhood along Rue St-Jean (outside the walls) is a good place to seek out inexpensive eats. **Au Petit Coin Breton (** (418) 694-0758, 1029 rue St-Jean, offers an almost overwhelmingly Breton experience, from crêpes and onion soup to waitresses in lacey collars, but it is fun and you can get a light meal. For reliably good Italian fare try **La Petite Italie (** (418) 694-0044, 491-2 rue St-Louis. **Sainte-Pub Alexandre (** (418) 694-0015, 1087 rue St-Jean, has 200 imported and local beers to nurse along with steak and fries.

HOW TO GET THERE

Although Jean Lesage International Airport, 15 km (9 miles) from the city center (about 20 minutes' drive), is served by many major airlines, most airborne visitors to the city come via Montréal or Toronto. The **airport shuttle**, La Québécoise (** (418) 872-5525, stops at various hotels in Haute-Ville and Vieille-Ville.

VIA Rail ((418) 692-3940 TOLL-FREE (888) 842-7245 WEB SITE www.viarail.ca has five daily trains to Québec City from Montréal and three daily from Toronto, arriving at the Gare du Palais, Basse-Ville. Coming from the Atlantic provinces, trains arrive at the Gare de Charny, Lévis, across the St. Lawrence, from where there is a regular ferry to Québec.

Les Dauphins de Saint-Laurent ((514) 288-4479 TOLL-FREE (877) 648-4499 WEB SITE www.dauphins.ca, operate hydrofoil ferries along the St. Lawrence Seaway between Montréal and Québec City.

If you are driving from the Maritime Provinces you will want to take the TransCanada Highway. From Montréal either the TransCanada Highway (Route 20) or Route 40 will take you to Québec City.

From the Atlantic coast of the United States (except Maine) the best route is up Interstate 91, which goes through Vermont becoming Route 55 when it crosses the border, joining the TransCanada Highway at Drummondville, 155 km (96 miles) southwest of Québec City. Those coming from New York will enter Canada via Interstate 87.

MONTRÉAL

Montréal has a lot in common with Manhattan: it is an island, it was once occupied by Native Americans, it is a major port, it is the most cosmopolitan and "European" city in the nation, it has hosted a memorable World's Fair, it has the

LEFT: Designed by Buckminster Fuller, Montréal's Biosphere explains the ecosystems of the St. Lawrence River and the Great Lakes. ABOVE: View from the tower of Notre-Dame-de-Bonsecours.

MONTRÉAL

ST LÉONARD

Rue Jeunesse
Rue Berri
Boulevard St-Michel
Rue Jarry
Lacordaire
Rue Beaubien
Boulevard Langelier
Rue Sherbrooke

Rue Jarry

Parc Jarry

MONT ROYAL

Rue Jean-Talon

Avenue Papineau
Rue d'Iberville
Rue St-Denis
Boulevard St-Laurent
Avenue du Parc

Rue Jean-Talon

Boulevard Rosemont

Boulevard St-Joseph

Olympic Park

Boulevard Pie IX
Boulevard Viau
Rue de Cadillac
Rue Dickson

Avenue Van Horne
Chemin de la Côte - Ste - Catherine

OUTREMONT

Chemin Queen Mary

Parc Lafontaine

Rue Sherbrooke

Rue Notre-Dame

St Lawrence River

Parc Hélène Champlain

LONGUEUIL

Rue Joliette

Parc Mont Royal
McGill University

Rue Sherbrooke
Rue Peel
Rue McGill
Rue Crescent

VIEUX MONTRÉAL
(see map below)

Île Ste. Hélène

WESTPOINT

Rue Notre-Dame

Autoroute Décarie
Avenue Victoria
Rue Atwater

Île Notre Dame

Rue St.Jacques

LA SALLE

Rue Wellington

VERDUN

Nuns Island

1.6km
1 mile

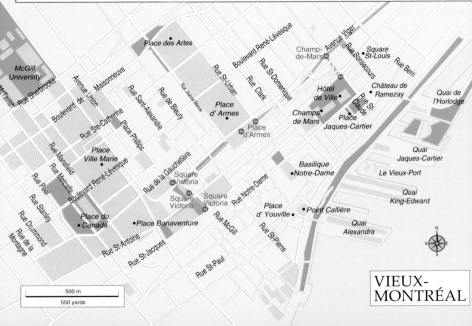

McGill University
Rue McTavish
Rue Sherbrooke

Place des Artes

Boulevard René-Lévesque
Rue St-Domenique

Champ-de-Mars
Square St-Louis
Rue Berri
Square Berri

Avenue Viger

Avenue de Maisonneuve
Avenue Union
Rue Saint-Alexandre
Rue de Bleury
Rue Jeanne Mance
Rue St-Urban
Rue Clark

Hôtel de Ville
Château de Ramezay

Quai de l'Horloge

Boulevard de Maisonneuve

Rue Ste-Catherine
Place Phillips

Place d'Armes

Champs de Mars
Place Jaques-Cartier
Rue St-Claude

Quai Jaques-Cartier

Rue Mansfield
Rue Metcalfe
Boulevard René-Lévesque

Place Ville Marie

Place d'Armes

Le Vieux-Port

Rue Peel
Rue Stanley
Rue Drummond
Rue de la Montagne

Place du Canada

Rue de la Gauchetière
Square Victoria
Square Victoria

Rue Notre-Dame

Basilique Notre-Dame

Quai King-Edward

Place Bonaventure

Rue McGill

Place d'Youville
Point Callière

Rue St-Antoine
Rue St-Jacques
Rue St-Pierre
Rue St-Paul

Quai Alexandra

Quai Alexandra

500 m
550 yards

VIEUX-MONTRÉAL

largest Jewish population in the country, it is noted for its excellent restaurants and exciting nightlife, it is home to more than 130 different ethnic groups, and it has a National League baseball team which is the annual source of much hope and much suffering among its devoted fans.

But this train of thought will take you only so far, after which point the landscape becomes notable — and illuminating — for the differences between the two places. Unlike Manhattan, Montréal is a large island (51 km or 32 miles long, and at its widest, 16 km or 10 miles across). It is a thousand miles from the ocean, it has a extensive and safe *métro* (subway) system, and the overwhelming majority of its three and a half million citi-

tions continued with the 1976 summer Olympics. This city of nearly 3.5 million people is efficiently modern without having sacrificed any of its Gallic zest for life.

BACKGROUND

Whereas Montréal's name apparently dates from 1535, when Jacques Cartier is said to have described the island's volcanic rock peak as "un mont réal" ("a royal mountain"), the city's foundation dates from 1611, when Samuel de Champlain established a fortified trading post on the island. Some 31 years later, in 1642, Paul de Chomeday, Sieur de Maisonneuve, arrived with

zens speak French as a first language. Indeed, it is the second largest French-speaking city in the world. And there is also a certain *je ne sais quoi* — let's call it *joie de vivre* — that clearly distinguishes Montréal from Manhattan, or from almost any other urban center you can think of. This is a city whose major festivals are devoted to food, jazz and comedy.

Built around a mound of volcanic rock (Mont-Royal, known locally simply as "the mountain"), Montréal stands as a living monument to the happy coexistence of two principal languages, two cultures, two traditions, two school systems (one French, one English), and even two eras: that of New France, which celebrates the past by preserving its landmarks, and that of the new Québec, which began celebrating the present and future with Expo '67, the World's Fair that brought more than 50 million visitors to the city. Such celebra-

53 Frenchmen and founded a permanent settlement named Ville-Marie on the site of what is now known as Vieux-Montréal. For the remainder of the century the settlers were under constant attack by the Iroquois. During the eighteenth century, the threat faded and the bustling town now known as Montréal prospered, thanks to its ever-expanding fur trade.

When the city fell to the British in 1760, it had a population of 5,000, all of whom lived in the present-day Vieux-Montréal. As a result of the British conquest, and the subsequent cession of Canada to Britain in 1763, there was a large exodus of French nobility and military officers back to France. At the same time there was an influx of immigrants from Scotland, who quickly became prominent in the burgeoning fur trade. In the

The 1705 Château de Ramezay, now a museum.

winter and spring of 1775–76, Montréal was occupied by the Americans under General Montgomery for seven months, but it had little impact on the city. The American Revolution did affect Montréal, when thousands of fleeing Loyalists resettled here.

In 1783, the North West Trading Company was set up by a partnership of Montréal's leading fur traders. This consolidated Montréal's preeminence in the fur trade and made possible the large-scale export of furs to Europe. In 1821, the company merged with its more powerful rival, the Hudson's Bay Company. The importance of the fur trade gradually diminished, but the economic boom continued with other industries

closed down. At the same time there was extensive redevelopment and renovation of derelict areas, a modern subway system was installed, and the ambitious Place Ville-Marie, a downtown underground shopping complex, was built. With the exception of a short spell in the early 1960s, Drapeau continued in office until the mid-1980s: a remarkable span of 30 years during which he literally changed the face of the city, with spectacular shopping complexes, the *métro*, the stunning array of buildings and structures associated with Expo '67, the magnificent cultural and performing arts center, Place des Arts, and many other less-obvious examples of his determination to beautify and modernize the city.

beginning to flourish. It was also the early nineteenth century that saw the arrival of a large wave of European Jewish immigrants, who brought with them skills crucial to Montréal's development as a major business and financial center. Thus, by the time the city was incorporated in 1832 it was already a significant force in Canadian life. By the time of Confederation in 1867 it was the most important city in Canada.

Its importance and growth continued into the twentieth century, although in the period between the two World Wars it acquired a rather unsavory reputation as "Sin City." Gambling, prostitution and gangsterism all thrived under the protection of corrupt authorities. This slide into decadence came to an abrupt end in 1954 with the election of Jean Drapeau as mayor. Corruption among city officials was weeded out, hoodlums were prosecuted, and brothels and gambling houses were

GENERAL INFORMATION

Infotouriste ((514) 873-2015 TOLL-FREE (877) 266-5687 WEB SITE www.tourism-montreal.org, 1001 rue du Square-Dorchester, has a range of services, such as hotel booking, bus tours, car rentals and currency exchange. There is also an information kiosk at Place Jacques-Cartier, 174 rue Notre-Dame est, Vieux-Montréal.

Museum buffs can reap savings by purchasing a **Montréal Museum Pass** ((514) 845-6873, which costs $20 from Infotouriste, participating museums and some hotels. The pass allows entry to 25 museums for two of any three days.

Getting Around

Many of Montréal's sites of interest can be reached on foot from downtown and Vieux Montréal hotels. For purposes of orientation, remember that the city is laid out on a grid and is divided into east and west, with St-Laurent at the center. East and west numbering is taken from St-Laurent, and north and south numbers begin at the Vieux-Port.

The city also has an excellent public transportation system, the STM (*Société de transport de Montréal*) WEB SITE www.stm.qc.ca, which operates the bus and *métro* (subway) systems on the island. They have a 24-hour recorded information service in both French and English ((514) 288-6287. STM offers the **Carte touristique (Tourist Pass)**, which comes in one-day, three-day or weekly (Monday to Sunday) versions, all considerably cheaper than buying individual ride tickets. You can also save by buying your tickets in a *lisière* of

Guidatour ((514) 844-4021 TOLL-FREE (800) 363-4021 run walking tours of Old Montréal (June to September). Bicycles can be rented from **Vélo Montréal** ((514) 236-8356, 3870 rue Rachel est, near the Olympic Stadium, or **La Maison des Cyclistes** ((514) 521-8356 WEB SITE www.velo.qc.ca, 1251 rue Rachel est. Both places also offer guided cycle tours of the city.

WHAT TO SEE AND DO

Vieux-Montréal

Vieux-Montréal, or the Old Town, is bounded by Rue Berri, Rue St-Antoine, Rue McGill and the waterfront (until the nineteenth century all of

six. Seniors and students with ID have reductions on tickets (though not passes). The Blue Line closes at 11 PM, otherwise the last *métro* is around 1 AM, after which a night bus runs between the popular nightspots. For information on commuter trains, call ((514) 287-8726.

Gray Line ((514) 934-1222 WEB SITE www.coach canada-montreal.com operates a range of year-round trolley sightseeing tours of the city and cruises on the St. Lawrence Seaway, with pickups at Infotouriste and many hotels. **Croisières AML** ((514) 842-9198 TOLL-FREE (800) 667-3131 WEB SITE www.croisieresaml.com, Quai de l'Horloge, and the **Bateau-Mouche** ((514) 849-9952 TOLL-FREE (800) 361-9952 WEB SITE www.bateau-mouche.com, quai Jacques-Cartier, also run cruises. For air tours over the city, contact **Delco Aviation** ((450) 663-4311 WEB SITE www.delcoavaiation.com, 335 boulevard Lévesque est, Pont-Vau, Laval.

Montréal was contained within this area). By the 1960s, no longer the city's center, the Old Town had fallen into disuse and disrepair, when the government stepped in and declared it a historic area — whereupon a program of restoration and renovation of its attractive older buildings began. It is now alive and well, bustling with restaurants, bars, shops, galleries, outdoor cafés and street entertainment. The best way to see the historic Old Town is to wander around on foot along its narrow streets and beautiful squares. Vieux-Montréal is served by three métro stations: Place d'Armes, Victoria Square and Champs-de-Mars.

The delightful Place Jacques-Cartier is a large cobbled square lined with old houses, restaurants,

OPPOSITE: Ornate façades LEFT of Montréal's Vieux Port contrast with downtown's soaring lines RIGHT. ABOVE: Cathédrale-Basilique Marie-Reine-du-Monde, a scaled-down version of St. Peter's in Rome.

cafés and craft shops. At the north end of the square a statue of Lord Nelson stands atop a high column erected in 1809 to honor his victory at Trafalgar. **Galerie le Chariot** ((514) 875-4994 WEB SITE www.galerielechariot.com, at No. 446, is one of Canada's foremost showcases for Inuit and Iroquois art. Running along the south side of the square is the **Rue St-Paul**, a lively main street that is filled with fashionable shops, art galleries and restaurants.

Moving up the incline from Place Jacques-Cartier, just across from the square on Rue Notre-Dame the **Hôtel de Ville** (City Hall) is a dignified Second Empire-style building. Just west of it is the domed **Old Courthouse** building. The broad

bottom of the road is the **Marguerite Bourgeoys Museum** ((514) 282-8670, 400 rue St-Paul, based around the excavations of the city's first church built here in 1657 by Marguerite Bourgeoys, the founder of an order of teaching nuns (open mid-May to mid-September). The museum covers the history of the city to prehistoric times and includes the lovely **Chapelle Notre-Dame-de-Bonsecours**, known as the Sailors' Chapel, which stood at the waterside until the land was reclaimed. It was built in 1678 and rebuilt in 1772, and has a quaint and interesting interior where model ships, votive offerings from sailors, hang from the ceiling. The life of its founder is depicted in a curious series of tableaux made with dolls. Climb up the

field that the city hall looks out onto, the **Champs-de-Mars**, was a parking lot until just recently. Facing the Hôtel de Ville on the corner of Notre-Dame and St-Claude is the elegant **Château de Ramezay** ((514) 861-3708 WEB SITE www.chateauramezay .qc.ca, 280 rue Notre-Dame est, which dates from 1705. Originally the home of the French governors, it has subsequently been used for a variety of purposes, with its most recent incarnation as a museum where you can see period furnishings, costumes, artifacts and displays on the history of the city, including the story of the area's original native inhabitants.

One block east of here, running between Rues Notre-Dame and St-Paul, is **Rue Bonsecours**, a beautiful little street that is well worth a visit. The **Maison Pierre-du-Calvet** stands here, an attractive French Colonial house that dates from 1725 (now a bed and breakfast and restaurant). At the

church tower for some good views of the old city and the harbor. Next door is the newly renovated **Marché Bonsecours** ((514) 872-7730 WEB SITE www.marchebonsecours.qc.ca, 350 rue St-Paul, an imposing neoclassical market, built in 1847, and busy once again with boutiques, restaurants, exhibitions and a farmer's market.

A few blocks west of Place Jacques-Cartier is the **Sir George Etienne Cartier National Historic Site** ((514) 283-2282 TOLL-FREE (800) 463-6769 WEB SITE www.parkscanada.gc.ca/cartier, 458 rue Notre-Dame est, a beautifully restored Victorian home covering the life and times of one of the fathers of Canadian Confederation.

Heading west along rue Notre-Dame, you come to **Place d'Armes**, which in 1644 was the site of a battle between settlers and the Iroquois. A statue of the Sieur de Maisonneuve in the center of the square commemorates the French victory.

To the north side of the square, the **Banque de Montréal** ((514) 877-6810, 119 rue St-Jacques ouest, a dignified classical building with its stately columned portico, houses a small and quite interesting banking museum. At the south end of the square, tucked away behind old stone walls, is Montréal's oldest building, the **Séminaire St-Sulpice**, which dates from 1685 and is still used by Sulpician monks (not open to the public).

Next to the seminary is the vast **Basilique Notre-Dame** ((514) 842-2925 WEB SITE www.basilique nddm.org, 110 rue Notre-Dame ouest, a twin-towered neo-Gothic structure, built over a period of 46 years and completed in 1869. The huge and richly decorated interior contains some very fine carving. There is an ornate main altar, made of red and white pine, and the pulpit was hand-carved from the trunk of a single walnut tree. The stained-glass windows, made in Limoges, France, tell of the religious history of Montréal. Notice the slope of the floor: architect James O'Donnell chose to rake the sanctuary, following the natural slope of the land downward toward the St. Lawrence. The sanctuary is occasionally used for concerts (Pavarotti once performed here). The lovely **Chapel of the Sacred Heart** was rebuilt after being all but destroyed by arson in 1978; many of the surviving 1888 elements were incorporated within the modern design. Its bronze sculpture depicting the stages of human life is one of the largest in the world. In the evenings, the basilica stages a slightly mawkish but entertaining sound-and-light show about the history of Montréal: **And Then There was Light** ((514) 790-1245 TOLL-FREE (800) 361-4595 WEB SITE www .admission.com (phone for performance times).

Down on the waterfront, the glass-and-steel **iSci Centre** ((514) 496-4724 TOLL-FREE (877) 496-4274 WEB SITE www.isci.ca, King Edward Pier (phone for opening times), is a splendid place for children, with a hands-on science museum, an IMAX cinema, interactive games and restaurants.

Pointe-à-Callière (Montréal Museum of Archeology and History) ((514) 872-9150 WEB SITE www.musee-pointe-a-calliere.qc.ca, 350 place Royale, is the pride of the city. An archeological dig in Vieux-Port found remains of Chomeday's 1652 original settlement, along with Amerindian remains. Rather than removing the artifacts, this museum was built on top of the site. A multimedia presentation on the founding of Montréal, "Montréal, a Crossroads of Cultures and Trade," kicks off the tour.

A block and a half west of Point-à-Callière is the **Centre d'Histoire de Montréal** ((514) 872-0238 WEB SITE www.ville.montreal.qc.ca/chm, housed in the old fire station at 335 place d'Youville, where the history of the city is described in a series of audiovisual displays. Just around the corner, **Musée Marc-Aurèle Fortin** ((514) 845-

6108, 118 rue St-Pierre, houses the works of Québécois landscape painter Fortin (1887–1970), and temporary exhibitions of the work of other local artists.

Just across from the Centre d'Histoire stands the **Écuries d'Youville**, a group of early nineteenth-century warehouse and factory buildings enclosed by old stone walls. The buildings have been renovated and function as offices and shops, and there are some pleasant restaurants here. The attractive courtyard provides a peaceful haven for tired sightseers.

There are plenty of tacky souvenir shops in Vieux-Montréal, but it also has its share of **boutiques, antique** and **craft shops**, especially around Rues St-Paul, St-Amble and St-Jacques. Notre-Dame ouest between Guy and Atwater is the main antiques area.

Downtown (Centre-Ville)

The downtown district of Montréal, bordered by Atwater, St-Denis, St-Antoine and Sherbrooke, has quite a different character. In the 1960s, steel and glass skyscrapers, high-rise hotels, and complexes began to appear here. This sweeping modernization was also happening below ground with the development of Montréal's **Cité Souterraine (Underground City)**, a huge 30-km (18-mile) network of passages among shopping and business centers, cinemas and restaurants, with access to hotels, railway stations and many other facilities. Whether or not you like the idea of shopping malls, going about your business without having to be outdoors can be quite an appealing prospect in the winter rain and snow. Underground walkways link such complexes as **Place Bonaventure, Place du Canada** and **Place Ville-Marie**, while others are a métro ride away.

The center of this system, and the first complex to have been built, is **Place Ville-Marie** (often referred to as the PVM). Above ground the square is dominated by the 45-story **Royal Bank Tower**, a remarkable cruciform structure designed by architect I.M. Pei and now one of Montréal's most famous landmarks. A couple of blocks south is the **Planetarium de Montréal** ((514) 872-4530 WEB SITE www.planetarium.montreal.qc.ca, 1000 rue St-Jacques (*métro*: Bonaventure; call for a schedule).

It could be said that **Dominion Square** is the heart of Montréal, and with *calèches* and tour buses waiting here, it's a good place to start your explorations. But before taking off, look around the square. On one side stands the **Sun Life Building**, a great gray wedding cake of a place that was Montréal's first skyscraper, and once Canada's largest building. The British crown jewels spent

The new Pointe-à-Callière museum of archeology and history is the pride of the city.

the World War II safely stored in its vaults. Facing it stands the **Bank of Commerce**, a slick, glass skyscraper, and the **Marriott Château Champlain** hotel, another vast modern structure sometimes referred to as "the cheese-grater" because of its semicircular windows. At the southern end of the square along the Boulevard René-Lévesque (formerly known as Boulevard Dorchester) **Cathédrale-Basilique Marie-Reine-du-Monde**, a scaled-down copy of St. Peter's in Rome, stands valiantly in the midst of the modern giants.

Eastwards along Boulevard René-Lévesque past the PVM, turn left (motorists: only after 6 PM) onto Rue de l'Université and two blocks along at 635 rue Ste-Catherine ouest, you'll find **Cathédrale**

where restored Victorian mansions house exclusive and trendy boutiques, cafés and restaurants.

For a cultural interlude, go eastwards along Rue Ste-Catherine to the **Place des Arts (** (514) 285-4200 WEB SITE www.pda.com, an arts complex for theater, opera, ballet, music and visual arts. It's the venue for the annual Festival International de Jazz (see NIGHTLIFE AND THE ARTS, page 141). The **Musée d'Art Contemporain (** (514) 847-6226 WEB SITE www.macm.org, 185 rue Ste-Catherine ouest, is part of the complex. It's Canada's only museum dedicated to contemporary art.

If you haven't had enough of shopping malls by this time, there's an underground link from Place des Arts to the nearby **Complexe Desjardins**

Christ Church ((514) 843-6577, a fine Gothic-style church dating from the 1850s. In summer there are free organ concerts here (phone for details). **Rue Ste-Catherine** is Montréal's main shopping street. At Rue Ste-Catherine ouest you'll find just about everything at the major department stores La Baie, Eaton, Simon (chic clothing) and Ogilvy's. However, the most exclusive fashion-only store, Holt Renfrew, is found along the "Gold Square mile" of Rue Sherbrooke Ouest, at the corner of Rue de la Montagne.

The **Canadian Guild of Crafts (** (514) 849-6091 WEB SITE www.dsuper.net/~cdnguild, 1460 rue Sherbrooke ouest, has an interesting permanent exhibition of Inuit art as well as a particularly good selection of Canadian arts and crafts, with knowledgeable staff to offer advice. Further west along Ste-Catherine, on and around **Rues Crescent** and **Bishop** is Montréal's center of chic,

((514) 845-4636, 150 rue Ste-Catherine ouest (*métro*: Place-des-Arts), an enclosed mall that extends above and below ground level. For a completely different kind of shopping, south of here near Place d'Armes *métro* and centered on Rue de la Gauchetière is Montréal's **Chinatown**.

On the north side of Rue Sherbrooke, where it intersects with Rue de l'Université, stands **McGill University**, where you might like to wander around the pleasant green campus lying at the foot of Mont-Royal. Facing the campus on the south side of Sherbrooke is the fascinating **Musée McCord de l'Histoire Canadienne (** (514) 398-7100 WEB SITE www.mccord-museum.qc.ca, 690 rue Sherbrooke ouest, which traces the history of Montréal and Canada as a whole with collections of art, costume, artifacts and a massive photographic collection, including the story and artifacts of the region's First Nations peoples.

Continuing westwards, Canada's first museum, the **Musée des Beaux-Arts** (Fine Arts Museum) ((514) 285-1600 TOLL-FREE (800) 899-6873 WEB SITE www.mmfa.qc.ca, 1379–1380 rue Sherbrooke ouest, houses an art collection that spans all ages and all parts of the world. As you might expect, it has a large collection of Canadian art, but European art movements are also well represented. Inuit sculptures, African masks and pre-Columbian figures are among the permanent exhibits and the museum also hosts major international exhibitions.

Le Centre Canadien d'Architecture ((514) 939-7000 WEB SITE www.cca.qc.ca, 1920 rue Baile, is one of the world's most important architectural

to many writers, artists and musicians. At the western end of the square runs **Rue Prince Arthur**, a lively pedestrian-only street that offers shops, ethnic food and street entertainment.

For more ethnic flavors, turn off Prince Arthur at **Boulevard St-Laurent**, an immigrant neighborhood that is rapidly becoming a fashionable culinary focal point. It's a busy area of shops, bars, cafés, delis and restaurants. St-Laurent, also known as "The Main," was once the ostensible dividing line between the French- and English-speaking communities, and although this is no longer strictly true, there are still hints of this cultural split. It remains the east–west dividing line for street numbers.

museums. Exhibition halls are open to the public with scale models and hands-on demonstrations.

Outside Downtown

Centered around **Rue St-Denis**, a few blocks east of the downtown area, is Montréal's **Quartier Latin**, traditionally the center of French-Canadian culture in the city, but now more associated with the many students from the local **Université du Québec** who hang out around here. St-Denis has an academic chic about it with its cafés, restaurants, nightclubs, bars, art galleries and trendy boutiques where local designers sell their one-of-a-kind conceptions: it's an area that's big on atmosphere, and relatively low on prices. Proceeding northwards, one block beyond the intersection with Sherbrooke you'll find **Square St-Louis** on the left, an attractive square of beautiful Victorian houses looking onto a small park and home

Parc Lafontaine ((514) 872-2644, rue Sherbrooke and avenue Parc-Lafontaine (*métro*: Sherbrooke), is an ideal place to do a spot of rowing, stroll around the French- and English-style gardens or have a picnic while enjoying the free open-air entertainment that is often presented here.

Just north of downtown, one of Montréal's most stunning features is, of course, the mountain that dominates the cityscape, Mont-Royal. **Parc du Mont-Royal** is the city's finest park, skillfully planned by the architect of New York's Central Park, Frederick Law Olmstead. In summer it's a popular place for walking, jogging, picnicking, riding, sitting, sunbathing, or just taking in the views of the city below. In winter, skates, sleighs,

OPPOSITE: An antique merchant LEFT buys and sells religious articles, while a "video sex" store RIGHT offers goods of a more secular nature. ABOVE: The Biodôme.

skis and snowshoes are brought here. How you get to the park depends on your mood: you can go there by *calèche*, drive most of the way there by car, or walk up from Rue Peel, Avenue du Parc or Rue Drummond. At the top is a 30-m (98-ft) cross erected in 1924. It commemorates a vow taken by Maisonneuve in 1643 to carry a wooden cross to the top of Mont-Réal if the fledgling colony were spared from flooding. The waters receded and he had to make good on the promise.

On the far, northwest, slope of Mont-Réal, is the **Oratoire St-Joseph** (St. Joseph's Oratory) ((514) 733-8211 WEB SITE www.saint-joseph.org, 3800 chemin Queen-Mary (*métro*: Côte des Neiges or Snowdon). In 1904, a monk called Brother André, who was said to have great healing powers, raised a chapel to St. Joseph here, from where he worked tirelessly to treat the sick. A vast domed basilica was built here in the late 1930s, although the interior was not completed until the 1960s; the original chapel still stands. Inside the basilica is a museum dedicated to Brother André: abandoned crutches and wheelchairs bear witness to his powers. If you are looking for a miracle yourself, you can light a candle or touch Brother André's tomb; hardcore pilgrims climb the long, steep stairs to the church on their knees saying a prayer at every step.

The Olympic Village

On the eastern edge of the city, several kilometers along Rue Sherbrooke, Parc Maisonneuve is the home of the Parc Olympique, originally built for the 1976 Summer Olympics (although not completed until 1987). This huge and vastly expensive complex is bold and striking in its design; the centerpiece is the gigantic **Stade Olympique (Olympic Stadium)** ((514) 252-8687 TOLL-FREE (877) 997-0919 WEB SITE www.rio.gouv.qc.ca, which can seat 80,000 spectators who come to see the Montréal Expos baseball games, rock concerts and trade shows. The striking tilted tower overlooking the stadium was designed for winching the retractable roof. The original roof, however, proved too expensive to maintain; it has recently been replaced by a stationary one. From the tower, which leans at a 45-degree angle, runs a funicular on which you can ride to an observation deck for a view over the metropolis. Daily guided tours of the Olympic complex, including its six swimming pools, leave from the tourist hall ((514) 252-8687 in the base of the tower. Tours at 12:40 PM and 3:40 PM are in English and the ones at 11 AM and 2 PM are in French. The pools are open for public swimming also.

Next to the Stade Olympique is the **Biodôme de Montréal** ((514) 868-3000 WEB SITE www.ville .montreal.qc.ca/biodome, 4777 avenue Pierre-de-Coubertin. Built as the Olympic vélodrome for the 1976 Olympics, it is now an environmental

museum and one of the city's most popular attractions. Replicas of four distinct ecosystems have been constructed inside the building: polar tundra, tropical forest, boreal forest and the St. Lawrence River. Each of the rooms features flora and fauna and appropriate temperatures, as well as changing seasons. Inclusive admission fees for the Biodôme, Olympic Tower and/or the Jardin Botanique and Insectarium are available.

A free shuttle bus links the Parc Olympique to the **Jardin Botanique** (Botanical Garden) ((514) 872-1400 WEB SITE www.ville.montreal.qc.ca/ jardin, rue Sherbrooke est, where about 26,000 species of plants from all around the world are displayed in a series of gardens and greenhouses, over an area of 72 hectares (180 acres). The summer is undoubtedly the time to see the gardens at their spectacular best, but in winter the visitor can escape into the exotic atmospheres of the greenhouses. The **Chinese Garden** was a joint

project of Montréal and Shanghai, and is the largest of its kind outside Asia. You can wander among its pavilions, courtyards, carp ponds and myriad indigenous Chinese plants. The truly celestial **Japanese Garden** is a must. There is a cultural pavilion and art gallery, a tearoom where the ancient tea ceremony is performed, and a Zen garden. Also within the grounds are the **Tree House** (all about trees), a new **butterfly house** and the Montréal **Insectarium** WEB SITE www.ville .montreal.qc.ca/insectarium, with more than 4,000 mounted insects including scarab beetles, locusts, butterflies, maggots, tarantulas and live creepy crawlers such as cockroaches, praying mantises and scorpions. A Greenhouse of Asian Medicinal Plants is planned. A train will take you on a guided tour of the gardens for a small fee.

The **Château Dufresne** ((514) 259-9201, 2929 avenue Jeanne d'Arc, could not be more of a contrast to the Olympic Village, an elegant beaux-arts

mansion, modeled after the Petit Trianon in Versailles. It is still sumptuously furnished as it was when it was built (1915 to 1918) by Marius Dufresne and his wife, Edna Sauriol. There are also regular exhibitions on the social history of Montréal.

The River

In the St. Lawrence River, facing Vieux-Montréal is **Île Ste-Hélène** (*métro*: Île Ste-Hélène), which was enlarged using landfill in the 1960s. To get there by car, take either La Concorde or Jacques Cartier bridges. Île Ste-Hélène and the completely manmade neighboring **Île Notre-Dame** were the setting for the World's Fair, Expo '67. Today, they make up the wonderful **Parc Jean-Drapeau**. At least half of both islands is given over to green space, with a lavish network of hiking, cycling

Inside Montréal's Biodôme visitors walk through the tropical forest exhibition.

and cross-country ski trails. The former French pavilion now houses one of the world's biggest gambling palaces — the Casino de Montréal (see NIGHTLIFE AND THE ARTS, below). The stunning giant geodesic dome was designed by Buckminster Fuller as the American Pavilion and now houses the **Biosphère (** (514) 283-5000 WEB SITE www.bio sphere.ec.qc.ca, an environmental exhibit area devoted to promoting awareness of the fragile St. Lawrence/Great Lakes ecosystem. There are multimedia shows, hands-on displays and good views of the river from the observation deck. The island is also home to Montréal's only fort, now housing the **Stewart Museum (** (514) 861-6701 WEB SITE www.stewart-musuem.org, 20 rue Tour-de-Isle (metro: Jean-Drapeau). Exhibits follow the history of the New World until the mid-nineteenth century, while costumed interpreters and seventeenth- and eighteenth-century military drills enliven the summer months.

For lighter entertainment there's **La Ronde (** (514) 397-2000 TOLL-FREE (800) 797-4537 WEB SITE www.laronde.com, 22 chemin Macdonald, Île Ste-Hélène's enormous amusement park, featuring some 30 rides, including Le Cobra, a stand-up roller coaster with a 360-degree loop.

Upstream, ships used to find the river virtually impassable because of the rough and tumble of the **Lachine Rapids**. In 1825, the **Lachine Canal (** (514) 637-7433 WEB SITE www.parkscanada.gc.ca/canallachine was built as a way to bypass them. **Jet-boating** over the Lachine Rapids is an exhilarating experience. Jet-boats depart from the Quai de l'Horloge (Clock Tower Pier) in Montréal's Vieux Port every two hours for the hour-and-a-half trip to the rapids and back. Trips run several times daily from May to October. For information and reservations contact **Saute Moutons–Lachine Rapids Tours (** (514) 284 9607 FAX (514) 287-9401 WEB SITE www.jetboatingmontreal.com, 47 rue de la Commune ouest. The company also offers rafting (minimum age 14) through the rapids and rides on a high-speed chase boat along the St. Lawrence River (see JET THE LACHINE RAPIDS, page 15 in TOP SPOTS). In 1970, the Lachine Canal was closed to traffic and has now become an idyllic 14-km (8.7-mile) green space with foot and cycle paths, picnic spots. Meanwhile work has begun on restoring the canal and reopening it to small boats.

Marché Atwater ((514) 937-7754 WEB SITE www.marchespublics-mtl.com, 138 avenue Atwater (*métro*: Lionel Giroulx), is a charming year-round farmer's market housed in a brick art deco building that also has cafés and delis and arts and crafts. On a sunny summer's day it's one of the most photogenic spots in the city, with crusty farmers chatting with customers over meticulously arranged vegetables. You can get some eastern Canadian food specialties here, such as maple syrup *(sirop d'érable)* and fiddlehead ferns.

EXCURSIONS FROM MONTRÉAL

In Laval, on the island north of Montréal, the **Cosmodome (** (450) 978-3600 WEB SITE www.cosmodome.org, 2150 autoroute des Laurentides, is Canada's first museum of space science, with interactive games and displays including an Apollo mission space suit and moon rock.

The **Five Nations Iroquoian Village (** (450) 638-7474 WEB SITE www.5ntions.qc.ca, Route 138, Kahnawake, is a traditional Mohawk site. Visit three longhouses, the art gallery and a horse, bison and deer farm and watch traditional dancing. The provincial tourist office publishes a thick brochure detailing all the First Nations tourism projects in Québec, for those who are interested in learning more.

From Montréal, Autoroute 10 runs east to Sherbrooke. This road takes you through the scenic terrain and tidy villages of **Les Cantons de l'Est** (Eastern Townships). It's a snow-belt region and a growing ski destination, yet on the whole much quieter and less bucolic than the pulsing Laurentian ski stations to the north (see above). The four main resorts have a total of 143 trails, verticals up to 540 m (1,770 ft), and 900 km (560 miles) of cross-country trails. As befits the birthplace of the inventor of the snowmobile, Joseph-Armand Bombardier, there are 2,000 km (1,200 miles) of trails for snowmobiling. Resorts include: **Mont Sutton (** (514) 538-2545, **Station Touristique de Mont Orford (** (819) 843-6548 TOLL-FREE (800) 361-6548, and **Station Touristique Owl's Head (** (514) 292-3342 TOLL-FREE (800) 363-3342, 40 chemin du Mont Owl's Head, Mansonville.

Accommodation is plentiful and varied in the region. For information on visiting the Eastern Townships, contact **Tourism Estrie (** (819) 820-2020 TOLL-FREE (800) 355-5755 FAX (819) 566-4445 WEB SITE www.tourisme-estrie.qc.ca, 25 rue Bocage, Sherbrooke, or visit the **Maison régionale du tourisme des Cantons-de-l'Est (** (514) 375-8774 TOLL-FREE (800) 355-5755 FAX (514) 375-3530 WEB SITE www.easterntownships.com, Eastern Townships Autoroute (10), Exit 68.

SPORTS AND OUTDOOR ACTIVITIES

General information on summer and winter sports activities in Montréal is available from the Sports and Leisure Department of the City of Montréal (** (514) 872-6211.

Parc Mont-Royal is a popular spot for **jogging**. There are over 20 **cycling** paths running through Montréal covering 240 km (149 miles); popular rides include the Lachine Canal, Vieux-Port, Angrignon Park, and Rue Notre-Dame, between the Parc Rivière-des-Prairies and Rue Berri. Maps are widely available. The *métro* allows cyclers to bring their bikes on board during non-rush-hour periods; use the last two doors of the tail car.

There are more than 200 **skating** rinks in Montréal, most of which are outdoors. The largest is the one-and-a-half-kilometer-long (one-mile) Olympic Basin on Île Notre-Dame. Winter also brings **cross-country skiing, tobogganing** and **snowshoeing** to the snow-covered city parks.

Two hours north of the city, **Les Laurentides** (the Laurentians) were named in 1845 by a French historian because they parallel the St. Lawrence River. For visitor information, call ((514) 436-8532 TOLL-FREE (800) 561-6673 WEB SITE www.laurentides.com, 14142 rue de Lachapelle, Saint-Jérôme. These hills are a Mecca for outdoor activities, from

100 theatrical companies, around 30 musical organizations, and over 40 festivals a year. There are also masses of bars and clubs to choose from, and a thriving gay scene. *Voir* (in French) and its English counterpart, *Hour*, are hefty free publications with all the listings of all the local events (available in shops and cafés all over town). **Tours Astral** ((514) 866-1001, at the Infotouriste office, 1001 Square-Dorchester, sells tickets to all of these sporting, as well as many cultural, events. Bars close at 3 AM.

The world-famous **Orchestre Symphonique de Montréal** ((514) 842-3402 WEB SITE www.osm.ca, performs at Salle Wilfrid-Pelletier, Place des Arts — when they're not on tour or playing in

paddling to sailing to trout fishing to mountain biking. But the region's greatest fame is as a ski destination. There are a wealth of slopes, including **Mont Tremblant** ((819) 681-2000 TOLL-FREE (800) 461-8711 WEB SITE www.tremblant.com, 3005 chemin Principal, and **Le Chantecler** ((514) 229-3555 or (514) 393-8884, chemin Chantecler, Route 15, in Ste-Adèle.

For spectator sports, the **Canadians Hockey Club** ((514) 790-1245 WEB SITE www.canadiens.com play at the Molson Centre ((514) 932-2582, 1260 rue de la Gauchetière.

NIGHTLIFE AND THE ARTS

Montréal has long had a well-deserved reputation for scintillating nightlife, with a choice of entertainment that ranges from the highbrow to the downright tacky. It has 65 theater stages, over

one of the city's parks or at the Basilique Notre-Dame. The **Orchestre Métropolitain du Grand Montréal** ((514) 598-0870 TOLL-FREE (800) 361-4595 WEB SITE www.orchestremetropolitan.com, an orchestra of younger musicians, also plays at Place des Arts. Classical music can also be heard at **Pollack Concert Hall** ((514) 398-4547, McGill University. L'**Opéra de Montréal** ((514) 985-2222 WEB SITE www.operademontreal.qc.ca, stages four or five major operas each year at the Place des Arts, with bilingual scripts projected on screens above the stage.

Balletomanes can see the excellent **Grands Ballets Canadiens** ((514) 849-8681 WEB SITE www.grandsballets.qc.ca, at the Salle Wilfrid-Pelletier (when they're not touring), the popular **Les Ballets**

The Casino de Montréal is a vast gambling palace, one of the world's largest.

Jazz de Montréal ((514) 982-6771, and several other thriving contemporary dance troupes.

Most theater productions are in French — the **Centaur Theatre** ((514) 288-1229, 453 rue St-François-Xavier in Vieux-Montréal, is the foremost English-language theater company. **Théâtre du Nouveau-Monde** ((514) 866-8667, 84 rue Ste-Catherine ouest, is the place for French classics, while **Théâtre du Rideau Vert** ((514) 844-1793, 4664 rue St-Denis, specializes in contemporary French works. Each July the 10-day **Just For Laughs Festival** ((514) 845-3155 is held in concert halls and outdoor venues around Rue St-Denis and all over the city.

The big-name pop and rock concerts take place at **Centre Molson** ((514) 932-2582, 1260 rue de la Gauchetière. The **Spectrum de Montréal** ((514) 861-5851, 318 rue Ste-Catherine ouest, is another biggy that hosts all kinds of shows, while the smaller **Club Soda** ((514) 270-7848, 5240 avenue du Parc, is a well-established venue for a variety of rock bands, including international acts.

The vast **Casino de Montréal** ((514) 392-2746 TOLL-FREE (800) 665-2274 WEB SITE www.casinosquebec.com, 1 avenue du Casino, on Île Notre-Dame in the St. Lawrence River, has five restaurants — including the Mobil-Five-Star awarded Nuances — and a bilingual cabaret theater, in addition to almost 3,000 slot machines and more than 100 gaming tables. Take the métro to Île Ste-Hélène and transfer to bus 167.

The 11-day **Festival International de Jazz de Montréal** ((514) 871-1881 (information) or (514) 790-1245 (tickets) TOLL-FREE (888) 515-0515 WEB SITE www.montrealjazzfest.com TICKETS www.admission .com, takes place both in- and outdoors from the end of June to the beginning of July at place des Arts. If you are looking for jazz and blues at other times, try **Kily Kun** ((514) 845-5392, 354 avenue du Mont-Royal est (*métro*: Mont-Royal), or **L'Air du Temps** ((514) 842-2003 in the Vieux-Montréal at 191 rue St-Paul ouest, Vieux-Port (*métro*: Place d'Armes). Downtown you could go to **Biddles** ((514) 842-8656, 2060 Aylmer (*métro*: McGill) and nibble a spare rib or a chicken leg while you enjoy the sounds.

For live Québécois folk music, head for **Aux Deux Pierrots** ((514) 861-1270, 104 rue St-Paul est, Vieux-Port (*métro*: place d'Armes). For world music and salsa, try **Cactus** ((514) 849-0349, 4416 rue St-Denis. For hard rock, the place to be is **Foufounes Electriques** ((514) 844-5539, 87 rue Ste-Catherine est (*métro*: Berri-UQAM).

With a huge young population, the city is stuffed full of funky clubs and bars, centered around several areas: **St-Denis** is more-or-less French, near the University of Québec; **Rue Crescent** is more-or-less English, and attracts McGill students; **St-Laurent** is the dividing line between east and west, and traditionally between English (east) and French (west) — and it's trendy right

now. It's a great place for a late-night espresso and people-watching at sidewalk cafés. There are also several great venues, of which the best is probably **Le Sergent Recruteur** ((514) 287-1412, 4650 boulevard St-Laurent (*métro*: Laurier / Mont-Royal), which offers a variety of entertainment from singers and storytellers (Sunday) to live jazz (Tuesday).

If you are looking to dance, try **Au Diable Vert** ((514) 849-5888, 4557 rue St-Denis, which attracts a crowd of academics and artists; **Karina** ((514) 288-0616, 1455 rue Crescent (*métro*: Concordia / Peel); **New Town** ((514) 284-9119, 1476 rue Crescent (*métro*: Concordia / Peel), which also has a ground-floor lounge, serving sushi and Thai food, a first-floor Mediterranean bar, and a roof terrace with a happy hour; **737 Altitude** ((514) 397-0737, 1 place Ville-Marie (*métro*: McGill / Bonaventure); or **Thursdays** ((514) 288-5656, 1449 rue Crescent (*métro*: Guy-Concordia / Peel).

WHERE TO STAY

Expensive

Directly above the railway station and a shopping mall, **Fairmont Le Reine Elizabeth** ((514) 861-3511 TOLL-FREE (800) 441-1414 FAX (514) 954-2256 WEB SITE www.fairmont.com, 900 boulevard René-Lévesque, with more than 1,000 rooms and suites, is the city's largest hotel. Unlike many of the chain's hotels, it is a modern building, but the decor is still sumptuous and the service excellent. There are many restaurants, but for a true treat, try the hotel's famous Beaver Club.

Hôtel Omni Mont-Royal ((514) 284-1110 TOLL-FREE (800) 843-6664 FAX (514) 845-3025 WEB SITE www.omnihotels.com, rue Sherbrooke ouest, is one of the very best hotels Montréal has to offer. The service is impeccable, the elegant rooms are equipped with just about everything you could want, and if it isn't there then it can probably be arranged. Its rival is the nearby **Ritz-Carlton Montréal** ((514) 842-4212 TOLL-FREE (800) 363-0366 FAX (514) 842-3383 WEB SITE www.ritz carlton.com, 1228 rue Sherbrooke ouest. Established in 1912, this was the first Ritz in North America and has catered to the whims of many of the rich and famous over the years. The rooms are elegant and spacious, the service is everything you could wish it to be, and afternoon tea in the garden is a tradition.

The **Montréal Marriott Château Champlain** ((514) 878-9000 TOLL-FREE (800) 200-5909 FAX (514) 878-6777 WEB SITE www.marriotthotels.com / yulcc, 1 place du Canada, is a tall and unmistakable building with crescent-shaped windows. Rooms are airy and fitted out with French-style furniture. Views of Dominion Square and the downtown are inspirational. It is connected to Place Bonaventure, shopping and restaurants via the city's underground network of walkways.

Directly on top of Place Bonaventure is the **Hilton Montréal Bonaventure (** (514) 878-2332 TOLL-FREE (800) 267-2575 FAX (514) 878-1442 WEB SITE www .hiltonmontreal.com, with a shopping mall, restaurants and *métro* below. There is a rooftop swimming pool in use year-round, a hectare (two and a half acres) of gardens, and the usual Hilton high standards.

The 37-floor **Centre Sheraton (** (514) 878-2000 TOLL-FREE (800) 325-3535 FAX (514) 878-3958 WEB SITE www.sheraton.com/lecentre, 1201 boulevard René-Lévesque, is conveniently situated for the smart shops and restaurants of the Rue Crescent area. The hotel has several bars of its own, a nightclub, restaurant and a smart, modern interior. The top five floors contain the most luxurious suites and rooms and have extra-special service.

One of Montréal's most charming downtown hotels is the **Château Versailles (** (514) 933-3611 TOLL-FREE (888) 933-8111 FAX (514) 933-8401 WEB SITE www.versailleshotels.com, 1659 rue Sherbrooke ouest, which now fills four lovely old stone houses and offers 65 comfortable, well-equipped rooms with bathrooms and friendly service. Across the street at No. 1808 is the 100-room Tour Versailles, a converted apartment hotel that has been added as an annex to the original town houses.

One of the most romantic places to stay in the city, the **Auberge du Vieux-Port (** (514) 876-0081 TOLL-FREE (888) 660-7678 FAX (514) 876-8923 WEB SITE www.aubergeduvieuxport.com, 97 rue de la Commune est, is an 1882 building with a cellar restaurant. Hardwood floors, massive beams and the original windows typify its cozy rooms, many of which have whirlpool baths. Light meals and cocktails are served on the rooftop terrace, which has good views of the Vieux-Port. Nearby, the **Hotel Place d'Armes (** (514) 842-1887 TOLL-FREE (888) 450-1887 WEB SITE www.hotelplacedarmes .com, 701 place d'Armes, is an elegant boutique hotel in a restored 1870 building, with a superb Vieux-Port location, 48 rooms, a fitness center, and a rooftop terrace, wine bar and restaurant.

Mid-range

Ideally placed for the restaurants and nightlife of the Latin Quarter, the **Crowne Plaza Métro Centre (** (514) 842-8581 TOLL-FREE (800) 477-0754 FAX (514) 842-3365 WEB SITE www.crowneplaza-montreal.com, 505 rue Sherbrooke est, has good facilities including an indoor pool.

Centrally situated, l'**Appartement-Hôtel (** (514) 284-3634 TOLL-FREE (800) 363-3010 FAX (514) 287-1431 WEB SITE www.appartementin.com, 455 rue Sherbrooke ouest, has 126 apartments of varying sizes, with an indoor swimming pool, a rooftop terrace and laundry facilities. Close to Rue St-Denis and to Old Town is the **Hôtel Lord Berri (** (514) 845-9236 TOLL-FREE (888) 363-0363 FAX (514) 849-9855 WEB SITE www.lordberri.com, 1199 rue Berri, where comforts include in-room movies and there's a bright and busy sidewalk café. Some floors are set aside for nonsmokers. **Le Jardin d'Antoine (** (514) 843-4506 TOLL-FREE (800) 361-6162 WEB SITE www.hotel-jardin-antoine.qc.ca, 2024 rue St-Denis (*métro* Berri-UQAM), is a restored nineteenth-century hotel, with 25 rather frilly rooms. The welcome is genuine, the rooms comfortable and the location excellent.

Les Passants du Sans Soucy ((514) 842-2634 FAX (514) 842-2912 WEB SITE www.lesanssoucy.com, 171 rue St-Paul ouest, near Pointe-à-Callière, is a delightful bed and breakfast in Vieux-Montréal, under the same ownership as the Auberge du Vieux-Port, although smaller and somewhat less expensive. There are nine guestrooms upstairs with stone walls, wood floors, wrought-iron beds and lace curtains.

People certainly don't stay at the **Hôtel de l'Institut (** (514) 282-5120 TOLL-FREE (800) 361-5111 WEB SITE www.hotel.ithq.qc.ca, 3535 rue St-Denis (*métro*: Sherbrooke), for the look of the place, but they do stay here for the service, convenient location and good value. Students of the Institute of Tourism and Hotel Management train here, and they are determined to please. The rooms are comfortable; the hotel looks across to Square St-Louis.

Inexpensive

Just off Sherbrooke, **Manoir Ambrose (** (514) 288-6922 FAX (514) 288-5757 WEB SITE www.manoirambrose.com, 3422 rue Stanley, offers an assortment of 22 accommodations in an attractive old building near the heart of downtown. Just south of Rue Sherbrooke Est is the clean and cozy **Hôtel Castel St-Denis (** (514) 842-9719 FAX (514) 843-8492 WEB SITE www.castelsaintdenis.qc.ca, 2099 rue St-Denis, which has 18 rooms. Nearby is the tiny **Maison Brunet (** (514) 845-6351 E-MAIL maison .brunet@freesurf.fr, 1035 rue St-Hubert (*métro*: Berri-UQAM), with only 14 rooms.

There is plenty of **bed and breakfast** accommodation in Montréal, ranging from basic to luxurious, and several agencies to help you find something to suit your needs, including **Bed and Breakfast City-wide (** (514) 738-9410 TOLL FREE (800) 738-4338 WEB SITE www.bbmontreal.com, 2033 rue St-Hubert; **Bed & Breakfast Downtown Network (** (514) 289-9749 WEB SITE www.bbmontreal .qc.ca, 3458 avenue Laval; or **Relais Montréal Hospitalité (** (514) 287-9653 TOLL-FREE (800) 363-9635 FAX (514) 287-1007 WEB SITE www.pages .infinit.net/pearson/BB, 3977 avenue Laval. Also downtown, **McGill University (** (514) 398-5200 FAX (514) 398-6770 WEB SITE www.residences .mcgill.ca/summer.htm, 3935 rue de l'Université; **Collège Français (** (514) 270-4459 FAX (514) 278-7508 WEB SITE www.vacancescanadamd.montreal plus.ca, 5155 avenue de Gaspé (*métro*: Laurier);

and the **Université de Montréal** ((514) 343-6531 FAX (514) 343-2353 WEB SITE www.resid.umontreal .ca, 2350 boulevard Édouard-Montpetit (*métro*: Édouard-Montpetit) all offer accommodation at low prices from mid-May to mid-August.

Hostelling International Montréal ((514) 843-3317 WEB SITE www.hostellingmontreal.com, 1030 Mackay Street (*métro*: Lucien-L'Allier), has both dormitory and private rooms.

WHERE TO EAT

It's easy to see why eating out is favorite pastime of Montréalers. With some 5,000 restaurants representing the national cuisines from more than

80 different ethnic groups, you could eat out every night of the year at a different restaurant without fear of monotony. In addition to ethnic, there is also an abundance of Québécois regional restaurants and bistros. A large number of restaurants in the Latin Quarter, around Rue St-Denis, allow you to bring your own wine, which will save on the final tab, so check this out in advance.

Expensive

The **Beaver Club** ((514) 861-3511, Le Reine Elizabeth, 900 boulevard René-Lévesque ouest, was a club formed by the early fur traders. By the 1800s, it had evolved into a gentlemen's club and now survives as a hotel-restaurant, where its origins are very much in evidence in its formal atmosphere and the pelts and mementos that are hung about the walls. The cuisine is both continental and Québécois regional, and the service and food are both superb.

Le Café de Paris ((514) 842-4212 at the Ritz-Carlton, 1228 rue Sherbrooke ouest, is classical in its cuisine and its elegant decor, and strains of piano music accompany your superb meal. Its venerable wine cellar provides an excellent list of wines ranging in price from moderate to very, very expensive. We recommend you pop in on a chilly morning for their delicous Japanese

breakfast — grilled salmon, spinach leaves with sesame dressing, miso soup, steamed rice, and dried toasted seaweed.

Toqué ((514) 499-2084, 3842 rue St-Denis, is one of Montréal's top tables. The contemporary Québec-Montréal cuisine emphasizes intense flavors and the freshest market ingredients.

At the splendid **Restaurant Nuances** ((514) 392-2708 TOLL-FREE (800) 665-2274, 1 avenue du Casino, in the Casino de Montréal on Île Notre-Dame, chef Jean-Pierre Curtat reigns over one of Montréal's most admired kitchens. The cuisine is authentically French with a nod to contemporary trends, so that Asian or Mediterranean flavors complement classic French dishes.

The relatively new **Area** ((514) 890-6691, 1429 Amherst Street, has come storming through to become one of the city's trendiest addresses, providing an ultra-modern fusion of Italian, French and Asian cuisine, along with an extensive wine list, in a contemporary setting. **Chez l'Epicier** ((514) 878-2232, 311 rue St-Paul est, has almost everything going for it: a superb Vieux-Port address, welcoming but stylish decor, delicious contemporary Canadian food, an extensive wine list and a mouth-watering delicatessen to entice people back for more. Book ahead for both restaurants.

The interior of **Le Lutetia** ((514) 288-5656 TOLL-FREE (800) 361-6262, in the Hôtel de la Montagne, 1430 rue de la Montagne, is an explosion of ornate decorative styles, baroque in the broadest sense and an ideal place for romantic *dîner à deux*. The excellent menu offers fine French and Italian cuisine, and the wine list is of a similarly high standard.

The old Jewish neighborhood around boulevard St-Laurent is now *très branché* (very trendy: literally "plugged in"), and here you'll find a host of excellent restaurants — and the who's who of Montréal dining in them. Your taste buds can literally travel the world. Ardent carnivores will think they have died and gone to heaven in **Moishe's** ((514) 845-3509, 3961 boulevard St-Laurent, a steak house of the highest order. The meat is expertly prepared and aged in the restaurant's own cold rooms, and steaks are grilled over wood. **Méditerraneo** ((514) 844-0027, 3500 boulevard St-Laurent, could be the best place on this gastronomic street. A glowing jet-set atmosphere and a menu that accents the flavors of southern France guarantee a memorable evening. **Soto** ((514) 842-1150, 3527 boulevard St-Laurent, offers divine sushi of all varieties as well as sashimi, yakitori and teriyaki. The setting is as elegantly styled as the food.

For good Greek food, **Milos** ((514) 272-3522, 5357 avenue du Parc, is an excellent choice. You select the ingredients of your meal from the fresh seafood, meat and vegetables that are displayed.

Moderate

Trendy Boulevard St-Laurent also offers some less loftily priced restaurants. Although **Pizzadelic** ((514) 522-2286, at No. 1250, is franchising its heart out, they haven't forgotten how to make an excellent pizza. Toppings range from the classic to the bizarre, and pastas, salads and other Italian specialties are also on offer. **L'Express** ((514) 845-5333, 3927 rue St-Denis, is another Montréal place to see and be seen. It is a crowded bistro and the food and the wine list are excellent. Try the *aiguillettes de canard*, slices of cold roast duck complemented by stir-fried vegetables with Thai peanut sauce, and save room for their famous *tarte au chocolat*. The kitchen is open until 3 AM making it a good late-night spot.

Formosa ((514) 282-1966, 2155 rue St-Denis, is a multi-purpose Asian restaurant serving everything from Cantonese to Thai cuisine in cleanly modernist surroundings. The food is good and the restaurant prides itself on catering to those with peanut allergies. Nearby **La Sila** ((514) 844-5083, 2040 rue St-Denis, is a cheerful Italian trattoria with a good list of Italian wines, cozy dining areas and an outdoor terrace for the summer.

One of the best Indian restaurants around is **Le Taj** ((514) 845-9015, 2077 rue Stanley, where the menu is northern Indian and includes tandoori dishes. **Katsura** ((514) 849-1172, 2170 rue de la Montagne, provides elegant and tranquil Japanese surroundings and a menu that includes an excellent range of sushi dishes. You can book a private tatami room to dine in the traditional Japanese manner, and there's also the option of the restaurant's sushi bar.

To sample Québécois food, head for **Auberge le St-Gabriel** ((514) 878-3561, 426 rue St-Gabriel, said to be North America's oldest restaurant.

Inexpensive

Laurier Barbeque ((514) 273-3671, 381 avenue Laurier ouest, is something of an institution, where traditional Québécois food is served and French-Canadian families gather; try their barbecued chicken, and save room for their legendary desserts.

Montréal has some excellent delicatessens in which smoked meat — brisket of beef that is marinated for two weeks then steamed and served with rye bread and pickle — is classic fare. Rue St-Laurent is home to the humble **Hoffner's** ((514) 845-9809, at No. 3671, where you can have sausage on a bun. **Ben's** ((514) 844-1000, 990 boulevard de Maisonneuve ouest, **Schwartz's** ((514) 842-4813, 3895 boulevard St-Laurent, and **Reuben's Restaurant Delicatessen** ((514) 861-1255, 888 rue Ste-Catherine ouest, all have their devoted customers.

Montréalers claim their city produces the best bagels in the world, and the best of the best are found at **St-Viateur Bagels** ((514) 276-8044, 263 rue St-Viateur ouest.

HOW TO GET THERE

Some 150 airlines from 47 destinations in Canada, 76 in the United States and 92 across the rest of the world fly into **Aéroport de Dorval** ((514) 394-7377 TOLL-FREE (800) 465-1213 WEB SITE www.admtl .com, 25 km (15 miles) west of the city (allow about 25 minutes). The **Airport Shuttle** ((514) 931-9002 operates a regular service with drop-offs at city center hotels. When flying out of Montréal you must pay a departure tax of $10.

VIA Rail's ((514) 989-2626 TOLL-FREE (888) 842-7245 WEB SITE www.viarail.ca intercity and transcontinental trains arrive at and depart from

Gare Centrale (Central Station), 935 rue de la Gauchetière ouest (*métro*: Bonaventure, McGill, and Peel). The station is connected underground to the *métro* and the Windsor railway station for local commuter trains. **Amtrak** TOLL-FREE (800) 872-7245 WEB SITE www.amtrak.com has daily services between Montréal and New York.

The main **bus** station is at 505 boulevard de Maisonneuve est (*métro*: Berri-UQAM). **Greyhound** TOLL-FREE (800) 667-0882 WEB SITE www .greyhound.ca has a regular bus service to Montréal from cities all over North America.

Les Dauphins de Saint-Laurent ((514) 288-4479 TOLL-FREE (877) 648-4499 WEB SITE www .dauphins.ca, 430 rue Ste-Hélène, Suite 202,

OPPOSITE: The gleaming dome of the Marché Bonsecours on Rue St-Paul. ABOVE: A water lily blossoms in Montréal's Jardin Botanique.

operates **hydrofoil ferries** along the St. Lawrence Seaway between Montréal and Québec City.

To reach Montréal by car, take the Trans-Canada Highway (Route 20) from the Maritimes; the TransCanada Highway and Route 40 both from Québec City; or Route 401 from Toronto. From the United States there are three principal routes: Interstate 87 through New York State, which becomes Route 15 at the Canadian border; Interstate 89 from Boston through New Hampshire and Vermont, becoming Route 133 at the border; and Interstate 91 from New Haven, Connecticut through western Massachusetts and Vermont, which becomes Route 55 at the border, before joining Route 10 into Montréal.

GASPÉ PENINSULA

Not far from Montréal, yet a world away, is the Gaspé Peninsula. Jutting out into the Gulf of St. Lawrence like a clenched fist, the peninsula is an ancient landmass bounded on the north by the vast estuary of the St. Lawrence River and on the south by the Baie des Chaleurs ("Bay of Warmth"). Rising out of the heavily forested interior are the Chic Chocs Mountains, a continuation of the Appalachian chain, with peaks of over 1,220 m (4,000 ft) above sea level, the highest in the province. Some of the world's best moose and deer hunting, as well as salmon fishing, is to be had in the uplands and river valleys of these mountains. The wild, boulder-strewn north coast, from Matane around to Percé, is punctuated at frequent intervals by tiny fishing villages. The gentler, warmer, less precipitous coastline of the south shore, though still dotted with little fishing villages, has most of the peninsula's farms and small industries.

But what is so striking about the Gaspé, apart from its stunning scenery, is its overwhelming sense of isolation. Not only is it geographically somewhat isolated from the rest of the country, but the little villages themselves are isolated from each other, even when they are only a few kilometers apart. And the villagers all seem cut off from the modern world, preferring to go about their business — the men usually as fishermen, but sometimes as merchants and craftspeople — in exactly the way that generations of their forebears did. It is this simplicity, this stubborn respect for tradition, that makes the Gaspé an enchanting as well as scenic place to visit.

BACKGROUND

The first European visitors to the Gaspé were the Vikings in the eleventh century, followed four centuries later by Basque fishermen who discovered

The twenty-first century arrives, modestly, in the Gaspé.

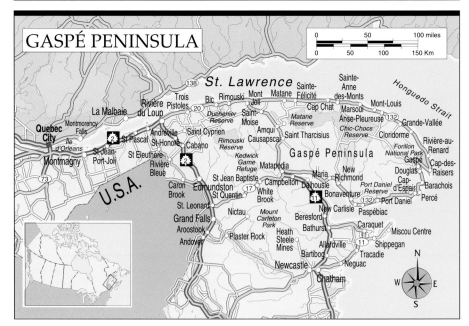

the rich fishing grounds protected by the Gulf of St. Lawrence. Then in 1534 Jacques Cartier landed at the present site of the city of Gaspé, where, in the presence of a small band of bewildered Mi'kmaq natives, he erected a tall wooden cross on a hill overlooking the bay and claimed the area for France. He named it Gaspéche, from the native word Gaspeg, meaning "land's end." It wasn't until the early seventeenth century that French fishermen began arriving and establishing little coastal villages, which, despite the harsh and primitive conditions, survived thanks to the rich harvest from the sea. Acadians deported by the British from Nova Scotia settled more villages in the mid-eighteenth century. At about the same time, English settlers began establishing farming communities along the south coast, which were then augmented by the arrival of Loyalists in the aftermath of the American Revolution.

Since then, it's as if time stood still. A few waves, or ripples, of immigrants arrived from Scotland and Ireland, but nothing much changed. The pattern of village life was set: cling to the coast, and the sea will provide. And the formula worked. The sea has provided not only fish in abundance, but in the eighteenth and nineteenth centuries it provided bonus extras in the form of shipwrecks along the Gaspé's rocky northern coastline. In fact, some survivors of shipwrecks founded entire villages with the stores and equipment they salvaged from their wrecked vessels. In cases where there were no survivors, the residents of existing villages would bury the dead sailors and then help themselves to the sunken cargo.

There are no longer any shipwrecks or roaming tribes of natives, or primitive outdoor plumbing, but in many essential respects the Gaspé today remains untouched — and therefore unspoiled — by the modern world.

GENERAL INFORMATION

You can get plenty of information from the provincial tourist information offices, but for more detail, contact the **Gaspé Tourist Association** ((418) 775-2223 TOLL-FREE (800) 463-0323 FAX (418) 775-2234 WEB SITE www.tourisme-gaspesie.com, 357 route de la Mer, Ste-Flavie. For information on Gaspé town, contact the **Office du Tourisme et des Congrès de Gaspé** ((418) 368-8525 FAX (418) 368-8549 WEB SITE www.tourisme.ville.gaspe.qc.ca, 27 boulevard York est, Gaspé. The area has many small museums and interpretation centers, covering everything from lighthouses to caves, leather to salted cod. Ask the tourist office for a full list.

WHAT TO SEE AND DO

As you make your way eastwards across the north coast of the Gaspé you really shouldn't pass through **Grand Métis** without stopping to see the magnificent **Jardins de Métis** ((418) 775-2221 WEB SITE www.jardinsmetis.com, 200 Route 132 (June to mid-October). When Elsie Reford inherited her uncle's estate near Grand Métis in 1919 she used her horticultural talents to create this series of landscaped settings for a vast variety of shrubs, perennials and annuals, and her achievement is all the more remarkable because many of the species are found nowhere else this far north. Her home, the elegant Victorian Villa Reford ((418) 775-3165, still stands in the park and is now a museum with a restaurant and shop.

Continuing eastwards on Route 132 you'll come to **Matane**, a fishing town well known for its salmon and shrimp, so it stands to reason that it's a good place to stop for a bite or to buy your fish and bite on it elsewhere. Starting in June, Atlantic salmon swim up the Matane River to their spawning grounds. The dam here has a specially constructed passage through which the salmon swim, and there's an observatory by the dam where you can listen to taped information as you watch them struggle by. South of Matane

a little way and just off Route 195, the **Réserve faunique de Matane** is a good place to pitch your tent and do some canoeing, boating or fishing, or just to take a hike.

Back along Route 132, **Cap-Chat** offers keen fishermen lots of opportunities. The lakes are brimming with trout, the river teems with salmon, and some of the locals will take you cod fishing at an hourly rate.

The next village is Ste-Anne-des-Monts, and from it Route 299 will take you south into **Parc de la Gaspésie** ((418) 763-3181 WEB SITE www .sepaq.com, 900 route du Parc, a magnificent wilderness area of some 802 sq km (310 sq miles) that encompasses lakes, forests and the wildlife reserve in the Chic Chocs Mountains, roamed by moose, caribou, deer and a few black bears. Mont Jacques-Cartier (1,268 m / 4,160 ft) is the tallest peak, and if you can take the cold, the wet and

the hike, the views are breathtaking. The park is laced with 130 km (78 miles) of hiking and cross-country ski trails and roads; there's some good fishing and canoeing.

About 40 km (25 miles) from Ste-Anne-des-Monts, along Route 299, is the **Gîte du Mont-Albert** ((418) 763-2288, a lodge from which all trails begin, and where you'll find accommodation, campsites, a restaurant, an information point and a nature center.

Return to the coast road at **Mont-St-Pierre**, a little village sheltering in a beautiful bay. It's one of the top Canadian spots for **hang-gliding**. If you fancy trying it yourself, a hang-gliding school operates between June and August. There's also a two-week hang-gliding festival, **La Fête du Vol Libre**, each summer. For information, contact Corporation Vol Libre ((418) 797-2222 FAX (418) 797-2558. It was at **Pointe-à-la-Renommée** ((418) 269-3310 WEB SITE www.gaspesie.net / gaspe2000, 884 boulevard L'Anse-à-Valleau, that Marconi installed North America's first maritime radio station in 1904. Today, there are displays here about the lives of lighthouse operators and some beautiful hiking trails (open June to mid-October).

Jutting out into the gulf, the northeastern tip of the peninsula forms the **Parc National Forillon** ((418) 368-5505 TOLL-FREE (800) 463-6769 WEB SITE www.parkscanada.gc.ca / forillon, 238 sq km (92 sq miles) of spectacular coastline and forest with a remarkable variety of flora and a wealth of wildlife, including moose, lynx and black bears. The northern side is characterized by dramatically sheer limestone cliffs, pebble beaches and impressive headlands, from which seals and whales can be sighted between May and October. Activities include guided tours and nature walks, with 70 km (42 miles) of hiking, cross-country skiing and snowshoeing trails. There are also boat trips to seal colonies and an island bird sanctuary, and whale-watching trips in season ((418) 892-5500 WEB SITE www.baleines-forillon .com. Scuba diving or fishing are other attractions — plus beaches to relax on after all that expending all that energy.

At Rivière-au-Renard, on the edge of the park, the **Modern Fishing Interpretation Centre** ((418) 269-5292, 1 boulevard Renard est, does what it says. It also has a display on historic fishing in the region. From here, Route 197 takes you south along the western side of the park to Gaspé, but follow Route 132 to see the magnificent northern coastline. This brings you along the coast to the old village of **Cap-des-Rosiers**, the site of many shipwrecks and Canada's tallest **lighthouse** ((418) 892-5577, 1127 boulevard de Cap-des-Rosiers, which dates from 1858. There's also a park interpretive center here. Some privately owned boats

The lighthouse at La Martre.

offer deep-sea fishing trips and cruises with the sanction of the park authorities. Route 132 continues along the south side of the Parc National Forillon, where the coastline along the Baie de Gaspé is softer and there are sandy beaches.

The port of **Gaspé** is the industrial and administrative center of the peninsula. It doesn't have a great deal to offer the tourist other than its historical significance, for it was here in 1534 that Jacques Cartier first landed on North American soil and claimed it in the name of the King of France, an event commemorated with a **monument** that depicts scenes of Cartier's journey in bas-relief. Near the monument and overlooking the bay stands the **Musée de la Gaspésie** ((418) 368-1534, 80 boulevard

The fishing village of **Percé** is a small and pleasant place set against a mountainous backdrop, with plenty of souvenir and craft shops, cafés and some excellent restaurants. It is chiefly renowned for the strange splendor of its geological landscape. Cliffs rise steeply from the sea, but nothing quite prepares you for the sight of **Percé Rock**. This majestic reddish-gold limestone rock is 427 m (1,400 ft) long, nearly 91 m (300 ft) wide and 88 m (270 ft) high and is pierced by a natural hole at its eastern end, from which the name Percé ("pierced") originates. Beside it stands a pillar of stone; all that is left of a second arch that collapsed in the nineteenth century. At low tide you can walk out to the rock and wonder at it from

Gaspé, where you can spend a pleasant hour learning about the peninsula's history.

Those interested in fishing should take note that three Atlantic salmon rivers run into the sea at Gaspé; these can be fished through prior arrangement with the government office that strictly controls the waters. The **Gaspé Fish Hatchery** ((418) 368 3395, 686 boulevard Youk ouest, is the oldest operating in North America (opened in 1874) and offers tours, tips and an opportunity to try fishing for salmon and speckled trout. They also have a variety of birds and animals and an art trail for those less enthused by fish. The **Gespeg Mi'kmac Interpretation Site** ((418) 368-6005, 783 boulevard Pointe-Navarre, Fontenelle, is a reconstructed seventeenth-century village where you can learn about the history, lifestyle and dress of the local First Nations people (June to October).

close quarters; if the tide is in, take a path that leads to a nearby cave.

Mont Ste-Anne affords some wonderful views of the area, including the Rock, and despite a height of 320 m (1,050 ft) it is not a difficult walk if you follow the trail near the church. Another trail, the Route des Failles, takes you to **La Grande Crevasse**, a dramatic split in the rock to the west of Mont Ste-Anne.

Regular boat trips run from the wharf to the **Parc de l'Île Bonaventure** ((418) 782-2240 WEB SITE www.sepaq.com, 4 rue du Quai, Percé, an island that is now a flourishing bird sanctuary, home to 250,000 seabirds including an enormous colony of over 75,000 gannets. You can either be content to circle the island or you can disembark walk around and catch another ferry back. Go armed with binoculars, sturdy walking shoes and a hat (June to mid-October).

Continuing southeast along Route 132, the south coast of the Gaspé assumes a very different character, with low rolling farmland and sandy beaches. During the American Revolution many Loyalists fled to this area and many of the towns bear English names as a result.

A little north of the town of Port-Daniel, **Port-Daniel Park** is a good spot for trout and salmon fishing, while further west the little town of **Bonaventure** sits in a pleasant bay, good for kayaking and canoeing. Its **Musée Historique Acadien** ((418) 534-4000 WEB SITE www.musee acadien.com, 95 avenue Port-Royal, describes the history of the Acadian people and features period furniture and old domestic appliances.

world show specimens from the area. You can take a look at the cliffs where the fossils are found and also see the laboratory processes used to separate them from the rock (June to mid-October). Further along Route 132 is **Restigouche**, where the final naval battle between the French and English was fought in 1760 — this is commemorated in the **Battle of Restigouche Historic Park** ((418) 788-5676 WEB SITE www.parkscanada.gc.ca, Route 132, Pointe-à-la-Croix. An interpretive center includes among its exhibits parts of the *Machault*, the French warship sunk during the battle (mid-June to mid-October).

Matapédia is an attractive little village at the confluence of the Matapédia and Restigouche

The **Village gaspésien d'héritage britannique** ((418) 392-4487 WEB SITE www.geocities.com/gbhcm, 351 boulevard Perron ouest, New Richmond, is an entertaining historical theme park with 23 buildings that recreate the life of the Breton pioneers (June to September).

At the attractive town of **Carleton**, it's worth a walk or bus ride to the top of 555-m (1,600-ft) **Mont St-Joseph** for a panoramic view of the south coast of the Gaspé and the shore of New Brunswick across the Baie des Chaleurs. At the top, the **Oratoire Notre-Dame du Mont-St-Joseph** ((418) 364-3520 is an elaborately decorated church built in 1935.

At **Parc de Miguasha** ((418) 794-2475 WEB SITE www.sepaq.com, 231 route Miguasha ouest, the cliffs are so fossil-rich that they have been declared a UNESCO World Heritage site. They date back around 370 million years. Museums around the

Rivers, both of which are full of salmon. From here Route 132 goes north to Ste-Flavie on the northern shore, a distance of around 160 km (100 miles). This is a very scenic route that takes you through the Matapédia valley with its pine-covered hills and tucked-away villages, so allow yourself time to enjoy it.

WHERE TO STAY

At Matane, the elegant **Riotel Matane** ((418) 566-2651 TOLL-FREE (888) 427-7374 FAX (418) 562-7365 WEB SITE www.riotel.com, 250 avenue du Phare est, has good facilities including a swimming pool, snowmobiling facilities and a good restaurant. There are 96 rooms, many of which offer pleasant

OPPOSITE and ABOVE: Bird watchers and watched birds flock to Île Bonaventure.

sea views (mid-range). The **Quality Inn Matane** ((418) 562-6433 TOLL-FREE (800) 463-2466 FAX (418) 562-9214 WEB SITE www.qualityinn.qc.ca, 1550 avenue du Phare ouest, has a swimming pool, a babysitting service and snowmobiling facilities, and some of its rooms come with fireplaces. Rates are slightly higher than those at the Riotel. **Motel la Vigie** ((418) 562-3664 TOLL-FREE (888) 527-3664 FAX (418) 566-2930 WEB SITE www.lavigie.com, 1600 avenue du Phare ouest, is an inexpensive 32-roomed motel near the dock, and the **Hôtel-Motel Belle Plage** ((418) 562-2323 TOLL-FREE (888) 244-2323 FAX (418) 562-2562 WEB SITE www.hotelbelle plage.com, 1310 rue Matane-sur-Mer, is reasonably good value (inexpensive to mid-range).

itself or the chalets around it (inexpensive to moderate; reservations essential). The rooms are basic, but pleasant, and offer a peaceful setting, fresh mountain air, views of Mont Albert, and a crackling fire in the grate. Camping is also possible.

In Mont-St-Pierre, the inexpensive **Motel au Délice** ((418) 797-2850 TOLL-FREE (888) 797-2955 FAX (418) 797-5032 WEB SITE www.audelice.com, at 100 rue Prudent-Cloutier, has 17 comfortable rooms and a restaurant, and is probably the best accommodation on offer. In Parc National Forillon there are some well-equipped **campsites**, and on the south coast of the Forillon peninsula there's a Hostelling International facility, **Auberge de Cap-aux-Os** ((418) 892-5153 TOLL-FREE (800) 461-

At Ste-Anne-des-Monts, both **Motel à la Brunante** ((418) 763-3366 TOLL-FREE (800) 463-0828 FAX (418) 763-7380 E-MAIL labrunante@globe trotter.net, 94 boulevard Ste-Anne ouest, and the smaller, slightly more expensive **Rîotel Monaco des Monts** ((418) 763-3321 TOLL-FREE (888) 427 7374 FAX (418) 763-7846 WEB SITE www.riotel.com, 90 boulevard Ste-Anne ouest, offer comfortable accommodation and reasonably good dining facilities at prices which are inexpensive to moderate. **Motel Beaurivage** ((418) 763-2291 TOLL-FREE (888) 763-2291 FAX (418) 786-5388 E-MAIL beau rivage@globetrotter.net, 100 avenue Première ouest, offers inexpensive accommodation and has a very good restaurant.

The **Gîte du Mont Albert** ((418) 763-2288 TOLL-FREE (888) 270-4483 FAX (418) 763-7803 WEB SITE www.sepaq.com, 2000 route du Parc, Parc de la Gaspésie, has accommodation either in the lodge

8585 FAX (418) 892-5292, 2095 boulevard Grande-Grève, Cap-aux-Os. The 56-bed inn is open year-round and offers a cafeteria in summer and kitchen in winter. The seasonal **Hôtel le Pharillon** ((418) 892-5200 TOLL-FREE (877) 909-5200 FAX (418) 892-5832 E-MAIL hotel-motelpharillon@globetrotter .net, 1293 boulevard Cap-des-Rosiers, Cap-des-Rosiers, has 38 inexpensive rooms with television and kitchenettes, and there's a restaurant.

At Percé, the best choice has to be the **Hôtel La Normandie** ((418) 782-2112 TOLL-FREE (800) 463-0820 FAX (418) 782-2337 WEB SITE www .normandieperce.com, 221 Route 132 ouest (inexpensive to mid-range). In this attractive wooden building, well situated for views of the sea and Percé Rock, there are 45 pleasant rooms with private bath and television, and a sitting area, a restaurant and a gym. The **Motel les Trois-Sœurs** ((418) 782-2183 TOLL-FREE (800) 463-9700 FAX (418)

782-2610 WEB SITE www.gaspesie.qc.ca / les3soeurs, 77-B Route 132 is also very comfortable, with good service and a restaurant (inexpensive to mid-range). In the same price range, the **Auberge du Gargantua** ((418) 782-2852 FAX (418) 782-5229 E-MAIL peresse@globetrotter.net, 222 Route des Failles, has 11 accommodations with great views of the Rock and probably the best restaurant in the Gaspé (breakfast and dinner only). There's an old-fashioned charm about the **Maison Avenue House** ((418) 782-2954, 38 avenue de l'Église, Percé G0C 2L0, where five simple and clean rooms are offered at very inexpensive rates.

Moving to the south shore of the peninsula, at Bonaventure the **Riôtel Château Blanc** ((418) 534-3336 TOLL-FREE (888) 427-7374 FAX (418) 534-4016 WEB SITE www.riotel.com, 98 avenue Port-Royal, is an attractive shorefront hotel built in 1906, with 32 rooms, bar, restaurant and private beach (mid-range).

At Carleton two of the best places to stay are the **Motel Carleton** (/FAX (418) 364-3288 TOLL-FREE (800) 510-3288, at 1746 boulevard Perron, which offers 33 inexpensive accommodations and a restaurant, and the **Manoir Belle Plage** ((418) 364-3388 TOLL-FREE (800) 463-0780 FAX (418) 364-7289 WEB SITE www.manoirbelleplage.com, 474 boulevard Perron, also with a restaurant (inexpensive to mid-range).

WHERE TO EAT

It is hardly surprising that the menus of Gaspésian cafés and restaurants are swimming with seafood that is well prepared and inexpensively priced. Cod tongues in batter are a Gaspésian specialty and have a surprisingly subtle flavor. As the Gaspé is such an outdoor place, there's always the option of buying your smoked fish from one of the many excellent fisheries and having a picnic somewhere along the way.

At the center of **Jardins de Métis** ((418) 775-3165, the Villa Reford has a busy restaurant where you can taste some traditional Canadian fare. In Matane there's a good and moderately priced restaurant at the **Hôtel-Motel Belle Plage** ((418) 562-2323, where you can sit watching the river flow.

At Ste-Anne-des-Monts it's again a case of looking to the hotels, with the best restaurant being at the **Hôtel Beaurivage** ((418) 763-2291, and another reasonably good one in **Monaco des Monts** ((418) 763-3321. Before leaving the town, you might want to gather the makings of a picnic for your trip to the Parc de la Gaspésie, in which case you can buy some smoked fish down by the dock.

In the Parc de la Gaspésie itself there's a real treat in store at the restaurant in the **Gîte du Mont-Albert** ((418) 763-2288, situated on Route 299. The highly acclaimed restaurant specializes in clas-

sic French cuisine and also regional dishes. Students from the Québec Institute of Tourism and Hotel Management serve here as part of their training and are eager to please. Prices are moderate and reservations essential.

Gastronomic delights await in Percé's **Auberge du Gargantua** ((418) 782-2852. Beautifully situated with a fine view of the Percé Rock, the restaurant specializes in French cuisine, seafood, Gaspésian dishes and a sinful array of desserts. Prices fall within the moderate category but are the most expensive in the area. Still, a meal here is a real must. The restaurant at the **Hôtel La Normandie** ((418) 782-2112 offers very good dining in attractive surroundings and with good

views of that rock. At the wharfside, **La Maison du Pêcheur** ((418) 782-5331, place du Quai, is also very good, moderately priced and serves excellent lobster. Its location makes it an interesting spot at lunchtime and its large windows afford views of you-know-what.

At Carleton, the good and moderately priced restaurant at the **Motel Baie Bleue** ((418) 364-3355, 482 boulevard Perron, Route 132, is probably the best spot to dine.

HOW TO GET THERE

VIA Rail TOLL-FREE (888) 842-7245 WEB SITE www.viarail.ca serves Gaspé and Percé via Halifax (Nova Scotia), Moncton (New Brunswick) and Matapédia, but to get the most out of being here, you'll need a car. From Montréal or Québec City, the TransCanada Highway (Route 20) goes to Rivière-du-Loup, from where the coastal highway, Route 132, does a complete loop of the peninsula. From New Brunswick, Routes 11 and 17 converge on Campbellton at the Québec border, where you cross over and pick up Route 132.

OPPOSITE: The famous Percé Rock stands sentry at the water's edge. ABOVE: A fisherman at Rivière-du-Renard, north of the port of Gaspé.

New Brunswick

New Brunswick, the "Gateway to Atlantic Canada," can lay claim to two of the wonders of the natural world: the tides in the Bay of Fundy and the leaves on its trees. Twice a day, 100 billion tons of water swirls up the funnel-shaped Bay of Fundy, creating tides of up to 15 m (50 ft), the highest in the world. Once a year, the trees of New Brunswick put on such a lavish show of color — as their leaves take on autumnal colors of gold, red, orange and purple — there is a toll-free hotline (800) 268-3255 with daily updates on the colors the leaves are turning.

There are a lot of leaves turning, as 85 percent of New Brunswick's 74,440 sq km (28,740 sq miles) is covered in forest. Bordered by Maine and Québec, and joined to Nova Scotia by the Isthmus of Chignecto, New Brunswick still has approximately 2,250 km (1,400 miles) of coastline. Along these shores are dozens of first-rate beaches and hundreds of charming fishing villages.

Like the other Maritimes, New Brunswick was inhabited by the Mi'kmaq for at least 2,000 years before it was "discovered" by Jacques Cartier in 1534. Seventy years later, Samuel de Champlain established a settlement on Saint Croix Island, but the French settlement of the province didn't begin in earnest until early in the eighteenth century. In 1751, with British pressure mounting, the French built Fort Beauséjour to protect the settlers. Four years later, in 1755, it fell to the British under Colonel Moncton, and shortly thereafter the order for the deportation of the French-speaking Acadians was proclaimed.

In 1783, the first ships bearing Loyalists from the former American colonies arrived at Parrtown (now Saint John). By the following year the Loyalist population had grown to 14,000, and the new province of New Brunswick was formally established. In 1785, Saint John became Canada's first incorporated city, while Fredericton was named the provincial capital. Around this time, some of the Acadians who had been deported 30 years before began to return, and today one-third of the province's 724,000 people are French-speaking. In fact, in 1969 New Brunswick was the first province officially to become bilingual.

FREDERICTON

As the home of the provincial legislature and the University of New Brunswick, and with a population of only about 47,500, it is not surprising that a majority of Fredericton's inhabitants work either for the government or the university, nor that Frederictonians seem to spend most of their free time planning or attending gala dinners, charity balls and garden parties. This "City of the Stately Elms," with its tree-lined avenues and elegant houses, is definitely the heartland of New Brunswick high society.

It is also, thanks to lavish benefactions from the city's most famous native son, Lord Beaverbrook, an important cultural center, with an excellent art gallery, theater and library. In addition, the city has become a center for all kinds of crafts. Fredericton, in other words, has managed the difficult feat of providing the perfect setting for both gentility and creativity.

BACKGROUND

Although the French built a fort here as early as 1692, at the confluence of the Nashwaak and St. John Rivers, it was several decades before the French settlement of Pointe-Ste-Anne was established. It lasted only until 1759, when British troops drove the settlers out and renamed it Fredericton, after the second son of George II. With the arrival of the Loyalists in 1783, Fredericton came into its own as a British town, the first major inland settlement. The following year New Brunswick was declared a province, with Thomas Carleton as its first governor, and in 1785 Carleton decided that Fredericton, rather than the larger Saint John, should be the provincial capital, because it was less vulnerable to attack from the sea. It quickly grew into an attractive and prosperous city.

GENERAL INFORMATION

Fredericton Tourism ((506) 460-2041 TOLL-FREE (888) 888-4768 WEB SITE www.city.fredericton.nb.ca, is at 11 Carleton Street. Ask for a copy of *Tourrific Tours*, which contains 32 coupons for attractions, accommodations, restaurants and shops (valid June to September).

WHAT TO SEE AND DO

Most places to visit in Fredericton are centrally located on Queen Street. The **Historic Garrison District** ((506) 460 2129 TOLL-FREE (888) 888-4768 was the site of the British Garrison from 1784 until 1869. Its various military buildings, which became a National Historic Site in 1964, now contain a range of attractions, from gift shops to live theatre.

Christ Church Cathedral ((506) 450-8500 is a fine Gothic edifice modeled on Saint Mary's parish church in Snettisham, Norfolk. Consecrated in 1853, it is generally considered to be the first cathedral built in North America. Sights within the cathedral include the working model for Big Ben. The silver-domed **Legislative Assembly** ((506) 453-2527, 706 Queen Street, is an imposing Victorian building (1882). Its library houses a number of rare books, including a priceless original hand-colored copy of *Birds of America* by John James Audubon. One volume is always on display.

Fredericton — autumn foliage frames St. Andrew's Church.

Opposite the Legislative Assembly, the **Beaverbrook Art Gallery** ((506) 458-8545 WEB SITE www.beaverbrookartgallery.org, 703 Queen Street, has one of the most impressive art collections in North America. Lord Beaverbrook designed the original building himself, and gave it, along with his personal art collection, to the people of New Brunswick. It is particularly renowned for its masterpieces by British artists including Thomas Gainsborough, Sir Joshua Reynolds, Joseph Turner, John Constable, Augustus John, Stanley Spencer and Graham Sutherland, although its most striking work is the huge *Santiago El Grande* by Salvador Dali. Another of Lord Beaverbrook's gifts to the city is the nearby **Playhouse** ((506) 458-8344 TOLL-FREE (800) 442-9779

There are several displays about life along the St. John River and a magnificent view of the city. In season, there are **cruises** along the St. John River aboard the *Carleton II* ((506) 454-2628 and the *Wood Duck* ((506) 447-7494.

Science East Science Centre ((506) 457-2340 WEB SITE www.scienceeast.nb.ca, 668 Brunswick Street, is housed in the Old York County Gaol, a formidable place with outer walls 12 m (40 ft) thick, built between 1840 and 1842. These days it has over 70 hands-on science exhibits (closed January).

Boyce's Farmers' Market ((506) 451-1815 WEB SITE www.boycefarmersmarket.com, George Street dates back to 1785, but these days offers a lively atmosphere and an excellent mix of local produce

WEB SITE www.theplayhouse.nb.ca, 686 Queen Street, built in 1964 and now the home of Theatre New Brunswick. Also on Queen Street, between Carleton and Regent, is **Officers' Square** ((506) 453-2324, an old parade ground that is now the site of lunchtime theater on weekdays during July and August, and free weekly band concerts. **Changing the Guard** ceremonies are held here in July and August, Tuesday to Saturday at 11 AM and 7 PM.

Between Queen Street and the river is the **Green**, a large landscaped park with monuments and trails. The **Lighthouse Adventure Centre** ((506) 460-2939, Regent Street, is the place to go for information and tickets for most of the city's attractions and events, from craft workshops to ghost walks, as well as kayak, canoe and bike rentals (mid-May through September, hours vary).

Pumpkins for sale outside Fredericton.

and souvenirs (Saturday 6 AM to 1 PM). Probably the best place to buy crafts however is the **New Brunswick Fine Craft Centre** ((506) 450-8989, 87 Regent Street (open summer and before Christmas).

The **Old Government House** ((506) 453-2505, 51 Woodstock Road, built in 1828, is the official seat of office for New Brunswick's Lieutenant Governor. Tours include the interpretation center, the staterooms and contemporary gallery spaces. The grounds stand on the site of the seventeenth-century Acadian settlement of Sainte-Anne. Nearby, there is an early burial ground for both Wolastoquewiyik (Maliseet) and Acadian peoples.

EXCURSIONS FROM FREDERICTON

For one of the finest examples of a nineteenth-century Canadian mill town, head towards **Marysville**, 10 km (six miles) from downtown. Its big

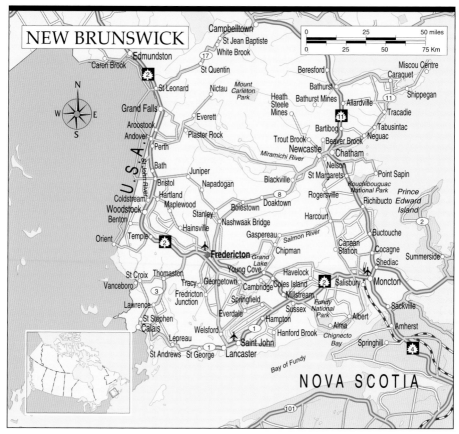

brick cotton mill, workers' tenements, stores and churches have survived almost intact. The tourist office has a self-guided walking-tour brochure.

The 550-hectare (1,375-acre) **Mactaquac Provincial Park** ((506) 363-4747, 24 km (15 miles) west of Fredericton on Route 105, is the largest park in New Brunswick and offers sailing, boating, water-skiing, fishing and lovely beaches for swimming. It also has an 18-hole golf course, supervised playgrounds, guided nature trails and 300 campsites.

Further along the St. John River, only 34 km (21 miles) west of Fredericton, **King's Landing Historical Settlement** ((506) 363-4999 WEB SITE www.kingslanding.nb.ca (Exit 253 off the Trans-Canada Highway, near Prince William), is a reconstruction of a typical nineteenth-century Loyalist village, with over 50 buildings including a working sawmill and grist mill, and 100 "villagers" who go about their daily routines exactly as they would have in the nineteenth century, demonstrating crafts from blacksmithing and weaving to herbal medicine (open June to mid-October). Typical period food and drink is served in the King's Head Inn. Nearby is the **River Valley Provincial Visitor Information Centre** ((506) 363-4994, 10 Prince William Road, Exit 253 from Route 2.

A scenic road continues northwest along the **St. John River Valley** to the Québec border. Attractions along the way include the **Hartland Covered Bridge** ((506) 375 4357 WEB SITE www.town.hartland.nb.ca, which at 390 m (1,282 ft) is the longest covered bridge in the world, and the **Grand Falls Gorge**, offering pontoon rides, walking trails and an Interpretive Centre ((506) 475-7717 TOLL-FREE (877) 475-7769 WEB SITE www.grandfalls.com. Just north of Edmundston, 278 km (173 miles) northwest of Fredericton, the seven-hectare (17.5-acre) **New Brunswick Botanical Garden** ((506) 737-5383 WEB SITE www.cuslm.ca/jardin, 15 Principale Street, Saint-Jacques, Exit 8 off Route 2, has eight stunning gardens and two arboreta.

WHERE TO STAY

The good news is that even the best hotels in Fredericton — and there are some very good ones — are moderately priced. The largest and most expensive is the **Sheraton Fredericton** ((506) 457-7000 TOLL-FREE (800) 325-3535 FAX (506) 457-4000 WEB SITE www.sheraton.com/fredericton, 225 Woodstock Road, with 222 rooms. It is located on the river a few minutes' walk from the city center.

The venerable **Keddy's Lord Beaverbrook Hotel** ((506) 455-3371 TOLL-FREE (866) 444 1946 FAX (506) 455-1441 WEB SITE www.lordbeaverbrookhotel .com, 659 Queen Street, across from the Playhouse, has all the luxuries one would expect of the city's leading hotel. Many of its 165 rooms overlook the St. John River (mid-range to expensive). Similarly priced and equipped is the **Auberge Wandlyn Inn** ((506) 452-4444 TOLL-FREE (800) 561-0000 FAX (506) 452-7658 WEB SITE www.wandlyninns.com, 958 Prospect Street West. Also in this category are the **Fredericton Inn Limited** ((506) 455-1430 TOLL-FREE (800) 561-8777 FAX (506) 458-5448, 1315 Regent Street, and the **Howard Johnson Hotel and Restaurant** ((506) 460-5500 TOLL-FREE (800) 596-4656 FAX (506) 472-0170 WEB SITE www.howardjohnson fredericton.com, 480 Riverside Drive.

The **Town and Country Motel** ((506) 454-4223 FAX (506) 454-6264, 967 Woodstock Road, has 17 units overlooking the river just west of the city (low end of moderate). The **Carriage House Inn** ((506) 452-9924 TOLL-FREE (800) 267-6068 FAX (506) 458-0799 WEB SITE www.bbcanada.com, 230 University Avenue, is a Victorian mansion adjacent to the Green, built in 1875 for the city's mayor, with excellent facilities for its 11 guestrooms (low end of moderate). There's no restaurant, but a full breakfast is served. In Mactaquac Park, near King's Landing, the inexpensive **Chickadee Lodge** ((506) 363-2759 TOLL-FREE (877) 363-2759 FAX (506) 363-2799 WEB SITE www.mactaquaccountry.com, 20 Lodge Lane, Prince William, is a superb bed and breakfast overlooking the headpond, with kayaks and canoes for guests' use.

WHERE TO EAT

Lord Beaverbrook Hotel (see WHERE TO STAY, above) offers several excellent dining possibilities. The elegant **Governor's Room** is generally rated among the finest restaurants in Canada. The **Terrace Room**, with a seasonal deck overlooking the river, has lunchtime buffets, Sunday brunch and evening specials; the **River Room** lounge offers light meals and snacks, a happy hour and live entertainment every evening.

The **Café du Monde** ((506) 457-5534, 610 Queen Street, serves good quality cuisine at reasonable prices. For Chinese cooking, **Mei's** ((506) 454-2177, 74 Regent Street, is very good. **Molly's Coffee House** ((506) 457-9305, 554 Queen Street, is a friendly coffee bar with garden decks in summer.

HOW TO GET THERE

Fredericton is served by **Air Canada**. The airport is 10 minutes' drive southeast of downtown on Route 102. Taxis run to downtown.

If you are coming by car, the TransCanada Highway (Route 2) enters New Brunswick from Québec near Edmundston, following the St. John River Valley into Fredericton. From Nova Scotia it crosses the Isthmus of Chignecto. Coming from Maine, Interstate 95 enters New Brunswick near Woodstock, where it links up with the Trans-Canada Highway.

SAINT JOHN

Known as "Loyalist City" to its inhabitants, Saint John is never known as St. John. It is Canada's oldest incorporated city, having been incorporated by its Loyalist settlers in 1785, and New Brunswick's largest, with a population of 125,000. Situated in the estuary of the St. John River, it has long been an important port and shipbuilding center, although today most of its income comes from oil refineries and its big pulp and paper mill.

More often than not the city is shrouded in fog, but the sea mists can have a welcome cooling effect on summer days when the rest of the province is sweltering. Saint John has never been famous for its beauty, although an ambitious development and restoration project worked has wonders for the waterfront and elsewhere has skillfully blended the past with the present. Now, when the fog lifts, it can be quite a pleasant city to look at.

BACKGROUND

Samuel de Champlain landed at the mouth of the river on Saint John the Baptist's Day in 1604, and in 1631 Charles de la Tour founded a fort and a trading post here. For the next century and a half the history of Saint John mirrored that of the region, with the Acadian population dispossessed by the British in 1755, and the city itself formally ceded to England in 1763. But its real birthday was May 18, 1783 — the day ships carrying more than 3,000 Loyalists arrived. What had been an obscure trading post instantly became a thriving Loyalist town, growing into a flourishing city that so prospered from its trade and shipbuilding it became known in the nineteenth century as the "Liverpool of America."

Growth and prosperity came to an abrupt end in the latter part of the century. As wooden sailing ships became obsolete, Saint John's shipyards sank into bankruptcy. Then, as if to demonstrate the cruelty of fate, a devastating fire in 1877 swept through the city's wooden buildings, wiping out over half the city. It was a long time before Saint John recovered. But recover it did, and the Saint John of today once again resembles the proud, bustling Saint John of yesteryear.

GENERAL INFORMATION

Tourism Saint John ((506) 658-2990 TOLL-FREE (866) 463-8639 FAX (506) 632-6118 WEB SITE www.tourism saintjohn.com can provide information. Motorists

arriving from the west should look for the **Visitor Information Centre** ((506) 658-2940 in the triangular building just off Route 1 (open mid-May to mid-October). Downtown, drop by the **City Centre Tourist Information Centre** ((506) 658-2855, inside Market Square, near the waterfront.

Saint John Transit Bus Tours ((506) 658-4700 operates two-hour sightseeing bus tours of the city from mid-June to September. Ask the tourist office for brochures for four self-guided **walking tours**.

WHAT TO SEE AND DO

There are sights and sights to see in Saint John, and then there is The Sight: the famous phenomenon of the **Reversing Falls** that occurs twice daily, when the mighty tides in the Bay of Fundy confront the St. John River and drive it back upstream. At the point where the river empties into the bay

the level of the river is over four meters (14 ft) above that of the bay at low tide, but at high tide the river is more than four meters (14 ft) below the oncoming sea water — so the river is forced to reverse its course. Because the river narrows dramatically and curls around a sharp bend just before it reaches the bay, whirlpools and plunging rapids are created: reversing falls. There is an observation point at Reversing Falls Bridge, which is ideal for witnessing this trick of nature. The **Interpretive Centre** ((506) 658-2937, 200 Bridge Street, explains it all. To get an even closer look, contact **Reversing Falls Jet Boat Rides** ((506) 634-8987 WEB SITE www.jetboatrides.com, Brunswick Square, which runs jet-boat tours through the whirlpools and rapids of the tidal swings. Those with no sense of fear can also experience the awe-

The happy, proud countenances of Legionnaires in Fredericton.

some power of the water in a three-meter (10-ft) bubble. The more timid can settle for a gentler harbor tour.

Also west of downtown is **Carleton Martello Tower ₵** (506) 636-4011 WEB SITE www.parkscanada .gc.ca, 454 Whipple Street (West), a stone fortification built during the War of 1812 that provides a commanding view of the city and the estuary. Exhibits show the powder magazine as it would have been in the 1840s, the barracks in 1866, and describe the tower's role in World War II.

Most of the sights in the city itself are within easy walking distance of King Square, and most have a distinctly Loyalist flavor. **King Square** advertises the city's past and present orientation:

Saint John is also the home of Canada's oldest market. The **Old City Market ₵** (506) 658-2820, 47 Charlotte Street, has been held in the same building since 1876, and many families have operated stalls here for generations (closed Sunday). For crafts or antiques, the place to go is **Prince William Street**, packed with shops and galleries. For more contemporary shopping, the **Market Square** complex offers several levels of shops.

Rockwood Park ₵ (506) 658-2883, off Mount Pleasant Drive, covers a stunning 890 hectares (2,200 acres) of woodland, coast and parkland, offering hiking trails, swimming, golf, canoeing and horseback riding. In winter, you can try skating, sleigh rides and cross-country ski trails. Within

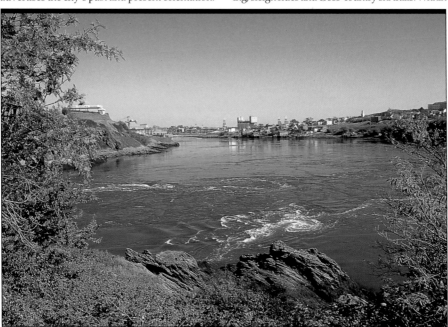

its flowerbeds and walkways are laid out in the form of a Union Jack. Nearby, **Loyalist House ₵** (506) 652-3590, 120 Union Street, is the oldest house in the city, an elegant Georgian mansion built in 1817 and one of the very few existing buildings to have survived the terrible fire of 1877 (open June to August). On the harborfront, **Barbour's General Store ₵** (506) 658-2939, Market Slip, is a red clapboard building dating from 1867, stocked with merchandise of the time and staffed by people in period costume (mid-June to mid-September). It also includes a vintage barbershop.

The **New Brunswick Museum ₵** (506) 643-2300 WEB SITE www.gnb.ca/culture, 1 Market Square, is Canada's oldest museum, founded in 1842. It features national and international art treasures, historic artifacts, a natural science gallery, a geological collection and a Hall of Great Whales. A tidal tube in the lobby follows the rise and fall of the Fundy.

the park, the small specialist **Cherry Brook Zoo ₵** (506) 634 1440 WEB SITE www.cbzoo.com, Sandy Point Road, has 35 species of exotic and endangered animals, including the rare Siberian tiger and gold lion tamarin. The Vanished Kingdom includes life-size replicas of extinct species.

The **Irving Nature Park ₵** (506) 653-7367 WEB SITE www.ifdn.com, Sand Cove Road West, is a 243-hectare (600-acre) coastal park on a peninsula of volcanic rock, with mud flats on one side and sandy beach on the other, all carefully restored, cleaned up and returned to the wild. It is not only an excellent place to watch the tidal range, but attracts over 250 species of marine and migratory birds, seen from eight walking trails, with boardwalks built out into the salt marshes and overlooking the seals' favorite hangouts. Naturalists are on hand to answer questions and give guided tours.

WHERE TO STAY

The best hotel in Saint John is the **Saint John Hilton** ((506) 693-8484 TOLL-FREE (800) 561-8282 FAX (506) 657-6610 WEB SITE www.hilton.com, 1 Market Square (expensive). Along with all the luxury comes its splendid location on Market Square. Larger and more moderately priced is the **Delta Brunswick Hotel** ((506) 648-1981 TOLL-FREE (800) 268-1133 FAX (506) 658-0914 WEB SITE www.delta hotels.com, 39 King Street (expensive). Luxurious and comfortable, it is also centrally located.

Possibly the best bargain in Saint John is the moderately priced **Coastal Inn Fort Howe** ((506)

In the western part of Saint John, just north of and parallel to Route 100 (Fairville Boulevard), is Manawagonish Road. Along this road you will find motels and guesthouses of every type and description, all inexpensive. Four of the best are: **Island View Motel** ((506) 672-1381 TOLL-FREE (888) 674-6717 FAX (506) 674-1089, at No. 1726, which has a heated pool and kitchenettes; the **Admiral's Quay Motel** (/FAX (506) 672-1125 TOLL-FREE (1-888) 612 4244 E-MAIL admirals_quay@excite.com, at No. 1711, which also has units and apartments; the **Econo Lodge** ((506) 635-8700 TOLL-FREE (800) 553-2666 FAX (506) 672-8853, at No. 1441, overlooking the bay; and the **Hillside Motel** ((506) 672-1273 TOLL-FREE (888) 625-7070, at No. 1131, which is the

657-7320 TOLL-FREE (800) 943-0033 FAX (506) 693-1146 WEB SITE www.coastalinns.com, at Main and Portland Streets, which has all the amenities of a luxury hotel — air conditioning, cable color television, indoor heated pool, on-site parking — and an excellent top-floor restaurant overlooking the city and harbor. Not quite so central, but again offering good value, is the **Colonial Inn** ((506) 652-3000 TOLL-FREE (800) 561-4667 FAX (506) 658-1664 WEB SITE www.colonial-inns.com, 175 City Road (inexpensive to moderate). Apart from the usual amenities, it has a 24-hour restaurant. There is no restaurant at the **Country Inn & Suites by Carlson** ((506) 635-0400 TOLL-FREE (800) 456-4000 FAX (506) 635-3818 WEB SITE www.countryinns .com, 1011 Fairville Boulevard, but there are compensations, such as videocassette players in all the rooms, free video movies and complimentary continental breakfast (moderate).

least expensive of the lot and has 19 units overlooking the bay.

WHERE TO EAT

Easily the three best places to eat in Saint John are the **Turn of the Tide** ((506) 693-8484 in the Hilton, the **Top of the Town** ((506) 657-7320 at Coastal Inn Fort Howe Hotel, and **Shucker's** ((506) 648-1981 in the Delta Brunswick (see WHERE TO STAY, above). You will pay handsomely to eat at these places, but you will eat handsomely as well.

For less sumptuous dining your best bet is to go to Market Square, where you will find an array of restaurants and cafés to appeal to every

OPPOSITE: The famous Reversing Falls at Saint John. ABOVE: Saint John's Old City Market, the oldest market in Canada.

appetite and every budget. As difficult as it is to single out any one of them, we would mention **Grannan's** ((506) 634-1555, a seafood restaurant and oyster bar which has delicious dishes at quite moderate prices. The **Food Hall** at Market Square is full of fast-food places. A short walk from Market Square is the popular **Incredible Edibles** ((506) 633-7554 at 42 Princess Street, which specializes in pastas and local desserts.

HOW TO GET THERE

Air Canada operates several direct daily flights to Toronto, Montreal and Halifax. Pan-Am affiliate **Boston-Maine Airways** TOLL-FREE (800) 359-7262 WEB SITE www.flypanam.com links Saint Johns with Portsmouth, New Hampshire, and Bangor, Maine. The airport ((506) 638 5555 WEB SITE www.saintjohnairport.com is 16 km (10 miles) east of the city on Loch Lomond Road. A shuttle service connects with arriving and departing flights.

If traveling by car, the principal north–south highway into the city is Route 1, which links with the TransCanada Highway about 70 km (43 miles) to the north at Sussex and in the south crosses the border into Maine at St. Stephen, becoming US Highway 1. From Fredericton the main road is Route 7, but the meandering Route 102, along the St. John River, is much more picturesque.

If you are coming by train, take the **VIA Rail** ((506) 857-9830 TOLL-FREE (888) 842-7245 WEB SITE www.viarail.ca network to Moncton and then change for one of the two daily (except Wednesday) buses to Saint John.

Bay Ferries ((504) 649-7777 TOLL-FREE (888) 249-7245 WEB SITE www.nfl-bay.com operates a year-round ferry service across the Bay of Fundy between Digby, Nova Scotia, and Saint John. The journey takes three hours. During peak season, the ferry sails three times daily. In Digby, contact Bay Ferries ((902) 245-2116.

Farm boys cycling on the road north of Saint John.

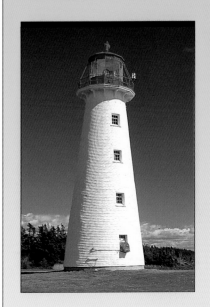

Prince Edward Island

Variously and affectionately known as Canada's "million-acre farm," "Spud Island" and "the Garden of the Gulf," Prince Edward Island is indeed small —half a million hectares (1.4 million acres) spread over an island 224 km (140 miles) long and 6 to 64 km (4 to 40 miles) wide. Lovely and unspoiled, much of the island is rolling farmland, famous for its potatoes.

Separated from the mainland by Northumberland Strait, when in 1534 Jacques Cartier came upon "the fairest land 'tis possible to see," named it Île St-Jean and claimed it for France, the island was inhabited by Mi'kmaq. French settlers didn't arrive in any numbers, however, until the early eighteenth century, reinforced in 1755 by Acadians expelled from Nova Scotia by the British, and again in 1758 by French colonists fleeing Nova Scotia after the fall of the fortress at Louisbourg. But it didn't remain a safe haven for long. Later that same year, a British expeditionary force under Lord Rollo captured the island and deported most of the

French-speaking population. Five years later Île St-Jean was renamed the "Island of St. John" and was annexed to Nova Scotia. In 1764, Charlottetown, named after Queen Charlotte, wife of George III, was designated the capital, and in 1769 the island became a colony in its own right.

In the years following the American Revolution, both the colony's population and its Anglophile orientation received a boost with the arrival of Loyalists fleeing the new republic to the south; and in 1799 it was renamed one final time, in honor of Prince Edward, later to be Duke of Kent and father of the future Queen Victoria. In 1851 the colony was granted self-governing status, and in 1864 it hosted the historic conference that led to the confederation of Canada in 1867. Prince Edward Island joined the Confederation in 1873.

Although the island's population is only 137,000, it is nonetheless Canada's most densely populated province — because it is also the smallest. It is even more crowded in summer, when over

a million visitors arrive to enjoy its idyllic scenery and long sandy beaches. Indeed, after agriculture, tourism is now the island's most important industry, fuelled in part by the global phenomenon of *Anne of Green Gables*, L. M. Montgomery's fictitious redheaded child whose exploits have remained popular since 1908 and are, apparently, red hot in Japan (for official memorabilia TOLL-FREE (800) 665 2663 WEB SITE www.annesociety.org).

Shoppers will find Prince Edward Island a treasure-trove of traditional crafts such as stitchery, quilting, pottery, glasswork, leather, woodwork and weaving. For information contact the Prince Edward Island Crafts Council ((902) 892-5152, 156 Richmond Street, Charlottetown.

CHARLOTTETOWN

This little city of tree-shaded streets and squares, stately Victorian clapboard houses and monumental churches is not only the provincial capital, but also the center of the island's commerce and tourism. It is situated on an arm of Hillsborough Bay, off the Northumberland Strait, 55 km (34 miles) from the ferry landing at Wood Islands.

BACKGROUND

Charlottetown lies just across the harbor from the spot where 300 French colonists founded the first European settlement on Prince Edward Island in 1720, naming it Port-la-Joye. After the British captured it in 1758 they built Fort Amherst on the site, and six years later founded Charlottetown. Over the next century, despite the influx of Loyalists following the American Revolution and successive waves of immigrants from Ireland and the Scottish Highlands, the town's population grew at a slow but steady pace — much like the pace of life in Charlottetown today. In 1864 it became the birthplace of Canada, when delegates from Britain's North American colonies convened in Province House and signed the articles that led to the Canadian Confederation.

GENERAL INFORMATION

Charlottetown Visitor Information Centre ((902) 368-4444 WEB SITE www.visitcharlottetown.com is on Water Street, next to Confederation Landing Park. The city operates a *Heritage Passport*, which gives you entry to all the local sights, a guided tour and lunch (price $28). Ask the Information Centre or any participating sights for details.

WHAT TO SEE AND DO

The heart and soul of Charlottetown is to be found in the **Confederation Centre of the Arts** ((902) 628-1864 TOLL-FREE (800) 565-0278 WEB SITE www .confederationcentre.com, 145 Richmond Street. Built in 1964 to commemorate the hundredth anniversary of the historic conference in which the first steps were taken towards a united, confederated Canada, it covers two city blocks and contains a memorial hall, a theater, and an art gallery and museum with a permanent collection of over 15,000 Canadian works and a wide range of changing exhibitions. There is also a library and restaurant. It is the principal venue of the annual, summer-long Charlottetown Festival, which always includes a popular musical based on the classic children's book, *Anne of Green Gables*.

Opposite the center on Richmond Street is **Province House National Historic Site** ((902) 566-7626 WEB SITE www.parkscanada.pch.gc.ca/parks/pei, a three-story, neo-Georgian sandstone edifice built between 1843 and 1847, and where the delegates met in 1864. The second floor **Confedera-**

A typical corner of Canada's "million-acre farm."

tion Chamber is set out exactly as it was in 1864. The building also houses the provincial Legislative Assembly. **Founders Hall** ((902) 368-1864 TOLL-FREE (800) 955 1864 WEB SITE www.founders hall.ca, Prince Street, Waterfront, tells the story of the birth of Canada through an imaginative range of audiovisuals, games, quizzes and displays (mid-May to mid-October).

South of Province House, on Richmond Street is **St. Dunstan's Basilica**, one of Canada's largest churches, easily recognizable by its twin Gothic spires. Inside you will find some exceptional Italian carvings. On Church Street is **St. Paul's Anglican Cathedral**, which dates from 1747, making it the oldest Protestant church in the province. Several murals by the portraitist Robert Harris distinguish its interior. The 1877 **Beaconsfield Historic House** ((902) 368-6603 WEB SITE www.peimuseum.com, 2 Kent Street, hosts a number of events throughout the year, including the Great PEI Children's Festival in July and August.

In summer, the Confederation Players TOLL-FREE (800) 955-1864 WEB SITE www.visitcharlotte town.com / walkingtours, in 1864 costumes, offer **walking tours** of the city.

West of the city, the **King's Byway Scenic Drive** (Route 1 / Route 4) skirts the coast to Murray River, where **Captain Scotty's Cruises** ((902) 962-2494 TOLL-FREE (800) 496-2494 WEB SITE www.tamotec .com / leszek / sealcruisespei.com, Route 4, northeast of town, offers **seal-watching** and **deep-sea fishing cruises** to the largest seal colony on Prince Edward Island. See seal pups and bull seals up to 450 kg (1,000 lbs), as well as Bird Island, where thousands of cormorants, great blue herons, terns and bald eagle. Further north along Route 4, just south of Montague, the **Buffaloland Provincial Park** ((902) 652-8950 has a boardwalk and observation deck overlooking a 100-acre enclosure with grazing herds of bison.

WHERE TO STAY

Expensive

The biggest and best hotel is the 10-story, 211-room **Delta Prince Edward Hotel** ((902) 566-2222 TOLL-FREE (800) 268-1133 FAX (902) 566-2282 WEB SITE www .deltaprinceedward.pe.ca, 18 Queen Street. Overlooking the waterfront, it has a swimming pool, an extensive health club and three dining choices. The other really top-flight hotel is the **Rodd Charlottetown** ((902) 894-7371 TOLL-FREE (800) 565-7633 FAX (902) 368-2178 WEB SITE www.rodd-hotels.ca, at the corner of Kent and Pownal Streets. Built originally by the Canadian National Railways, it is grand and luxurious, set in fine grounds but only a short walk from the theatre and shopping district.

The **Dundee Arms Inn and Motel** ((902) 892-2496 TOLL-FREE (877) 638 6333 FAX (902) 368-8532 WEB SITE www.dundeearms.com, 200 Pownal

Street, is a restored century-old mansion furnished with antiques and offering one of the best restaurants on the island (see below). Rooms in the motel wing are less expensive than those in the inn.

The city also has several other gracious old bed-and-breakfast inns, set in carefully restored mansions filled with antiques, and worth the price. Among the best are **Elmwood Heritage Inn** ((902) 368-3310 TOLL-FREE (877) 933-3310 FAX (902) 628-8457 WEB SITE www.elmwoodinn.pe.ca, on elmlined North River Road; **Edenhurst Inn** ((902) 368-8323 TOLL-FREE (877) 766-6439 FAX (902) 894-3707 WEB SITE www.peisland.com / edenhurst / inn; and **Fairholm National Historic Inn** ((902) 892-5022 TOLL-FREE (888) 573-5022 FAX (902) 892-5060 WEB SITE www.fairholm.pe.ca.

Moderate to Inexpensive

Of the less expensive accommodation, the two best-equipped places are conveniently clustered together on the TransCanada Highway just a couple of kilometers (a little over a mile) west of the city. The fanciest of these is the **Queen's Arms Econo Lodge** (/ FAX (902) 368-1110 TOLL-FREE (800) 539-1241 WEB SITE www.choicehotels.ca / cn437, 20 Lower Malpeque Road. Its 55 rooms and eight housekeeping units are all air-conditioned and have cable television. **Royalty Maples Cottages and Motel** ((902) 368-1030 TOLL-FREE (800) 831-7829, Rural Route 7, two kilometers (1.3 miles) west of Charlottetown, has 16 housekeeping units, 10 of them cottages, set in spacious grounds near a shopping mall and a golf course.

Happily for the bargain-hunter, there is an abundance of **tourist homes** and **bed-and-breakfast** accommodations in Charlottetown, as well as in the rest of the island. Contact **Tourism PEI** ((902) 368-7795 TOLL-FREE (888) 268-6667 FAX (902) 566-4336 WEB SITE www.peiplay.com for accommodation information throughout the island.

WHERE TO EAT

One of the best places to eat in town, perhaps in the whole province, is the colonial-style **Griffon Dining Room** ((902) 892-2496 in the Dundee Arms Inn. It is expensive, of course, but not quite as expensive as the **Selkirk** ((902) 566-2222 in the Prince Edward Hotel. Both are excellent, as is the **Carvery** ((902) 894-7371 in the Rodd Charlottetown, which is somewhat easier on the wallet. **Samuel's** ((902) 894-8572, at the Quality Inn on the Hill, serves delicious seafood at reasonable prices. **McAssey's** ((902) 892-1223, inside Founders' Hall, 6 Prince Street, is probably the best (expensive) option outside the hotels, with a historic waterfront setting, fine seafood and local specialties (open May to December).

Charlottetown has a good selection of moderately priced eateries serving above-average

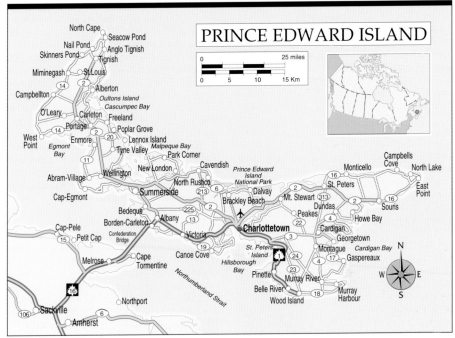

PRINCE EDWARD ISLAND

food. The **Lobster-on-the-Wharf** ((902) 368-2888, Prince Street Wharf, overlooks the harbor; the clams and mussels are delicious. Another popular place is the **Town & Country Restaurant** ((902) 892-2282, at 219 Queen Street, which has good steaks and salads.

The **Merchantman** ((902) 892-9150, Queen at Water Street, is a fine old historic house on the waterfront with a good collection of draught beer and fine Thai and Cajun food alongside the inevitable seafood and steak. The **Gahan House** ((902) 626-2337 WEB SITE www.peimenu.com, 126 Sydney Street, is a brew pub serving handcrafted ales and good old-fashioned pub food such as fish and chips.

Charlottetown also has some worthwhile ethnic restaurants, such as **Cedar's Eatery** ((902) 892-7377, 81 University Avenue, a welcoming place that specializes in Lebanese dishes and mountainous servings.

THE NORTH SHORE

Prince Edward Island's North Shore is home to some of the island's finest beaches, with their attendant family fun, from roller coasters to dinosaurs, and lines of motels mainly centered on Cavendish. It also has the island's finest national park, and a frenzied *Anne of Green Gables* souvenir trade.

Prince Edward Island National Park ((902) 672-6350, 2 Palmers Lane, is the province's premier tourist attraction. The park stretches for 40 km (25 miles) along the spectacular north shore and is hugely popular thanks to some of the finest white-sand beaches in North America and beautiful clear water warmed by the Gulf Stream. **Dalvay Beach**, at the eastern end, is usually the least crowded of the park's beaches, while **Cavendish Beach** WEB SITE www.cavendishbeachresort .com at the other end of the park is one of the busiest in all of Canada. All are accessible from Route 6, which after **Brackley Beach** becomes part of the scenic Blue Heron Drive that loops around the central part of the island. The drive is named for the birds that make their home in **New London Bay**, just beyond Cavendish at the western end of the park. **Greenwich** protects a rare system of parabolic sand dunes and the sites of Aboriginal, French and Acadian occupation. There are park information centers in Cavendish (Routes 6 and 13), Brackley (Routes 6 and 15) and Greenwich (Route 313).

"Anne" tourism has spawned everything from theme parks to museums and chocolate shops, including Lucy Maud Montgomery's birthplace and home. At the center of it all, **Green Gables House** ((902) 963-3370, off Route 6, Cavendish, is the old green and white farmhouse that belonged to cousins of the grandfather of Lucy Maud Montgomery, who used it as Anne's home in her novel. Now carefully restored, it is visited by thousands of people every year (May to October). Also in Cavendish, **Avonlea Village** ((902) 963-3050 WEB SITE www.avonlea.ca is an entertaining little theme park based around the Belmont Schoolhouse and Long River Church where Montgomery taught and worshipped (June to September).

Those looking for peace and quiet could try walking part of the 300-km (180-mile) **Confederation Trail**, a hiking and cycling trail laid on an old rail bed; it stretches across the north of the island and forms the easternmost section of the proposed TransCanada Trail, which will eventually run all the way to British Columbia.

WHERE TO STAY

At the eastern end of the national park is the magnificent **Dalvay-by-the-Sea Inn** ((902) 672-2048 WEB SITE www.dalvaybythesea.com, Little York.

Built in 1895 as the summer residence of Alexander Macdonald, a Standard Oil tycoon, it is set in lovely grounds only 180 m (590 ft) from Dalvay Beach, with 26 rooms, an excellent restaurant, a two-hole fairway, a bowling green, tennis courts, playgrounds, nature trails and a lake with canoes. Breakfast and dinner are included in the expensive rates (open June to September).

Further west, the moderately priced **Stanhope by the Sea** ((902) 672-2047 TOLL-FREE (877) 672-2047 FAX (902) 672-2951 WEB SITE www.peisland .com/stanhopebythesea, Little York, on Route 25, near the beach overlooking Covehead Bay, has been a country inn since 1817. There are 34 rooms in the original inn and 86 resort units (open June to mid-October).

At Brackley Beach the class act is **Shaw's Hotel & Cottages** ((902) 672-2022 FAX (902) 672-3000 WEB SITE www.peisland.com/shaws, on Route 15. Run by the Shaw family since 1860, it has 16 rooms in the hotel proper and 25 cottages (including 15 luxury chalets) on the well-manicured grounds, not far from the beach. Meals are included in the expensive rates (cottages open year-round; inn open June to early October). Around Rustico Bay are several delightful places to stay, all very reasonably priced. The moderately priced **Barachois Inn** ((902) 963-2194, Hunter River Rural Route 3,

is a Victorian house built in 1870 and recently refurbished, with eight tastefully decorated rooms and suites.

The entire area around Cavendish is crammed with places to stay. **Sundance Cottages** ((902) 963-2149 TOLL-FREE (800) 565-2149 FAX (902) 963-2100 WEB SITE www.peisland.com/sundance, Hunter River, Rural Route 2, offers 20 deluxe cottages with everything from kitchens and barbecues to hot tubs, a pool, exercise room and mountain bike rental (expensive).

In the heart of town, the **Kindred Spirits Country Inn and Cottages** ((902) 963-2434 FAX (902) 963-2619, Route 6, Memory Lane, Cavendish, is an antique-filled inn on a beautiful estate right next to Green Gables House and Golf Course. There are 25 large rooms at the inn, 14 cottages and a large swimming pool (mid-May to late October; expensive). Also next to Green Gables Golf Course is the **Lakeview Lodge and Cottages** ((902) 963-2436 TOLL-FREE (800) 565-7550 FAX (902) 963 2493 WEB SITE www.lakeviewlodge.ca, Cavendish, which has two rooms in the lodge, along with cottages and motel units (late May to early October; mid-range). On Route 13 in the center of Cavendish is the **Shining Waters Country Inn and Cottages** (/FAX (902) 963-2251 TOLL-FREE (877) 963-2251 WEB SITE www.peisland.com/shiningwaters, with 10 rooms in the main lodge, 20 cottages and a splendid array of recreational facilities (moderate).

Nor should one forget that all along this coast excellent budget accommodation can be found in farmhouses and bed and breakfasts. Contact **Tourism PEI** for accommodation information (see WHERE TO STAY, above under CHARLOTTETOWN).

WHERE TO EAT

The dining room at **Dalvay-by-the-Sea** ((902) 672-2048 is excellent; the Australian chef uses fresh local ingredients to create an exciting range of dishes from across the globe (open June to September). The seafood is similarly scrumptious, if not as elaborate, at **Stanhope by the Sea** ((902) 672-2047 (open June to September). When you get to Brackley Beach, you are in for a treat at the dining room of **Shaw's Hotel & Cottages** ((902) 672-2022 (open June to September), especially if you arrive in time for the Sunday buffet. A bit further down the road, you can enjoy a delightful meal in delightful surroundings at delightfully reasonable prices at **Café St. Jean** ((902) 963-3133, on Route 6 in Oyster Bed Bridge (open early June to late September).

In North Rustico the whole world, or so it seems, heads for **Fisherman's Wharf** ((902) 963-2669 on the harbor (open mid-May to early October), where it is claimed that 10 tons of live lobsters are kept for the hundreds (yes, hundreds) of customers who can be accommodated at one sitting.

In Cavendish there are many — too many — diners, snack bars and fast-food places, but little of decent quality. One happy exception is the **Galley** ((902) 963-2354, Route 13, which has steaks as well as seafood and lobster dinners.

HOW TO GET THERE

Air Canada has daily flights to Charlottetown from Toronto, while its partner, **Air Nova** WEB SITE www.airnova.ca, operates six daily flights from Halifax, Nova Scotia, and a summer daily direct service from Montreal.

The 13-km-long (nine-mile) **Confederation Bridge** links Prince Edward Island to the mainland, with a crossing time of only 12 minutes. You pay your toll on the return trip — as the tourism brochures say — "if you decide to leave" the province. There's a free shuttle service for pedestrians and cyclists.

The *Confederation* is a car ferry that crosses from Caribou, Nova Scotia, to Wood Islands, Prince Edward Island, sailing 18 times daily (May to December; journey time 75 minutes). For information and schedules call **Northumberland Ferries** ((902) 566-3838 TOLL-FREE (888) 249-7245 WEB SITE www.nfl-bay.com, 94 Water Street, Charlottetown.

The **PEI Express Shuttle** ((902) 462-8177 TOLL-FREE (877) 877-1771 WEB SITE www.peishuttle.com, is an express passenger service from Halifax, Nova Scotia, to the island, using 10-passenger minibuses.

There is no train service to the island.

OPPOSITE: The House that Anne Built — Green Gables House, near Cavendish, is a perennial tourist attraction. ABOVE: A small Prince Edwardian takes it easy.

Nova
Scotia

Formed as if to honor its most celebrated culinary delight, the lobster-shaped province of Nova Scotia is Canada's anchor in the Atlantic. Its 52,842 sq km (20,402 sq miles) is divided into a long peninsula connected to the adjoining province of New Brunswick by the narrow Isthmus of Chignecto, and Cape Breton Island, linked by a one-and-a-half-kilometer-long (one-mile) causeway. The province is only 560 km (350 miles) long, but its ragged shore gives it a staggering 7,400 km (4,598 miles) of coast. With Prince Edward Island and New Brunswick, it is one of the three Maritime Provinces.

Like Newfoundland, Nova Scotia is thought to have been visited by the Vikings around AD 1000, but dates its "discovery" to 1497, when John Cabot arrived at the northern tip of Cape Breton Island and claimed the territory for England. The first settlement, however, was French: Samuel de Champlain founded Port Royal, now Annapolis Royal, on the peninsula's northwest coast in 1605. Sixteen years later, England's Scottish King James I granted the region to another Scot, Sir William Alexander, so that he might establish a "New Scotland" there. Which he did, though using the Latin form of the name in the original charter.

For the next century Nova Scotia was caught up in the Anglo-French struggle for possession of eastern North America. Finally, in 1737 it was agreed that the British would have sovereignty over the peninsula while the French would control Cape Breton Island. In the early 1740s the French completed their great fortress at Louisbourg, which had a commanding position on the east coast of the island, prompting Britain to send a large group of settlers to establish a fortified settlement at Halifax, as a counterweight to France's military stronghold.

In 1755, as Britain and France squared up to fight another war, the British governor of Nova Scotia ordered the deportation of all French settlers, or Acadians, who refused to take an oath of allegiance to the British Crown. Over the next few years 15,000 Acadians were forcibly removed from their homes and shipped off to the American colonies, where they found themselves equally unwelcome. Most of them eventually settled in the bayou country of Louisiana, where they survive to this day as Cajuns. Some later returned to Cape Breton, which still has a strong French influence.

In 1763, after the end of the Seven Years' War, all of Nova Scotia, including Cape Breton Island, came under British rule. The Anglicization of the region received a further boost after the American Revolution, when 30,000 Loyalists fled the new republic and resettled here, mainly along the Atlantic coast. In 1867 it became one of Canada's four founding provinces.

Today, with a population of around 950,000, Nova Scotia is by far the most populous of the Maritime Provinces. Fishing has always been at the heart of the province's economy, and today still accounts for the largest share of its revenues. There is also a thriving timber industry, along with orchards and dairy farms in the Annapolis Valley. But its fastest growing industry is undoubtedly tourism, thanks to its excellent recreational facilities, its strong Celtic heritage and its great natural beauty, which includes the spectacular Cape Breton Highlands National Park.

HALIFAX

Originally founded purely for strategic reasons, Halifax remains the home of Canada's largest naval base. But this bustling provincial capital with a metropolitan population of around 345,000 is now more important as the largest city and commercial center of the Maritime Provinces.

On a small peninsula on the western shore of a deep inlet of the Atlantic, Halifax has a superb natural harbor that shelters the busiest port on Canada's east coast. The oldest British town on the Canadian mainland, and home of Canada's first Protestant church, Halifax wears its age gracefully. At the same time, the city has a liveliness and sophistication seldom found in cities of comparable size. In short, Halifax is in the enviable position of being able to boast both small-town virtues and big-city amenities.

BACKGROUND

Although the Mi'kmaq had long inhabited the area, the town of Halifax came into being almost overnight when, in 1749, Colonel Edward Cornwallis led a flotilla of 20 ships, carrying 3,000 settlers, into the harbor. Built in response to the perceived threat posed by the new French fortress at Louisbourg, the town was named after the Earl of Halifax, then the president of England's Board of Trade and Plantations.

Ironically, having been established in the first place solely because of its strategic location in case of war, Halifax went on to prosper greatly from wars fought in other lands. First, the British victory in the Seven Years' War removed any potential threat from Louisbourg. Then during the American War of Independence the harbor became an important naval base for British warships. After the British defeat, the resulting influx of fleeing loyalists, many educated and well to do, further invigorated the local economy and had a profound impact on the local culture. Then came the War of 1812, which brought the warships back from Britain, and with them more money to swell the municipal coffers. Even the American Civil War led to increased military activity, spending and employment here.

Twentieth-century wars, too, were profitable for the town. During World War I, thanks to the 16 sq km (10 sq miles) of deep-water anchorage in the harbor's Bedford Basin, Halifax was used as a distribution center for supply ships heading for Europe. During World War II it was the port from which the great convoys — some 17,000 ships in all — sailed across the North Atlantic.

The past half-century, however, has shown that Halifax can flourish in peacetime just as well as in wartime, remaining an important transportation hub. In 2001, the people of Halifax took in some 9,000 travelers whose flights were rerouted during the September 11 aftermath.

GENERAL INFORMATION

The **International Visitors Centre** ((902) 490-5946 TOLL-FREE (800) 565-0000 E-MAIL nsvisit@fox.nstn.ca

and kayaks. For **Autumn Leaf Watch**, on the state of the fall colors throughout Nova Scotia, contact TOLL-FREE (1877) 353 5323. The **Nova Scotia Museum Pass** TOLL-FREE (800) 632-1114 WEB SITE www.museum.gov.ns.ca offers a family ticket to 25 sites throughout the island.

WHAT TO SEE AND DO

Thanks to a city ordinance banning the construction of buildings that interfere with various views across the city, Halifax has successfully preserved a human scale as it has grown. Since the founding of the city, the center of Halifax has been the **Grand Parade**, a square running along the west side of

WEB SITE www.explorenovascotia.com, corner of Barrington and Sackville Streets, has video kiosks and a small theater as well as brochures and booking desks. There are also information offices at Sackville Landing ((902) 424-4248 and Halifax International Airport ((902) 873-1223. For Halifax information, see WEB SITE www.halifax.info.com.

Atlantic Tours ((902) 423-6242 TOLL-FREE (800) 565-7173 WEB SITE www.atlantictours.com operates sightseeing trolley tours of the city, and **Double Decker Tours** ((902) 420-1155 WEB SITE www.double deckertours.com does city tours in an old London bus. For an amphibious tour of town and harbor, call **Harbour Hopper Tours** ((902) 490-8687 WEB SITE www.harbourhopper.com. For local evening **ghost walks**, contact ((902) 469-6176 E-MAIL macrev@ns.sympatico.ca.

Freewheeling Adventures ((902) 857-3600 WEB SITE www.freewheeling.ca rents out bicycles

Barrington Street, Halifax's main shopping thoroughfare. At the north end of the square is **City Hall**, built in 1888, with its enormous wooden flagpole, and at the south end is the timber-framed **St. Paul's** (1750), the oldest Protestant church in Canada. Going up George Street from the Grand Parade towards the citadel, you come upon the symbol of Halifax, the **Old Town Clock**, erected in 1803 by the Duke of Kent, then head of the garrison.

Further up is the **Citadel** ((902) 426-5080 WEB SITE www.parkscanada.gc.ca (open May to October), one of Canada's foremost attractions. This many-angled, star-shaped fortress was originally built by Cornwallis on his arrival in 1749. It was rebuilt and expanded after the American Revolution and then again after the War of 1812.

Long after the flames died, the story of a terrible forest fire still lives in Cape Breton Highlands National Park.

Finally, in 1828, the Duke of Wellington ordered a permanent fortress of masonry to be built. Completed in 1856 it remained in use as a barracks until after World War II. The Citadel has been restored to its 1856 state, with guides dressed in 78th Highland Regiment uniforms. Its Army Museum ((902) 426-5979 housed in the Cavalier Building, has an extensive collection of local military memorabilia.

Down on the harborfront north of Duke Street, the **Historic Properties** ((902) 426-0530 is a group of restored and refurbished wharves and buildings dating from 1800, now an all-pedestrian area with shops, galleries, restaurants and street entertainers. The **Privateers' Warehouse** is the oldest

ing display on local shipwrecks, and items illustrating Halifax's maritime history make up the rest of the museum's excellent collection. Outside are several historic ships, including **HMCS Sackville** ((902) 429-2132 WEB SITE www.hmcssackville-cnmt.ns.ca, a World War II convoy escort corvette restored as a floating museum of the Canadian navy (June to September). A replica of Canada's most famous boat, the unbeaten racing schooner **Bluenose II** ((902) 634-1963 TOLL-FREE (800) 763 1963 WEB SITE www.bluenose2.ns.ca offers daily two-hour harbor cruises June to September.

Canada's answer to Ellis Island, the **Pier 21 National Historic Site** ((902) 425-7770 WEB SITE www.pier21.ns.ca, 1055 Marginal Road, is an innovative

structure in the area, where nineteenth-century pirates stashed their loot; it is now a restaurant and entertainment center.

Alexander Keith's Nova Scotia Brewery ((902) 455-1474, Lower Water Street, is the nineteenth-century home of Keith's beer, a Nova Scotia legend, still very much in evidence in modern bars. The brewery tour, led by costumed interpreters, goes back to its 1834 roots, but offers a taste of the modern brew.

The **Maritime Museum of the Atlantic** ((902) 424-7490 WEB SITE www.maritime.museum.gov.ns.ca, 1675 Lower Water Street, traces the link between the *Titanic* disaster and Halifax — the closest major port to the disaster site — telling the story of the search and rescue ships chartered from this city. Ship models, naval instruments, weapons, a haunt-

and imaginative museum set in Canada's last remaining immigration shed, telling the stories of over a million immigrants who flooded through these halls between 1928 and 1971.

In a restored heritage building a block back from the water, the **Art Gallery of Nova Scotia** ((902) 424-7542 WEB SITE www.agns.ednet.ns.ca, 1723 Hollis Street, houses a permanent collection of Canadian and international art and offers a wide array of events and educational workshops. Nearby is the **Nova Scotia Centre for Craft & Design** ((902) 424-4062 WEB SITE www.craft-design.gov.ns.ca, 1683 Barrington Street. A block away, the **Discovery Centre** ((902) 492-4422 WEB SITE www.discoverycentre.ns.ca, 1593 Barrington Street, is an entertaining hands-on science center with over 80 interactive exhibits.

On the far side of the hill from downtown, the **Nova Scotia Museum of Natural History** ((902)

A fisherman with his catch in picturesque Peggy's Cove, west of Halifax.

424-7353 WEB SITE www.nature.museum.gov.ns.ca, 1747 Summer Street, has exhibits covering every aspect of the province's history — geographical, natural, social and industrial. The **Public Gardens** (open spring to late fall) just south of the museum were first opened in 1867 and remain a classic work of Victoriana: a bandstand, fountains, statues, duck pond and formally planted Oriental trees. Even more attractive for would-be strollers and picnickers is **Point Pleasant Park**, Point Pleasant Drive, at the southern tip of the Halifax peninsula. This heavily wooded 75-hectare (186-acre) park has a restaurant in addition to its many walking trails and picnic spots. Within the grounds stands the **Prince of Wales Martello Tower** ((902) 426-5080

NIGHTLIFE AND THE ARTS

Halifax is lively at night, especially along **Grafton Street** and **Spring Garden Road**, which on Friday and Saturday nights is the scene of one long party. There is multilevel partying at **Privateers' Warehouse** ((902) 422-1289 in the Historic Properties: with the Upper Deck restaurant (see WHERE TO EAT, below), the **Middle Deck** lounge, where rock and jazz bands play, and the **Lower Deck**, where maritime folk music fills the air.

The **Economy Shoe Shop** ((902) 423-7463, 1663 Argyle Street, is a hip café and bar with live jazz, open-mike nights and local art exhibitions.

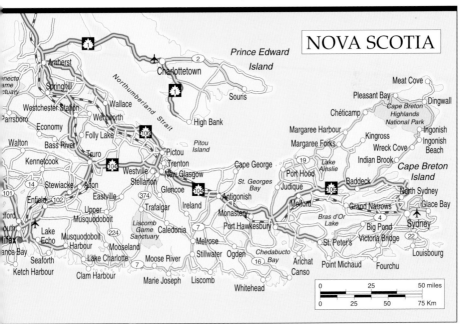

WEB SITE www.parkscanada.gc.ca, built from 1767 to 1797 as one of the mainstays of the local naval defense network FAX (902) 496-8118. In July and August, the park hosts the open-air theater festival **Shakespeare by the Sea** ((902) 422-0295.

Dating back to 1811, **Peggy's Cove**, 43 km (27 miles) west of Halifax on Route 333, is built around a narrow ocean inlet and is dominated by a lighthouse perched on massive granite boulders. Here brightly colored clapboard houses cling to the granite cliffs surrounding the lovely little harbor where the fishing boats are moored and where the fishermen's shacks stand on stilts in the water. Unfortunately, it is packed with tourists during summer, so go in early morning before the hoards descend. **Peggy's Cove Express** ((902) 422-4200 WEB SITE www.peggyscove.com is a round-trip boat excursion from Halifax to Peggy's Cove, searching for whales and dolphins en route.

The **Old Triangle** ((902) 492-4900, 5136 Prince Street, has Cape Breton and Nova Scotian music.

Concerts of all kinds are performed regularly at the **Metro Centre** ((902) 451-1202, 5248 Duke Street, near the Citadel, while the intimate **Neptune Theatre** ((902) 429-7070 TOLL-FREE (800) 565 7345 WEB SITE www.neptune.ns.sympatico.ca, 1593 Argyle Street, stages drama and comedy.

Casino Nova Scotia ((902) 425-7777 TOLL-FREE (888) 642-6376 WEB SITE www.casinonovascotia .com, 1983 Upper Water Street, has live entertainment and five restaurants and bars.

WHERE TO STAY

Expensive
The most luxurious hotel is the **Sheraton Halifax** ((902) 421-1700 TOLL-FREE (866) 42564329 FAX (902) 422-5805 WEB SITE www.sheratonhalifax.com, in

the Historic Properties, 1919 Upper Water Street. Although large, modern and equipped with all the luxuries, it manages to blend in beautifully with the historic buildings around it. Connected by underground walkway to the World Trade and Convention Centre, the **Prince George Hotel** ((902) 425-1986 TOLL-FREE (800) 565-1567 FAX (902) 429-6048 WEB SITE www.princegeorgehotel.com, 1725 Market Street, is an elegantly appointed hotel in a handy downtown location; it has 260 rooms and an award-winning restaurant. The downtown **Westin Nova Scotian** ((902) 421-1000 TOLL-FREE (877) 993-7846 FAX (902) 422-9465 WEB SITE www.westin.ns.ca, 1881 Hollis Street, has been around for 70 years, but has been tastefully

burton House Inn ((902) 420-0658 FAX (902) 423-2324 WEB SITE www.halliburton.ns.ca, 5184 Morris Street. This registered heritage property with 29 rooms and a courtyard garden was built in 1820 and has been completely renovated and modernized without sacrificing any of its original charm. It also has one of the best restaurants in Halifax.

Opposite the Public Gardens, the **Lord Nelson** ((902) 423-6331 TOLL-FREE (800) 565-2020 FAX (902) 491-6148 WEB SITE www.lordnelsonhotel.com, 1515 South Park Street, is another venerable, recently renovated, hotel, with 243 rooms. The friendly 30-room **Waverley Inn** ((902) 423-9346 TOLL-FREE (800) 565-9346 FAX (902) 425-0167 WEB SITE www.waverleyinn.com, 1266 Barrington

refurbished and now enjoys the addition of a number of luxury rooms.

Mid-range

Halifax is blessed with many superb mid-range hotels. The **Citadel Halifax** ((902) 422-1391 TOLL-FREE (800) 565-7162 WEB SITE www.citadelhalifax .com, 1960 Brunswick Street, has 267 luxurious rooms, some on no-smoking floors and some overlooking the harbor. The twin **Delta Barrington and Halifax** ((902) 429-7410 TOLL-FREE (800) 268-1133 WEB SITE www.deltahotels.com, 1875 and 1990 Barrington Street, near the Historic Properties, are classic examples of how to build a modern hotel without upsetting the neighbors. The Barrington has more down-home charm; the Halifax, built originally by Canadian Pacific, more elegance. Both have pools, fitness centers and restaurants.

For elegance it would be hard to beat **Halli-**

Street, has been here since 1876, and boasts Oscar Wilde among its former guests. Now fully modernized, it is an attractive bargain.

Inexpensive

The **Garden Inn** ((902) 492-8577 TOLL-FREE (877) 414-8577 FAX (902) 492-1462 WEB SITE www.garden inn.ns.ca, 1263 South Park Street, is a registered Heritage Home (built 1875) near downtown, attractively and comfortably restored into a small hotel with 23 rooms.

The **Travelers Motel** ((902) 835-3394 TOLL-FREE (800) 565-3394 FAX (902) 835-6887 WEB SITE www .travelersmotel.com, 773 Bedford Highway, Bedford, on the Halifax city limits, has 25 motel units, an outdoor pool and a restaurant. Across the harbor from Halifax, in Dartmouth, the **Country Inn & Suites** ((902) 465-4000 TOLL-FREE (800) 456-4000 FAX (902) 465-6006 WEB SITE www.countryinns.com,

101 Yorkshire Avenue Extension, has 77 rooms, and offers complimentary videos and light breakfasts.

From May to August, cheap accommodation is available in the student residences of **Dalhousie University** ((902) 494-8840 FAX (902) 494-1219 WEB SITE www.dal.ca/confserv and **Saint Mary's University** ((902) 420-5486 TOLL-FREE (888) 347 5555 WEB SITE www.stmarys.ca/conferences.

There are many excellent **bed and breakfasts** in Halifax and throughout Nova Scotia. Contact the tourist office for an up-to-date list.

WHERE TO EAT

As with many smallish cities, the best restaurants are often in the best hotels. In Halifax, we would recommend the superb restaurant in the **Halliburton House Inn** ((902) 420-0658, 3184 Morris Street. An excellent alternative would be the **Press Gang** ((902) 423-8816, 5218 Prince Street, a cozy, dark basement restaurant in one of the city's oldest properties, serving a wonderfully eclectic range of food from Thai soup to clam chowder, beet salad to filet mignon.

The **Upper Deck Restaurant** ((902) 422-1289, Third floor, Privateers' Warehouse in the Historic Properties, has excellent food as well as courteous service to go with its maritime decor. Also part of the complex, the **Harborfront Market** ((902) 422-3077 houses a luscious variety of delis and food stalls, cafés and a microbrewery, with plenty of outdoor waterfront tables.

Of course, it's not difficult to find wonderful seafood in Halifax, but if you want to find it in an unusual and lovely setting, go to the **Five Fishermen** ((902) 422-4421, 1740 Argyle Street across from the Grand Parade. The restaurant is upstairs in a converted schoolhouse and is lit by genuine Tiffany lamps.

Ryan Duffy's Steak and Seafood ((902) 421-1116, Spring Garden Place Shopping Center, 5640 Spring Garden Road, is as moderate (or as expensive) as you want it to be. If you order a steak, the meat is cut and trimmed to your specifications at your table before it is cooked, and the price is strictly according to the weight of the cut you have chosen. Also excellent for steak and seafood, **McKelvies Restaurant and Bar** ((902) 421-6161, 1680 Lower Water Street, opposite the Maritime Museum, is a lively, cheerful place in a renovated fire station.

Rogue's Roost ((902) 492-2337, 5435 Spring Garden Road, is a trendy microbrewery where you can watch five craft ales being brewed while sampling and snacking.

HOW TO GET THERE

Air Canada has daily flights to Halifax from New York, Boston, Toronto and Montréal. For information on Halifax Airport visit WEB SITE www.hiaa.ca.

Halifax is the eastern terminus of **VIA Rail**, with one train daily (except Tuesday) from Montréal via Moncton, New Brunswick. **Greyhound** runs buses from the United States and **Voyageur** buses from Montréal link up with the SMT bus lines in New Brunswick, which in turn connects at Amherst with the Nova Scotian company, **Acadian Lines** ((902) 454-9321, 6040 Almon Street, Halifax.

If you are driving, highways from all over the United States and Canada join the TransCanada Highway, which crosses from New Brunswick into Nova Scotia at Amherst. For ferry connections to Nova Scotia, see HOW TO GET THERE, page 195 under OUTSIDE HALAFAX.

OUTSIDE HALIFAX

Nova Scotia may divide into two parts geographically, but ethnically it is a jigsaw puzzle. While Halifax is English both in its history and its character, the rest of the province shows English, Irish, French, German and Scottish influences. Place names, from Windsor to Lunenburg or Bras d'Or are a clear indication of who settled where. Traveling around Nova Scotia these influences become apparent in other ways, from French Acadian food to Scottish pipes and tartans.

THE SOUTH SHORE

On Route 3 southwest of Halifax, the charming seaside village of **Chester** is on a peninsula at the

OPPOSITE: Halifax's Historic Properties. ABOVE: The Victorian bandstand, focal point of the Public Gardens.

head of scenic, island-strewn Mahone Bay. Settled by New Englanders in 1760 (who originally gave it the name Shoreham), it is still the summer home of quite a few American families — as well as a favored retirement home of wealthy Canadians. Although visitors are welcome to use its tennis courts and its 18-hole golf course on a promontory overlooking the bay, most people come for the sailing and yachting. Indeed, the high point of the summer season is **Chester Race Week** ((902) 275-3876 (mid-August), the largest sailing regatta in the Maritimes.

The little town of **Mahone Bay**, 21 km (13 miles) southwest of Chester on Route 3, is best known as a crafts and antiques center, with its trademark three churches standing side-by-side at the head of the harbor. There was a time, in the century after its founding by Captain Ephraim Cook in 1754, when it was known primarily as a haunt of pirates and smugglers. Many of the town's shops, studios, galleries and restaurants are housed in historic early nineteenth-century buildings.

Just down the coast from Mahone Bay is **Lunenburg**, a UNESCO World Heritage Site, long considered Nova Scotia's premier fishing port. Like its neighbor, it was a favorite haven for pirates until well into the nineteenth century. On a picturesque peninsula with a front and back harbor, Lunenburg has lately become an important tourist stopover, with shops, galleries and all sorts of recreational facilities, including the nine-hole **Bluenose Golf Course** overlooking Front Harbour. The area was first settled in 1753 by Protestants from the German town of Lunenburg, and has a long and colorful seafaring heritage, and one of the finest surviving town centers in Canada. For **walking tours** of the historic area, contact ((902) 634-3848.

Lunenburg is probably best known as the town that in 1921 built the *Bluenose*, the famous racing schooner — depicted on the Canadian dime — that never lost an international race. In 1963 Lunenburg also built its replica, *Bluenose II*, which can usually be seen in the harbor at Halifax, but is sometimes moored at the **Fisheries Museum of the Atlantic** ((902) 634-4794 WEB SITE www.fisheries.museum.gov.ns.ca, 68 Bluenose Drive, which has three floors of exhibits about fishing, whaling and the fishing communities, an aquarium, a good restaurant and several historic ships. There are **whale-watching trips** from the Fisheries Wharf ((902) 527-7175, and *Bluenose II* runs cruises when in town TOLL-FREE (800) 763 1963 WEB SITE www.bluenose2.ns.ca.

Continuing west along the coast, **Whitepoint Beach** TOLL-FREE (800) 565-5068 WEB SITE www.whitepoint.com, near Liverpool, is one of Nova Scotia's favorite seaside resorts, with a one and a half kilometers (a mile) of sand and plenty of child-friendly entertainment and water and land sports on offer.

The 381-sq-km (147-sq-mi) **Kejimkujik National Park** ((902) 682-2772 WEB SITE www.parkscanada.gc.ca, 25 km (15 miles) southwest of Liverpool, protects a stunning section of wooded lake country and wild, glacier-carved cliffs and coves. Fifteen trails crisscross the park. Canoeing is possible on many of the lakes and rivers; park staff lead walks and cycle rides.

Further along Route 103 is **Shelburne**, "The Loyalist Town," settled in 1783, when 3,000 Loyalists fleeing New York City, many of them rich, arrived in 30 ships and instantly created a prosperous town where there had been nothing but wilderness — and one of the best natural harbors in the world. Within a few years the population

had quintupled, making it the largest community in British North America. However, the population shrank almost as quickly as it had expanded, whereupon Shelburne turned into a fishing and shipbuilding center — in fact, it went on to become the birthplace of many of the world's great yachts. There are still a number of houses in Shelburne that date from the Loyalist period, notably **Ross-Thomson House** ((902) 875-3141 WEB SITE www.rossthomson.museum.gov.ns.ca, 9 Charlotte Lane, built in 1784. Originally a general store, today it is a Loyalist museum, its shelves stocked with goods in demand in the 1780s (June to mid-October). **David Nairn House**, built in 1787, is now the home of the **Shelburne County Museum** ((902) 875-3219 WEB SITE www.historicshelburne.com, 8 Maiden Lane (shorter hours in the off-season).

The three villages of **West Pubnico**, **Middle West Pubnico** and **Lower West Pubnico**, on the west coast, were first settled in 1653 and make up the oldest Acadian settlement in Nova Scotia. West Pubnico's **Historic Acadian Village** ((902) 762-2530 WEB SITE www.tusket.com, Old Church Road, off Route 335 (open mid-June to September) features

OPPOSITE TOP: A barn and farmhouse in their wooded context. BOTTOM: The shingled exterior of a barn. ABOVE: Preparing salmon for smoking.

a number of restored nineteenth-century buildings and the **Musée Acadien** ((902) 762-3380 WEB SITE www.ccfne.ns.ca, an 1864 homestead with a summer-long program of events and demonstrations about the Acadian lifestyle.

With a great shipping tradition going back to its settlement in 1761, **Yarmouth**, Nova Scotia's largest seaport west of Halifax, is notable for its well-preserved **Victorian architecture** and for its famous **Runic Stone** on Main Street, which bears inscriptions suggesting that the Vikings reached here 1,000 years ago. The **Yarmouth County Museum** ((902) 742-5539, 22 Collins Street, is excellent, with displays of seafaring artifacts, Victorian furniture, costumes and early decorative arts.

Chester also has the informal, inexpensive **Mecklenburgh Inn** ((902) 275-4638 E-MAIL frnthrbr @auracom.com, 78 Queen Street, a Victorian-style hotel in a residential neighborhood, with large porches on its two floors. The comfortable rooms have shared bath.

A short distance out of town, **Oak Island Inn and Marina** ((902) 627-2600 TOLL-FREE (800) 565-5075 FAX (902) 627-2020 WEB SITE www.oakisland inn.com, Exit 9 or 10 off Highway 103 between Chester and Mahone Bay, is a recently renovated oceanfront resort with 106 rooms and 13 chalets and a full set of facilities.

Nearby in Hubbards there are two delightful places on Shore Club Road. One is the **Anchor-**

Yarmouth is principally of interest today, however, as the "Gateway to Nova Scotia": the terminus for ferries from Portland and Bar Harbor in Maine.

There are **visitor information centers** in Mahone Bay ((902) 624-6151, Chester ((902) 275-4616, Lunenburg ((902) 634-8100, Blockhouse Road, Shelburne ((902) 875-4547 at the corner of King and Dock Streets, and Yarmouth ((902) 742-5033, 228 Main Street, up the hill from the ferry terminal.

Where to Stay

In Chester, enjoy stylish luxury at **Haddon Hall** ((902) 275-3577 FAX (902) 275-5159 WEB SITE www .haddonhallinn.com, 67 Haddon Hill Road, perched atop a hill with unobstructed views of Mahone Bay (expensive). Four rooms have wood fireplaces, three have Jacuzzis and two have kitchenettes. The (expensive) dining room is very good; reserve a table on the front porch for its lovely vistas.

age House & Cottages ((902) 857-9402 TOLL-FREE (800) 565-2624 WEB SITE www.anchoragehouse .com, Rural Route 2, which has 14 housekeeping cottages and four rooms in the main lodge (moderate). It has fishing charters and small-boat rentals from its own private wharf. The **Dauphinee Inn** ((902) 857-1790 TOLL-FREE (800) 567-1790 FAX (902) 857-9555 WEB SITE www.dauphineeinn.com, 167 Shore Club Road, has only six moderately priced rooms along with a licensed dining room and lounge, a gift shop and boat-docking facilities.

In Lunenburg, the most elegant accommodation is in some of its many restored Victorian mansions. Among the finest are the **Boscawen Inn** ((902) 634-3325 TOLL-FREE (800) 354-5009 FAX (902) 634-9293 WEB SITE www.ns.sympatico.ca/boscawen, 150 Cumberland Street (mid-range to expensive); the mid-range **Kaulbach House Historic Inn** (/FAX (902) 634-8818 TOLL-FREE (800) 568-8818

WEB SITE www.kaulbachhouse.com, 75 Pelham Street; and **Lincoln House B&B** ((902) 634-7179 TOLL-FREE (877) 634 7179 E-MAIL lincoln@fox.nstn.ca, 130 Lincoln Street (inexpensive). An excellent bargain is the **Homeport Motel & Cottages** ((902) 634-8234 TOLL-FREE (800) 616-4411 E-MAIL home port.motel@ns.sympatico.ca, 167 Victoria Road.

The **Whitepoint Beach Resort** ((902) 354-2711 TOLL-FREE (800) 565-5068 FAX (902) 354-7278 WEB SITE www.whitepoint.com is a large, luxurious beachfront resort, with 44 cottages, 74 rooms, all the facilities you could ever need and a huge range of activities (expensive).

In Shelburne you should try to get into the **Cooper's Inn** ((902) 875-4656 TOLL-FREE (800) 688-

edly celebrated, while its bar, Hawthorne's Lounge, is a most convivial watering hole. The **Harbour's Edge Bed and Breakfast** ((902) 742-2387 WEB SITE www.harboursedge.ns.ca is a lovely Italianate historic house, with three guest rooms, set in grounds overlooking Yarmouth Harbour (moderate). Four kilometers (two and a half miles) from Yarmouth on Route 1 at Dayton, the **Voyageur Motel** ((902) 742-7157 TOLL-FREE (800) 565-5026, has 29 motel units and four housekeeping units, overlooking Doctors Lake (moderate).

Where to Eat

In Chester, if you are staying at **Haddon Hall** ((902) 275-3577, eat there. Otherwise go down Route 3

2011 WEB SITE www.ns.sympatico.ca/coopers, 36 Dock Street, a splendidly refurbished 1784 house on the waterfront with six antique-furnished rooms and one large suite; breakfast is included (moderate). If you are looking for something inexpensive, try the **Loyalist Inn** ((902) 875-2343 FAX (902) 875-1452, 160 Water Street, which has 18 air-conditioned rooms with bath and cable television, a bar and dining room.

The poshest hotel in Yarmouth is easily the **Rodd Grand Hotel** ((902) 742-2446 TOLL-FREE (800) 565-7633 FAX (902) 742-4645 WEB SITE www.rodd-hotels.ca, 417 Main Street, whose 138 comfortable rooms occupy seven floors overlooking Yarmouth Harbour (mid-range). Its lower-priced sister hotel, the **Rodd Colony Harbour Inn** ((902) 742-9194 TOLL-FREE (800) 565-7633 WEB SITE www.rodd-hotels .ca, is across from the ferry terminal, at 6 Forest Street. The hotel's Colony Restaurant is deserv-

to the **Galley** ((902) 275-4700, 115 Marina Road, which has an enchanting view over the marina at Marriott Cove as well as fine, and inexpensive, seafood and homemade desserts. In Mahone Bay, **Mimi's Ocean Grill** ((902) 624-1342, 662 Main Street, provides good food using local ingredients in an attractive seaside setting.

In Lunenburg, the best dining is at the **Boscawen Inn** ((902) 634-3325. Also good is the **Old Fish Factory** ((902) 634-3333, 68 Bluenose Drive, on the second floor of the Fisheries Museum of the Atlantic, which offers several traditional Lunenburg dishes.

In Shelburne, apart from the **Cooper's Inn** (((902) 875-4656 and the **Loyalist Inn** ((902) 875-

OPPOSITE: The church in Grand Pré National Historic Site that memorializes the deported Acadians. ABOVE: Annapolis Royal's Historic Gardens.

2343, try the award-winning Swiss-run **Charlotte Lane Café and Crafts** ((902) 875-3314, 13 Charlotte Lane, which is far more about innovative fine dining than its rather cozy name suggests.

In Yarmouth, once again, the best places to eat are in the best places to stay: **Rodd Colony Harbour Inn** ((902) 742-9194 and the **Rodd Grand Hotel** ((902) 742-2446. After those you ought to check out **Captain Kelley's Restaurant** ((902) 742-9191, 577 Main Street, which serves very good food at popular prices. Also, out on Route 1 across from the Voyageur Motel, there is **Harris's Quick 'n' Tasty** ((902) 742-3467, which is much better than it sounds — and also boasts of "cholesterol-free frying."

port. There are others in Annapolis Royal ((902) 532-5769; Kentville ((902) 678-7171 WEB SITE www.town.kentville.ns.ca, 125 Park Street; Wolfville ((902) 542-7000 WEB SITE www.town.wolfville.ns.ca, Main Street; and Windsor ((902) 798-2690, Highway 101, Exit 6.

Digby is the first town of any size that you come across, home of the (justly) celebrated Digby scallops. The town itself celebrates its best-known product with the Digby Scallop Days in August. Almost as well known are the locally cured smoked herring, called Digby Chicks. Digby's site, on an inlet of the Bay of Fundy, is not only beautiful but handy: it is the terminus for the ferry from Saint John, New Brunswick. **Basin Charters** ((902)

ANNAPOLIS VALLEY

Route 1 from Yarmouth to Windsor, through the beautiful Annapolis Valley region, is known as the **Evangeline Trail** WEB SITE www.evangeline trail.com, after the heroine of Longfellow's famous poem about the tragedy of the Acadians who were expelled from here in 1755. This was the heartland of Acadia, celebrated each July during the **Festival Acadien de Clare**. The other major festival in the area is the spring **Apple Blossom Festival**. The whole area is strewn with little local museums focusing on the area's history: from schooling to fishing to a restored sawmill. Ask at the tourist office for a full list, if you have time to linger.

There are two **Tourist Information Centers** in Digby ((902) 245-5714, on the harbor at 110 Montague Row and at 237 Shore Road, next to the ferry

245-8446 operates sports fishing charters and whale-watching cruises from the Digby Marina.

Founded in 1605 by Samuel de Champlain, **Annapolis Royal** was originally called Port-Royal, and for over a century was at the center of the battles that raged between the French and English for control of the area. Finally, in 1710, the English triumphed and renamed the town Annapolis Royal in honor of Queen Anne. Although it then became the capital of Nova Scotia until the founding of Halifax, it remained an English island in a sea of French-speaking Acadians until 1755, when the Acadians were expelled from the province. The centerpiece of the town is the **Fort Anne National Historic Site** ((902) 532-2321 TOLL-FREE (888) 773-8888 WEB SITE www.parkscanada.gc.ca, with its well-preserved earthwork fortifications, a museum, and a gunpowder magazine dating from 1708 (mid-May to mid-October; out of season by appointment). The **Annapolis Royal Historic Gardens** ((902) 532-7018 WEB SITE www.historic gardens.com, near the fort on Upper George Street, has a magnificent four hectares (ten acres) of gardens, which include a Victorian Garden and Acadian Cottage Garden (mid-May to mid-October). At **Port Royal National Historic Site** ((902) 532-2898 TOLL-FREE (888) 773 8888 WEB SITE www .parkscanada.gc.ca, 10 km (six miles) west of Annapolis Royal, you will find a restoration of the original French fur-trading post that stood here from 1605 to 1613 (mid-May to mid-October). The final stop here should be at the **Tidal Power Project** ((902) 532-5454, where an interpretation center explains how they use the force of the ferocious

thoroughly New England feel to it. The reason for this ambiance is clear: The region was largely populated in the wake of the American Revolution by transplanted New Englanders. These new inhabitants forced out the Acadian settlers who had been working the land here since the late 1600s.

Grand Pré, the "great meadow" of diked land along the shore a few kilometers (a couple of miles) east of Wolfville, was the most important Acadian settlement before the Deportation, and was the setting for Longfellow's *Evangeline*. The **Grand Pré National Historic Site** ((902) 542-3631 WEB SITE www.grand-pre.com commemorates the expulsions of the Acadians, with a bronze statue of Evangeline, as well as an Acadian well, a black-

local tides to generate significant amounts of Nova Scotia's electricity (mid-May to mid-October).

This coast marks the southern edge of the Bay of Fundy, which has some of the highest tides in the world, reaching up to 16 m (40 ft). The area around **Harbourville**, **Halls Harbour** and **Kingsport Beach** are the best from which to view the **tidal bore**, a massive wave created when the incoming tides meet the water gushing from the mouth of a significant river, a phenomenon that occurs twice daily; ask the tourist office for tide timetables and the best places to view the spectacle.

Kentville is a pretty old town which truly comes to life for the **Harvest Festival** (October) ((902) 678-7170, when the whole town is decorated with a vast, bizarre, often funny and occasionally creepy army of pumpkin people, from Cinderellas to nativities. **Wolfville** (population 3,500) is a trim little Victorian village with a

smith's shop, and a stone church that stands as a memorial to the Acadians and houses an exhibit on the Deportation (mid-May to mid-October). **Domaine de Grand Pré** ((902) 542-1753 TOLL-FREE (866) 499-4637 WEB SITE www.grandpre wines.ns.ca, 11611 Highway 1, three kilometers (two miles) east of Wolfville, is a relatively new vineyard that is already producing some excellent wines, including rich, sweet ice wine, made in January from grapes frozen on the vine.

The Evangeline Trail ends at **Windsor**, at the eastern end of the Annapolis Valley, which also happens to be located exactly midway between the equator and the North Pole. Settled by the Acadians at the end of the seventeenth century, not long after the founding of Grand Pré, it disappeared as an Acadian town in 1755 and became

Lobster pots piled up on Cape Breton Island.

a Loyalist stronghold shortly thereafter. **Fort Edward National Historic Site** ((902) 798-4706 is a military blockhouse, built in 1750 and the oldest military structure surviving in North America (open mid-June to August).

Today Windsor is best known as the home of Judge Thomas Chandler Haliburton, the "Canadian Mark Twain" who created the memorable character of Sam Slick. **Haliburton House** ((902) 798-5619 WEB SITE www.museum.ednet.ns.ca/hh, 414 Clifton Avenue, which he built in 1833, is now a museum (June to mid-October). Less well known is that this is the birthplace, in 1800, of ice hockey, Canada's national obsession. There is a **Hockey Heritage Centre** ((902) 798-1800 WEB SITE www.birthplaceofhockey.com, 128 Gerrish Street, while **Long Pond**, site of the first game, is now open to those who wish to worship.

Where to Stay

The **Pines Resort Hotel** ((902) 245-2511 TOLL-FREE (800) 667-4637 FAX (902) 245-6133 WEB SITE www.signatureresorts.com, Shore Road, is expensive — and well worth it. It has an 18-hole golf course, floodlit tennis courts, a heated swimming pool, croquet lawns, hiking trails … you name it.

In Annapolis Royal there is no shortage of delightful places to stay. For creature comforts, you can't do better than the **Annapolis Royal Inn** ((902) 532-2323 TOLL-FREE (888) 857-8889 FAX (902) 532-7277 E-MAIL wandlyna@atcon.com WEB SITE www.portroyalinn.com, Route 1, with its modern rooms and its restaurant. It is just west of town. The **Bread and Roses Inn** ((902) 532-5727 TOLL-FREE (888) 899-0551 WEB SITE www.breadandroses.ns.ca, 82 Victoria Street, is a brick mansion built in 1882, in which the nine rooms all have en suite bathrooms and antique furnishings. The **Garrison House** ((902) 532-5750 TOLL-FREE (866) 532-5750 FAX (902) 532-5501 WEB SITE www.cometo/garrison, 350 St. George Street, is directly across from Fort Anne and was built in 1854. It has only seven rooms, and an excellent restaurant. The **Queen Anne Inn** ((902) 532-7850 FAX (902) 532-2078 WEB SITE www.queenanneinn.ns.ca, 494 Upper St. George Street, is a registered Heritage Property with 10 antique-furnished rooms, all with private bath.

In Wolfville, the **Blomidon Inn** ((902) 542-2291 TOLL-FREE (800) 565-2291 FAX (902) 542-7461 WEB SITE www.blomidon.ns.ca, 127 Main Street, has 25 elegantly furnished and moderately priced rooms, as well as recreational facilities and a first-class dining room. The **Evangeline Motel** ((902) 542-2703 TOLL-FREE (888) 542-2703 WEB SITE www.evangeline.ns.ca, 11668 Highway 1, Grand Pré, at the intersection of Route 101 and the road into the park, is an attractive place with 21 comfortable

Rural scenes on Cape Breton Island.

rooms — and it costs what you would pay in tax alone at some other places.

In Windsor, the pick of the accommodations is easily the **Hampshire Court Motel and Cottages** ((902) 798-3133, 1081 King Street. In beautiful surroundings, with air conditioning, tennis courts, cable television and a lovely picnic area, it is surprisingly inexpensive.

Where to Eat

In Digby, the **Annapolis Room**, Pines Resort Hotel ((902) 245-2511 is tops. In Annapolis Royal, the **Secret Garden** ((902) 532-2200, at 471 St. George Street, serves delicious light meals in a Victorian house overlooking beautiful gardens. **Newman's** ((902) 532-5502, 218 St. George Street, is more for gourmands than gourmets, but its basic and well-prepared dishes are very reasonably priced.

In Wolfville, the best place to eat is **Chez La Vigne** ((902) 542-5077, at 117 Front Street, where you will find classic French cuisine in a romantic setting. **Le Caveau** at the Domaine de Grand Pré ((902) 542-1753, 11611 Highway 1, is an excellent Swiss-French restaurant serving light lunches and full dinners — and of course, fine house wine — with a charming garden patio in summer.

More homespun is the **Colonial Inn Restaurant** ((902) 542-7525, on Main Street across from the post office in the center of town. Everything here is homemade, including the pastries, and served in a colonial setting. For elegant food in an elegant atmosphere, you can't beat the **Blomidon Inn** ((902) 542-2291.

CAPE BRETON ISLAND

Connected to the mainland by the one-and-a-half-kilometer-long (one-mile) Canso Causeway, Cape Breton Island consists of 10,300 sq km (3,980 sq miles) of some of the most beautiful scenery in North America. There are nine tourist information centers on the island. The main branch and a wise first stop is the **Port Hastings Tourist Information Centre** ((902) 625-4201, on the right after crossing the causeway. There is also a **Cape Breton Highlands National Park Information Office** ((902) 285-2691 at Ingonish Beach, another at Chéticamp, and the **Louisbourg Visitor Centre** ((902) 733-2720.

Consider visiting Cape Breton in October, when the fall colors are at their spectacular best, the **Celtic Colors Festival** is in full swing and the weather can be surprisingly warm and sunny. The fog and the cold can sweep in at any time of year, however, so whenever you go, bring along a sweater and a raincoat just in case. As an additional warmer, make your first stop the **Glenora Distillery** ((902) 258-2662 TOLL-FREE (800) 839-0491 WEB SITE www.glenoradistillery.com, nine kilometers (five and a half miles) north of Mabou on

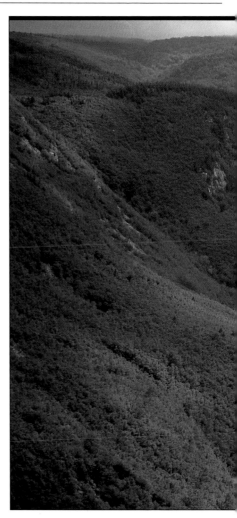

Route 19 (tours mid-June to October. Admission for tours only). This is North America's only distiller of single malt whisky, using peaty water imported from Scotland to get the correct smoky flavor.

There are half a dozen scenic routes, but once across the causeway, most visitors continue on up the TransCanada Highway as far as **Baddeck**, an attractive little town beside the huge Bras d'Or Lakes; it is chiefly famous as the home for 37 years of the father of the telephone, Alexander Graham Bell. His estate, Beinn Bhreagh, can only be seen from the water, but there are several boat companies that offer cruises, including the schooner *Amoeba* ((902) 295-2481 (June to September). This is also one of the best places in the world to spot **bald eagles**, with some 300 nesting pairs in the vicinity.

Back on land, stop at the **Alexander Graham Bell National Historic Site** ((902) 295-2069 WEB SITE www.parkscanada.gc.ca, 559 Chebucto

Street (Route 205), Baddeck. This museum tells the extraordinary story of an extraordinary man, fleshing out the bones of his numerous inventions and discoveries with film and memories of his family. The **Wagmatook Culture and Heritage Centre** ((902) 295-2999 WEB SITE www.wagmatook .com, 16 km (10 miles) west of Baddeck, explains the heritage and lifestyle of the Mi'kmaq people. If a more hands-on approach is your style, **Mi'kmaq Learning Adventures** ((902) 379-1284 operates overnight camping trips, hiking through the Ekasoni Hills, staying in a traditional Mi'kmaq dwelling, and a morning's kayaking.

From Baddeck, take the **Cabot Trail**, a 294-km (184-mile) loop that rivals California's famous Highway 1 for unbelievably spectacular views. Heading clockwise, it crosses Hunter's Mountain into the Middle River Valley before joining the Margaree River in a lush valley renowned for its salmon pools. The highway then cuts across gentle farmland until it reaches Margaree Harbour on the coast, where it crosses the estuary of the Margaree River and heads up the coast, affording excellent views of the Northumberland Strait and the Gulf of St. Lawrence. About half an hour's drive up the coast from Margaree Harbour is **Chéticamp**, an Acadian, French-speaking fishing village known for the hooked rugs and mats handmade by the local women. In addition to the large number of craft shops, of which the best is **Flora's** ((902) 224-3139 WEB SITE www.floras.com, the **Musée Acadien**, 744 Main Street, has a good collection of hooked rugs. To the north, in Pleasant Bay, the **Whale Interpretive Centre** ((902) 224-1411 offers a fascinating look at the gentle giants who visit the area each year (open mid-May to October).

The forested mountains and steep, verdant valleys of Cape Breton Highlands National Park provide a paradise for hikers and campers. OVERLEAF: The rugged beauty of Cape Breton Island's coastline.

About five kilometers (three miles) east of Chéticamp is the entrance to **Cape Breton Highlands National Park (** (902) 285-2691 TOLL-FREE (888) 773-8888 WEB SITE www.parkscanada.gc.ca, which covers the whole northern end of the island, 958 sq km (370 sq miles) of steep mountains, stony shores, deep forests, green valleys, sandy beaches and stunning ocean views — not to mention all kinds of wildlife — in a wilderness area furnished with many campgrounds, picnic sites and walking trails.

The most important resort area along the Cabot Trail is in the **Ingonish** region at the eastern entrance to the park, 105 km (65 miles) from Chéticamp. Here you will find the park's administrative headquarters and a great variety of recreational facilities: a golf course, tennis courts, supervised swimming, campsites, picnic areas, hiking trails, boating, sailing and, in winter, skiing. **Ingonish Beach**, south of Ingonish, is a stunning white-sand beach that is also the home of the Keltic Lodge, one of the finest resort hotels in eastern Canada (see WHERE TO STAY, below). At nearby **Englishtown**, **Puffin Boat Tours (** (902) 929-2563 TOLL-FREE (877) 278-3346 WEB SITE www.baddeck.com/puffins, operate two-and-a-half-hour cruises to see the puffin colonies on **Bird Island**.

From Ingonish, you climb the 366 m (1,200 ft) of Cape Smokey, a mist-capped promontory whence the trail plunges back to the coast and continues along the "North Shore," an area originally settled by Highland Scottish pioneers down to South Gut St. Ann's, below St. Ann's Harbour. Just before getting there, you pass North River, home of **North River Kayak Tours (** (902) 929-2628 TOLL-FREE (888) 865-2925 WEB SITE www.northriver kayak.com, which runs a variety of river and sea kayaking trips. From St Ann's, the road rejoins the TransCanada Highway for the final 18 km (11 miles) back to Baddeck, completing the loop.

If you take the TransCanada Highway (Route 105) in the other direction — east — it will take you to North Sydney, where it is met by the ferry to Newfoundland. Before entering North Sydney, if you turn right onto Route 125 it will take you across the Sydney River to the outskirts of Sydney, the "Steel City," Nova Scotia's third largest (and certainly drabbest) urban area. From there you take Route 22 south for 37 km (23 miles) to reach the **Fortress of Louisbourg National Historic Site (** (902) 733-2280 WEB SITE www.fortress.uccb.ns.ca, the largest in Canada (June to September, May and October guided tours only). The fortress itself, guarding the entrance to the St. Lawrence and therefore the approach to Québec, took the French a quarter of a century to build (1719–44) and it wasn't completely finished when it was attacked in 1745 by an army of 4,000 New Englanders who captured it after a 49-day siege. It was handed back to France in 1748 under the

Treaty of Aix-la-Chapelle, but was retaken by the British in 1758. Two years later Prime Minister William Pitt ordered the fortifications blown up. Since 1961 the fortress and the town have been the site of the largest historical reconstruction project ever undertaken in Canada. Over 40 buildings have been meticulously reconstructed, while the streets and shops are full of people in period dress and the inns and taverns serve authentic eighteenth-century food and drink. It is remarkable in the way it captures the feel of a French colonial outpost of the time.

Where to Stay

On the Canso Causeway at the junction of Routes 19, 104 and 105, **Skye Lodge (** (902) 625-1300 TOLL-FREE (888) 832-7593 FAX (902) 625-1966 E-MAIL skye@ns.sympatico.ca, 160 Highway 4, Port Hastings, is a comfortable and moderately priced motel with 49 rooms and a reasonable restaurant.

In Baddeck, the **Inverary Resort (** (902) 295-3500 TOLL-FREE (800) 565-5660 FAX (902) 295-3527 WEB SITE www.capebretonresorts, Route 205 and Shore Road, offers a wide variety of motel rooms and cottages — 160 in all — in addition to a private beach on Bras d'Or Lake, spacious grounds, indoor and outdoor swimming pools, tennis courts, and a wonderful restaurant (mid-range to expensive). The town also has an excellent crop of bed and breakfasts; a couple of the best are the **Broadwater Inn and Cottages (** (902) 295-1101 TOLL-FREE (888) 818-3474 WEB SITE www.broadwater .baddeck.com, Bay Road, and the **Lynwood Country Inn (**/FAX (902) 295-1995, 23 Shore Road — both moderate. Ask the tourist office for a full list.

In Chéticamp, the cream of the crop is **Laurie's Motor Inn (** (902) 224-2400 TOLL-FREE (800) 959-4253 FAX (902) 224-2069 WEB SITE www.lauries.com, Main Street (expensive). It has 54 rooms, some with private balcony, a children's playground, good restaurant, and operates whale-watching cruises in season. A good deal cheaper, but still mid-range, is the **Parkview Motel (** (902) 224-3232 FAX (902) 224 2596 WEB SITE www.parkviewresort.com, on Route 19 north of town, with a view of the Gulf of St. Lawrence and 17 riverfront units, a licensed dining room and friendly lounge. The inexpensive **Laurence Guest House (** (902) 224-2184, 15408 Main Street, is an attractive, antique-furnished bed and breakfast in a historic house (circa 1870).

In Ingonish, the **Glenghorm Beach Resort (** (902) 286-2049 TOLL-FREE (800) 565-5660 WEB SITE www.capebretonresorts.com, has 74 motel units and 11 housekeeping cottages on nine hectares (22 acres) with ocean frontage and a swimming pool (mid-range). Near the eastern entrance to the park at Ingonish Beach is the spectacular, and spectacularly expensive, **Keltic Lodge (** (902) 285-2880 TOLL-FREE (877) 375 6343 WEB SITE www.signaturere sorts.com. Set on a peninsula jutting out into the

Atlantic, it features a baronial main lodge with 32 rooms, the **Inn at the Keltic** with 40 rooms, and nine cottages. It has a world-class 18-hole golf course and everything else the dedicated vacationer might want, including an excellent restaurant.

Where to Eat

About three kilometers (two miles) off the Cabot Trail, the **Normaway Inn (** (902) 248-2987, 691 Egypt Road, Margaree Valley, has a wonderful dining room in the main lodge. In Chéticamp, **Laurie's Motel (** (902) 224-2400 has a very fine restaurant, although it closes a bit early. You probably don't have to be told that the place to eat in Ingonish is the **Purple Thistle** at Keltic Lodge **(** (902) 285-

operated by **Northumberland Ferries (** (902) 566-3838 TOLL-FREE (800) 565 0201 FAX (902) 566-1550 WEB SITE www.nfl-bay.com. There is also a ferry to Yarmouth from Portland, Maine, operated by **Scotia Prince Cruises** TOLL-FREE (866) 412-5270 WEB SITE www.scotiaprince.com; and a high-speed catamaran service from Bar Harbor, Maine, from May to October — contact **Bay Ferries (** (902) 566-3838 TOLL-FREE (888) 249-7245 FAX (902) 566-1550 WEB SITE www.nfl-bay.com.

From Halifax, follow the TransCanada Highway (Route 104) to Cape Breton. There are no airports on the island. The only direct ferry connection is the service from Port-aux-Basques, Newfoundland, to Sydney operated by **Marine**

2880, which probably has the best food on the island — and the dearest. In Baddeck, **Flora's** restaurant in the Inverary Resort **(** (902) 295-3500 is worth a visit even if you're not staying there. Between Baddeck and Louisbourg, the **Old General Store (** (902) 736-9643, TransCanada Highway (Route 105), has been in business since 1907. In Sydney, head for **Joe's Warehouse and Food Emporium (** (902) 539-6686, 424 Charlotte Street, where you can get excellent seafood and steaks.

Atlantic Reservations TOLL-FREE (800) 341-7981 WEB SITE www.marine-atlantic.ca.

The **Bras d'Or**, operated by VIA Rail TOLL-FREE (888) 842-7245 WEB SITE www.viarail.ca, is a weekly sightseeing train from Halifax to Sydney that winds its way through some of the island's most spectacular scenery (from June to October). The train is first class only, with observation cars, regional cuisine and music to keep you entertained.

HOW TO GET THERE

There are no ferries into Halifax, but there are ferries from Newfoundland to North Sydney through **Marine Atlantic Reservations** TOLL-FREE (800) 341-7981 WEB SITE www.marine-atlantic.ca; and a daily ferry from Wood Islands, Prince Edward Island, to Caribou, Nova Scotia, from May to December,

Nova Scotia

Fishing boats moored in Peggy's Cove.

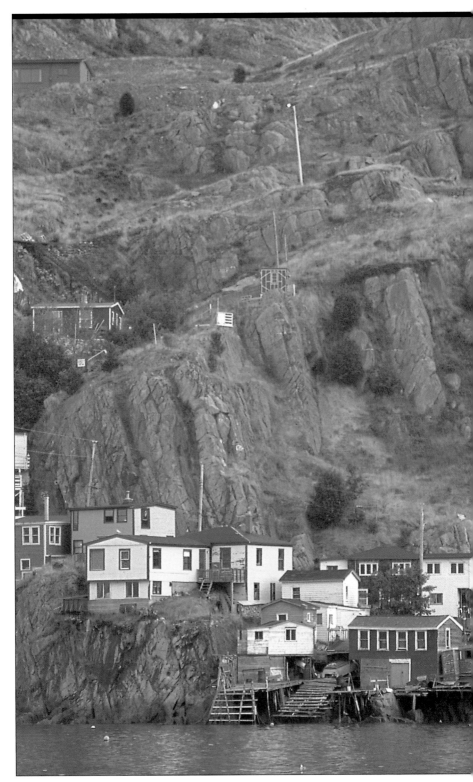

New-
foundland
and
Labrador

It is almost impossible to read or hear anything about Newfoundland and Labrador without the word "rugged" being used describe both the place and its people. It is an apt word. Island Newfoundland is indeed very rugged, as you would expect of a land that only 10,000 years ago was still covered by glaciers, and today is regularly lashed by Atlantic winds and rain, while mainland Labrador is even more remote, inhospitable and less populated. The people are every bit as rugged as the landscape they inhabit. They are also ruggedly independent.

Although a confederated Canada was formed in 1867 and spanned the continent by 1905, the Newfoundlanders and Labradorians stubbornly refused to join the Confederation until 1949. The islanders still refer to their compatriots from the mainland as "Canadians," while inquiring of visitors if they come "from Canada." They have their own distinctive accents and dialects, with their own colorful (if not always comprehensible) vocabulary. They even have their own time zone — "Newfoundland Time" — which is a half-hour ahead of Atlantic Standard Time. They are happy to point out that the provincial capital, St. John's, is closer to Europe than it is to Winnipeg in the middle of Canada.

Given this fiercely independent streak, no wonder they have become the butt of countless "Newfie jokes" among other Canadians. For the most part, the Newfoundlanders themselves take all this in good-humored stride, although the nickname is considered insulting. In turn, the island has its own little jokes: just look at the map. There you will find places with names like Stinking Cove, Useless Bay, Sitdown Pond, Come By Chance, Blow Me Down, Tickle Cove, Witless Bay, Joe Batt's Arm, Jerry's Nose, Nick's Nose Cove, Cuckold's Cove, Dildo Pond, Happy Adventure, Heart's Desire, Heart's Content and Little Heart's Ease.

The island of Newfoundland, known to locals as "The Rock," is the eighteenth largest in the world, and was inhabited by Inuit and natives when the Vikings arrived a thousand years ago, establishing a settlement near L'Anse aux Meadows at the northern tip. The next Europeans to arrive came with John Cabot in June 1497. He reported back to Henry VII that he had discovered a *"new founde lande"* surrounded by rich fishing grounds. Thirty years later Captain John Rut arrived and wrote to the new king, Henry VIII, urging that a permanent settlement be established here. This was done the following year, but it was not until 1583 that Queen Elizabeth I sent Sir Humphrey Gilbert to claim the island officially for England. Thus did Newfoundland become the first British colony in the New World.

Anchored in the then-rich Grand Banks fishing grounds, the island became the scene of repeated military confrontations between the British

claimants and others, usually the French. Under the Treaty of Utrecht in 1713, Newfoundland was formally recognized as belonging to Britain, but there was to be another half-century of hostilities before the British finally secured undisputed control of the island by defeating the French at St. John's in 1762.

There followed a period of increased immigration from Britain, swelling the colony's population to 40,000 by 1800. In 1832 it was granted self-government in domestic affairs, and in 1855 achieved full dominion status in the British Commonwealth. Especially hard hit by the Depression, Newfoundland suffered the dual humiliation of bankruptcy and reversion to being a mere colony in 1934. Finally, in 1949, but only by the narrowest of margins, Newfoundlanders and Labradorians voted to end their long holdout and join the rest of Canada as the nation's tenth province.

With its population of 560,000 concentrated almost exclusively along its 9,660 km (6,000 miles) of deeply indented coastline, Newfoundland and Labrador's economy was for 500 years based on fishing. There was a time when the island's fishermen brought in an annual haul of well over 500,000 tons of fish, mostly cod. (In fact, in Newfoundland "fish" always means cod; other types of fish are given their individual names.) But overfishing has destroyed what was the greatest fishing ground in history, Grand Banks. With the death of the cod-fishing industry, Newfoundland and Labrador struggle to set a new economic course based on tourism, mining, oil and hydroelectric activity.

ST. JOHN'S

Although supposedly settled in 1528, there is no evidence of permanent settlement in St. John's until 1620. Even so, St. John's has a claim to be the oldest city in North America. Its past has not only been long but colorful and sometimes violent. The city was a prize to be coveted, blessed with a wonderfully sheltered natural harbor, alongside what were some of the richest fishing grounds in the world, and strategically located as the nearest point to Europe in the New World.

It is markedly quieter today, but still colorful, with brightly painted clapboard houses crowding the waterfront and lining narrow winding streets that climb up from a harbor where the fishing boats of many nations lie at anchor. Even with some modern buildings and high-rises, the oldest city in North America has lost little of its character. Perhaps the sailors who went to war over it, and the pirates who took refuge in it, would

Cape Spear, North America's most easterly point — The new lighthouse shines its beacon out into the Atlantic.

have trouble recognizing it today, but they would still find something awfully familiar about it.

BACKGROUND

The 178,000 citizens of St. John's date their city from June 24, 1497, the saint's day of St. John the Baptist, when John Cabot landed at Cape Bonavista. It was repeatedly fought over by the British and French (and occasionally the Dutch), until British supremacy was finally and lastingly established in 1762, at the end of the Seven Years' War. Yet just because there was peace doesn't mean that St. John's was suddenly peaceful. As a rough-and-ready port town, by the end of the

Tourism Division ((709) 576-8106. There is a seasonal **information booth** ((709) 758-8500 in the baggage claim area at the St. John's airport. Off-season, you'll find a supply of brochures and maps free for the taking.

British Island Tours ((709) 738-8686 WEB SITE www.bigkahoona.com operates city sightseeing tours in a British double-decker bus. For smaller groups, contact **Jiffy Tours** ((709) 722-2222 WEB SITE www.7222222.com; and for walking tours, try **St. John's Historic Walking Tours** ((709) 738-3781 or the evening **St. John's Haunted Hike** ((709) 685-3444 WEB SITE www.hauntedhike.com. If a late-night bar crawl is more your style, hook up with **Downtown St. John's Entertainment Tours** ((709)

eighteenth century there were 80 taverns and over 750,000 liters (200,000 gallons) of rum was being imported annually.

The nineteenth century was one of rapid growth interrupted by devastating fires: St. John's burned down no fewer than five times. Each time the townspeople, undaunted, rebuilt it — in wood. It has escaped the flames in the last 100 years, but only a handful of buildings date back to before the Victorian period.

GENERAL INFORMATION

In summer, visitor information is available at the **Tourist Information Rail Car** ((709) 576-8514, Harbour Drive, along the waterfront. The rest of the year, you can get information at **City Hall** ((709) 576-8106 E-MAIL cityedev@nfld.com, New Gower Street, or contact the **City of St. John's**

727-7522. Most operators only run in the summer months, but phone for details.

WHAT TO SEE AND DO

Much to the chagrin of the tourism association, which has given St. John's the sobriquet "City of Legends," St. John's is more widely known as "Fog City." Nowhere is this aspect of the city seen from greater advantage than on **Signal Hill** ((709) 772-5367 WEB SITE www.parkscanada.pch.gc.ca/parks/newfoundland, with its sunlight and fog, mist-shrouded ponds, crying seagulls and, on a good day, a magnificent view of the Narrows — the inlet that leads into St. John's Harbour. Signal Hill rises steeply at the mouth of the harbor, and was originally used by the various sailing companies to hoist their flags to signal dockworkers and merchants that one of their ships was approaching.

It was also the birthplace of modern telecommunications, for this is the site where, on December 12, 1901, Guglielmo Marconi received the first transatlantic radio message from his station in Cornwall. **Cabot Tower** was built in 1897 to mark Queen Victoria's diamond jubilee and the fourth centenary of Cabot's landing. Outside are cannons from the Queen's Battery dating from 1796 and ruined fortifications from the War of 1812. Cadets perform nineteenth-century military drills here in summer.

The **Johnson Geo Centre** ((709) 737-7743, 175 Signal Hill Road, is a fascinating geological exhibit using the ancient rocks of Newfoundland to tell the story of the earth's four-billion-year history.

The Anglican **Cathedral of St. John the Baptist** ((709) 726-5677 WEB SITE www.infonet.st-johns .nf.ca / cathedral, 22 Church Hill, was founded in 1847, designed by Sir Gilbert Scott it is considered one of the finest churches in North America (open June to September; off season by appointment). There is a tearoom in the crypt. The Roman Catholic **Basilica Cathedral of St. John the Baptist** ((709) 754-2170, 200 Military Road, is also well worth a visit. Completed in 1855, it has a Romanesque façade, twin granite-and-bluestone towers that dominate the city's skyline, and 66 fine stained-glass windows. The Basilica Palace Library leading off the cathedral has a fine collection of ecclesiastical art and literature. Further

Over the north side of the hill is the picturesque fishing village **Quidi Vidi** (pronounced "kiddy viddy"), set on a small inlet. It's a good place to get a feel for this type of hamlet. Among the little wharves and boats are some wonderful seafood restaurants, and a nearby trail circles Quidi Vidi Lake. **Water Street**, one of the oldest streets in North America, runs parallel to the harbor. At the corner of Duckworth and Prescott Streets is the **Provincial Museum of Newfoundland and Labrador** ((709) 729-0917 WEB SITE www.nfmuseum.com, with exhibits on local naval history, the early native peoples of Newfoundland, and the history of St. John's, with particular emphasis on daily life in the nineteenth century. **Quidi Vidi Battery Provincial Historic Site** ((709) 729-2977 TOLL-FREE (800) 653-6353, Cuckold's Cove Road, is an old fort, first built by the French in 1762. The British rebuilt it and used it through much of the nineteenth century.

along Military Road is the distinctly more modest **St. Thomas' Anglican Church** (also known as the Old Garrison Church), which dates from 1836 and is one of the few buildings to be spared in the terrible fires that swept the city in the nineteenth century. In fact it is the oldest church still standing anywhere in the province. There is a small museum in the crypt (open July to August).

Next door to the church, **Commissariat House** ((709) 729-6745, King's Bridge Road, is a clapboard structure with tall chimneys that dates from 1821. It, too, escaped the fires and was used by the military commissariat until 1871, when it became the rectory for the church, and is now beautifully restored and furnished with period pieces (open June to October).

Although St. John's is the oldest city in North America, almost all of its oldest buildings were built in the twentieth century.

The **Art Gallery of Newfoundland & Labrador** ((709) 737-8209 WEB SITE www.mun.ca/agnl, Arts and Culture Centre, Allendale Road at Prince Philip Drive, has a permanent collection of local art along with regular touring exhibitions. The **Arts and Cultural Centre** ((709) 729-3904 WEB SITE www.artsandculturecentre.com/stjohns includes two theaters and three libraries (September to June).

Other small museums and exhibits include the **James O'Mara Pharmacy Museum** ((709) 753-5877, 288 Water Street, a replica of an 1895 apothecary's shop (mid-June to mid-September), and **Newman Wine Vaults Provincial Historic Site** ((709) 739-7870, 440 Water Street, inside one of the city's oldest buildings (open June to August). Several fine parks and gardens with walking trails include the 81-hectare (200-acre) **Bowring Park** ((709) 576-6134 WEB SITE www.bowringpark.com, Waterford Bridge Road, with an open-air amphitheatre offering a wide range of performances, and the 45-hectare (110-acre) **Mun Botanical Garden** ((709) 737-8590 WEB SITE www.mun.ca/botgarden, 306 Mount Scion Road (May to November; tours available on request).

The shopping center **Murray Premises** ((709) 754-1090, 5 Beck's Cove, built in 1846 as a trade and fishing warehouse and office, is one of the best places to go for boutiques and luxury goods. It is also home to the **Newfoundland Science Centre** ((709) 754-0823 WEB SITE www.sciencecentre.nf.ca, an entertaining hands-on interactive science exhibition. **Duckworth Street** is also good for boutiques and antique shops and the excellent **Craft Council Gallery** ((709) 753-2749 WEB SITE www.craftcouncil.nf.ca, 59 Duckworth Street. For arts and crafts, try the area around the War Memorial at the eastern end of Water Street. New and used books, notably on Newfoundland travel and history, are sold at **Wordplay** ((709) 726-9193 WEB SITE www.wordplay.com, 221 Duckworth Street.

NIGHTLIFE AND THE ARTS

St. John's has an excellent folk music scene. There are many places, but you might start with **Bridie Molloy's** ((709) 576-5990, George Street, which features Newfoundland and Irish folk music; arrive early to get a seat. **Trapper John** ((709) 579-9630, 2 George Street, is also known for outstanding provincial folk music. Bars come and go, but there's a wide variety of music on George Street.

In keeping with its rum-soaked past, St. John's probably has more drinking spots per capita than any other city in Canada. Most of them seem to be clustered downtown on and around George Street, with bars, clubs and discos to suit almost any state. We also like the **Ship Inn** ((709) 753-

Here at Cabot Tower on Signal Hill, Guglielmo Marconi received the first transatlantic radio message in 1901.

3870, at 265 Duckworth Street, down the stairs, off the alley, a hangout for the local arts community with live music.

The city also has two dinner theaters: **Spirit of Newfoundland Productions** ((709) 579-3023, 223 Duckworth Street; and **Steele N' Steps** ((709) 739-7837 TOLL-FREE (866) 819 8687 WEB SITE www .newfoundlandtours.com.

WHERE TO STAY

Expensive

The **Fairmont Newfoundland Hotel** ((709) 726-4980 TOLL-FREE (800) 441-1414 WEB SITE www.fairmont.com, 115 Cavendish Square, is easily the grandest hotel in Newfoundland, located downtown, with excellent views of Signal Hill and the Narrows. It has 301 elegantly furnished rooms and suites, a formal dining room, a restaurant and a lounge, an indoor swimming pool, squash courts and a disco. Rates are very reasonable for what it has to offer — and there are discount weekend packages. The 11-story **Delta St. John's Hotel** ((709) 739-6404 TOLL-FREE (800) 268-1133, WEB SITE www.deltahotels.com, 120 New Gower Street, overlooks the harbor, with 276 rooms and nine suites. It has non-smoking floors, a pool and health center, and a highly rated restaurant.

Mid-range

Though bland from the exterior, **Battery Hotel and Suites** ((709) 576-0040 TOLL-FREE (800) 563-8181 WEB SITE www.batteryhotel.com, 100 Signal Hill Road, is a comfortable choice, offering good value, with 125 rooms and 20 suites, glorious views over the harbor and city, and an indoor swimming pool.

Holiday Inn St. John's ((709) 722-0506 WEB SITE www.holidayinnstjohns.com, 180 Portugal Cove Road, two and a half kilometers (one and a half miles) from downtown, near the Confederation Building, has all the amenities one associates with Holiday Inns, including an outdoor pool, an above-average restaurant and 24-hour room service.

Inexpensive

About three kilometers (just under two miles) from downtown, **Best Western Traveler's Inn** ((709) 722-5400 WEB SITE www.bestwestern.com, 199 Kenmount Road, has 88 rooms and an outdoor pool. The **Airport Plaza Hotel** ((709) 753-3500 TOLL-FREE (800) 563-2489 WEB SITE www.cityhotels.ca, 106 Airport Road, is right next to the airport, within walking distance of the terminal. Its rooms and suites are nicely furnished, and its restaurant and lounge are both good.

For a real bargain in civilized surroundings, try the **Prescott Inn** ((709) 753-7733 WEB SITE www.prescottinn.nf.ca, 19 Military Road, which has 12 large rooms with balconies, and 10 suites overlooking the harbor, each decorated with lo-

cal arts and crafts, and each with color television and private bath. Five suites are equipped with kitchens. A delicious full breakfast is included.

There are around three dozen **bed and breakfasts** sprinkled throughout the city and the province. They're listed in the *Newfoundland and Labrador Travel Guide*, available free from Tourism Newfoundland and Labrador (see TOURIST INFORMATION, page 238 in TRAVELER'S TIPS).

WHERE TO EAT

Expensive

The best restaurant in St. John's is **Bianca's** ((709) 726-9016, 171 Water Street. Menu selections are

seasonal, preparation and service are impeccable, and the wine selection is the best in town. Of the hotel restaurants, we prefer the elegant **Bona Vista** ((709) 726-4980 in the Fairmont Newfoundland Hotel (see WHERE TO STAY, above). A mix of traditional Canadian fare — such as caribou medallions — and continental cuisine gives variety to the menu. This is a formal place and jackets are required for men.

The **Classic Café** ((709) 579-4444, 364 Duckworth Street, offers a casual ambiance and warm service, in a cozily rustic room. Seafood is expertly prepared and reasonably priced. It's open 24 hours a day and big breakfasts are served at all hours. At 108 Duckworth Street, the **Casa Grande** ((709) 753-6108 serves award-winning Mexican and Canadian food in cozy surroundings. If you are willing to stray a bit further afield, head out along Route 60 about 11 km (seven miles) to the **Wood-**

stock **Colonial Inn** ((709) 722-6933, where delicious food is served (generously) in a delightful colonial setting.

Inexpensive

For fish and chips, **Ches's** is something of an institution in St. John's. Its four restaurants are at 655 Topsail Road ((709) 368-9473, 9 Freshwater Road ((709) 722-4083, 29-33 Commonwealth Avenue ((709) 364-6837, and 8 Highland Drive ((709) 738-5022.

For something a bit more sophisticated, wander over to **Nautical Nellie's** ((709) 738-1120, 201 Water Street, which looks as though it might serve typical pub grub, but there's nothing me-

ELSEWHERE ON THE ISLAND

It is known that bands of First Nations peoples roamed the island up to 4,000 years before the Vikings landed, some left behind stone tools that are among the most delicate ever discovered. Whether due to the arrival of the Vikings or to some other phenomenon, the island's original inhabitants disappeared around AD 1000, replaced by the Beothuks. These were the natives that Cabot and the later settlers encountered. As they tended to cover their bodies in red powdered ochre, they became known as the "Red Paint People" — possibly the origin of the term "Red

diocre about the excellent-value menu. Try the curried scallop pasta with peach chutney.

How to Get There

St. John's International Airport is eight kilometers (five miles) from the city, and the drive to downtown takes 10 to 15 minutes. **Air Canada** ((709) 726-7880 operates regular service to Newfoundland and Labrador airports, with connections from all major centers in Canada and the United States. **Air Labrador** ((709) 896-6777 WEB SITE www.airlabrador.com and **Provincial Airlines** ((709) 576-1666 WEB SITE www.provair .com provide regular services within the province and offer daily scheduled services from St. John's to points throughout the province. There are also regularly scheduled services from St. John's to the island of St-Pierre.

Indian." In any case, the arrival of the white man spelled doom for the red man. Over the next three centuries, Europeans gradually displaced the Beothuks from their traditional coastal habitat. Battles and diseases also took a toll. The last known Beothuk died in 1829.

Except around its edges, the island that the Beothuks and their predecessors occupied for millennia is still pretty much the way it was throughout its prehistory. Perhaps the only real difference, apart from the obvious inroads made by the modern world, is that the forests are being nibbled away — not devoured, just nibbled — by the timber, paper and pulp manufacturing industries which have now surpassed fish-

OPPOSITE: A St. John's softball team gets ready to take the field. ABOVE: Quidi Vidi village is set on a small inlet on the north side of St. John's.

ing in the economy of the western part of Newfoundland. Otherwise the land, or most of it anyway, retains the same wild beauty that the natives enjoyed long before Europeans ever set foot on it.

THE AVALON PENINSULA

With its coastal fog-bound cliffs and inland bogs, the Avalon has some of Newfoundland's most dramatic scenery. Most of the peninsula is accessible on day trips from St. John's, making it a good choice for travelers with limited time. Listen for the Irish burr in the speech of the local residents. Many of the original settlers came from the southeastern Irish counties of Cork and Waterford in the seventeenth century as part of the migratory fishery industry. Much of the peninsula's shore is lined by hiking trails of extraordinary scenic beauty.

Cape Spear National Historic Site is only 11 km (seven miles) southeast of St. John's. Here, at North America's most easterly point, you will get a stunning view of the ocean (which in springtime includes the sight of humpback whales heaving their way up and down the coast). There is also a square, white clapboard **lighthouse (** (709) 772-6367 WEB SITE www.parkscanada.gc.ca/newfoundland dating from 1836, which makes it the oldest lighthouse in Newfoundland. It has been restored to its appearance in 1839 (tours daily mid-June to mid-September).

About 35 km (21 miles) south of the capital there is world-class birding at **Witless Bay Ecological Reserve (** (709) 729-2424 WEB SITE www.gov.nf.ca/parks&reserves, a cluster of islands located a few kilometers off shore (refer to SEE THE WONDERS OF WITLESS BAY, page ## in TOP SPOTS). Each spring the largest Atlantic puffin colony in North America descends on the islands to nest. Murres, kittiwakes and gulls also inhabit the tiny islands. Tour boats take visitors out of Bay Bulls (an anglicized version of the French name for the bullbirds — *baie boules* — or dovekies that are common wintering birds in the area) to observe the birds, as well as the humpback whales and icebergs. Many companies offer whale, 'berg and birdwatching boat tours. Among the best are **Gatherall's Puffin & Whale Watch (** (709) 334-2887 TOLL-FREE (1-800) 419-4253 WEB SITE www.newfoundland-whales.com and **O'Brien's Puffin and Whale Tours (** (709) 753-4850 WEB SITE www.netfx.ca/obriens.

For hiking, sea kayaking and sailing in the area, contact **Whales and Bergs (** (709) 726-8104 WEB SITE www.whalesandbergs.nf.ca, **Wilderness Newfoundland Adventures** TOLL-FREE (888) 7476353 WEB SITE www.wildnfld.ca, or **Trapper John's Tours and Promotions (** (709) 579-8687 WEB SITE www.trapperjohns.com. **Dive Adventures (** (709)

754-8687 TOLL-FREE (866) 819-8687 WEB SITE www.divenewfoundland.com runs wreck diving trips off the southern shore.

About 40 km (24 miles) south of Witless Bay is **Ferryland**, a seaside town with a major **archeological dig (** (709) 432-3200 WEB SITE www.heritage.nf.ca/avalon, Route 10. A 380-year-old cobblestone street has been unearthed here. The street section was part of the Colony of Avalon, established in the 1620s by Lord Baltimore. The site includes an archeology laboratory and exhibit center. In the town courthouse, the **Historic Ferryland Museum (** (709) 432-3200 TOLL-FREE (877) 326-5669 tells the story of Ferryland's role in the colonization of North America (open mid-June to August). Just inland from here is **Avalon Wilderness Reserve (** (709) 729-2424 WEB SITE www.gov.nf.ca/parks&reserves, an untamed sanctuary for many species of plants and wildlife, including Canada's most southerly herd of caribou.

The drive down Route 100 south of Placentia is dotted with lovely coves and cliffy viewpoints. At the end of the line is **Cape St. Mary's Ecological Reserve** ((709) 635-4520 WEB SITE www.gov .nf.ca / parks&reserves. This remote corner of the island is worth the effort it takes to get here. Some 25,000 northern gannets nest here, along with 10,000 pairs of murres, 20,0000 kittiwakes and 100 razorbills. The nesting birds are approached from the top of a 100-m (300-ft)-high cliff, so visitors can get quite close without disturbing them, while the visitor center (open May to October) offers a good introduction to the cape's bird life and interpretive hikes.

If you are heading west from Witless Bay you can circle back towards St. John's around the northern Avalon Peninsula and Conception Bay. On a small island off the northern tip of the peninsula, **Baccalieu Island Ecological Reserve** ((709) 729-2424 WEB SITE www.gov.nf.ca / parks

&reserves, Route 70, has 11 species of nesting seabirds, including a staggering three million pairs of Leach's Storm Petrel, the largest colony in the world. There is an exhibition about the island in **Heritage House** ((709) 587-2766, Blundon's Point, Bay de Verde, a three-story merchant's house, built in 1896 (open June to September).

Heading south along Route 70, **Harbour Grace** was the headquarters of the seventeenth-century pirate, Peter Easton. From 1919, this town was the takeoff point for numerous attempts at trans-Atlantic flight. Amelia Earhart departed from here in 1932 to become the first woman to fly solo across the Atlantic. The town also has a charming heritage district of historic houses and shops.

The beautiful little village of **Brigus** (19 km or 12 miles off Route 1 and Route 80) provides a

The old lighthouse at Cape Spear with its signature red and white striped dome.

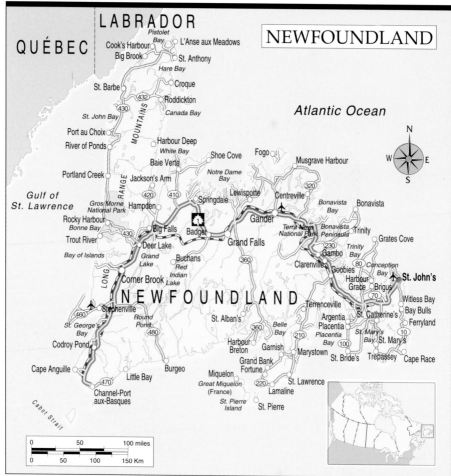

public garden, winding lanes and a pleasant teahouse. Brigus is the birthplace of Captain Bob Bartlett, who accompanied Admiral Peary on polar expeditions during the first decade of the twentieth century. His house, **Hawthorne Cottage** ((709) 528-4004, Irishtown Road, dates from 1830 and is a National Historic Site (mid-May to October; off-season by appointment). Nearby is **Cupids**, the oldest English colony in Canada, founded in 1610 by John Guy. You can visit the **Cupids Archeological Site and Museum** ((709) 596-1906, Main Road, where archeologists have unearthed remnants of the original colony (open July to September).

Where to Stay and Eat
In Ferryland there is the inexpensive **Downs Inn** ((709) 432-2808 TOLL-FREE (877) 432-2808 E-MAIL acostello@nf.sympatico.ca, Irish Loop Drive, a handsome Victorian-style building overlooking the harbor. Formerly a convent, the furnishings are uninspired — tending to reflect its history as

an institution — but if you can get one of the front rooms you can watch for whales from your windows. There is a tearoom for light lunches and desserts. The innkeepers offer customized touring packages.

At the southwest corner of the peninsula, **Bird Island Resort** ((709) 337-2450 TOLL-FREE (888) 337-2450 WEB SITE www.birdislandresort.com, Main Road, St. Bride's, is an inexpensive modern motel with five rooms and 15 cottages offering basic amenities, including some rooms with kitchenettes. It is set in rolling green landscape overlooking the bay.

Fish and chips are offered just about anywhere you eat in Newfoundland. When you're on the road look for a branch of the Irving chain; they're always open and are among the few places serving cod broiled, not fried. Try their Jigg's Dinner

RIGHT: Clouds gather over Conception Bay, just north of St. John's. OVERLEAF: The village of Brigus, Avalon Peninsula.

(meat, potatoes, cabbage and carrots all cooked together) on Sunday. Though cod fishing is officially banned, "by-catch" (cod that happens to be collected during other fishing operations) has thus far insured a steady supply to the island.

BONAVISTA PENINSULA

Cape Bonavista, at the northern tip of Bonavista Peninsula, is said to have been Cabot's first North American landfall. He named it in 1497 — accurately, one should add, because there is a beautiful view from the cape. The fishing village of **Bonavista**, five kilometers (three miles) away, has an outer harbor as well as a sheltered inner har-

bor for smaller fishing boats. It was a favorite port of European fishing fleets in the sixteenth century before the British settled it, and is now a favorite spot for whale-watchers in early summer.

The little village of **Trinity** on Trinity Bay (not be confused with the village of the same name on Bonavista Bay) was discovered by the Portuguese navigator Gaspar Corte Real in 1501. The first Admiralty Court in North America was convened here in 1615. Thanks to a program of renovation and restoration, the character of the village has been beautifully preserved and several of the houses are open as small museums. The main summer attractions are the **Summer in the Bight Theatre Festival**, with a season of 10 plays performed indoors and outdoors, and the **New-Founde-Lande Trinity Pageant**, a comedic walking tour of the town, both staged by Rising Tide Theatre ((709) 464-3847 or 464-3232 TOLL-FREE (1-888) 464-3377 WEB SITE www.risingtidetheatre.com.

From Trinity, you can explore **abandoned fishing villages**, such as Kerleys Harbour, a short drive south of the village. The last inhabitants left the Kerleys Harbour in the 1950s but the remnants of their lives still remain. From the churchyard in New Bonaventure it's a 20-minute walk past ponds and stands of trees to the site. The Trinity-New Bonaventure area is also where the Holly-

wood feature *The Shipping News* and the television miniseries *Random Passage* were filmed. The *Random Passage* set is now a tourist draw.

Where to Stay and Eat

Trinity boasts the best place to stay on the island: **Campbell House** ((709) 464-3377 (summer) or (709) 753-8945 (winter) TOLL-FREE (877) 464-7700 WEB SITE www.trinityvacations.com. Proprietor Tineke Gow personally oversaw the authentic restoration of the historic 1840s home. Rooms are spacious and comfortable with luxurious touches such as down comforters and views of the lovely harbor. Loyal guests return here year after year for Tineke's hospitality and hearty breakfasts. A

cottage nearby is also part of the property. Reserve well in advance for July and August.

On the TransCanada Highway (Route 1) at Clarenville, just before you turn off to head out onto the Bonavista Peninsula, the mid-range **Clarenville Inn** ((709) 466-7911 WEB SITE www .clarenvilleinn.ca, Routes 1 and 1A, is a convenient and comfortable pit stop with 64 rooms. If you are keen on whale-watching, or other types of oceangoing expeditions, the inexpensive **Village Inn** ((709) 464-3269 WEB SITE www.ocean contact.com, Trinity, is small (12 rooms) but very comfortable, with a licensed dining room and a private bar. The hotel organizes trips and charters with their resident marine biologist.

Also in Trinity, the **Dock Marina Restaurant** specializes in juicy, thick steaks. Upstairs is a gallery of local arts and crafts. The dependable **Cooper's Meat Market, Restaurant and Convenience Store**

☏ (709) 464-3832 in the nearby hamlet of Port Rexton is open year-round. It's a friendly, family-run place where fried cod is always a good choice.

TERRA NOVA NATIONAL PARK

The older and smaller of Newfoundland's two national parks, 396 sq km (153 sq miles) **Terra Nova National Park** is divided north to south by the TransCanada Highway. To the east are beaches, tidal flats and rocky coast along Bonavista Bay, as well as the park's two developed campgrounds at **Newman Sound** (400 campsites, a general store, laundry, cabins, showers, fireplaces — the works) and **Malady Head** (165 campsites, and a little

Main Street, Burnside, Route 310, is a fascinating heritage interpretation center, describing 5,000 years of local aboriginal history, based around artifacts found at the Bloody Reach archeological digs (mid-June to October).

Where to Stay and Eat
The **Terra Nova Golf Resort** ☏ (709) 543-2525 FAX (709) 543-2201 WEB SITE www.terranovagolf .com, Route 1, Port Blandford, south of the park's southern entrance (moderate) is a modern resort with 89 rooms and suites. Though somewhat characterless, it is clean, comfortable and a good base from which to explore the park. The course is probably one of the more scenic in Atlantic

more Spartan). There are also more primitive campsites spread around the park.

To the west of the highway are the woods, lakes, ponds, streams and bogs so typical of the island's interior. And on both sides of the highway — indeed sometimes on the highway itself — the area teems with wildlife: black bear, moose, beaver and otter. There is a seaside golf course, from which in early summer you can see any number of icebergs floating in the coastal waters. There are 80 km (50 miles) of nature trails in the park, and both canoes and bicycles can be rented at the **Marine Interpretation Centre** ☏ (709) 533-2801 WEB SITE parkscanaada.pch.gc.ca/parks/ newfoundland at the Saltons Day-Use Area, about five kilometers (three miles) north of the Newman Sound Campground (May to mid-October).

North of the park, **Burnside Archeology Centre** ☏ (709) 745 4687 WEB SITE www.burnsideheritage.ca,

Canada. The lodge's dining room is open for all meals, with standard island fare such as fried cod dinners and surf-and-turf.

The seasonally operated **Clode Sound Motel** ☏ (709) 664-3146 WEB SITE www.clodesound.com, Charlottetown, has 19 units, a heated pool and a tennis court, and is only 10 minutes from the golf course.

GANDER

About the only thing Gander has going for it is its **airport**, which in the pre-jet era was the west-

Ready for winter in Trinity, Bonavista Peninsula — OPPOSITE: Newfoundlanders still store their winter vegetables in root cellars such as this one. Wood is stacked RIGHT for a long cold spell. ABOVE: Afternoon sunbeams play on an antique cupboard at the circa 1840s Campbell House inn.

ern takeoff and landing point for transatlantic flights. It was chosen for this role not only because of its proximity to Europe, but also because it is far enough inland to be not affected by the fog that often shrouds the coast. It played a critical part in World War II as a refueling stop for the thousands of military aircraft headed for Europe, but its importance has declined since the advent of the jet engine. The town is home to the **North Atlantic Aviation Museum** ((709) 256-2923, 135 TransCanada Highway, with several fine restored aircraft and a host of aviation memorabilia on display.

Gander's only other point of interest, unless you are excited by shopping centers, lies west of

the 62-room **Irving West Hotel** ((709) 256-2406, 1 Caldwell Street, has a heated outdoor swimming pool and a children's activity room. The **Albatross Motel** ((709) 256-3956 TOLL-FREE (800) 563-4900 WEB SITE www.albatrosshotel.nf.ca, is on the Trans-Canada Highway and has 100 nicely furnished rooms. **Sinbad's Motel** ((709) 651-2678 TOLL-FREE (800) 563-8330 WEB SITE www.sinbadshotel.nf.ca is on Bennett Drive, across from the Gander Mall. Many of its 112 rooms and suites are efficiency units. At the 154-room **Hotel Gander** ((709) 256-3931 TOLL-FREE IN CANADA (800) 563-2988 WEB SITE www.hotelgander.com, 100 TransCanada Highway, you can enjoy an indoor pool, fitness facilities and a restaurant.

the town, where the **Gander River** flows under the TransCanada Highway. Apart from being beautiful to look at, either from the bank or a canoe, it is one of the island's best salmon rivers. Bring your angling gear.

North of town, along the **Kittiwake Coast** is a series of pretty small inlets and villages, many with fine historic houses and small museums. There are good hikes and excellent opportunities for bird, whale and 'berg watching. **Boyd's Cove Beothuk Interpretation Centre** ((709) 656-3114, off Route 340, Boyd's Cove, is a reconstruction of a late seventeenth-century Beothuk village, based on a real archeological site (June to October).

Where to Stay and Eat
The four best hotels in Gander are all mid-range in price. Marginally more expensive than the others,

GROS MORNE NATIONAL PARK

Gros Morne ("Big Knoll") is probably the most spectacular national park in eastern Canada. Within its 1,815 sq km (700 sq miles) are mountains, gorges, lakes and fjords of stunning beauty. The flat-topped **Long Range Mountains**, which rise to a barren plateau some 600 m (2,000 ft) tall, are cut by deep lakes and fjords bordered by towering rock cliffs. It was at Tablelands, a mesa-like rock formation within the park, that geologists finally confirmed the theory of continental drift. Its geological importance and beauty have earned the park UNESCO World Heritage status.

The **Visitor Reception Centre** ((709) 458-2417 or 458-2066 WEB SITE www.parkscanada.gc.ca/grosmorne is just south of Rocky Harbour on Route 430.

The entire park is glorious, and crisscrossed by around 100 km (60 miles) of hiking trails, but there are two areas of special beauty. One is **Western Brook Pond**, 29 km (19 miles) north of Rocky Harbour, which is reached by hiking about four kilometers (two and a half miles) through the forest from the highway. When you get there, the "pond" turns out to be a lake 16 km (10 miles) long that resembles a fjord because of the soaring, near vertical cliffs rising alongside it. It is truly breathtaking. There are three boat tours of the lake daily during the summer.

The other must-see scenic spot is **Bonne Bay**, a deep fjord on the Gulf of St. Lawrence, with two arms thrusting deep into the park. The drive along

The architecturally impressive **Victorian Manor** ((709) 453-2485 WEB SITE www.grosmorne .com/victorianmanor, Main Street, Woody Point, a short walk from the harbor, has three Victorian era rooms within the 1920's built manor, three fully equipped efficiency units on the property, (one with Jacuzzi) and a guesthouse. A continental breakfast is included in the inexpensive to moderate rates.

A few minutes drive away from the Manor in Trout River, the **Seaside Restaurant** ((709) 451-3461, Main Street, is a cut above the usual island offerings, serving excellent pan-fried cod and a number of other seafood dishes. There is a splendid view of the harbor from the dining room.

the South Arm must be one of the most gorgeous drives in the world, and only slightly less so is the drive up along the East Arm to Rocky Harbour.

Where to Stay and Eat
You can get details of all the campgrounds in the park from the Visitor Center (see above). The handiest private campground is the **Juniper Campground** ((709) 458-2917 EMAIL juniper @nf.sympatico.ca, Pond Road, off Route 230, close to Rocky Harbour. It has 72 campsites, 25 of them full-service. For inexpensive accommodation in Rocky Harbour, try **Gros Morne Cabins** ((709) 458-2020 or (709) 458-2369 TOLL-FREE (888) 603-2020 WEB SITE www.grosmornecabins .com, which has 22 log, ocean-view cabins well equipped with kitchenette and gas barbecue. The complex includes a store, a laundromat and a recreation area.

L'ANSE AUX MEADOWS NATIONAL HISTORIC SITE

At the northern tip of Newfoundland's Northern Peninsula is the site of the only authenticated Viking settlement in North America, preserved as **L'Anse aux Meadows National Historic Site** ((709) 623-2608 WEB SITE www.parkscanada.gc.ca/ parks/newfound/anse_meadows, Route 436 (open mid-June to mid-September). It had long been known that Norsemen sailing from Iceland landed somewhere along North America's Atlantic coast, and named the spot Vinland after the wild grapes they found there, but it was not until

OPPOSITE: Kerley's Harbour, a fishing village abandoned in the 1950s, bears witness to the island's changing economy. ABOVE: Fishing boats at rest along the Viking Trail.

1960 that the Norwegian explorer Helge Instad came upon a cluster of overgrown mounds near L'Anse aux Meadows. For the next seven years his team excavated the site, and established beyond doubt that here were the remains of a 1,000-year-old Norse settlement.

In 1978 L'Anse aux Meadows was named the first cultural UNESCO World Heritage Site. Today three of the original six sod houses have been reconstructed, and artifacts from the site are on display in the Visitor Reception Centre, together with an exhibit on the Norse way of life. Period costumed staff bring the center to life with stories and displays including textile production, food preparation and woodworking.

Where to Stay
The nearest accommodation to the historic site is the **Viking Village/Viking Nest Bed-and-Breakfast** ((709) 623-2238 TOLL-FREE (877) 858-2238 WEB SITE www.bbcanada.com/vikingvillage, one kilometer (about half a mile) away. The Viking Village building is newer. St. Anthony, 27 km (17 miles) away from L'Anse aux Meadows, has the **Vinland Motel** ((709) 454-8843 TOLL-FREE (800) 563-7578 E-MAIL vinland.motel@nf.sympatico.ca with 40 rooms and two cottages (mid-range).

CORNER BROOK

A population of a little under 22,000 makes Corner Brook Newfoundland's second largest town.

Lichen covers some seaside rocks in the abandoned fishing village of Kerleys Harbour.

With an economy based almost exclusively on the town's giant pulp and paper mill and the herring fishing industry, it cannot be said to have overpowering appeal for the visitor, unless one needs to buy the sort of goods and services generally unavailable in smaller places.

However, Corner Brook does have the advantage of being near some appealing places. To begin with, it is an ideal starting point for a drive along either the northern or southern shore of the scenic Humber Arm of the **Bay of Islands**. A drive out along the southern shore will take you to **Bottle Cove**, where there is a lovely public beach as well as campsites and hiking trails up into the mountains. Also, there is fabulous salmon fishing in the **Humber River** near Corner Brook: catches of salmon weighing over 13 kg (30 lb) have been recorded here. Finally, there is excellent hunting nearby, and only eight kilometers (five miles) away is the **Marble Mountain Ski Resort**, the only proper ski resort in Newfoundland.

Where to Stay and Eat
The three best hotels in Corner Brook are all midrange in price, and all three belong to hotel chains. The 55-room **Mamateek Inn** ((709) 639-8901 TOLL-FREE (800) 563-8600 WEB SITE www.mamateek .nf.net is on the TransCanada Highway at Maple Valley Road. Nearby at 41 Maple Valley Road, the **Comfort Inn** ((709) 639-1980 TOLL-FREE (800) 228-5150 WEB SITE www.choicehotels.ca/245 is the least expensive of the four. The best of the three is the Tudor-style **Glynmill Inn** ((709) 634-5181 TOLL-FREE (800) 563-4400 WEB SITE www.glynmill inn.ca, 1 Cobb Lane. Overlooking Glynmill Pond, it has 80 handsome rooms and suites, and a splendid steak house, as well as a more intimate restaurant downstairs.

PORT AUX BASQUES

Named for the Basque fishermen who were fishing the waters of the Cabot Strait as early as 1500, and probably earlier, Port aux Basques is still an important fishing port as well as being the island's main ferry port. If you arrive in Newfoundland by ferry, and are intending to do some hunting and fishing, you will be happy to discover that you needn't go further than 200 km (125 miles) beyond Port aux Basques to find the best hunting and fishing on the island.

Taking the TransCanada Highway north towards Corner Brook, you go through the wooded valley of the **Grand Codroy River**. This whole region, all the way to Corner Brook, is noted for its abundance of game, especially moose and caribou.

Where to Stay and Eat
The best hotel in this area is the **Hotel Port aux Basques** ((709)695-2171 WEB SITE www.hotelpab.com,

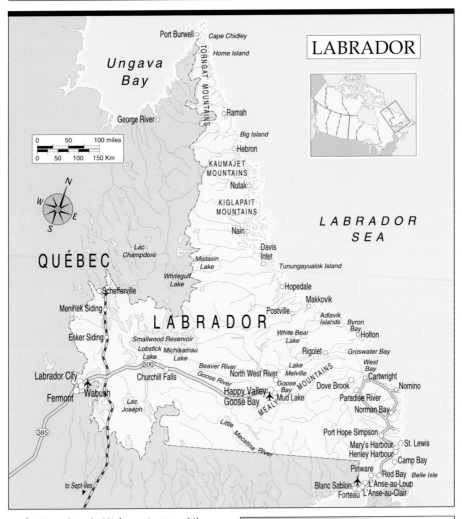

LABRADOR

At the top of the Gulf of St. Lawrence, a strip of water 16 km (10 miles) wide separates the island of Newfoundland from mainland Labrador. At 293,347 sq km (113,261 sq miles), Labrador is almost three times the size of the island, yet has only 35,000 inhabitants. Until fairly recently it was virtually uninhabited except for the Air Force base at Goose Bay and the dozens of tiny villages huddled in coves and inlets along the eastern seaboard.

Although Labrador remains one of the world's last great wilderness areas, its fabulous natural resources are a draw. At Labrador City and Wabush near the Québec border, large mining complexes produce almost half of Canada's iron ore, while a giant hydroelectric plant at Churchill Falls supplies power to the eastern United States. Development has also begun on one of the world's

on the TransCanada Highway just two kilometers (a bit over a mile) from the ferry terminal. It has 50 rooms and a good restaurant. Another inexpensive option, **St. Christopher's Hotel (** (709) 695-7034 TOLL-FREE (800) 563-4779 FAX (709) 695-9841 WEB SITE www.stchrishotel.com, Caribou Road, has a pleasant restaurant and a welcoming lounge.

HOW TO GET THERE

There is an international airport at Gander, as well as airports at Stephenville, St. Anthony and Deer Lake. **Provincial Airlines (** (709) 576-1666 WEB SITE www.provair.com and **Air Canada/Air Tango** WEB SITE www.aircanada.ca, provide air services. For information on the ferry from North Sydney, Nova Scotia, to Port aux Basques, contact **Marine Atlantic Reservations Bureau** TOLL-FREE (800) 341-7981 WEB SITE www.marineatlantic.ca.

richest nickel deposits at Voisey's Bay near Nain. At the same time, Labrador's other great natural resources, its fish and wildlife, are attracting anglers and hunters in ever-increasing numbers.

BACKGROUND

You could say that Labrador looks its age: it forms the eastern edge of the Canadian Shield, one of the oldest unchanged geological formations on the planet. As a result, it apparently looks very much the same as it did before animal life appeared on earth. The first humans are thought to have arrived in Labrador almost 9,000 years ago. In any case, it is known that the Inuit and other natives were here for thousands of years before the arrival of the first Europeans: Basque whalers who established a settlement at Red Bay, just across the strait from the northern tip of Newfoundland, in the sixteenth century. New arrivals since then have been few and far between, but this will undoubtedly change as more people begin to realize the extent of the unspoiled beauty that awaits them here.

WHAT TO SEE AND DO

Labrador's untamed wilderness contains some of the most spectacular scenery in North America. Don't think in terms of specific sights you ought to see or specific things you ought to do at a particular time or place. Labrador is just *there*, in all its vastness and prehistoric splendor, to be enjoyed by anyone who likes to hunt or fish or hike or ski or camp or simply breathe fresh, unpolluted air. With the gradual building of new roads along the coast and inland, the area is becoming more accessible, but most organized hunting and fishing excursions into the interior are by plane, while many coastal villages still communicate by boat in summer and on skis in winter. For details of operators, contact Tourism Newfoundland & Labrador (see TOURIST INFORMATION, page 238 in TRAVELERS' TIPS).

WHERE TO STAY

As you might expect, Labrador is not exactly chock-a-block with hotels, and what accommodation there is tends to be overpriced.

Happy Valley–Goose Bay has three comfortable, moderately priced hotels. The largest and plushest is the **Labrador Inn** ((709) 896-3351 TOLL-FREE (800) 563-2763 WEB SITE www.labradorinn .nf.ca, 380 Hamilton Road, with 73 rooms and a superb restaurant. The 40-room **Aurora Hotel** ((709) 896-3398 TOLL-FREE (800) 563-3066 WEB SITE www.aurorahotel.com, 382 Hamilton River Road, is similarly comfortable. The smallest and in many ways the most charming of the three is the **Royal**

Inn ((709) 896-2456 TOLL-FREE (888) 440-2456 E-MAIL royal.inn@nf.sympatico.ca, at 3 Royal Avenue, with nine rooms and nine units.

In L'Anse-au-Clair, the **Northern Light Inn** ((709) 931-2332 WEB SITE nli.labradorstraits.net, on Route 510, is similarly priced and offers most of the same facilities, plus self-contained units and all kinds of recreational opportunities and facilities nearby.

Flowers River Lodge ((709) 781-2091 TOLL-FREE (877) 725 6664 FAX (709) 781-1759 WEB SITE www.flowersriver.com is a beautiful red cedar lodge in Northern Labrador, accessibly only by float-plane (expensive). It is an excellent base for nature hikes, canoeing and 'berg watching.

HOW TO GET THERE

For information on air services to Labrador, contact **Air Labrador** ((709) 896-6777 WEB SITE www .airlabrador.com. **Québecair** ((514) 376-1682 flies to Blanc-Sablon from Montréal, Québec City and Sept-Îles.

From May to November a car-and-passenger **ferry** ((418) 461-2656 operates between St. Barbe on Newfoundland's west coast and Blanc Sablon, Québec, just five minutes drive from L'Anse-au-Clair in Labrador. Route 510 is paved 88 km (55 miles) to Red Bay, then gravel from there to Cartwright, 323 km (201 miles) on. A summer car-and-passenger ferry TOLL-FREE (866) 535-2567 operates between Happy Valley-Goose Bay and Cartwright. There is a separate coastal boat service between Pinsent Arm and Nain. A ferry ((418) 461-2656 also operates between Blanc Sablon and ports along the north shore of the St. Lawrence River in Quebec as far west as Sept-Îles, from April to January. For information on these services call TOLL-FREE (866) 535-2567 WEB SITE www.gov.nf.ca/ FerryServices or contact **Tourism Newfoundland and Labrador** (see TOURIST INFORMATION, page 238 in TRAVELERS' TIPS).

Motorists can reach Labrador City and Wabush via Route 389, a partially paved highway from Baie-Comeau, Québec. The total distance is 581 km (366 miles) and travel time is eight and a half hours. The TransLabrador Highway, Route 500, is a gravel road between Labrador City and Happy Valley-Goose Bay.

Rail service between Sept-Îles, Québec, and Labrador is provided by the **Québec, North Shore & Labrador Railways** (QN&L) ((418) 968-7808 (in Québec) or (709) 944-8205 (in Labrador).

Black water — sunlight glints off a northern stream.

Manitoba

In 1612, Englishman Thomas Button sailed into Hudson Bay and spent the winter at the mouth of the Nelson River. He came in search of the fabled Northwest Passage to the Orient. Although disappointed at coming up against the mass of mid-Canada, the area turned out to be a hunter's paradise, teeming with furry animals and cut by rivers brimming with fish. In 1668, the ketch *Nonsuch* sailed from England to Hudson Bay and returned laden with furs. As a result, the Hudson's Bay Company was formed and was granted the vast territory, then known as Rupertsland, by Charles II. Trading posts were established around the province.

French trappers were the first white settlers in the prairie, the fathers of the Métis race, a half-French, half-Indian people who followed the Catholic faith but led the native way of life. The fur trade continued to flourish and eventually the French posts were surrendered to the British. With the success of trade and transportation, the province began to open up, threatening the Métis way of life.

In 1870, the Hudson's Bay Company sold its land to the Dominion of Canada, which immediately surveyed the area in preparation for land allotment to new settlers. The Métis people rose in defense of their land rights and, under the leadership of the young Louis Riel, they set up their own provisional government. As a result, a small area around the Red River Valley was declared the province of Manitoba, with land allocated to the Métis. In 1870 Manitoba was incorporated into the Dominion of Canada.

The coming of the Canadian Pacific Railway in the 1880s heralded a period of great change, bringing with it immigrants from Ontario, Iceland, Eastern and Western Europe and the Ukraine. By 1912 the ever-growing province had been extended to its present-day boundaries, farming was flourishing, and good communications increased the province's supply lines, thus strengthening the economy.

Often referred to as Canada's "keystone province" because of its central position, Manitoba stretches across a vast 650,088 sq km (251,000 sq miles), between Saskatchewan to the west and Ontario to the east. Rivers and lakes cover about one-sixth of its land. It has a population of just over one million.

Agriculture — primarily wheat, cereals and cattle — continues to play an important role in the province's economy. Food processing and manufacturing are the province's main industries, and the rich mineral deposits of the Canadian Shield form the basis of several others. However, of the three Prairie Provinces, Manitoba has the smallest portion of prairie land, its wheat belt only in the southwest corner. Beyond the prairies lie the great lakes of Winnipeg, Manitoba and Winnipegosis;

beyond them a vast, rugged, rocky wilderness of forests, bogs and more lakes stretch northwards to the subarctic coastline of Hudson Bay. With the Northern Lights and polar bears of Churchill, over 100,000 lakes, the desert-like landscape of Spruce Woods Provincial Park, and numerous parks offering escape routes into the wilderness, there is a lot more to Manitoba than farms.

Outdoor enthusiasts can paddle broad and wild rivers, hike through a variety of terrain, ride horse trails, learn many winter sports and participate in wildlife-spotting safaris: black and polar bears, bison, lynx, moose, badgers, golden eagles and beluga whales are among the possible sightings. The climate, however, is a limiting factor. Summer temperatures sometimes run upwards of 30°C (86°F), while in winter they can drop to -20°C (-4°F). Snow and blizzards chill to the bone, even in southerly Winnipeg.

WINNIPEG

Halfway across Manitoba, at the very center of Canada, the city of Winnipeg, Manitoba's only major city, rises out of the prairies like a mirage, so far is it from any other city. It lies at the junction of the Assiniboine and Red Rivers, 2,093 km (1,300 miles) west of Toronto, and 572 km (355 miles) east of Regina, connected by rail and the TransCanada Highway. Around 667,000 people live in western Canada's oldest city — over half the entire population of the province.

Winnipeg is a very likeable, fairly cosmopolitan place. Its nucleus is, and always has been, the junction of Main Street and Portage Avenue, streets that stretch out for miles across the prairie, following the direction of the city's two rivers. It has pleasant parks, lovely riverside walks, wealthy suburbs with old mansion houses, and at the northeastern end of the city an old area of warehouses and depots reminds visitors of its early importance as a distribution center. The buildings along the wide, flat downtown streets testify to a policy of urban development that has respect for the city's stately older buildings, while remaining unafraid of change and innovation.

The corner of Portage Avenue and Main Street has benefited from such innovation, with an underground mall and walkways now offering shelter from what is billed as the windiest spot in Canada. Winnipeggers seem to take pride in their ability to withstand the bitterness of their long winters. The combination of harsh weather and Winnipeg's isolation from other urban centers may be why it has created such a rich cultural scene for itself. It boasts the world-famous Royal Winnipeg Ballet, a widely acclaimed symphony orchestra, the Manitoba Opera, the excellent Manitoba Theatre Centre and one of the country's finest museums, the Manitoba Museum.

Another enriching factor in Winnipeg's cultural life is the diverse ethnic mix of its population. It started out with a mixture of Indians, British, French and Métis, but the coming of the Canadian Pacific Railway added more to the mix. Chinese came as laborers working on the construction of the railway, then came other Western and Eastern Europeans, Ukrainians, Mennonites and Icelanders. The various nationalities tended to settle in ethnic-based communities around the city, and though this arrangement has to a large extent broken down, certain districts still retain a strong cultural identity. The downtown area has a sizable Chinatown, while the St. Boniface district to the east of the river has a large French-speaking community, and the southern part of town generally tends to be British in origin. Each August the city celebrates its rich ethnic mix with Folklorama: the world's largest multi-cultural event of its kind (see FESTIVE FLINGS, page 30).

Maybe the city's isolation and self-sufficiency underlies its strong character. Even the cityscape, with its cut-stone buildings, huge stockyards, warehouses and mansion-like houses, has solidity and a sense of security about it. Winnipeggers are themselves a resilient bunch, proud of their city, with an intense loyalty binding them to it wherever they wander.

BACKGROUND

Once a region where Cree, Ojibway and Assiniboine roamed, change began when the first white man arrived in 1738. He was a French explorer and fur trapper, Pierre Gaultier de la Verendrye, who established Fort Gibraltar near the confluence of the Red and Assiniboine Rivers. The fur trade flourished, albeit with a good deal of friction between rival factions. In 1812 the Hudson's Bay Company gave land in the Red River valley to Lord Selkirk, allowing him to establish a Scottish settlement and supply center for the traders.

Regular flooding and pestilence made a difficult start for the Scottish Highlanders who came here in search of a more prosperous life, but slowly they began to farm the area. For the Métis people, who lived by hunting buffalo, the settlement and farming of the area was a threat to survival, and in 1816 they attacked the settlement, killing 20 of the Scots in what has become known as the Seven Oaks Massacre. The colony faltered, but continued to grow slowly. A commercial center developed around the junction of the two rivers, with river and road transportation linking it to the United States.

In 1870 the province of Manitoba was created, and by 1873, the city of Winnipeg was incorporated. The Canadian Pacific Railway arrived in 1886, sparking the rapid expansion of the city and bringing in large numbers of immigrants. The

agricultural industry flourished, strengthening Winnipeg's position as a distribution center and financial capital. Today it has a thriving manufacturing industry, and the city remains a major financial and distribution center with a large Commodity Exchange. The junction of Portage Avenue and Main Street, shadowing the two old trade routes, remains at the center of the city's financial district.

GENERAL INFORMATION

At The Forks waterfront complex (next to the Johnston Terminal), you can visit the huge **Explore Manitoba Centre (** (204) 945-3777 TOLL-FREE (866) 626-4862 WEB SITE www.travelmanitoba.com, where exhibits and travel counselors will help you sort through your options. Information on camping in Manitoba's provincial parks can be obtained from **Manitoba Conservation (** (204) 945-6784 TOLL-FREE (800) 214-6497.

For information specifically about Winnipeg, there is **Tourism Winnipeg (** (204) 943-1970 TOLL-FREE (800) 665-0204, 279 Portage Avenue, a second location at the **Winnipeg International Airport (** (204) 982-7543 TOLL-FREE (800) 665-0204 WEB SITE www.tourism.winnipeg.mb.ca.

WHAT TO SEE AND DO

The **Exchange District (** (204) 942-6716 WEB SITE www.exchangebiz.winnipeg.mb.ca, a national historic site, lies at the very heart of Winnipeg, a 20-block area stretching from Portage Avenue and Main Street to the Manitoba Museum. Guided walking tours are offered June to September, Tuesday to Sunday at 11 AM and 2 PM.

The **Market Square**, at King Street and Bannatyne Avenue, is the hub of Winnipeg's visual arts activities, with numerous galleries and studios in historic buildings. There are shops, trendy restaurants, market stalls selling arts and crafts, and street entertainment during the summer months. This is also the location of the Fringe and Jazz Festivals, and a lively nighttime spot when the theaters, clubs and restaurants open up.

On the edge of the Exchange District, at Main Street, stand several significant buildings, including the **Centennial Concert Hall (** (204) 949-3950 (information), (204) 949-3999 (box office) or (204) 986-6069 (tours). Another is the excellent **Manitoba Museum** (until recently the Museum of Man and Nature) **(** (204) 956-2830 or (204) 943-3139 (24-hour recorded information) WEB SITE www .manitobamuseum.mb.ca, 190 Rupert Avenue. Consistently among Canada's "Top Ten Museums," this splendidly presented establishment is devoted to the province's geology, nature, history and culture. Realistic dioramas of Manitoba's various natural regions combine sight, sound and

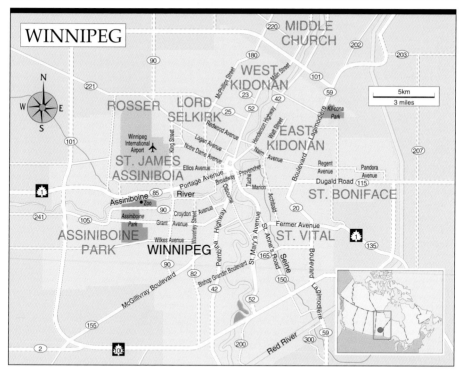

smell, and a gallery focuses on the prairie lands, with reconstructions of pioneer dwellings and displays describing the native way of life. Highlights include a gallery devoted to the Hudson's Bay Company and the *Nonsuch*, a full-scale and seaworthy replica (which can be boarded) of the ketch that left London in 1668 for Hudson Bay. Within the museum are a 280-seat **Planetarium** ((204) 943-3139 and the hands-on **Science Centre** ((204) 956-2830.

Close by stands the **Ukrainian Cultural and Educational Centre (Oseredok)** ((204) 942-0218, 184 Alexander Avenue East. This old building houses an art gallery and museum containing archives and changing exhibitions on the history and culture of the Ukrainian people, the second largest group of immigrants to settle in the province. Many of the refugees brought with them smuggled documents, which now form the most complete archive about the country outside the Ukraine itself. Exhibits include samples of embroidery, ceramics, carving, costumes and the delicately painted Easter eggs called *pysankys*.

Moving south along Main Street, opposite the railway station there's a tiny park in which you can see **Upper Fort Garry Gate**, all that remains of the early nineteenth-century Hudson's Bay Fort. To the east along Broadway, another Winnipeg landmark carries on the name — **The Fort Garry**, a château-like hotel built by the Grand Trunk Railway in 1913.

Behind the station, 5.5-hectare (13.6-acres) **Forks National Historic Site** ((204) 983-6757 WEB SITE www.parkscanada.pch.gc.ca/forks has interpretive displays about the region's history, heritage entertainment — Parks Events Hotline ((204) 983-6757 — and riverside pathways.

Next to the historic site, sharing the riverside promenade, is **The Forks** ((204) 943-7752 WEB SITE www.theforks.com, a sprawling complex of renovated railway buildings and parkland. There's a lively public market in a former stable, a skating rink in winter and Johnston Terminal — with shops, restaurants, a viewing tower, an outdoor stage, a railway museum, a children's theater and **Manitoba Children's Museum** ((204) 924-4000 WEB SITE www.childrensmuseum.com, a state-of-the-art, hands-on space that appeals equally to adults. Seven galleries cover history, science, nature, technology — and hockey. Kids can climb aboard a vintage steam engine or try out a fully functioning television studio.

The **Splash Dash Water Bus** ((204) 783-6633 offers a dock-to-dock service on the Red and Assiniboine Rivers (May to October daily 7 AM to sunset, with departures from The Forks every 15 minutes). It also rents canoes for individual river trips.

The magnificent **Legislative Building** ((204) 945-5813, Broadway and Osborne Street, is an excellent example of neoclassical architecture, designed by English architect Frank Worthington

Simon and built in 1919. This H-shaped structure is made of fossil-rich Tyndall limestone. Atop its dome stands the recently re-gilded figure of the **Golden Boy**, symbolically facing north. He holds the torch of economic progress in one hand and carries a sheaf of wheat in the other to symbolize agriculture. The work of French sculptor Charles Gardet the statue has become the symbol of the city. The building is set in lovely grounds dotted with statuary honoring the city's various ethnic groups with depictions of some of their distinguished countrymen, including Louis Riel. The interior of the building is also quite spectacular; guided tours allow visitors a look at the Legislative Chamber (hourly tours July through Labor Day daily, 9 AM to 6 PM).

South of Broadway, take a look at what high-tech meant to the late Victorians at the **Dalnavert Museum** ((204) 943-2835, 61 Carlton Street, a house that was built for the son of John A. Macdonald, Canada's first prime minister. It is a red brick building that was built with indoor plumbing and electric lighting, and was fitted with all kinds of household gadgetry.

The superb **Winnipeg Art Gallery** ((204) 786-6641 WEB SITE www.wag.mb.ca, 300 Memorial Boulevard, is housed in an unmissable wedge-shaped building. It has a varied collection of international art, but is most famous for the world's largest collection of contemporary Inuit works of art (over 9,000 pieces), which are exhibited in continually changing displays. Cultural events are often staged in the roof garden.

Across the Red River, the **St**. **Boniface** district is home to the oldest French-speaking community in Canada. French traders lived in the area from 1738 when Pierre Gaultier de la Verendrye arrived. In 1819, following the building of a church here, a French community began to develop that included French Canadians and Métis. The 1906 City Hall, 219 Provencher Boulevard, now houses a tourist information center and gallery with works by francophone artists.

St. **Boniface Cathedral**, 190 Cathedral Avenue, is a modern structure built among the ruins of an earlier cathedral that burned down in 1968. In the old cemetery lies the body of Louis Riel, who was executed following the defeat of the Northwest Rebellion. *In Riel's Footsteps* is a 45-minute play staged in the cemetery July to August, Wednesday to Sunday at 2 PM and 7 PM, Saturday and Sunday at 4 PM too — French and English versions alternate, so check.

Next to the basilica stands Winnipeg's oldest building, an oak structure dating from 1846, which was a convent for the Grey Nuns who arrived here from Montréal. It now contains the **St**. **Boniface Museum** ((204) 237-4500, 494 Taché Avenue, which has a large collection of artifacts belonging to the Métis and other early settlers,

including some Louis Riel memorabilia. Also in the area is the **Church of the Precious Blood**, an interesting modern structure that is shaped like a tipi.

At the southern edge of the city you can visit **Riel House** ((204) 257-1783, 330 River Road (mid-May to early-September, daily 10 AM to 6 PM), which stands close to the river in St. Vital. It was the home of the Riel family, although Louis Riel never lived here. It has been restored to the year 1885, when Riel was executed, and bilingual tours and exhibits offer glimpses into Métis life of the period.

Moving eastwards, a striking glass pyramid houses the **Royal Canadian Mint** ((204) 257-3359, 520 Lagimodière Boulevard, which produces coins for Canada and over 30 foreign nations: it's estimated that a quarter of the world's population carry coins minted here. Guided tours (by appointment only; English and French) show you the processes and high-tech equipment involved in making money, but the product is out of reach!

Assiniboine Park ((204) 986-3130, 2355 Corydon Avenue, accessible by footbridge over the Assiniboine River from Portage Avenue, west of the city — about 11 km (seven miles) from downtown — is a 153-hectare (378-acre) park with the Leo Mol sculpture garden, an English garden with a statue of Queen Victoria, and the Lyric outdoor theater. There's a Winnie-the-Bear statue (the beloved Pooh was named after a Canadian bear in the London Zoo named Winnepeg, but the Disney Corporation has the copyright on the name "Winnie-the-Pooh") and an attractive old pavilion ((204) 888-5466, with an art gallery containing the only known E. H. Shepard oil painting of Winnie. The park also contains a **zoo** ((204) 986-6921, with around 1,700 animals of over 300 species, many indigenous, and a **conservatory** ((204) 986-5537, a small but delightful spot filled with orchids and other flowers.

The **Fort Whyte Centre for Family Adventure and Recreation** ((204) 989-8355 WEB SITE www .fortwhyte.org, 1961 McCreary Road, has 215 hectares (600 acres) of land in Winnipeg's southwest corner. Here the natural habitat of the province's lakes and rivers has been recreated in and around several former cement quarries — you can canoe on the lakes, see (usually) a 40-strong herd of bison, and feel a bear's fur. Self-guided nature trails and an interpretive center tell all about it.

Excursions from Winnipeg

Lower Fort Garry ((204) 785-6050 TOLL-FREE (877) 534-3678, about 32 km (20 miles) north of Winnipeg along Highway 9 (mid-May to Labor Day daily 9 AM to 5 PM), was built by the Hudson's Bay Company in the 1830s and is the only remaining stone fort of that era in North America. It has been carefully restored and visitors can see the various living quarters, the fur loft and the governor's residence, as they were when the fort functioned as an important trading post. Before you begin your tour of the buildings, watch the background film shown in the reception center. Inside the compound, costumed "workers" demonstrate crafts in the various workshops. In the grounds you'll see a restored York boat, a vessel designed for transporting furs.

The **Mennonite Heritage Village** ((204) 326-9661 WEB SITE www.mennoniteheritagevillage .mb.ca lies 61 km (38 miles) southeast of Winnipeg. To get there from Winnipeg, take Highway 1 to Highway 12 North, and watch for signs just north of Steinbach. This living museum runs a

working mill and has Mennonites demonstrate their nineteenth-century crafts. The Mennonites who settled in Manitoba came from Russia in the 1870s and 1880s, and this heritage village presents a colorful picture of their way of life. The sect is totally committed to pacifism and has been frequently persecuted because of its beliefs. The Livery Barn Restaurant serves traditional Mennonite food and the general store sells traditional goods.

The *Prairie Dog Central* ((204) 832-5259 WEB SITE www.vintagelocomotivesociety.mb.ca is an early twentieth-century steam train that takes you on a delightful 45-km (28-mile), two-and-a-half-hour trip to **Warren**. It leaves from Inkster Junction, just north of Inkster Boulevard (with free bus service from The Forks) at 10 AM and 3 PM every Sunday from May to September; in July and August there are Saturday trips too.

SPORTS AND OUTDOOR ACTIVITIES

There are **hiking** trails and **cycling** paths in the city parks (details available from information centers) and several **skating** rinks throughout Winnipeg. When the snow comes, there's also **snowmobiling** at Birds Hill Provincial Park, about 32 km (20 miles) northeast of the city.

There's excellent **fishing** in the province, as you would expect with so many lakes, but you need to venture outside Winnipeg. The tourist information centers can help you on where to go and how to get there, and with details of the many **canoe** routes for which the province is famous.

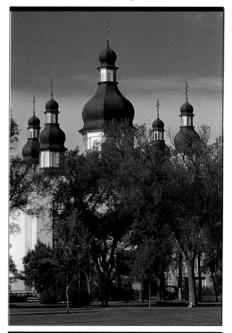

NIGHTLIFE AND THE ARTS

Winnipeg has a lively nightlife. To find out what's going on, check the entertainment listings that appear in the daily *Winnipeg Free Press* and the *Winnipeg Sun*. Hotels and other places distribute the free *Uptown*, a weekly arts and entertainment paper, and there's a useful monthly publication, *Where Winnipeg*.

The theater season in Winnipeg is really under way between September and early May, but in July the **Manitoba Theatre Centre (MTC)** ((204) 942-6537 (box office), 174 Market Avenue, promotes the 11-day **Fringe Theatre Festival** E-MAIL fringe@mtc.mb.ca, as well as staging a variety of comedy and serious drama throughout the

ABOVE: Part of the façade of the Legislative Building LEFT and the towers of the Ukrainian church at the Ukrainian Cultural and Educational Centre RIGHT.

theater season. Nearby, the smaller **MTC Warehouse Theatre ℂ** (204) 956-1340 or (204) 942-6537 (box office) stages experimental productions.

There are several other companies scattered around town, including the **Prairie Theatre Exchange ℂ** (204) 942-5483, Portage Place Shopping Centre, and the **Rainbow Stage ℂ** (204) 780-7328, which specializes in musicals. In summer, productions are staged at the outdoor amphitheater in Kildonan Park. The most cherished and famous of Winnipeg's cultural institutions is the **Royal Winnipeg Ballet**, which performs a program of classical and modern works at the **Centennial Concert Hall ℂ** (204) 956-0183 (information) or (204) 956-2792 (box office), Room 101, 555 Main Street (season October to May), and also gives a free open-air performance on the Lyric Stage in Assiniboine Park in the summer. The acclaimed **Winnipeg Symphony Orchestra ℂ** (204) 949-3950 (information) or (204) 949-3999 (box office) (season September to May) and the **Manitoba Opera ℂ** (204) 942-7479 (information) or (204) 780-3333 (box office) (season November to May) also perform at the Centennial Concert Hall. Also with a November to May season, **Winnipeg's Contemporary Dancers ℂ** (204) 452-0229 are famous for pushing the boundaries of modern dance. They perform at different venues. The **Manitoba Theatre for Young People ℂ** (204) 942-8898, The Forks, offers productions October through March that are aimed at children and teenagers. For summer visitors, varied entertainments are presented at the Festival Park outdoor **Scotiabank Stage ℂ** (204) 942-6302 WEB SITE www.theforks.com.

A mixture of jazz, folk, and classical music can often be heard at the **Winnipeg Art Gallery ℂ** (204) 786-6641 WEB SITE www.wag.mb.ca, 300 Memorial Boulevard.

You'll find rock and other live music playing at various bars and clubs in the town, often in hotel lounges. The **Palomino Club ℂ** (204) 772-0454, 1133 Portage Avenue, is a country music hangout. **Pyramid Cabaret ℂ** (204) 957-7777, 176 Fort Street, offers top local and national bands, as well as DJs covering a wide variety of styles.

Winnipeg has a lively and rapidly changing club scene, especially in the Exchange District, and two **casinos**, with a common TOLL-FREE number (800) 265-3912 and a common WEB SITE www.casinosofwinnipeg.com. Both operate Monday through Saturday 10 AM to 3 AM, Sunday from noon. Nobody under 18 is admitted. **Club Regent ℂ** (204) 957-2700, 1425 Regent Avenue West, is set-up as a Disney-type jungle with ersatz palm trees, beasts and temples on all sides, as well as a genuine walk-through aquarium with a small shark and less fearsome creatures. **McPhillips Street Station ℂ** (204) 957-3900, 484 McPhillips Street, has a less-striking decor but incorporates the **Millennium Express ℂ** (204) 957-3900 TOLL-FREE (800) 265-3912,

a mind-blowing 3D combination ride/history/entertainment. In addition to these attractions and the usual mass of gaming tables, both casinos feature Vegas-style live entertainment, restaurants and lounges.

WHERE TO STAY

Expensive

The **Delta Winnipeg ℂ** (204) 942-0551 TOLL-FREE (800) 268-1133 FAX (204) 943-8702, 350 St. Mary Avenue, is part of a recently renovated complex that connects with the Convention Centre. The 390 pleasant rooms include several suites. Facilities include indoor and outdoor pools and a good range of services, a choice of restaurants within the hotel and several more inside the complex.

The **Fairmont Winnipeg ℂ** (204) 957-1350 TOLL-FREE (800) 441-1414 FAX (204) 949-1486, 2 Lombard Place, one of the city's top-rated hotels, is in the

very center of town. Service is excellent, there are 340 luxurious rooms and guests have the use of an indoor swimming pool, a choice of restaurants, a café and in-house entertainment.

For some old-style grandeur, go to **Hotel Fort Garry** ((204) 942-8251 TOLL-FREE (800) 665-8088 FAX (204) 956-2351, 222 Broadway. This castle-like hotel was built by the Grand Trunk Railway in 1913 and has undergone extensive but careful renovation to preserve its original splendor. There are 240 elegant rooms and suites and two beautiful dining rooms. A full breakfast is included in the rate.

The **Sheraton Winnipeg** ((204) 942-5300 TOLL-FREE (800) 463-6400 FAX (204) 943-7975, 161 Donald Street, is another top downtown hotel, located close to the Convention Center. It has an indoor pool, a sundeck, and nightly entertainment. Some rooms are mid-range. Their **Just Off Broadway** restaurant specializes in regional cuisine.

Mid-range

The **Radisson Winnipeg Downtown** ((204) 956-0410 TOLL-FREE (800) 333-3333 WEB SITE WWW .radisson.com/winnipeg.ca, 288 Portage Avenue, is a downtown high-rise hotel with 272 rooms above its multistory parking facility. The rooms are smart and have good views. The service is first-rate and amenities include a recreation center with indoor swimming pool, sauna, whirlpool and exercise room, and a business center with secretarial services and free Internet access.

For accommodation with lots of character and excellent service, book in at the **Ramada Marlborough Hotel** ((204) 942-6411 TOLL-FREE (800) 667-7666 FAX (204) 942-2017, 331 Smith Street, in the town's financial district. This Victorian Gothic building has a grand interior of vaulted ceilings, stained glass and polished wood. The rooms and

Feathers for sale in the Old Market Square.

suites are stylish, with modern conveniences, and the hotel has a restaurant, an English pub and a coffee shop.

Canad Inns TOLL-FREE (888) 332-2623 (central reservations) WEB SITE www.canadinns.com, have half a dozen establishments scattered around town. They are big, new and spotlessly clean, with pools and waterslides for the kids and good-quality family restaurants. One is attached to the Club Regent Casino. Some rooms are inexpensive.

Inexpensive

The **Charter House Hotel** ((204) 942-0101 TOLL-FREE (800) 782-0175 FAX (204) 956-0665, 330 York Avenue, is a good downtown choice. It has 90 rooms

(some with balconies), a very good steak house and an outdoor swimming pool.

The **Ivey House International Hostel** ((204) 772-3022 FAX (204) 784-1133, 210 Maryland Street, is located in a turn-of-the-twentieth-century residence within walking distance of the city's cultural attractions. It's open year-round.

The *Bed & Breakfast of Manitoba* listing is available from the information centers or **Manitoba Bed and Breakfast** ((204) 661-0300 WEB SITE www.bedandbreakfast.mb.ca, 893 Dorchester Avenue. If a rural retreat appeals, get in touch with the **Manitoba Country Vacations Association (MCVA)** (/FAX (204) 776-2176 E-MAIL ffamfarm @escape.ca WEB SITE www.countryvacations.mb .ca, c/o Ernest Fraser, Box 93, Minto R0K 1M0. The tourist information centers can also tell you about campgrounds in the region.

WHERE TO EAT

Winnipeg's diverse ethnic mix makes for some exciting dining, and there is a surprisingly large number of restaurants for a city of its size.

Expensive

The restaurant **529 Wellington** ((204) 487-8325, 529 Wellington Crescent, is unashamedly the priciest place in town — but worth it. The elegant uncrowded surroundings, superb service and connoisseurs' wine list match the quality of the superb steaks. Excellent jumbo prawns and fresh Atlantic lobster also feature on the menu.

Wasabi ((204) 774-4328, 588 Broadway, is a top Japanese establishment, the funkiest sushi bistro in town. Don't miss the soft-shell crab. **Fusion Grill** ((204) 489-6963, 550 Academy Road at Lanark Street, takes a lot to beat it if you enjoy the imaginative use of spices. Fresh local ingredients prepared in a way that reflects the city's mixed ethnic influences are delicious enough to attract many well-known clients, as well as "normal" folk who enjoy the simple bistro atmosphere.

Moderate to Expensive

Dubrovnik Restaurant ((204) 944-0594, 390 Assiniboine Avenue, is in a large Victorian house on the riverbank, with a charming interior and many original features. Some beautiful examples of Yugoslavian crafts adorn the walls. The food is continental with Yugoslavian specialties, and it is delicious.

Tre Visi ((204) 949-9032, 173 McDermot Avenue, is a comfortable but elegant California/ modern-Italian restaurant with a great wine selection to accompany brilliant salads and wonderful dishes made with fresh ingredients.

Moderate

Earls ((204) 989-0103, 191 Main Street, is a popular rendezvous with a wide-ranging good-quality menu, reasonable prices and a pleasantly casual ambiance. The **Dim Sum Garden** ((204) 942-8297, 277 Rupert Avenue, lives up to its name, with over a hundred delicious choices of authentic Cantonese-style dim sum brought round on carts.

Mona Lisa ((204) 488-3687, 1697 Corydon Avenue, is the place for classic Italian pizzas, excellent pastas and the like. It's family-oriented with a casual atmosphere. **Stella's Café and Bakery** ((204) 453-8562, 166 Osborne Street, is a great place for brunch, with excellent quiches and other baked goods, but it's always busy, so get there early. **Rae and Jerry's Steak House** ((204) 783-6155, 1405 Portage Avenue in the west end of the city, is a popular 1950s-style steak house that includes chicken and fish dishes on its menu. Prices vary between inexpensive and moderate.

If you like Vietnamese food, try **Nhu Quynh** ((204) 786-1182, 510 Sargent Avenue, which offers rice-flour pancakes wrapped round blanched vegetables and delicious sauces. Again, it's moderate to inexpensive.

Inexpensive

The north end of town has a plethora of delis and cafés that make for some interesting and enjoyable dining. **Alycia's Restaurant** ((204) 582-8789,

559 Cathedral Avenue, serves homemade Ukrainian food in cozy surroundings decorated with traditional arts and crafts. This is a place where Winnipeggers hang out. Both **Oscar's Deli** ((204) 947-0314, 175 Hargrave Street, and **Simon's Delicatessen** ((204) 589-8269, 1322 Main Street, are well-established Jewish delicatessens open into the small hours.

Mrs. Mike's Burgers ((204) 237-3977, 286 Taché Avenue, opens only in summer for outdoor dining or takeaway. It is Winnipeg's oldest burger joint, and consistently popular as it is both good and very cheap. The two **Soup Pierre** TOLL-FREE (888) 7687, 238 Portage Avenue, and ((204) 453-7687, 651 Corydon Avenue, offer a large selection of homemade soups, some vegetarian, and sandwiches. You can eat in or take away.

Winnipeg's **Chinatown** lies to the north of the Exchange District, stretching between James and Logan avenues and covering an eight-block area. You'll find good-value Chinese restaurants here.

How to Get There

Winnipeg International Airport ((204) 987-9402, is approximately 10 km (six miles) northwest of downtown, about a 20-minute drive away, but allow longer during rush hours. An airport shuttle runs between the airport and some of the big hotels. Apart from Air Canada, the only scheduled airlines covering the city are **Westjet** ((403) 444-2552 TOLL-FREE (800) 538-5696 WEB SITE www.westjet .com (within Canada) and **Northwest Airlines** TOLL-FREE (800) 447-4747 or (800) 225-2525 WEB SITE www.nwa.com (primarily from Minneapolis).

The **VIA Rail** station ((204) 949 1830 TOLL-FREE (888) 842-7245 WEB SITE www.viarail.ca is downtown at 123–146 Main Street. Trains run to Vancouver via Kamloops, Jasper, Edmonton and Saskatoon. From the east the line runs into Winnipeg from Toronto, while VIA Rail runs the *Hudson Bay* train to Churchill via Dauphin, The Pas and Thompson.

The bus station is downtown at 487 Portage Place. **Greyhound** ((204) 783-8857 TOLL-FREE (800) 661-8747 WEB SITE www.greyhound.ca operates buses to and from this terminal. **Grey Goose Bus Lines** ((204) 784-4500, 301 Burnell Street, links Winnipeg with other towns in Manitoba.

Winnipeg is quite isolated, so if you're driving, the chances are that wherever you're coming from (unless it's the airport), you'll have quite a long drive. The TransCanada Highway (Highway 1) runs through the city, linking it with Toronto, 2,093 km (1,300 miles) to the east, and Calgary, 1,359 km (844 miles) to the west. Minneapolis in Minnesota is 734 km (456 miles) from Winnipeg via Interstate 94 and Interstate 29 in the United States, becoming Highway 75 in Manitoba.

ELSEWHERE IN MANITOBA

WHITESHELL PROVINCIAL PARK

Nature sets the stage for all kinds of outdoor pursuits in this large wilderness park (272,090 hectares / 672,334 acres) close to the Ontario border, 144 km (89 miles) east of Winnipeg. It is Canadian Shield country, an area rich in clear, deep lakes, rushing rivers, forest, sandy beaches and wildlife — ideal for hiking, mountain biking, canoeing, horseback riding, fishing and all kinds of water sports in summer. In winter these give way to cross-country skiing, ice fishing, skating, snowmobiling and snowboarding. Areas of the park have been developed for tourism and offer such things as shops, a golf course, tennis courts and small museums about local features. Specific points of interest include centuries-old aboriginal petraforms, a goose sanctuary, a fish hatchery, a lily pond and rock tunnels through which canoes can pass.

LAKE WINNIPEG

This vast lake lies to the north of Winnipeg and is lined with sandy beaches, making it an excellent place for relaxation and water sports. Grand Beach, on the eastern shore, is one of North America's best for swimming, windsurfing and fishing, with powdery sand, dunes up to eight meters (26 ft) high and a lagoon crowded with waterfowl.

The **Visitor Centre** is operated by the **New Iceland Heritage Museum** ((204) 642-4001, which focuses on Icelandic settlement in the area and inter-cultural history.

The fishing town of **Gimli** (meaning "paradise" in Norse mythology) has the largest Icelandic community outside Iceland. It stands on the western shore of the lake, 90 km (56 miles) north of Winnipeg. Back in the 1870s, Icelanders came to the area in search of a new volcano-free home. They found that this area could offer them a good living through fishing and farming, and for a time the region was an independent country known as New Iceland. The community of Gimli retains a strong Icelandic identity and culture, and in August it celebrates the **Icelandic Festival**, a celebration of sports, music, parades, art and traditional food.

Hecla/Grindstone Provincial Park ((204) 378-2945, Riverton, encompasses a collection of islands in Lake Winnipeg. These islands are wildlife preserves and a bird-watcher's delight, while hikers, fishermen, canoeists and winter sports enthusiasts also find much to enjoy here. Hecla Island is accessible by car, and at its northern end the **Gull**

Winnipeg's skyline.

Harbour Resort and Conference Centre ((204) 279-2041 TOLL-FREE (800) 267-6700 WEB SITE www.gullharbourresort.com, offers recreation facilities, attractive accommodation and good Icelandic hospitality without marring the natural beauty of the island. The hotel is open year-round.

RIDING MOUNTAIN NATIONAL PARK

Riding Mountain National Park is an outdoor playground 248 km (154 miles) northwest of Winnipeg, on the highlands of a prairie escarpment. The resort town of **Wasagaming**, on the shores of Clear Lake, offers a variety of accommodation and extensive recreational facilities, but the area remains largely unspoiled, with 60 species of mammal, including bison, moose, elk, white-tailed deer, black bears and beaver inhabiting the parkland. In the winter there are cross-country skiing trails through the park.

The **Visitor Centre** in Wasagaming ((204) 848-7275 or 7272 TOLL-FREE (800) 707-8480 E-MAIL RMNP_Info@pch.gc.ca will provide guides, maps and information, as well as offering films and other worthwhile educational aids.

On the outskirts of Wasagaming, the **Elkhorn Resort & Conference Centre** ((204) 848-2802 WEB SITE www.elkhornresort.mb.ca/www.rci.com, has chalets and suites, a nine-hole golf course and organized horseback riding treks. Prices vary from mid-range to expensive.

Rather less hectic is **Riding Mountain Guest Ranch** ((204) 848-2265 E-MAIL wildlifeadventures @mts.net WEB SITE www.wildlifeadventures.ca, Lake Audy, a peaceful spot run by animal lovers Jim and Candy Irwin, whose guests are made to feel part of the family. Horseback riding in the park and canoeing on the lake that laps at their front lawn are among the activities arranged to work off the excellent food, while less strenuous pursuits include billiards, board games, books, a sauna, and bear-watching from a comfortable "hide" (an old school bus). A great place to really get away from it all and relax. Many guests become friends and regular visitors.

CHURCHILL

The small town of Churchill lies on the southwestern shore of Hudson Bay at the estuary of the Churchill River, and is one of the few places in the north accessible from the south by rail or air. It is one of the world's largest grain-handling ports, with huge grain elevators looming overhead, but it has become an international tourist destination because of its substantial natural attractions. Although weather conditions are very difficult here, with snow during most of the year creating a sparse, subarctic vegetation, the wildlife draws visitors.

Churchill is the world capital for **polar bear watching**, especially during October and early November, when migration is at its height and the bears are regularly seen wandering around the outskirts of town.

Tundra Buggy Tours ((204) 675-2121 TOLL-FREE (800) 544-5049 operates specially built buggies that take visitors out on bear-spotting safaris on the tundra. Half-day tours run July through September, full-day tours October and early November.

This is also one of the best places on earth to see the **Northern Lights** in their full glory: they are visible for around 190 nights a year! Their appearance is determined by the weather but you would be unlucky not to see them if you were to stay for more than a couple of nights any time from October through April. At this time they may well be visible from other parts of the province: March is the peak in the north, a little later in the south.

The town is not without a summer attraction, too: from July through mid-August **beluga whales** congregate at the mouth of the Churchill River, and there are daily tours in a hydroplane-equipped boat to listen to these most vocal whales with **Sea North Tours** ((204) 675-2195 WEB SITE www.cancom.net/seanorth.

The **Eskimo Museum** ((204) 675-2030, in downtown Churchill, has an excellent collection of Inuit artifacts, including walrus tusks carved with scenes from mythology and everyday life.

Calm Air ((204) 778-6471 TOLL-FREE (888) 225-6247 WEB SITE www.calmair.com, 90 Thompson Drive, runs flights between Winnipeg and Churchill year-round, at least once a day.

There's also the option of a two-night **VIA Rail** journey from Winnipeg. In peak seasons (July, and mid-September to mid-November) there are three trains a week in each direction. For information, contact VIA Rail ((506) 857-9830 TOLL-FREE (888) 842-7245 WEB SITE www.viarail.ca, 146-123 Main Street, Winnipeg R3C 1A3.

FURTHER NORTH: NUNAVUT AND THE NORTHWEST TERRITORIES

A vast frontier covering an area nearly half the size of the United States and one-fifth of Canada (1,994 million sq km or nearly 770 million sq miles), Nunavut and the Northwest Territories form the North American continent's last true wilderness: a "don't miss" experience for those who love outdoor activities in totally unspoiled — and spectacular — surroundings.

The approximately 1,367,000 caribou that roam the land far outnumber the population of 67,500 Dene, Athapaskan, Inuit, Inuvialuit, Métis and Europeans who call these territories home. These two territories have the world's lowest population density, averaging one person for every 100 sq km (39 sq miles).

In the eastern areas, the Inuit (singular Inuk) form a majority of the population. Although their traditional culture has suffered from contact with Anglo-European settlers, they remain a strong cultural force, and in recent decades have won significant victories in the fight to preserve a way of life that is intimately tied to the land. Their land-rights negotiations finally led to the partitioning, on April 1, 1999, of the old Northwest Territories into today's eastern Nunavut and western North-west Territories. Although twenty-first-century amenities are encroaching, the basic lifestyle is still much as it has been for centuries, and the local people see few enough visitors to retain a welcoming attitude to those who do make it their way.

snowmobiles and all-terrain vehicles (ATVs), as there are no roads linking many communities. Dog teams are still used in winter and boats travel during warmer months, when the ice comes off the water.

GENERAL INFORMATION

If you hear the call of the North, advance planning is essential. Your first response should be to get in touch with the government tourism agencies: **Northwest Territories Tourism** ((867) 873-5007 TOLL-FREE (800) 661-0788 WEB SITE www.nwt travel.nt.ca., Box 610, Yellowknife X1A 2N5, and **Nunavut Tourism** ((867) 979-6551 TOLL-FREE (866)

Outdoor activities are ubiquitous, largely based on the necessity to employ non-road-using forms of transportation: from dog-sledding and snowmobiling in winter, to hiking, rafting and canoeing/kayaking in summer. Sport fishing and hunting are also options.

Winter provides an excellent chance to see the Northern Lights, as they are visible for some 190 nights a year. Be prepared to stay three or four nights to ensure you have clear skies. In summer, the long, long days are warm and sunny.

For the adventurer, the Northwest Territories and Nunavut offer incomparable scenic wonders, along with abundant wildlife, world-class fishing, and opportunities to visit and learn from the native inhabitants. However, you do need to plan your trip in advance, and confirm accommodations and guide services before departure. In much of the area, transportation is limited to airplanes,

686-2888 WEB SITE www.nunavuttourism.com, Box 1450, Iqaluit, Nunavut X0A 0H0.

Many northern communities have **regional and local visitor centers** offering information and assistance, as well as interpretive displays on the local culture and history. In communities that don't have visitor centers, you can usually get assistance at the community center and from hotel staff.

Recommended (if not indispensable) publications include *The Nunavut Handbook* (Marion Soubliere, ed., Nortext Press), *NWT Explorers' Guide* (a free annual publication produced by Northwest Territories Tourism and available from them) and *The Milepost* (Vernon Publications). Nunavut Tourism also publishes a free annual Travel Planner.

Moose graze in the unspoiled beauty of Riding Mountain National Park.

Travelers'
Tips

The best tip we can offer any traveler is to get on the Net, do your homework and get a good travel agent. In a world where fares, schedules, even routes are changing hourly, only access to the latest information can ensure a hassle-free vacation.

GETTING THERE

BY AIR

Almost all of the major international airlines fly to Canada, but Air Canada has more flights to more Canadian cities than any other airline. Also, as you would expect, Air Canada has an extensive network of domestic airlines linking cities within Canada (see GETTING AROUND, below). Contact numbers for **Air Canada** are as follows: TOLL-FREE IN CANADA (888) 247-2262 TOLL-FREE IN THE UNITED STATES (800) 268-0024 IN AUSTRALIA ((02) 9286-8900 IN NEW ZEALAND ((09) 379-3371 IN THE UK ((0870) 524-7226 WEB SITE www.aircanada.ca.

Other major airlines offering flights to Canada from the United States include **American Airlines** TOLL-FREE (800) 433-7300 IN THE UK (0845) 778-9789 WEB SITE www.aa.com; **Delta** TOLL-FREE (800) 221-1212 TOLL-FREE IN THE UK (0800) 414-767 WEB SITE www.delta.com; **United** TOLL-FREE (800) 241-6522 IN THE UK (0845) 8444-777 WEB SITE www.ual.com; **Northwest** TOLL-FREE (800) 447-4747 WEB SITE www.nwa.com; **US Airways** TOLL-FREE (800) 428-4322 IN THE UK (0845) 600-3300 WEB SITE www.usairways.com; and **WestJet** ((403) 444-2552 TOLL-FREE (888) 937-8528 WEB SITE www.westjet.com.

Other major airlines offering flights to Canada from Europe include: **Air France** TOLL-FREE IN CANADA (800) 667-2747 TOLL-FREE IN THE US (800) 237-2747 IN THE UK ((0845) 084-5111 IN FRANCE ((08) 2032-0820 WEB SITE www.airfrance.com; **British Airways** TOLL-FREE (800) AIRWAYS IN THE UK ((0845) 773-3377 WEB SITE www.britishairways.com.

BY RAIL

Amtrak TOLL-FREE (800) 872-7245 WEB SITE www.amtrak.com, the United States passenger railway system, has several routes serving Canada's east coast and one route serving the west coast. Major eastern routes are: New York–Montréal, New York–Buffalo–Niagara–Toronto, Chicago–Sarnia–Toronto, Cleveland–Buffalo–Niagara–Toronto, and Detroit–Windsor–Toronto.

BY ROAD

There are 13 principal border-crossing points where the American highway system connects directly with the Canadian. Crossing into Canada by car is usually a quick, simple matter, although in peak season you might want to avoid the busier crossing points such as Detroit–Windsor and

Niagara Falls. Once in Canada, no matter where you've crossed, you are only a short drive from the TransCanada Highway.

Greyhound TOLL-FREE (888) 842-8747 WEB SITE www.greyhound.ca is the only company operating a cross-border service, but it has such a huge route system that you should have no difficulty in getting to most points in Canada from virtually anywhere in the United States. It also has a hugely complicated system of fares, discount fares, seasonal rates, unlimited-travel passes, including the 7- to 60-day Canada Pass.

BY WATER

There are several **car-ferries** operating to Canada from points in the northeastern and northwestern United States. For address details see BY FERRY, page 239 under GETTING AROUND.

Although there is no regular passenger ship service between Europe and Canada, some **cargo lines** leaving from European ports accept passengers. Accommodations on board are usually comfortable and food plentiful if plain. Costs are less per day than they are on luxury cruise liners, but the trip is longer, so this option is not for those in a hurry. (The trip from Le Havre, France, to Montréal, for example, takes 18 to 20 days.) For information on freighter travel, contact your travel agent or **Freighter World Cruises** ((626) 449-3106 TOLL-FREE (800) 531-7774 WEB SITE www.freighterworld.com, 180 South Lake Avenue, Suite 335, Pasadena, California 91101-2655.

For more information about cruise ships that ply Canada's coasts see TAKING A TOUR, page 38 in YOUR CHOICE.

ARRIVING AND LEAVING

United States citizens require only proof of citizenship to enter Canada (passport, birth certificate, voter registration card or naturalization certificate). United States residents who are not citizens must show their Alien Registration Receipt Card. Nationals from all other countries need a full valid passport, with at least six months' validity. United States, European, Australian and New Zealand nationals do not require a visa; those of other nationalities should check in advance.

Travelers crossing the border with children should carry identification for them (passport or birth certificate), as Canadian and United States Customs and Immigration are taking measures to reduce parental and other kinds of child abduction. Children traveling with one parent or adult should bring a letter of permission from the other parent, the parents or legal guardian. Divorced parents with shared custody rights should carry legal documents establishing their status.

CUSTOMS

Customs regulations are similar to those in most countries, including the usual restrictions on bringing in meats, plants and animals. Items intended for personal or professional use do not have to be declared, and you are allowed up to 200 cigarettes or 50 cigars, and 1.5 liters of wine or 1.1 liters of spirits or 8.5 litres of beer duty-free. The minimum drinking age is 18 in Québec, Manitoba and Alberta, and 19 in all other provinces.

You can bring in gifts up to $60 per gift in value. There are no currency restrictions.

Personal hunting and fishing equipment may be brought in duty-free as well, but all firearms and ammunition must be declared and a written description of each item, including serial numbers of guns, must be provided. Certain non-firearm weapons are also prohibited. Details of Customs regulations are available from Customs Canada ((204) 983-3500 TOLL-FREE (800) 461-9999 WEB SITE www.ccra-adrc.ga.ca.

If you are planning on purchasing furs or other animal products (e.g., antlers) check with your country's customs regulations to find out which animals are considered endangered and cannot be imported. The same consideration applies to Inuit art, which may be made of whalebone or mastodon ivory, neither of which can be brought into the United States or the United Kingdom.

TAXES

Provincial and federal taxes are added to the published price of all goods. With federal GST of 7 percent and provincial sales tax of up to 15 percent, this can add significantly to the price. Alberta makes a great play of the fact that it is the only province in Canada with no provincial sales tax.

As a visitor to Canada, you can claim a **tax refund** for some of the tax you pay on accommodation, as long as you stay less than one month in that accommodation. In addition, you may claim a tax refund for certain goods you take home. Look for the "Tax Refund for Visitors" brochure at Visitor Information Centres, ask for it at your hotel front desk, or write the Visitor Rebate Program, Revenue Canada, Summerside Tax Centre WEB SITE www.ccra-adrc.ga.ca, 275 Pope Road, Suite 104, Summerside, Prince Edward Island C1N 6C6.

EMBASSIES AND CONSULATES

FOREIGN REPRESENTATION IN CANADA

Australian High Commission ((613) 236-0841 WEB SITE www.ahc-ottawa.org, Suite 710, 50 O'Connor Street, Ottawa K1P 6L2. There are consulates in Toronto and Vancouver.

Irish Embassy ((613) 233-6281, 130 Albert, Ottawa K1P 564.

New Zealand High Commission ((613) 238-6097 FAX (613) 238-5707 WEB SITE www.nzcottawa.org, Metropolitan House (suite 727), 99 Bank Street, Ottawa K1P 6G3. There are consulates in Toronto and Vancouver.

South African High Commission ((613) 744-0330 FAX (613) 741-1639, 15 Sussex Drive, Ottawa K1M 1M8. Consulates in Montréal and Vancouver.

United Kingdom High Commission ((613) 237-1530 WEB SITE www.britainincanada.org, 80 Elgin Street, Ottawa K1P 5K7. There are consulates in Calgary, Halifax (NB), Montréal, Québec City, St John's, Toronto, Vancouver and Winnipeg.

United States Embassy ((613) 238-5335 TOLL-FREE (800) 529-4410 WEB SITE www.usembassy.state.gov, 490 Sussex Drive, Ottawa, Ontario K1N 1G8. There are American consulates in Calgary, Halifax (NB), Montréal, Québec, Toronto, Vancouver and Winnipeg.

CANADIAN REPRESENTATION ABROAD

Australia: Canadian High Commission ((02) 6270-4000 FAX (02) 6273-4081 E-MAIL cnbra@dfait-maeci.gc.ca, Commonwealth Avenue, Canberra ACT 2600. There are consulates in Melbourne, Perth and Sydney.

Ireland: Canadian Embassy ((01) 417-4100 FAX (01) 417-4101 E-MAIL cdnembsy@iol.ie, 65 St. Stephen's Green, Dublin 2.

New Zealand: Canadian High Commission ((04) 473-9577 FAX (04) 471-2082 E-MAIL wlgtn@dfait-maeci.gc.ca, Third Floor, 61 Molesworth Street, Thorndon, Wellington.

South Africa: Canadian High Commission ((012) 422-3000 FAX (012) 422-3052 E-MAIL pret@dfait-maeci.gc.ca, 1103 Arcadia Street, Hatfield 0028, Pretoria. There is also an office in Cape Town and a consulate in Durban.

All aboard! A railway station, though it may be small, is never far away.

United Kingdom: Canadian High Commission ((020) 7258-6600 FAX (020) 7258-6333 E-MAIL Ldn@dfait-maeci.gc.ca, located in Macdonald House, 1 Grosvenor Square, London WIK 4AB; Consular and Passport Services ((020) 7258-6600 FAX (020) 7258-6533, Canada House, Pall Mall East, London SW1Y 5BJ. There are consulates in Belfast, Birmingham, Cardiff and Edinburgh.

United States: Canadian Embassy ((202) 682-1740 FAX (202) 682-7726 E-MAIL wshdc-outpack @dfait-maeci.gc.ca, 501 Pennsylvania Avenue NW, Washington DC 20001. There are consulates in Atlanta, Boston, Buffalo, Chicago, Detroit, Los Angeles, Miami, Minneapolis, New York, San Francisco and Seattle.

TOURIST INFORMATION

Rather than having a central source of information for all of Canada, each of the provinces maintains a bureau that dispenses information on subjects of interest to tourists. In the GENERAL IN-FORMATION sections of the preceding chapters we have listed the local agencies; here, then, are the provincial tourism offices for eastern Canada.

Tourism New Brunswick ((506) 444-4097 TOLL-FREE (800) 561-0123 WEB SITE www.tourismnew brunswick.ca, 26 Roseberry Street, Campbelltown, New Brunswick E3N 2G4. In the United Kingdom ((0906) 871-5000 (premium rate).

Tourism Newfoundland and Labrador ((709) 729-2830 TOLL-FREE (800) 563-6353 FAX (709) 729 0057 E-MAIL tourisminfo@mail.gov.nf.ca WEB SITE www.gov.nf.ca/tourism, Box 8700, St. John's, Newfoundland A1B 4K2. In the United Kingdom ((0906) 871-5000 (premium rate).

Northwest Territories Arctic Tourism ((867) 873-7200 TOLL-FREE (800) 661-0788 FAX (867) 873-4059 E-MAIL arctic@nwttravel.nt.ca WEB SITE www.nwttravel.nt.ca, Box 610, Yellowknife, Northwest Territories X1A 2N5.

Check-In Nova Scotia ((902) 453-8400 TOLL-FREE (800) 565-0000 FAX (902) 453-8401 E-MAIL nsvisit@fox.nstn.ca WEB SITE www.explorenova scotia.com, 2695 Dutch Village Road, Suite 501, Halifax, Nova Scotia B3L 4V2. In the United Kingdom ((0906) 871-5000 (premium rate).

Nunavut Tourism ((867) 979-6551 TOLL-FREE (800) 491-7910 FAX (867) 979-1261 WEB SITE www.nunatour .nt.ca, Box 1450, Iqaluit, Nunavut X0A 0H0.

Ontario Travel ((416) 314-0944 (English) or (416) 314 0956 (French) TOLL-FREE (800) ONTARIO (English) or (800) 268-3736 (French; Canada only) WEB SITE www.ontariotravel.net, Queen's Park, Toronto, Ontario M7A 2E5.

Tourism Prince Edward Island ((902) 368-4444 TOLL-FREE (800) 734 5259 E-MAIL tourpei@gov.pe.ca WEB SITE www.peiplay.com, Box 940, Charlottetown, Prince Edward Island C1A 7M5. In the United Kingdom ((0906) 871-5000 (premium rate).

Tourisme Québec ((514) 873-2015 TOLL-FREE (877) 266-5687 FAX (514) 864-3838 EMAIL info @tourisme.gouv.qc.ca WEB SITE www.bonjour quebec.com, CP 979, Montréal, Québec H3C 2W3. In the United Kingdom ((0870) 556-1705 E-MAIL brochures@quebectourism.co.uk.

NATIONAL PARKS

National parks are federally administered, but locally supervised by park information centers. These are excellent sources of information, and are the place to pickup permits for fishing or backcountry camping. Interpretive talks, exhibits on flora and fauna, nature walks with park natural-

ists and reports on weather and road conditions are often also part of the package.

Drivers must pay a modest entry fee to all national parks, usually purchased from a roadside booth at the park boundary. A day pass is valid from the day of issue until 4 PM the following day. It is also possible to buy an excellent-value 12-month National Parks Pass to 27 national parks, or a Discovery Package that also includes 67 national historic sites. They are sold at park gates and information centers, over the Internet, or by telephoning **Parks Canada** ((819) 997-0055 TOLL-FREE (888) 773-8888 (trip planning) E-MAIL parks_webmaster@pch.gc.ca WEB SITE www .parkscanada.pch .gc.ca, 25 Eddy Street, Hull, Québec K1A 0M5.

Parks Canada also runs a wide range of campgrounds within the parks, ranging from the fully serviced to the most basic. Advance booking is strongly recommended in high summer. To do longer trails and go wilderness camping, you will need to buy a daily or annual Wilderness Pass ((780) 852-6177. For additional information and reservations, contact Parks Canada or the local parks offices listed in each chapter.

GETTING AROUND

BY AIR

The country's,major carrier, **Air Canada** TOLL-FREE IN CANADA (888) 247-2262 TOLL-FREE IN THE UNITED STATES (800) 268-0024 IN AUSTRALIA ((02) 9286-8900 IN NEW ZEALAND ((09) 379-3371 and IN THE UK ((0870) 524-7226 WEB SITE www.aircanada.ca and its regional partners handle the bulk of the middle- and long-distance air traffic. Dozens of local independent carriers connect the remaining dots on the map. Thus there are very few places in Canada, even the remote islands, that are not accessible by air. The principal regional carriers not owned by Air Canada include: **Air Labrador** ((709) 896-6730 WEB SITE www.airlabrador.com, serving the Maritime Provinces; **Air Transat** TOLL-FREE (800) 388-5836 WEB SITE www.airtransat.com, with connections between the major cities; and **WestJet** ((403) 444-2552 WEB SITE www.westjet.com, with a wide range of flights to major cities and throughout western Canada.

BY BUS

Where,there's a way, there's a willing bus to take you just about anywhere you want to go in Canada. Greyhound Canada has a nationwide route system, and there are five or six large regional companies that reach into the nooks and crannies Greyhound misses. Bus service is frequent, quick and inexpensive, whether it's intercity or cross-country. The 5,000-km (3,000-mile) trip from Montréal to Vancouver, for example, takes about 69 hours. Greyhound offer various passes, some covering Canada, some the whole of North America. For detailed information contact **Greyhound Canada** ((403) 265-9111 TOLL-FREE (800) 661-8747 WEB SITE www.greyhound.ca. Other, more local bus companies are listed in the HOW TO GET THERE sections of city listings.

BY CAR AND MOTORHOME

Canada, only slightly less,than the United States, is a driver's dream. The highway system may not be as sprawling as in the United States, but it doesn't have to be, since most of the places visited by tourists and natives alike are within easy driving distance of the TransCanada Highway. The gasoline may not be as cheap as in the United States, but it's far cheaper than in Europe.

The major car-rental firms are represented across the country, including: **Avis** TOLL-FREE IN CANADA (800) 272-5871 TOLL-FREE IN THE UK (0870) 606-0100 TOLL-FREE IN THE US (800) 230-4898 WEB SITE www.avis.com; **Hertz** TOLL-FREE IN CANADA (800) 654-3001 TOLL-FREE IN THE UK (0870) 840-0084 TOLL-FREE IN THE US (800) 854-3131 WEB SITE www.hertz.com; **Alamo** TOLL-FREE (800) 462-5266 TOLL-FREE IN THE UK (0870) 599-4000 WEB SITE www.alamo.com; **Budget** TOLL-FREE (800) 527-0700 TOLL-FREE IN THE UK (0870) 156-5656 WEB SITE www.budget.com; **Holiday Autos** TOLL-FREE IN THE UK (0870) 400-4400 WEB SITE www.holidayautos.com; **National Car Rental** ((954) 320-6600 TOLL-FREE (800) 227-7368 WEB SITE www.nationalcar.com;

and **Rent-a-Wreck** TOLL-FREE IN CANADA (800) 327-0116 TOLL-FREE IN THE US (800) 944-7501 WEB SITE www.rentawreck.ca.

If you are planning to rent a car in the summer, it's a good idea to reserve before you leave home. In order to rent a vehicle in Canada, you must be at least 25 years old and have a credit card.

Perhaps you had in mind something a bit larger. Each year, hundreds of travelers hit the backroads of Canada in rented motorhomes (recreational vehicles) and truck campers. This is the American equivalent of a "caravan," especially attractive for those who want to explore Canada as a family or group of friends. In order to rent an RV, you must have a driver's license (that you've held for more than one year) and be at least 25 years old. It is strongly recommended that you reserve your RV several weeks prior to departure. Contact your travel agent for information and reservations.

BY FERRY

There are both car and passenger ferry services available on most of Canada's major lakes and rivers, as well as between the mainland and the

OPPOSITE: Winter in Canada is a time for bundling. ABOVE: Autumn leaves in New Brunswick attract droves of leaf-peepers.

offshore islands, and Canada and the United States. Ferries across the St. Lawrence and to Vancouver Island don't require reservations, but other ferries should be booked in advance — well in advance if you are taking a car with you.

Information on ferry transportation within various regions is listed under HOW TO GET THERE in the relevant chapters.

In eastern Canada, **Bay Ferries (** (902) 245-2116 WEB SITE www.nfl-bay.com operates services between Bar Harbor, Maine, and Nova Scotia, Prince Edward Island and New Brunswick. **Marine Atlantic (** (902) 794-5700 FAX (902) 564-7480 WEB SITE www.marine-atlantic.ca operates a wide range of ferry routes year-round between New Brunswick, Prince Edward Island, Nova Scotia, Newfoundland and Labrador. There is also a seasonal ferry between St. Barbe, on Newfoundland's Northern Peninsula, and Blanc Sablon, Québec. **Prince of Fundy Cruises (** (207) 775-5616 TOLL-FREE (800) 845-4073 WEB SITE www.scotiaprince.com connects Portland, Maine, with Yarmouth, Nova Scotia.

BY RAIL

Canada's main passenger rail,carrier is the government-owned **VIA Rail (** (514) 871-6000 (headquarters) TOLL-FREE (888) 842-7245 WEB SITE www .viarail.ca, 3 Place Ville-Marie, Suite 500, Montréal, Québec H3B 2C9. The VIA Rail network was cut back severely but there are still regular services between the major cities, and it is still possible to make the transcontinental journey by train, although the southern route has been closed.

VIA Rail issues the **Canrailpass**, which makes possible substantial savings by allowing 12 days of coach-class travel over a 30-day period. Prices are $423 (low season) and $678 (high season). Sleeping cars are also available, but must be reserved at least a month in advance during the May to October high season. The pass must be purchased prior to arrival in Canada. There are several other passes on offer, such as the **Corridorpass**, for use only in the Eastern cities.

For United Kingdom information and bookings for VIA Rail, contact **Leisurail (** (0870) 750-0222 WEB SITE www.leisurail.co.uk, 12 Coningsby Road, Peterborough PE3 8XP.

BY LOCAL TRANSPORTATION

Taxis can always be found at airports, railway stations and major hotels. They can also be hailed in the street fairly easily in the larger cities; elsewhere they can be ordered by telephone. Rates are quite reasonable by American or European standards, and a tip of 15 percent or so is normal. In some provinces not all the taxis have meters, making it advisable to agree on the fare before beginning a journey.

Most major cities have good bus networks. If you choose to travel by bus, be sure to have the exact fare with you, as bus drivers do not carry change — or buy a pass. Details are given under each city chapter.

DRIVING

You will be able to drive on a valid national driver's license for three months, however, it is recommended that you get an international driving permit (see WHAT TO TAKE, below). Any standard United States car insurance policy is valid in Canada; get a Canadian Non-Resident Inter-Provincial Motor Vehicle Liability Insurance Card from your insurance company. All other nationals must take out insurance for a minimum of $200,000 ($50,000 in Quebec and the Northwest Territories).

If the car you're driving is not registered under the name of one of the drivers or one of the passengers, bring written proof that you have permission from the owner to take the car into Canada.

The driving regulations will be familiar to anyone used to driving in the United States or in continental Europe: drive on the right and pass on the left, vehicles approaching from the right have the right-of-way at intersections, the use of seat belts is compulsory, and driving under the influence of alcohol will incur stiff penalties. In Newfoundland, Prince Edward Island, Québec, Ontario, Manitoba, the Yukon, Northwest Territories and Nunavut, radar detectors are illegal even if not in use.

The speed limit on highways is 100 km/h (60 mph), on smaller roads 80 km/h (50 mph), and in towns 80 km/h down to 50 km/h (30 mph). You must stop if you come upon a school bus with its red lights flashing. You may turn right at a red light (except in Québec) if you stop first and make sure the road is clear. Some provinces require drivers to keep headlights on for periods after dawn and before sunset. In the Yukon, the law requires drivers to keep headlights on at all times when using territory highways. Pedestrians have the right of way at all intersections without stoplights and at crosswalks. Note: Fines for traffic offenses in Québec are much harsher there than elsewhere in Canada.

There are plenty of 24-hour service stations flanking the major highways, while those in town tend to close around 9 PM (7 PM in small towns, and all day on Sundays). Gasoline (or petrol) is sold by the liter (one liter equals about one quart; there are 3.8 liters to the gallon). Gas is a good deal more expensive than it is in the United States, but cheaper than in Europe. Most stations take credit cards, and most are now self-service.

In the event of an accident, you should get to a telephone and dial the operator ("0"), who can connect you with the police and emergency services. Members of automobile clubs affiliated with the Canadian Automobile Association (the American Automobile Association and most European automobile clubs are) should bring their membership cards along with them, as they are entitled to membership benefits. For more information contact the **Canadian Automobile Association** ((613) 247-0117 FAX (613) 247-0118 WEB SITE www .caa.ca, 1145 Hunt Club Road, Ottawa, Ontario K1V 0Y3; the **American Automobile Association** TOLL-FREE (800) 564-6222 WEB SITE www.aaa.com; the **United Kingdom Automobile Association** ((0870) 600-0371 WEB SITE www.the-aa.com; or the **Royal Automobile Club** ((0800) 092-2222 WEB SITE www.rac.co.uk.

you want to get into serious rusticity, there is no better way than to stay on one of the hundreds of working farms and ranches that offer accommodation as well as hearty meals and healthy activities (see SPECIAL INTERESTS, page 36 in YOUR CHOICE). If you just want to get away from it all and hunt or fish or think about the human condition, there are some wonderful lodges in remote wilderness areas where Nature starts at your front door.

If you will be staying in one place for a longish period, particularly with children or in a group, you will get both privacy and savings (on food) in an efficiency apartment in one of Canada's many apartment hotels.

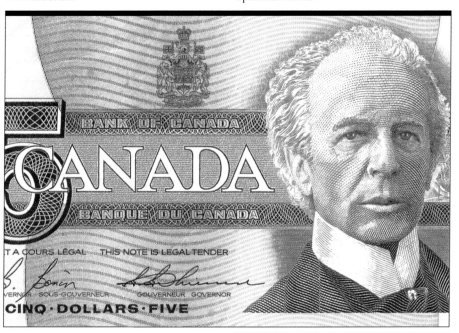

ACCOMMODATION

When it comes to accommodation in Canada, one is spoiled for choice. Wherever you go in Canada, you will find places to stay that appeal to every taste and suit every budget. If luxury and comfort are your priorities, there are deluxe hotels to rank with any in the world. If convenient locations while driving are important, there are motels in every price range sprinkled along the nation's main roads and highways. If economy is the paramount consideration, you will be able to get rooms at a YMCA, YWCA, university, or hostel in all but the most remote spots — and sometimes even there (see BACK-PACKING, page 23 in YOUR CHOICE). If conversation and "character" count alongside economy, there is bound to be a bed and breakfast nearby.

If rustic charm is what you're looking for, there are delightful inns spread across the country. If

CAMPING

There are thousands upon thousands of campgrounds throughout Canada, of every size and description. Many are in the national and provincial parks, some are municipally owned, others are privately run. Most are open from May until late September, with campsites costing from $10 to $20. Facilities usually include toilets, showers, a laundry, picnic tables, campfire sites and power hookups for recreational vehicles. The fancier ones will also have a shop and a restaurant. Generally speaking, the privately run campgrounds will have more amenities and will be more expensive, while the public ones in the national and provincial parks will be more scenically situated.

Sir Wilfred Laurier (1841–1919), first French-Canadian prime minister of Canada, appears on Canada's five dollar bill.

As most campgrounds are run on a first-come, first-served basis, during the high season — July and August — it's a good idea to start looking for a site no later than mid-afternoon.

There are three **nocturnal nuisances** that can thoroughly spoil a camping vacation if you come unprepared. The first is that familiar bane, the mosquito. Bring plenty of insect repellent, as well as a tent fitted with a mosquito net. The second nuisance is scavenging animals — often, in Canada, bears. These creatures can be discouraged by never keeping food in or near the tent (unless it's in the car), and by always disposing of uneaten food and washing up the dishes immediately after meals. No leftovers, no problems. Third, even

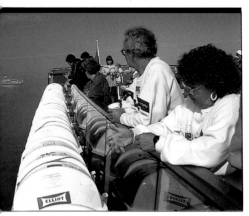

in midsummer, the temperature at night can suddenly drop, leaving you shivering unless you have brought enough warm clothing.

For lists of campgrounds write to the provincial tourism office in the area you plan to visit or contact Parks Canada (see NATIONAL PARKS, above).

PRICES

We have deliberately avoided giving exact restaurant and accommodation prices. This is because we have learned that the only thing you can absolutely depend on in this business is that the prices will have changed before the ink is dry (sometimes, surprisingly, for the better — as special offers and new types of discounts are introduced). We have therefore confined ourselves to price categories where hotels and restaurants are concerned. Hotels in the **expensive** category, for example, will generally charge over $150 a night for a double room; **mid-range** hotels will charge between $75 and $149; **inexpensive** hotels will charge less, sometimes much less.

At restaurants listed as **expensive** you can expect to pay more than $50 per person for a meal, excluding wine; **moderate** restaurants will charge between $25 and $50; **inexpensive** ones will cost you less — sometimes, again, much less. When

hotels or restaurants fall at either of the two extremes — very expensive or very inexpensive — we have so indicated.

Another word about prices: All the prices given in this book, and the categories outlined above, are in **Canadian dollars**. Most travel guides tell you to remember that the Canadian dollar is worth about 20 percent to 30 percent less than the American dollar. My advice is precisely the opposite: forget that the Canadian dollar is worth less. Don't translate; think in United States dollars. This is because all the prices quoted in Canada are exclusive of the layers of taxes that are added later — sales taxes, goods and services taxes, even "taxes on taxes," as one hotel owner wanly pointed out to me. So by the time your bill is added in Canadian dollars, it will come to almost exactly the original, untaxed figure in American dollars. If you keep in mind this one simple trick, you will know a real bargain when you see one.

BASICS

BUSINESS HOURS

Business hours are generally more or less from 9 AM to 6 PM, Monday through Friday, with late-night shopping in some stores until 9 PM on Thursday and Friday. Most shops and stores are also open Saturday and some local stores, especially during the summer, are open on Sunday from noon until 5 PM. Stores may have longer hours in summer months.

CURRENCY

Canadian currency resembles American currency in every important respect except value. The coins are in the same denominations and go by the same names (penny, nickel, dime, etc.), the paper notes are of uniform size (but in different colors according to value). There are no longer $1 and $2 bills. Instead there is the $1 "loonie" coin, nicknamed after the bird that appears on it, and the $2 "toonie."

At press time the **exchange rate** was: US$1 to C$1.56; UK£1 to C$2.43; and €1 to C$1.53. Should you wish to be precisely *au courant*, visit the Universal Currency Converter WEB SITE www.xe.net/currency, or check your local newspaper. American dollars are widely accepted, but using them introduces an unnecessary complication into a transaction, as well as an unnecessary discourtesy.

As in all countries with hard currencies, the banks offer the best exchange rates — much better than hotels, for example. Normal banking hours are Monday to Friday 10 AM to 3 PM. Trust companies and credit unions tend to have longer hours and may also be open on Saturday morning. Most major credit cards are accepted anywhere you are likely to go — including American Express, MasterCard, Visa, Diners Club, Enroute and Carte Blanche; consequently you are advised to carry a minimum of cash. If you prefer using non-plastic money, take it in the form of travelers' checks. They can be cashed everywhere, with proper identification (e.g. passport, driver's license), although the larger denominations will not always be welcome in places like restaurants that don't like being used as banks.

In general, however, we recommend floating through Canada on a raft of plastic: your bank debit or credit card. All Canadian financial institutions have automatic teller machines (ATMs), and you'll find ATMs located in large and small shopping

(second Monday in October), Remembrance Day (November 11), Christmas Day (December 25), Boxing Day (December 26).

In addition to the national holidays, each territory and province has its own local holidays, many on the first Monday in August.

TIME

Canada is divided into six time zones, including Newfoundland's own, typically quirky, time zone, which is only a half-hour ahead of Atlantic Standard Time in the Maritime Provinces. The other four time zones correspond to, and are continuations of, the four United States time zones: Eastern

centers, airports, train stations and even many gas stations and corner stores. Before you leave home check with your bank to be certain your ATM card is on the Plus or Cirrus network; they can also provide you with a booklet listing networks worldwide on which your card with operate.

ELECTRICITY

The electric current is 110–120 volts AC, the same as in the United States, and the sockets only take American-type plugs with two flat prongs.

PUBLIC HOLIDAYS

National holidays include: New Year's Day, Good Friday, Easter Monday, Victoria Day (Monday nearest May 24), Canada Day (July 1), Labor Day (first Monday in September), Thanksgiving

Standard Time, Central Standard Time, Mountain Standard Time and Pacific Standard Time.

Atlantic Standard Time is four hours behind Greenwich Mean Time, so when it is 8 PM in London, it is 4 PM in the Maritimes (4:30 PM in Newfoundland). Québec and all of Ontario to the east of Thunder Bay are on Eastern Standard Time, five hours behind GMT. Manitoba and the eastern half of Saskatchewan are on **Central Standard Time** (GMT minus six); the rest of Saskatchewan, Alberta and northeast British Columbia are on **Mountain Standard Time** (GMT minus seven). All of British Columbia west of the Rockies is on **Pacific Standard Time**, eight hours behind GMT.

OPPOSITE: The ferry across the St. Lawrence to Rivière-du-Loup, at the base of the Gaspé Peninsula. ABOVE: Made in America — a '57 Chevy sports Québec plates by the banks of the St. Lawrence.

All of Canada — with the mysterious exception of eastern Saskatchewan — observes Daylight Savings Time from the first Sunday in April, when the clocks are put forward one hour, until the last Sunday in October.

TIPPING

In general, you should tip more or less 15 percent — more if the service is outstanding, less if it is not so good. Tip porters $2 a bag, chambermaids $2 a day — rounding off the total upwards in deserving cases, downwards in undeserving ones.

WEIGHTS AND MEASURES

Canadians, like just about everybody else in the world except their American neighbors, rely almost exclusively on the metric system.

To make life easier for those not yet numerate in metrics, we have devised our own rough-and-ready (and of course approximate) system for making instant conversions on the spot. It is not only simple, but easy to memorize, so long as you remember that the colloquial term "a bit" here represents one-tenth of whatever it is next to. Thus: a meter equals a yard and a bit; a kilometer equals a half-mile and a bit; a kilogram equals two pounds and a bit (500 grams equals 1 lb and a bit); a liter equals an American quart and a bit.

For converting to degrees Fahrenheit, simply double the figure you are given in Celsius and add 32, topping it up by a couple of degrees when you get above 20°C. The temperature you come up with won't be precisely accurate, but it will be close enough. Note that when temperatures descend into the negative numbers the two scales begin to converge, thus: -40°C equals -40°F. (This may seem like an arcane piece of knowledge, but remember, this is Canada.)

COMMUNICATION AND MEDIA

MAIL

Although main post offices in Canada may open as early as 8 AM and close as late as 6 PM on weekdays, and some are open on Saturday mornings, you can avoid disappointment by going between 9 AM and 5 PM, Monday to Friday. In fact, you can avoid post offices altogether for most purposes, as stamps can be bought at hotels and from vending machines in airports, railway stations, shopping centers and drugstores. Letters and postcards can be mailed at most hotels' front desks or at any red mailbox.

If sending mail to a Canadian address, be sure to include the postal code. Also, we are told by the postal authorities that every year there are some Americans who think it is just as good to use American stamps as Canadian ones. It's not. Following are **postal abbreviations** for the provinces and territories: Alberta AB, British Columbia BC, Saskatchewan SK, Manitoba MB, New Brunswick NB, Newfoundland and Labrador NF, Northwest Territories NWT, Nunavut NT, Nova Scotia NS, Ontario ON, Prince Edward Island PEI, Québec QP, Yukon Territory YT.

If you want to **receive mail** in Canada, you can have mail sent to you $^c/_o$ General Delivery at the mail post office in the town or city where you wish to pick it up. But remember that it must be picked up within 15 days or it will be returned to sender. If you have an American Express card, or traveler's checks from American Express or Thomas Cook, you can have mail sent to you at any office of either company. It should be marked "Client Mail," and it will be held for you for as long as a month.

Telegrams are handled by CN/CP Telecommunications, while most good hotels now have Internet and fax facilities available for guests' use.

TELEPHONES

The Canadian telephone system is completely integrated with that of the United States, which means that it is splendidly efficient and economical, and that no international codes are necessary for calls between the United States and Canada. As in the United States, for information on local telephone numbers dial 411; for information on long-distance numbers dial 1-555-1212. For calls requiring operator assistance — such as long-distance personal or collect calls, or for emergency calls — dial "0."

To place a long-distance call within the same area code, dial 1 + the number you are calling. To place a call outside your area code, dial 1 + area code + telephone number. Do the same for dialing toll-free numbers. For direct dialing of overseas calls, dial 011 + country code + city code + telephone number.

Calls placed in the evening or on the weekend are less expensive, although any call from a hotel will incur a (usually steep) surcharge. There are public telephones just about everywhere; they only accept Canadian quarters, and/or prepaid phone cards.

We have made an effort to provide the specific geographic limitations of the toll-free numbers listed in this book when this information was available. Generally speaking, TOLL-FREE refers to numbers available throughout North America, whereas limitations to Canada, the United States, or a specific province are indicated. TOLL-FREE IN WESTERN CANADA means just that: you can use this number in British Columbia, Alberta, Saskatchewan, Yukon and Manitoba, but will not get through if you dial from elsewhere.

THE INTERNET

Canada is wired. Just about everywhere you go, you will find a bookstore, café or public library offering access to the Internet for a nominal fee (and sometimes free). If you've signed up for one of the free global e-mail accounts such as HotMail or Yahoo before leaving home, then you are wired, too.

We found that most libraries offered access, but that actual availability varied greatly because of lack of equipment and high demand. Many hotels have access points now. If that doesn't work, ask around for the latest cybercafé where you can settle down with a coffee and get warming news from home.

The Internet is also becoming a powerful tool for researching and planning trips. Most organizations, hotels, and tour operators listed in this book have home pages on the **World Wide Web**. We have listed web addresses where we could find them, but with new web sites coming online faster than we can type, if the address is not there, you may be able to find it via a simple search on your web browser (e.g., Netscape Navigator™ or Microsoft Internet Explorer™).

Web sites are of varying quality. Some are quite useful, allowing you to retrieve information quickly, make contact via e-mail direct from the site, or even make a reservation at the touch of a button. Others will have you pulling your cyber hair out. All the provinces and major cities now have excellent tourism web sites with detailed links to other local sites, listed along with the office addresses throughout the book. The prize for the best we have discovered in writing this edition goes to the city of Saskatoon, whose web site is a joy to use and filled with useful, up-to-date information.

RADIO AND TELEVISION

We are tempted to say that if you are in Canada you shouldn't be indoors, and leave it at that. We are further tempted to say that if you do find yourself indoors in North America, you certainly shouldn't be watching television. It's difficult to convey the feeling of dull despair that comes over you when you contemplate a galaxy of up to 40 television channels — not one of which is shining brightly enough to engage your attention for more than a few minutes.

If it's any consolation, though, you are better off watching television in Canada then in the United States, simply because you have a choice of programs aside from the American ones (which nonetheless predominate even in areas beyond the reach of American stations). Its precarious finances notwithstanding, the CBC (Canadian Broadcasting Corporation) manages to produce some worthy

programming of its own, while the French-language channels serve up the occasional treat. But don't be surprised when you switch channels to escape Teenage Mutant Ninja Turtles only to be confronted with *Popeye et son fils*.

The Canadian radio dial, like the American, features end-to-end music — classical, pop, rock, country, jazz — interspersed with talk shows, phone-ins, and news.

NEWSPAPERS AND MAGAZINES

Canadian journalism, too, closely resembles its American counterpart. With the exception of the *Globe and Mail*, which is published in Toronto, the

newspapers are all local papers. Certainly, some big-city papers such as the *Toronto Star* are national, even international, in stature; but their main emphasis remains on coverage of their own communities. This enlightened parochialism benefits the visitor not only by providing a useful introduction to topics of local interest, but also by providing, through its listings and advertisements, a comprehensive guide to local events and entertainment. So don't neglect this valuable resource whenever you arrive in a new place.

All of the larger newsagents in Canada have shelves that are identical to the ones you would expect to find in comparable shops in the United States — except that in addition to all the American newspapers and magazines you get the Canadian ones as well.

Tucking in to an adult-size portion of *moules-frites* (steamed mussels and fries) in Montréal.

HEALTH AND SAFETY

You really haven't much to worry about in Canada, because health hazards are few and healthcare is excellent. It can be expensive, though, so visitors should check to make sure that they are either covered for Canada by their existing health insurance or take out full travel insurance. An excellent medical emergency policy, which also includes personal travel insurance, is available from the **Europ Assistance Group** through its affiliates in a dozen or so countries, including the United Kingdom ((01444) 442-365 FAX (01444) 416-348, Sussex House, Perrymount Road, Haywards Heath,

West Sussex RH1 IDN. A similar policy, similarly priced, is offered by **Wexas International** ((020) 7589-3315 E-MAIL mship@wexas.com, 45-49 Brompton Road, Knightsbridge, London SW3 1DE.

Another wise precaution is to carry a card in your wallet giving your blood type and listing any allergies or chronic conditions (including the wearing of contact lenses) that might affect treatment in an emergency. Also take a letter from your doctor detailing any prescriptions for ongoing medication, and a copy of your glasses prescription, in case you need to replace them.

Beyond that, it's always a good idea to have insect repellent with you, because in summer Canada has plenty of insects to repel, especially black flies and mosquitoes. A sunscreen lotion is also advisable, as the Canadian sun has a burning power out of all proportion to its heating power.

Emergency fire, ambulance, and police services are usually reached by dialing 911. For other emergencies or for areas not serviced by 911 (e.g., the Northwest Territories and Nunavut), you should contact the operator by dialing "0." In the Yukon Territory, only Whitehorse operates a 911 emergency call system. For the rest of the territory, dial Royal Canadian Mounted Police ((867) 667-5555, or for medical assistance ((867) 667-3333. Yukon

communities also have local police and medical emergency numbers, which you can get a list of from a visitor information center when you begin your trip.

CRIME

Crime? What crime? Canada may well be the most law-abiding of the world's industrialized nations. Violent crime isn't exactly unheard of, but it's not heard of very often. Most streets in Canada's cities are as safe at night as they are in the daytime.

All this law-and-orderliness notwithstanding, one should still take sensible basic precautions here: leave valuables in the hotel safe; lock your hotel room and car; don't leave valuable items visible in your car when unattended; don't carry all your cash and cards with you when you go out; use a handbag with a shoulderstrap slung diagonally and a zip, or put your wallet in an inside pocket, to avoid pickpockets; don't go for late-night strolls through questionable areas. In short, exercise your common sense, secure in the knowledge that Canadians can be counted on to exercise their common decency.

DISABLED TRAVELERS

In general, Canada is extremely well set-up for disabled access. Information may be obtained from the **Canadian Paraplegic Association** (CPA), National Office ((613) 723-1033 FAX (613) 723-1060 WEB SITE www.canparaplegic.org, 1101 Prince of Wales Drive, Suite 230, Ottawa, Ontario K2C 3W7, who will be able to offer general advice and refer you to the various provincial organisations. In the United Kingdom, contact **Tripscope** ((0845) 758-5641 E-MAIL tripscopesw@cablenet.co.uk or the **Holiday Care Service** ((01293) 774-535 E-MAIL holiday.care@virgin.net WEB SITE www.holiday care.org.uk for details.

WHEN TO GO

The decision of when to go will depend on what you are going *for*, and by now you should have a pretty good idea of what each region has to offer at what time of the year.

Generally speaking, the seasons in Canada's more temperate climes divide up as follows: winter occupies most of the long stretch from November to the end of March, summer occurs in June, July, and August, while the "shoulder" seasons of spring and autumn are largely confined to April through May and September through October.

In Newfoundland and the Maritimes, winter temperatures seldom rise above freezing and can often fall far below, especially in the inland areas. Spring is brief — just time for the countryside to change from its winter to its summer wardrobe.

The summer is comfortably mild, with temperatures in the high teens and 20s Centigrade (60s and 70s Fahrenheit). The autumn is gloriously colorful, as trees erupt in a blaze of reds and golds.

In Ontario and Québec the winters are just as cold — often, in places, colder — and tend to be gray and damp in southern Ontario and snowy, bright and chilly elsewhere in the region. Spring is very pleasant and autumn is lovely, as in the Maritimes, but summer is considerably warmer and more humid, particularly in Toronto.

Not surprisingly, weather conditions in the Far North are more extreme than those in the southern provinces. But some visitors are surprised to find out that northern summers can be hot. With the sun out as much as 24 hours a day (above the Arctic Circle), the temperature can reach a balmy 31°C/88°F. But even in July, you should be prepared for cool weather and take sweaters and a fall jacket.

Average monthly temperatures for five Canadian cities are as follows:

Inuvik

January	-29°C/-20°F
April	-14°C/7°F
July	14°C/57°F
October	-8°C/18°F

Montréal

January	-8°C/18°F
April	6°C/43°F
July	21°C/70°F
October	9°C/48°F

St. John's

January	-5°C/23°F
April	1°C/34°F
July	15°C/59°F
October	7°C/45°F

Toronto

January	-5°C/23°F
April	6°C/43°F
July	21°C/70°F
October	10°C/50°F

Yellowknife

January	-28°C/-18°F
April	-7°C/19°F
July	16°C/61°F
October	1°C/34°F

In the North, daylight hours are an important seasonal factor. Average daylight hours for seven northern Canadian cities are as follows:

	DEC	JUNE
Cambridge Bay	0.0	24.0
Dawson City	4.2	21.1
Inuvik	0.0	24.0
Iqaluit	4.5	20.8
Rankin Inlet	4.5	20.8
Whitehorse	5.4	19.1
Yellowknife	6.5	20.0

WHAT TO BRING

To choose what to pack think not about the desirability of having a particular article with you at any given time, but the undesirability of *not* having a particular article with you when you really need it. On that principle, here is our list of things you should never leave home without. On the other hand, you can buy anything you need in Canada, so unless you are going into the remote back country, you won't have any problems.

At the top of the list, by a wide margin, is a Swiss Army knife (or, to put it another way, two knives, two screwdrivers, a bottle opener, a can opener, a corkscrew, a toothpick, tweezers, nail file and scissors). We would also throw in a miniature flashlight and a small travel alarm clock. You will need an adapter and/or transformer if you plan to bring electrical appliances that don't run on 110 volts or don't have an American-style plug.

Because even the most minor physical irritations or afflictions can ruin a trip if they strike at the wrong time (which is the only time they strike), we would be sure to include a small first-aid kit with such items as lip balm for chapped lips, aspirin, anti-diarrhea tablets, antiseptic ointment, a few bandages and a few packets of tissues (which can also serve as toilet paper in an emergency). Resealable ziplock plastic bags come in handy when traveling — not least when you have items that you want to keep apart, or you want to segregate items that are damp or dirty or might be inclined to leak.

If you are planning to travel by air and you want to take a Swiss Army knife, or anything else that might conceivably be considered a "weapon" — even a nail file or scissors — be sure to pack it in the luggage you intend to check in. You don't want to be mistaken for an armed passenger, and security these days is tight. On the other hand, if you are taking any battery-powered gadgets — shavers, cassette players, etc. — carry them with you on the airplane or take the batteries out before packing them; airline security personnel get understandably jumpy when unidentified objects with batteries in them show up on their X-ray screen.

Be sure to take with you lists of the numbers of all travel documents, cards and checks you will be carrying, along with any telephone numbers included on them. This will greatly facilitate their quick replacement if lost. Also, take photocopies

---

At Montréal's busy Dorval Airport, workers keep up their nonstop pace.

of your passport and any travel tickets: duplicates are issued more speedily if people can see a copy of the original — much more speedily in the case of tickets or refunds. It is a good idea to get an international driver's license, obtainable from your automobile club, so that you can keep your home driver's license tucked away in a safe place. Always leave your inessential credit cards behind when you go on a trip, and of those you take with you carry only a couple in your wallet: any others should be tucked away in the same safe place as your passport, driver's license, extra travelers' checks, etc. It's just another way of ensuring that any loss causes only a temporary inconvenience.

When it comes to clothing, toiletries, jewelry and gadgetry, it's up to you to decide what and how much you want to take. Canadians are very casual in their dress, so there is no need to take formal or semiformal wear beyond what your taste and your expected engagements require. There is, however, a need to take some warm clothing — a sweater or two perhaps, the odd woolen or corduroy garment, and a windbreaker — because even in summer, even in the hottest spots, it can turn quite cool in the evenings, especially if you happen to be on or near the water.

LANGUAGE

Canada's two official languages are English and French, although the province of New Brunswick is the only officially bilingual area in the country. There are also 53 native languages spoken. Though French is the official language of the province of Québec, English is the mother tongue of 18 percent of the population of Québec, and is widely spoken, particularly around Greater Montréal.

French-speakers who wish to know more about the nuances and vocabulary specific to French as it is spoken in Québec can refer to the *Dictionnaire de la Langue Québécoise* by Léandre Bergeron (Éditions VLB), where they'll learn that a *dépanneur* is a convenience store (corner grocery store), *magasiner* is "to shop," and so on.

Even though English is widely spoken in Québec it helps to know a few phrases of French, especially if you are venturing outside of the province's urban areas.

Driving
arrêt stop
autoroute expressway
centre-ville downtown
est east
ouest west
nord north
sud south
droite right
gauche left
pont bridge

sens unique one way
stationnement interdit no parking
virage turn
vitesse speed

Conversations
au revoir goodbye
bienvenue welcome
bonjour hello
bonsoir goodnight, good evening
merci thank you
s'il vous plaît please
Comment ça va? How are you?
Pouvez-vous m'aidez? Can you help me?
Où puis-je trouver…? Where can I find…?
Combien ça coûte? How much does it cost?
Quelle heure est-il? What time is it?

Shopping
ascenseur elevator
chaussures shoes
comptant cash
cuir leather
étage floor, story
escalier roulant escalator
prix réduit/rabais discount or reduced price
rez-de-chaussée ground floor
sortie exit
sous-sol basement
vente sale
vêtements clothing

General
aller-retour round trip (ticket)
billets tickets
calèche horse-drawn carriage
gratuit free
métro subway
renseignements information
reçu receipt
salle de bain washroom
souterrain underground

RECOMMENDED WEB SITES

Web sites are listed throughout the book alongside address and telephone numbers. This list adds a few particularly useful or interesting sites without direct connections to sights or associations within the book.

Sympatico www.sympatico.ca. This is a comprehensive site, operated by Bell Canada, with all things Canadian and more. It's very well organized, easy on the eye, and an excellent place to start research on the country in any category. The travel sections are especially good.

Universal Currency Converter www.xe.net/ currency. A nifty way to find out what your dollar or euro is worth against any other currency, in real time.

Travelocity www.travelocity.com. The best choice for straightforward air travel fare search and booking. Sign-up for automatic updates on air routes of your choosing. When the rate drops by $50 or more, you'll be notified via e-mail

Where Magazine www.wheremagazine.com. These are locally edited, ad-oriented destination magazines. The web site is useful and attractive. You can order magazines from the site, or browse information on a number of Canadian cities, including Toronto, Winnipeg and Vancouver.

North American Bear Center www.bear.org. Everything you've ever wanted to know about bears.

Mooseworld www.mooseworld.com. And about moose ...

Whales www.cetacea.org or www.whaleslife .com. ... and about whales.

Rec.Travel Library — Canada www.travel-library.com/north_america/canada/index.html. A homespun and rather out-of-date site that has plenty of information, including personal advice and a list of answers to frequently asked questions about traveling in Canada. Strong on links to many other Canadian sites.

Lost Moose, the Yukon Publishers www.Yukon web.com/business/lost_moose/. These publishers specialize in northern literature, including the legendary *Lost Whole Moose Catalog.*

National Archives www.archives.ca. In English and French, this site contains written records, artwork, photographs and maps that document the history of Canada and the workings of its government.

Canadian Yellowpages www.yellowpages.ca. This is a fairly well organized tool for address and telephone searches. It also offers classified ads, pictures of Canada and links to other sites.

RECOMMENDED READING

ATWOOD, MARGARET. *Alias Grace.* Doubleday, 1997.
BACKHOUSE, FRANCES. *Women of the Klondike.* Whitecap Books, 1995.
BERTON, PIERRE. *The Mysterious North.* Toronto: McClelland and Stewart, 1956. *The Klondike Fever.* New York: Carroll and Graf, 1958.
BERTON, LAURA BEATRICE AND PIERRE BERTON. *I Married the Klondike.* Toronto: McClelland and Stewart, 1996.
BROOK, STEPHEN. *Maple Leaf Rag.* London: Pan Books, 1989.
CRAVEN, MARGARET. *I Heard the Owl Call My Name* and *Again Calls the Owl.* Laureleaf, 1993.
DRISCOLL, CYNTHIA BRACKETT. *One Woman's Gold Rush: Snapshots from Mollie Brackett's Lost Photo Album 1898–1899.* Kalamazoo: Oak Woods Media, 1996.
GALE, DONALD. *Shooshewan, Child of the Beothuk.* Breakwater Books, 1988.

HARDY, ANNE. *Where to Eat in Canada 2002-2003.* Oberon Press.
MACKAY, CLAIRE. *The Toronto Story.* Toronto: Annick Press, 1990.
MACKAY, DONALD. *Flight from Famine: The Coming of the Irish to Canada.* Toronto: McClelland & Stewart, 1990.
MACLENNAN, HUGH. *Papers.* Calgary: University of Calgary Press, 1986.
MALCOLM, ANDREW H. *The Canadians.* New York: Times Books, 1985.
MCNAUGHT, KENNETH. *The Penguin History of Canada.* London: Penguin Books, 1988.
MILEPOST, 54th edition. Bellevue, Washington: Vernon Publications, 2002.
MORGAN, BERNICE. *Random Passage.* Breakwater Books, Ltd., 1992.
MORTON, DESMOND. *A Peculiar Kind of Politics.* Toronto: University of Toronto Press, 1982.
MORTON, WILLIAM L. *The Canadian Identity.* Madison: University of Wisconsin Press, 1973.
PATTERSON, FREEMAN. *The Last Wilderness: Images of the Canadian Wild.* Vanier, Ontario: Canadian Geographic Society, 1991.
PROULX, E. ANNIE. *The Shipping News.* New York: Simon & Schuster, 1994.
RABAN, JONATHAN. *Passage to Juneau: A Sea and its Meaning.* Vintage Books, 2000. Veteran British travel writer retraces Captain Vancouver's 1792 voyage up the Inside Passage.
RICHLER, MORDECAI. *The Apprenticeship of Duddy Kravitz.* London: Penguin Books, 1991. Broadsides. London: Vintage Books, 1991. Papers. Calgary: University of Calgary Press, 1987.
SKOGAN, JOAN. *The Princess and the Sea-Bear and Other Tsimshian Stories.* Polestar Press, 1990.
SOUBLIERE, MARION, editor. *The Nunavut Handbook: Traveling in Canada's Arctic.* Iqaluit, NWT: Nortext Press, 1998.
WATERMAN, JOHATHAN. *Arctic Crossing: A Journey through the Northwest Passage and Inuit Culture.* New York: Knopf, 2001.
WELLS, E. HAZARD and RANDALL M. DODD, editor. *Magnificence and Misery: A Firsthand Account of the 1897 Klondike Gold Rush.* Garden City, New York: Doubleday & Company, 1984.

Quick Reference A–Z Guide
to Places and Topics of Interest

Photography Credits

All photographs taken by Robert Holmes and Nik Wheeler, with the exception of those listed below:
David Henry: pages 10, 12, *left and right*, 13 *top and bottom*, 14, 16, 24, 25, 27, 32, 33, 37 *top and bottom*, 38, 84, 91, 97, 99, 119 *left*, 120 *left*, 121, 122, 123, 124, 126, 132 *left and right*, 134, 137, 139, 143, 198, 205, 206, 212 *left and right*, 213, 214, 216, 219, 237, 243, 246.
Yukon Archives: Claude Lidd Collection: 49.